TRULY UNDERSTOOD

Truly Understood

CHRISTOPHER PEACOCKE

OXFORD
UNIVERSITY PRESS

OXFORD

UNIVERSITY PRESS

Great Clarendon Street, Oxford OX2 6DP

Oxford University Press is a department of the University of Oxford.
It furthers the University's objective of excellence in research, scholarship,
and education by publishing worldwide in

Oxford New York

Auckland Cape Town Dar es Salaam Hong Kong Karachi
Kuala Lumpur Madrid Melbourne Mexico City Nairobi
New Delhi Shanghai Taipei Toronto

With offices in

Argentina Austria Brazil Chile Czech Republic France Greece
Guatemala Hungary Italy Japan Poland Portugal Singapore
South Korea Switzerland Thailand Turkey Ukraine Vietnam

Oxford is a registered trade mark of Oxford University Press
in the UK and in certain other countries

Published in the United States
by Oxford University Press Inc., New York

British Library Cataloguing in Publication Data

Data available

Library of Congress Cataloging in Publication Data

Data available

Typeset by Laserwords Private Limited, Chennai, India
Printed in Great Britain
on acid-free paper by
Biddles Ltd, King's Lynn, Norfolk

ISBN 978–0–19–923944–3

1 3 5 7 9 10 8 6 4 2

Preface

This book came as a surprise. Almost three years ago, when I was thinking once again about the way in which justificationist and other conceptual-role theories of meaning might attempt to treat the concept of the past, it occurred to me that the most plausible kind of rival truth-conditional theory of that subject matter could be generalized to concepts of other domains. The generalization gives a special role to reference in the theory of understanding; it subsumes various other special treatments of particular concepts that had seemed plausible to me; and it suggests a way forward on certain problematic mental concepts. This book is an attempt to give a unified statement of the generalized treatment and some of its applications.

My intellectual debts and sources are recorded in another section. On a more personal level, I would not have been able to carry out this work without the happy atmosphere in the Philosophy Department at Columbia University. The range of views, and friendly critical discussion, that I have encountered here have often brought me to locate my position in a much wider context than I would otherwise have attempted.

Once again, my family has given me much more than background support. In an emergency meeting held to avoid the various boring titles for this book that had occurred to me, the present title was proposed by my daughter Antonia, during a family discussion with my son Alexander and my wife, Teresa.

C.P.

Columbia University in the City of New York
July 2007

Acknowledgements

Most of the material in this book was developed for my seminars and courses at Columbia University in 2004–7, and at New York University in 2003–4. Some of the ideas were presented in series of lectures elsewhere, including my Immanuel Kant Lectures at Stanford University in October 2003, and in series and events at the University of London's Institute of Advanced Study, the University of St Andrews (at the Arché Centre), the University of Toronto, the University of Texas at Austin, the University of Southern California, and the University of Washington, St Louis. I learned a great deal from the discussions in New York and at all of these universities.

Special thanks are due to John Campbell for his highly perceptive comments on a complete draft of the material, comments that prompted revisions both of thought and of formulation. The same applies to two anonymous further referees for Oxford University Press. I blush to think of the state this material would be in without their advice. Special thanks too to the authors, identified below, of the no fewer than six commentaries I received on three lectures, drawn from this material, that I gave at the University of Toronto in the fall of 2006. Once again, Peter Momtchiloff's timely and diplomatic encouragement has been important to me. Normally, in a book such as this, the copy-editor is invisible to the reader. But Laurien Berkeley's work has improved the presentation of this material so substantially that I take this opportunity to thank her too.

Acknowledgements for the individual chapters follow.

Chapter 1. An early version of this chapter was presented at a conference on my work in National Tsing-Hua University, Taiwan, in 2004. I thank the National Science Council of Taiwan for support for this conference. That version was published as 'Justification, Realism and the Past', *Mind*, 114 (2005), 639–70; and it was improved by comments from Philip Kitcher, Joseph Raz, Ruey-Yuan Wu, and the two anonymous referees for *Mind*. Michael Dummett replied to this paper in his article 'The Justificationist's Response to a Realist', *Mind*, 114 (2005), 671–88. I am indebted to Dummett for his energetic and revealing 'Response'. This chapter engages with some of his principal points. Jerry Fodor's vigorous comments at our joint seminar in 2005 have also assisted me.

Chapters 2 and 3. This material has not been previously published (and is not due to appear elsewhere). I have been helped in developing it by the comments of José Bermúdez, Paul Boghossian, James Higginbotham, Paul Horwich, Mark Johnston, Philip Kitcher, Sydney Shoemaker, and James van Cleve; by the participants at the Conference on Epistemic Normativity at Chapel Hill in the spring of 2006; by my commentator on that occasion, Fred Dretske; by the comments of Carrie Jenkins and Crispin Wright at the Arché Centre in St Andrews; and by the comments of Imogen Dickie, Gurpreet Rattan, and Sonia Sedivy at Toronto.

Chapter 4. This is the material in this book that goes back farthest in time. I first developed the ideas for an Invited Lecture at the 1996 Barcelona meeting of the European Society for Philosophy and Psychology, and as seminars at the universities of Hamburg and St Andrews, and at New York University. At a presentation at the Pittsburgh meeting of the Central Division of the American Philosophical Association in 1997, my commentator was Tyler Burge; and at a presentation at the 1997 meeting of the Conference on Methods in New York, my commentators were Georges Rey and Gideon Rosen. This material involved a significant change of view from the position I occupied in *A Study of Concepts* (Cambridge, Mass.: MIT Press, 1992). It was the points in this material that began to move me to a position more characteristic of rationalism. In grappling with these issues, I was helped by the advice of Ned Block, Paul Boghossian, Bill Brewer, John Campbell, Martin Davies, Hartry Field, Wolfgang Künne, Barry Loewer, Eric Margolis, Stephen Schiffer, Stewart Shapiro, John Skorupski, and Crispin Wright. Once again, I acknowledge with gratitude the support of the Leverhulme Trust in the period 1996–2000, without which this work would not have been possible. Versions of this material were published as 'Implicit Conceptions, Understanding and Rationality', in M. Hahn and B. Ramberg (eds), *Reflections and Replies: Essays on the Philosophy of Tyler Burge* (Cambridge, Mass.: MIT Press, 2003); and in E. Villanueva (ed.), *Concepts, Philosophical Issues 9* Atascadero, Calif.: Ridgeview, 1998). The first of these volumes contains comments on this position by Tyler Burge; the second contains commentaries from Eric Margolis, Georges Rey, Stephen Schiffer, and Josefa Toribio, together with a reply by me. Those interested in pursuing these issues further are encouraged to read these exchanges.

Chapter 5. This material is also previously unpublished, and is not currently scheduled for publication elsewhere. It has benefited from the comments

of Nicholas Asher, Jerry Fodor, Philip Kitcher, Carol Rovane, Mark Sains-
bury, and Crispin Wright; from discussions at the joint Columbia–Rutgers
Seminar on Concepts that Jerry Fodor and I ran in the fall of 2005; and
from the commentaries of Benj Hellie and Diana Raffman at Toronto,
and of Bill Child at the conference in June 2007 on Wittgenstein and the
Philosophy of Mind at the University of California at Santa Cruz.

Chapter 6. I presented some of these ideas in the first of my Immanuel
Kant Lectures at Stanford University. My thanks to José Bermúdez, Michael
Bratman, John Campbell, Victor Caston, Mark Crimmins, Alison Gopnik,
Stephen Schiffer, Susanna Siegel, Elliot Sober, and an anonymous referee
for helpful comments. An earlier version appeared as ' "Another I": Rep-
resenting Conscious States, Perception and Others', in J. Bermúdez (ed.),
Thought, Reference and Experience: Themes from the Philosophy of Gareth Evans
(Oxford: Oxford University Press, 2005). Section 5 of this chapter differs
in substance from the version in Bermúdez's collection. My formulation in
that collection confused conscious trying with apparent action-awareness.
Though no doubt closely causally related, these are distinct things, as
Chapter 7 argues. Section 5 also differs from the version in Bermúdez's
collection in generalizing the Core Rule for the concept of perception to
the case of action in general, rather than to the case of doing something
intentionally.

Chapter 7. Earlier versions of these ideas were presented in 2004 to the Lan-
guage and Mind Seminar at New York University and to the Santa Barbara
Conference on Content and Concepts; and in 2005 to the Conference on
Mental Action at the School of Advanced Studies, University of London. I
have been helped by the comments of Ned Block, David Chalmers, Jerry
Fodor, Jim John, James Pryor, Michael Rescorla, Nathan Salmon, Susanna
Schellenberg, Stephen Schiffer, Sydney Shoemaker, Susanna Siegel, and
Aaron Zimmerman. This chapter unifies material presented in my paper
'Mental Action and Self-Awareness (I)', in J. Cohen and B. McLaughlin
(eds), *Contemporary Debates in the Philosophy of Mind* (Oxford: Blackwell,
2007) and in its sequel, 'Mental Action and Self-Awareness (II): Episte-
mology', forthcoming in L. O'Brien and M. Soteriou (eds), *Mental Action*
(Oxford: Oxford University Press, forthcoming, 2008).

Chapter 8. No version of this material has been published previously. Special
thanks to Tyler Burge for much intensive and illuminating discussion and
correspondence over what is now a decade on the issues of this chapter, and

Richard Heck for more recent valuable comments. Sebastian Watzl's comments have also helped me. There is much more to be said on the relation of the present chapter to Burge's and to my other published contributions on these issues; but it has to be left for another occasion if this chapter is to remain within reasonable bounds.

Contents

Introduction

The principal claim of this book is that reference and truth have an explanatory role to play in the nature of understanding and concept-possession, an explanatory role that is deeper and more extensive than is commonly envisaged—either by opponents of truth-conditional theories, or even by some of their supporters.

One can argue for this principal claim by considering various specific concepts of philosophical interest. For some particular concept, we can argue that some of its distinctive features are adequately explained only by a possession-condition that involves reference and truth essentially. Such a concept-specific approach can hope to illuminate the nature of the particular concepts it treats. The concept-specific approach will be significant for the metaphysics and epistemology of the domain in which that concept applies.

Yet the concept-specific approach, however important it may be for understanding some particular domain and our thought about it, can carry you only so far. The desire for generality and the possibility of philosophical explanation that accompanies it is hard to resist. Once we have accepted, for some sample concepts of interest, that their possession-conditions involve reference and truth in some ineliminable way, it becomes irresistible to ask: why is this so? Is the explanation one that applies to other concepts too? Is there some general model here that is instantiated by the correct treatment of various specific concepts? What is that general model, and can it explain some facts about concepts in general?

I attempt to extract a general model of understanding from examples, and to defend it by its explanatory powers, in the four chapters that comprise Part I of this book. The general model is expounded in Chapter 2. The character of the model is motivated in part by reflections on the nature of the problems inherent in approaches to content that try to dispense with an essential role for reference and truth.

The chapters in Part II aim to apply the general model outlined in Part I to various mental concepts. These include the concept of a subject of conscious states, and the concepts of perception and action, both bodily and mental. The mental is, then, twice over the concern of this study. Understanding, or concept-possession, is itself a mental state, whatever the subject matter of the concept; and my particular aim is a better philosophical understanding of concepts of the mental, by drawing on the particular theory of understanding I am offering. A further particular concern throughout this material is a proper account of the relations between the mental and the non-mental worlds, and the ways in which these relations contribute to the very nature of the mental, and to the nature of ways of thinking of mental events, states, and things made available by our own mental lives.

The background methodology of the chapters in this book is that of inference to the best explanation. The facts for which we seek an explanation concern features of the grasp of specific concepts, or classes of concepts. Here are some diverse examples of facts about concepts that are in need of explanation:

- You can understand what it is for something that is too small (or too large) to be perceived nevertheless to be square in shape without knowing what would be evidence that it is square, and without knowing what would be the consequences of its being square.
- When you engage in first-person thought, your thought normally is self-conscious, in the sense that you know that you are thinking about yourself, without your needing to rely on any further empirical information. This is apparently something unique to the first-person concept, and to concepts explained in terms of it.
- You can understand what it is for some organism to be in pain without knowing what would be evidence that it is in pain, and without knowing what would be the consequences of its being in pain.

I aim to explain such facts by appealing to an account of concepts and their possession that makes essential use of reference and truth in the explanation. Explanations of that sort for the three displayed facts are attempted in Chapters 1, 3, and 5 respectively.

For the purposes of this book, what matters is the correct explanation of such facts, rather than the philosophical status of such explanations. As is so often the case, one can reasonably have a greater degree of confidence that something is the explanation of some datum than one has in any particular philosophical theory of explanation in general; or than one has in the epistemic status of the explanation of the datum in question. In particular, the approach I develop here is in itself neutral on the issue of whether the explananda and the explanations are themselves a priori. Those who are sceptical either of the extent, or even the intelligibility, of the notion of the a priori, could consistently accept the explanations offered here. The explanations are, as far as I can see, in no way proprietary to a rationalist stance. My own view, of course, is that the explanatory resources I draw on here do have a bearing on the explanation of a priori status, where it exists. I have signalled some such points in the various chapters. But my central claims about concept-possession and about the explanation of various facts about understanding, and about reasons that support particular judgements involving certain concepts, do not in themselves require any particular stance on the a priori.

The contribution that I try to make in this book stands squarely in the tradition of efforts to develop, exploit, and apply Frege's conception in his *Grundgesetze* of sense as individuated by (contribution to) truth-conditions. Undoubtedly the development of this conception of sense and its attendant conception of understanding has taken a meandering course in the near century and a quarter since the publication of Frege's work. I hope that I myself am not moving orthogonally to the direction of progress. In any case, the Fregean roots of the enterprise in which I am engaged here are very clearly visible. The entire project of this book can be seen as generated by the Fregean ur-idea that a sense is individuated by the fundamental condition for something to be its reference. As soon as we accept that ur-idea, it follows that anything distinctive of a particular sense—facts about grasp of the sense, facts about certain attitudes involving it—must be traced back to the nature of the sense, which on this Fregean conception is given by the condition for something to be its reference.

In a project such as this, there is no natural, feasible, and satisfying stopping point. Any territory selected for attention will be adjacent to equally important areas lying outside the selected area. Topics I do not attempt to cover here, but to which the position outlined here can contribute, and from which its further elaboration needs to draw, include the following: philosophical issues of concept-acquisition; the ontology of properties, relations, and such individuals as mental subjects; the finer-grained analysis of awareness, including awareness of others, and what it makes possible; and the nature of rule-following—to mention only a few. The topics I have covered, however, seem to me to be those on which any treatment of these further issues needs to take a stance.

PART I

A THEORY OF UNDERSTANDING

1

Truth's Role in Understanding

Truth and reference play an essential part in the nature of meaning, intentional content, and understanding. Meaning, intentional content, and understanding cannot be elucidated solely in terms their relations to evidence, justification, inference, or consequences. A conception of understanding as involving truth and reference has significant explanatory powers that are unavailable if we neglect this role of truth and reference.

These are claims for which I will be arguing directly and indirectly throughout this book. In this first chapter, I will be arguing for these claims directly in the case of some contents whose subject matter is the non-mental spatio-temporal world. My strategy will be to examine detailed proposals that aim to elucidate meaning, content, and understanding independently of truth and reference; to consider respects in which these proposals fail where their truth-involving rivals succeed; and to propose some elements of a positive account of meaning, content, and understanding for the subject matter of the non-mental spatio-temporal world. If meaning and content are not to be philosophically explained in terms of the notions of evidence, justification, and the like, part of the challenge of developing a positive account is to say how we should understand the relation of truth to evidence, justification, and consequences.

1. CRITIQUE OF JUSTIFICATIONIST AND EVIDENTIAL ACCOUNTS

I will take as an example of a treatment of meaning and understanding in terms of justification the account of past-tense statements in Michael Dummett's book *Truth and the Past*, together with his more recent elaboration of the view.[1] The explicitness of Dummett's account is one of its virtues.

---

[1] Dummett (2004); page references in this chapter to Dummett's writings are to this book, unless otherwise specified. The more recent, and at one important point, different, elaboration is to

Many accounts of meaning and understanding that aim to dispense with any fundamental role for truth and reference do not actually state in detail how the meanings of many basic concepts are to be specified. Dummett's account is not one of these. The account Dummett offers is also one that he thinks of as 'repudiating anti-realism about the past—the view that statements about the past, if true at all, must be true in virtue of the traces past events have left in the present' (p. ix). So in considering Dummett's position, we are not taking as a target of investigation something that is presupposing an extreme anti-realism about the past. As we shall see, Dummett's account is also of interest because it develops a model which may also seem to be applicable to a range of other contents, including contents about other places.

A justificationist theory of meaning, in Dummett's treatment, specifies the meaning of a statement in terms of the grounds for asserting the statement (p. 26). The intuitionistic theory of meaning for arithmetical sentences is one such justificationist theory for that mathematical domain. Under this treatment, the meaning of an arithmetical sentence is given by its proof-conditions. These meaning-specifying proof-conditions are determined componentially. The meaning of an individual arithmetical expression is given by its contribution to the proof-conditions of the complete sentences in which it occurs. The meaning of a complete arithmetical sentence is given by the proof-conditions which are determined by the contribution to proof-conditions made by its component expressions, together with their mode of combination in the sentence. The proof-conditions so determined can be described as the canonical proof-conditions of the sentence. A canonical ground, or a canonical justification, for an arithmetical sentence is a proof meeting the specifications in these canonically determined proof-conditions. Providing such a meaning-determined proof is the most direct way of establishing the sentence, in a technical sense of directness proprietary to a justificationist semantics. A direct method of establishing a sentence is a method of a kind that is mentioned in the canonical specification of the sentence's meaning.

Dummett emphasizes that an arithmetical sentence can also be proved by non-canonical means. A sentence may be a surprising consequence of the axioms of arithmetic, or of some other a priori theory, and there may be a way of establishing the sentence that is not a canonical proof of the sentence in question. His illustration of this possibility is drawn

be found in his article 'The Justificationist's Response to a Realist' (Dummett 2005); I refer to this article as Dummett's 'Response'.

from Euler's solution of the problem of whether any path that crosses all the bridges in Königsberg crosses some bridge twice. Euler proved that any such path does cross some bridge twice. Take the existential sentence 'Some bridge is crossed twice on the particular path p that crosses all the bridges'. This existential sentence is most directly verified by first identifying some particular bridge; by then verifying that this particular bridge is crossed twice on path p; and then inferring by existential generalization that some bridge is crossed twice. But Euler's proof of the general proposition 'Any path crosses some bridge twice' equally establishes the existential generalization without identifying any particular such bridge, given only the information that every bridge was crossed on a particular path. Similarly, the proposition that $13^2 = 169$ can be established by all sorts of complicated proofs other than simply a computation that involves adding 13 to itself the requisite number of times. All of these proofs are indirect, non-canonical, and genuine. They are not, however, the ground or justification of the sort canonically determined by the meaning of the statement itself. The canonical justification of $13^2 = 169$ involves a series of successive, cumulative additions of 13:

$$13 + 13 + 13 \ldots = 169 \text{ (for thirteen occurrences of '13').}$$

Dummett holds that the recognition that there are non-canonical, "indirect" means of establishing sentences should come 'as a relief' (p. 44) to the justificationist attempting to give an account of past-tense sentences. Dummett's thought is that a non-canonical proof is still a proof, and what a non-canonical proof shows is that the proposition in question could have been verified in the direct way that corresponds, on a justificationist theory, to the sense of the sentence as determined by its components and syntactic structure. In applying this idea to the case of the past, Dummett's *Truth and the Past* offers a treatment of the meaning of past-tense statements that contains the following five theses:

(A) The truth of a past-tense sentence 'consists of its being the case that someone suitably placed *could have* verified it' (p. 44).

(B) Thesis (A) amounts to what Dummett regards as a modified justificationist theory. His view is that a purely justificationist theory would involve a stronger anti-realism about the past, one to the effect that the past exists only in what we would call its present traces. Such an anti-realism was formulated and discussed in Dummett's earlier writings on the past, notably in his paper 'The Reality of the Past', and in his Gifford Lectures.[2] In *Truth and the Past*, at least, Dummett is experimenting with a rejection of this stronger anti-realism.[3] He notes that on the modified justificationist theory with which he is experimenting, a central general principle of justificationism is still maintained: 'a statement about the past can be true only in virtue of an actual or possible direct verification of it' (p. 70).

(C) The distinction between direct and indirect means of establishing statements is preserved in this modified justificationist account. Consider the statement 'Your sister must now be sitting down to her breakfast'. According to Dummett, we credit to even a child the consciousness that if he were to go downstairs and, a little later, observe his sister having her breakfast, 'this would not be the most *direct* way of verifying the statement' (p. 53). To be already in the place referred to, and to observe the relevant state of affairs at the time referred to, 'is the only *direct* way to verify the statement' (p. 54).

(D) The grasp of a statement about what is happening elsewhere 'falls into two parts: one is an understanding of what it is for a state of affairs of the type in question to obtain or an event of the type in question to occur; the other is our knowledge of how to locate it on the grid which serves to particularize the place referred to' (p. 57). Dummett eventually concludes that an analogous account of thought about what obtains, or is happening, at other times is equally correct (pp. 65 ff.).

(E) It is a mistake 'to argue that a conception of reality as existing independently of being observed must be prior to and inform the observational practice that we learn: it is by learning that practice that we acquire such a conception' (p. 71). The idea of observation as revealing something that would have been so even if the observation had not been made 'is a sophisticated thought, which ought not to be attributed to a child who had been taught to say how things are by looking, feeling, or listening' (pp. 70–1).

---

[2] See especially the formulation of anti-realism in Dummett (1978*b*: 373). The Gifford Lectures are now published in Dummett (2006).

[3] Dummett should not be regarded as having changed his view, but rather as trying out different philosophical options at different times. 'I do not think anyone should interpret everything that a philosopher writes as if it was just one chapter in a book he is writing throughout his life. On the contrary, for me every article and essay is a separate attempt to arrive at the truth, to be judged on its own' (p. x).

The Dummettian child does not have the conception of reality as existing independently of being observed.

The justificationist position in (A)–(E) has to face the critical observation that there is a fundamental difference between a proof that establishes an arithmetical statement and a perception that establishes a statement about the observable world. A proof, considered as a sequence of sentences that are themselves expression-types, is something whose existence is entirely mind-independent. The proof exists whether or not anyone has ever given it, or contemplated it, or stood in any other psychological relation to it. A perception by contrast is a mental state or event. It is essentially something mind-dependent. Even if the content of the mental state is conceived, as on McDowell's account, as some kind of fact involving a state of affairs in the non-mental world, the perception itself involves a psychological relation to that fact. This contrast between the mind-independence of proofs and the mind-dependence of perceptions has consequences that ramify throughout the theory of intentional content. In my judgement, the contrast is a symptom of the deep difference between the nature of arithmetical thought and the nature of thought about the spatio-temporal world.

Is this contrast a mere artefact of treating proofs as sequences of expression-types? Does the contrast disappear if we regard proofs as sequences of actual expression tokens, or, like Brouwer, as subjective mental constructions? The contrast remains, on any plausible view of arithmetical truth. Even if a proof is an actual sequence of expression tokens, or an actual corresponding mental construction, what makes such a sequence a proof of a given proposition is something mind-independent. What, for an intuitionist for example, makes it such a proof is that its transitions conform to the proof-conditions given in specifying the meaning of the logical constants, or it is an indirect proof that such a proof can be constructed. This condition is not about minds or mental states. But we should also allow that it is enough for a proposition of arithmetic to be true that there could be a proof of it, even when proofs are sequences of expression tokens or mental constructions. The condition that there could be a proof, a sequence of expressions or a corresponding mental construction, of a certain proposition is mind-independently true or false. That means that the move away from expression-types has not affected the conclusion, and that the contrast between the arithmetical case and the spatio-temporal world is not an artefact of treating proofs as sequences of expression-types. This conclusion holds unless we are strict finitists, or subjectivists about modality, or believe that providing a proof actually makes a proposition of arithmetic true.[4] These all seem to me implausible claims. They certainly do not feature as premises in Dummett's argument.

There are substantial internal tensions that emerge when we try to carry through an application to the spatio-temporal case of the distinction between direct and indirect methods of justification in the way Dummett's justificationism proposes.

Take an arithmetical equation built only from canonical numerals, together with vocabulary for addition, multiplication, and identity. Whenever such an equation is true, there exists a proof of it. (Realists and arithmetical intuitionists will agree thus far.) The intuitionist holds more generally that in every case in which any arithmetical sentence is true, there exists a proof of it. Both in the case of the equations, and in the case of other arithmetical sentences, an indirect method of proof of an arithmetical sentence quite properly establishes for the justificationist that a canonical proof of that sentence exists, even if no one has written out or encountered such a proof. By the justificationist's standards, this means that the indirect method establishes the truth of the arithmetical sentence. Since we can know that there is a proof that $1,257^2$ is $1,580,049$ (it is) without having seen or worked through a proof of that fact, this use and application in the arithmetical case of the direct–indirect distinction is not intrinsically problematic. In the spatio-temporal case, however, as expounded by Dummett, we confront a crucial disanalogy. A successful use of an indirect method of establishing what is going on at some place-time other than one's current location does not establish that there is a *perception* of what is going on at that other place-time.

It is no simple matter for the justificationist, as characterized by Dummett, to explain away or discount this disanalogy. Certainly it does not seem plausible from the justificationist standpoint to modify the account of the arithmetical case. It is not as if it were open to the justificationist to say that we have some grasp of what it is for an arithmetical sentence to be true even when there is no proof of it, so that the apparent disanalogy disappears. That would be to abandon justificationism (or at least proof-based justificationism). The

---

[4] As John Campbell remarked to me, the last of these three options involves a kind of radical justificationism about arithmetic that is an analogue for arithmetic of a species of radical anti-realism about the past. These anti-realisms about the past are rejected in Dummett's *Truth and the Past*, so it is reasonable to take it that there is no such analogous commitment about arithmetic in his position in that book.

very attraction of the direct–indirect distinction, and its applicability in the mathematical case, is wholly dependent upon the idea that a sound indirect method establishes the truth of a sentence on a conception of truth that is characterized independently of any mention of indirect methods.

We can distinguish at least three types of intended justificationist theory. Theories of the first type give as the canonical justification—the direct, meaning-specifying justification—for a predication (of an observational property) of another place-time the perception of something being the case then and there. This is the type we have just rejected as clearly false. One of the other two types, the second type, takes as the direct, canonical justification the condition that the other place-time has the same property as is observed to be instantiated when the thinker makes a present-tense, observationally based predication of the property in question. This second type takes the indirect method to be given by the counterfactual about what would be observed to be the case at the other place-time. The third conceivable type of intended justificationist theory takes the counterfactual as the direct justification-condition. The three types of theory can be shown as in the following table.

	Meaning-specifying condition for a predication of observational concept of a place-time	Indirect method
Type One	Perception of state of affairs there	Counterfactual, or maybe same-kind condition
Type Two	Same kind as in observational application	Counterfactual
Type Three	Counterfactual	?

There are also difficulties with theories of Type Two and of Type Three, both in themselves, and in reconciling either one of them with everything Dummett says about the kind of theory he accepts.

Theories of Type Two aim to take the meaning-specifying, direct justification-condition for a statement about another place-time to be that it has the same property as is observed to be instantiated when the thinker makes a present-tense predication of an observed place or object, on the basis of perception. How are we to conceive of the uniform, single property that can be recognized by observation to be instantiated in some event or object at one's current location, and can also be instantiated unperceived elsewhere? In order to make sense of this conception, we must think of what is observed to be the case as something that can also hold unobserved. Pre-theoretically, this seems to be entirely intuitive and unproblematic. From the theoretical stand-point of a justificationist theory of Type Two that employs a direct–indirect distinction, it may also seem to be just what is needed. For to say that the property could be instantiated unperceived may seem to be the analogue for the spatio-temporal case of saying, in the mathematical case, that there is a proof that has not in fact been written out. So, it may seem, "could have been established" characterizes what Dummett calls the indirect case in both the mathematical and the spatio-temporal case, just as he said. Type Two theories seem to have just the properties that Dummett at some points endorses. Sometimes he insists, rightly in my view, that a counterfactual about what would be observed if one went to the place is not what is actually said in a statement about what is going on elsewhere. 'What it [a statement about what obtains elsewhere] says is that at that particular location on the spatial map is something of a kind he can recognize when he himself is at the right location' (p. 51). This is just what a Type Two theorist would also say.

Someone might read Dummett's statement about what is said in a statement about elsewhere as using merely a pleonastic notion of sameness of kind, of the sort discussed by Stephen Schiffer in his *Remnants of Meaning*.[5] For a pleonastic notion of sameness of kind, it would suffice that the same linguistic predicate is used in a thinker's accepted sentences about his current location and those about other locations. But this pleonastic reading, whatever its virtues elsewhere, cannot be relevant to question about the nature of understanding, because it implies no positive account at all about the relations between understanding of the local and understanding of the non-local predications. The pleonastic reading simply says that the same linguistic predicate is used in the local and the non-local cases, without saying why there is a genuine identity of meaning or understanding in the two cases. Our concern at this point is precisely with how justificationism could address such issues about meaning and understanding.

The inadequacy of the pleonastic conception to this particular task is parallel to the inadequacy of trying to explain the relation of third-person

---

[5] Schiffer (1987).

ascriptions of conscious states to first-person ascriptions by saying only that the third-person ascriptions apply the same concept. They do apply the same concept; but how this is possible needs philosophical explanation. No account of how it is possible—a unified account of first-person and third-person understanding—is supplied merely by saying that they are the same concept. The issue for the case of concepts of conscious states is addressed below, in Chapter 5 section 3. Exactly the same points could be made against someone who construes 'same kind' in Dummett's condition as one involving merely substitutional quantification, which requires only an identity of expression for a claim of sameness of kind, so understood, to be correct.

Are the resources used in theories of Type Two really available to Dummett's justificationist? The intended position of such a theory holds that what is said in a statement about the instantiation of an observational property at another place is that, in Dummett's words, 'at that particular location on the spatial map is something of a kind he [the thinker] can recognize when he himself is at the right location'. If a justificationist is to appeal to contents like this, he must give a justificationist account of their nature. The content itself involves an identity of kind: an identity of a kind instantiated by the unperceived thing or event with a kind instantiated by things or events that the thinker perceives. How is this identity itself to be explained in justificationist terms? There are two problems here, a general problem which arises for any justificationist theory, and a special problem for Dummett which arises in the context of the other theses he holds.

The general problem for the justificationist is to explain, in justificationist terms, grasp of identity of shape, or other kind, as between a perceived and an unperceived object or event. There is a problem here that does not arise in the arithmetical case. In the arithmetical case, we do have a justificationist account of identities formed with complex arithmetical terms on each side of the identity. If the terms are formed from certain canonical arithmetical vocabulary (successor, plus, multiplication), the identities are decidable, and appreciation of the canonical decision procedure can be appealed to by the justificationist when asked for an account of grasp of the sense of the identity, even if it is one that is actually proved by indirect means. But what can the justificationist offer in the case of an identity of kind between observed thing or event, and thing or event unobserved by the thinker?

Dummett himself does not address this question. One apparent option would be to appeal to counterfactuals again. That option holds that for the identity of kind to hold between the observed and the unobserved cases is for certain counterfactuals about what would be observed to be true. But this is an answer which implies that the counterfactual is not being treated as an indirect method, but as something independently written into the grasp of the sense of predications about other places—the answer is being offered as something to put in column one of our table, an answer that addresses the question of meaning-specifying conditions. The defence is, consequently, not a defence of a theory of Type Two. The defence then also incidentally has no account of what an indirect method is, once counterfactuals are included in the direct method. This defence does not fit Dummett's description of his theory at all.

Alternatively, it may be suggested that the justificationist can simply say that what justifies a judgement of identity of shape or other property as between a perceived and an unperceived case is simply evidence that the identity holds. The problem with this suggestion is that, in the absence of a non-circular characterization of what such evidence is, it makes the justificationist account parasitic on grasp of what it is for the identity really to hold—that is, parasitic on a truth-conditional account. No one can or should deny that evidence that p can justify the judgement that p, but this by itself is not material that can support a justificationist account. If a thinker has to employ his truth-conditional grasp of p in working out what is evidence that p, there is no support here for a justificationist theory of the content p. In fact it seems to be an empirical matter what would justify a claim that some thing, currently unperceived, has the same shape as some currently perceived object. Mere memory of the unperceived thing having the same shape as an object is currently perceived to have justifies the identity only on the wholly empirical premiss that the unperceived thing is not changing in shape. We do not seem to have any non-circular specification of a justifying condition that stands to a claim of identity of shape, or other property, between something perceived and something unperceived, as decision procedures associated with numerical operators stand to a decidable identity between two numerical terms. But that is what the justificationist would need to support his position.

If this argument is sound, it is already enough to show that theories of Type Two are not available to the justificationist. But there is also a problem special to Dummett's own conception of justificationism and of observation. The commitments of theories of Type Two are apparently incompatible with Dummett's view of observation as stated in his Thesis (E) above. Thesis (E) implies that the ability to make observational reports does not involve possession of the conception that what is observed is something that would or could exist even if not observed. Theories of Type Two, as construed under this option, require the child to grasp something that is, by the terms of Dummett's conception of observation in (E), unintelligible. Dummett says that the child who is capable of making observational judgements does not, simply in virtue of that, have any conception that what is observed can also exist unobserved. But theories of Type Two, under this option, imply that the child, in understanding predications about locations other than his own, appreciates that what is being said is that something is going on, or exists, that is of the same kind as he observes when such events or objects are at his own location. For this identity to be so much as intelligible, the child must be capable of grasping that something of the form 'It's F here and it's F at such-and-such place', where the place such-and-such is in fact unperceived by him, is on occasion true. If the child is not capable of grasping this, then giving the child the information that things elsewhere are F if they have the same property as the local things he in fact observes to be F is not going to make it any more intelligible that the property that can be observed to be instantiated can also be instantiated unperceived. The information involved in such an understanding of predications of other places presupposes some grasp of this as an intelligible possibility. The information by itself cannot make that possibility intelligible if the child does not already find it intelligible.

There seem to exist some types of perceptual experience that are both enjoyed by an infant prior to language-acquisition, and whose content makes rational the assertion of observational sentences once the more elementary parts of language are acquired. Observational shape concepts are the most obvious examples. If it is the very same content of experience both before and after the acquisition of language, and possession of the concept *oval* (say) involves appreciation that an arbitrary oval thing has the same shape as things perceived to be oval, it follows that pre-linguistic experiences have a correctness-condition that concerns the objective spatial world. An experience's having a correctness-condition that concerns the objective world is not something that comes only with the acquisition of language.

There is a substantial body of developmental psychological data best explained by the hypothesis that infants have a rich pre-linguistic conception of an objective world, and some conception of the constraints to which it conforms. Young children and infants have a rich conception of the world that is not currently perceived by them. This conception affects their knowledge and action, and it pre-dates by years their ability to use language to make observational reports on their surroundings. Later linguistic practice draws in part on this rich conception, rather than contributing to making it available, contrary to Dummett's assertion. The detail and characteristics of the infant's and young child's conception of the world as unseen by him at a given time have been extensively confirmed in a justly famous body of work in developmental psychology in the past twenty years. I mention two examples. Consider an object whose centre is occluded by a closer object. Philip Kellman and Elizabeth Spelke showed that 4-month-old infants perceive the occluded object as continuing behind the closer object when the visible parts of the occluded object move together.[6] The infants are surprised if the occluded object is revealed to be discontinuous. Renee Baillargeon showed that infants from the ages of 4.5 months to 5.5 months who see an object that is then obscured by a second object expect the second object not to be able to move into a location occupied by the first (and now unperceived) object.[7] These, and many other cases, are ones in which the phenomena are best explained by the hypothesis that the infant has a specific conception of how the world is in the regions he is not currently perceiving. Real children are not Dummettian children (in the full sense of his Thesis (E)).

It would not help if Dummett's view is that the child, in making judgements based on observation, is also to be ascribed the conception of other subjects as also capable of making observations. We have to explain understanding of a predication of, say, a shape property of an object as something that can be true even if the object is unobserved by anyone at all. There would still be a problem of unintelligibility on such a more socially oriented account. The problem would be transferred to the transition from a conception of a property of which the thinker need not have any conception that it can be instantiated unperceived by anyone, to a conception which requires that the thinker grasp that possibility. Such a transition still cannot intelligibly be effected simply by the thinker's use of an identity relation if Thesis (E) is in place.

The upshot of the discussion to this point seems to be that attempting to give theories of Type Two justificationist credentials via counterfactuals is making the direct–indirect distinction inapplicable in those theories; and that making sense of the identity of kind required in Type Two theories is

---

[6] Kellman and Spelke (1983). For an important defence of the methodology of these and related experiments, see Spelke (1998).
[7] Baillargeon (1987); and, for a more general survey, see Baillargeon (1993).

difficult to square with justificationism; and is problematic on Dummett's conception in Thesis (E) of observation and observational judgements.[8]

We turn to theories of Type Three. Would it be correct to take the meaning-specifying justification-condition for a predication of another place-time to be given by the counterfactual (regardless of what we go on to count as an indirect method)? That is the distinctive claim of theories of Type Three. This position would have to say something about the fact that when, for instance, we experience it to be sunny here, and take the experience at face value, we do not, before making the judgement *It's sunny here*, make a transition to a counterfactual 'If someone were to be here, he would observe it to be sunny'. But, the defender may continue, this would be a sound inference. The inference from the pair set of premisses {A, B} to the counterfactual 'If A were to be the case, B would be the case' is intuitively valid, and it is rightly treated as valid in both Stalnaker's and Lewis's semantics for counterfactuals.[9] We may not explicitly insert the counterfactual step in coming to make an observational judgement about how things are here, this justificationist may say, but our practice is legitimate, and there is a uniform account of the sense of sentences about place-times, only because it could be validly inserted.

The objection to this account is not from its lack of uniformity, but from the fact that the counterfactual condition is incorrect, both for predications of the thinker's current location, and for predications of other place-times. At least some of these points are familiar from other literature, and I will go through them briefly.

(1) Its being sunny at a place, either here or somewhere else, is what causally explains the truth of the counterfactual 'If someone were there, they would perceive it to be sunny'. Since nothing can causally explain itself, its being sunny at a place cannot be analysed in terms of the truth of that counterfactual.

---

[8] In his 'Response', Dummett writes that in these objections to Type Two theories, I am making a 'wholly illicit use' (p. 681) of the passage (E) from *Truth and the Past*. He attributes to me the view that a 'child's grasp of the logically presupposed item must temporally precede any grasp of what presupposes it' (p. 681). Saying that would be incompatible with an acknowledgement of a long-standing favourite theme of mine, the existence of ineliminable local holisms within a given family of concepts. When there is a local holism in a family of concepts, possession of a concept C can presuppose possession of D, and possession of D can also presuppose possession of C. It immediately follows that such a presupposition cannot sustain an asymmetrical relation of temporal priority in the account of acquisition of the concepts C and D. There is no commitment to a connection between what is 'logically presupposed' and temporal priority in the text above.

[9] Stalnaker (1968); Lewis (1973).

(2) It is widely held, and asserted by Dummett himself in some of his writings, that counterfactuals cannot be 'barely true'. This doctrine has more than one reading. But a very natural reading under which it is plausible would say that a counterfactual 'If someone were there, they would perceive it to be sunny' is, when true, true in virtue of a certain condition, the condition in (1) that explains its truth. An account of understanding of predications of places owes us some theory of what it is to conceive of these underlying conditions in virtue of which the counterfactuals are true. Once we have this, the counterfactual explication may be unnecessary.

(3) It is by now a very old point that the counterfactual explication is not extensionally correct. The presence of an observer may affect whether a place has a certain property, so it is not correct to say that a place has an observable property F just in case if someone were at the place, he would perceive it to be F. The point should not be breezily dismissed as one easily met by a minor qualification. To say 'For some place to be F is for it to be true that someone there would perceive it to be F, unless his being there affects whether that place is F' is to embed the very condition 'That place is F' that was to be explicated in justificationist terms. If the counterfactual was meant to explain what it is for a place to be F, it should not include the very condition of a place's being F that was to be explicated. The additional qualification makes the account circular.

This point also tells against a justificationist who holds that proofs are sequences of expression tokens (or corresponding mental constructs), and who tries to use a counterfactual explication of what it is for a place-time to be F to restore a parallel between the arithmetical and the empirical case. Such a theorist might propose that just as an indirect proof establishes that someone could write out a canonical proof of a true arithmetical equation, so similarly an indirect means of establishing that some other place-time is F establishes that someone there could have a perception of that other place-time being F. This proposal fails because someone could have a perception of the other place-time as F without the other place-time actually being F. That would be the case if the person's being at that other place-time caused it to be F.

(4) Some theorists, in the case of statements about what is the case elsewhere now, might offer justificationist accounts that talk about what someone would observe if he were now to travel to the place in question, and arrive there a little later. Even in a case in which there are no interference problems of the sort mentioned in (3), however, it is always an empirical, and certainly not an a priori, truth that how a place is now is the same as it was

a little time earlier. Anyone who grasps spatio-temporal thought will be in a position to appreciate this fact. It follows that we must give some account of understanding statements about what is the case at other places that makes this an empirical, and not an a priori, truth. We will not be doing this if we try to identify the truth of the predication with a counterfactual about what would be experienced by someone who travels to the place in question.

(5) These issues cannot be separated from the question of what individuates the intentional contents of mental states and events, both perceptions and judgements. Suppose it is true that a thinker elsewhere would experience it to be sunny there, and would judge it to be so. The fact that his experience and judgement would have this content is constitutively dependent upon the complex relations his experience and judgement bear to their occurrence and production in situations in which the thinker finds himself and in which it really is sunny.[10] This involves a philosophical-explanatory priority of the condition of its being sunny at a given place in relation to a thinker's experience or judgement that it is so.

(6) The ability to think of how it is at one's own, and at other, places and times does not seem to me to require the ability to think about other minds at all. There is no difficulty in principle in the idea of a very deeply autistic child, with no conception of other minds as having experiences and making judgements, nevertheless having the conception of places and times, both local and distant. In fact, part of what is involved in having the conception of a subject of experience who may be located elsewhere is that his states and judgements are suitably sensitive to what is objectively the case at other places. Again, this means that the conception of a subject who is elsewhere and has certain perceptions and makes certain judgements is philosophically posterior to the conception of how it really is at those places. This implies that no modified justificationist account of thought about other places and times that appeals to counterfactuals about what other thinkers would perceive or judge there can be correct. This objection would not apply to a more radical justificationism that holds that there is no more to the past than exists in the present. But this more radical, and less credible, form of justificationism about the past is just what Dummett was trying to avoid in developing his modified version.

There are genuine contrasts between the direct and the indirect that do apply to the distinction between observing some place-time to have a

---

[10] For further discussion, see Peacocke (2004, ch. 2 sect. 3).

property, and establishing the counterfactual 'If someone were to go to that place-time, she would observe it to have that property'. One such contrast is this: a thinker's understanding of the counterfactual depends upon his ability to know what it would be to establish by observation that a place-time has the property in question. When a thinker has information that there is no interference from the presence of an observer (as described in point (3) above), establishing the counterfactual is also an indirect way of establishing what could be established more directly by observation. These highly intuitive points are, however, equally available to, and should be endorsed by, truth-conditional, non-justificationist theories of meaning and content. These kinds of distinction between the direct and the indirect are not to be identified with the distinction introduced in justificationist semantics between the direct and the indirect. They involve no commitment to justificationism.

Is there some diagnosis of how Dummett arrived at his position? There must surely be more going on in the thought of such a substantial thinker than a simple conflation of features of the different theories of Types One, Two, and Three. I conjecture that there is, and that the explanation of what motivates Dummett's position lies partly in his conception of observation, as elaborated in his Thesis (E) about observation. Dummett's discussion of his conception is very brief (it is on one paragraph spanning pages 70–1), and it would be unfair to pin on him any specific elaboration. There are many distinct ways in which it can be true that a thinker lacks the conception of observation as revealing what would have been so even if the observation had not been made. One way is for the subject not to have the concept of perception at all; another is for the subject to possess the concept of perception, but to remain neutral on the thesis of independence from observation. But one tempting way to specify a Dummettian conception of observation in the child, a way consistent with each of these various elaborations, is to say that in making observational judgements about the world, the child bases those judgements on the content of her perceptual experience without needing to take any stand on the question of observation-independent existence. Then from the point of view of the Dummettian child, it may seem to make no difference whether we give the meaning-specifying condition for a predication of an observational concept in terms of the perception of a state of affairs, or in terms of the state of affairs itself. It may seem that under these conditions, and from the point of view of the Dummettian child, theories of Type One and of Type Two can be identified. The canonical justifying condition for such an observational sentence is given indifferently, for the Dummettian child, as the holding of an observational property or the perception thereof; and the indirect condition is given by the counterfactual.

This makes it much more intelligible how Dummett might come to hold such a position. It does not, however, make it more defensible. Either the canonical, meaning-specifying condition for an observational sentence requires perception of a state of affairs, or it does not. If it does, then the objections above to Type One theories apply. If it does not, then the objection to Type Two theories applies. In short, what makes it more intelligible that Dummett should have come to hold his position is also what makes it hard to see how his conception of observation will also permit an account, on his lines, of grasp of the instantiation of observational properties in the non-local cases. These issues are not avoided by saying that the content in the observed cases is simply indeterminate as between a content concerning the perceiver's world, and a content concerning his perceptions of the world. An acceptable account of the "direct" specification of meaning in Type Two theories requires that the property attributed in the observed case is in fact one that could be instantiated unperceived (whether or not the child conceptualizes that possibility). If the property could be instantiated unperceived, that is incompatible with its being a property of which it is indeterminate whether its instantiation concerns the subject's perceptions—it determinately does not.

We could of course form a genuinely different, intelligible justification-condition that requires that a state of affairs both obtains and is also perceived. But it is not the justification-condition for a content like *It is raining in the next village*. It is at best the justification-condition for the different content *It is raining in the next village and is perceived to be so*.

This discussion of theories of Types One, Two, and Three prompts two observations. One concerns the relations between metaphysics on the one hand, and the theory of meaning and understanding on the other. Many of the points on the above list (1)–(6) support the position that a good account of meaning and understanding has to draw on a correct metaphysics of counterfactuals, of explanation, and of perceptual experience. Far from settling questions of metaphysics, the theory of meaning and understanding requires distinctions and points drawn from metaphysics. So my position here also diverges from the contrary view of the relations between the theory of meaning and metaphysics for which Dummett argued in his book *The Logical Basis of Metaphysics*.[11]

---

[11] Dummett (1991).

The other observation concerns a curious feature of the theory in *Truth and the Past*: that there is in that book little discussion of memory in our understanding of past-tense statements. 'Memory' and 'remembering' do not feature in the index to the book, and such discussions of memory as there are concern such matters as the extreme version of anti-realism under which 'only what exists now can render any statement true or false' (p. 67). Dummett's own version of justificationism as applied to past-tense thought, and the justification-conditions he offers, each presuppose the subject's ability to think about past times. It is implausible that someone can think about past times without having some form of memory capacity, some ability to perceive temporal order and possibly intervals.[12]

Further examination of the metaphysics of the past and of our thought about the past seems to me to emphasize further some of the difficulties for the justificationist that we have noted. Here are two.

First, on the side of the metaphysics of the past: if we accept that past-tense statements are equi-categorical with their present-tense counterparts, it follows that a past-tense predication of an observational property should not be explained in counterfactual terms (even when we prescind from interference, pre-emption, and the like). In the present-tense case, the presence of the observational property causally explains the truth of the counterfactual about what a perceiver would experience when perceiving the object. It follows that the past-tense counterpart is equally causally explanatory of the corresponding past-tense counterfactual. The truth of the past-tense counterpart should not be identified with the truth of the counterfactual, under the thesis of equi-categorical character.

Second, on the side of thought about the past: we need to reflect on what individuates memory states with their past-tense intentional contents, and the consequences of a plausible account of this individuation. It seems to me that these memory states have the contents they do in part because they are, when all is functioning properly, caused by the past-tense states of affairs they represent as obtaining. That is, states with past-tense contents have their contents in virtue of certain of the causes of some such states, just as spatial perceptions have their content in part in virtue of the spatial states of affairs that, when all is functioning properly, cause those spatial perceptions. Both the memory states with temporal contents, and the perceptual states with

---

[12] A version of this thesis is actually formulated in highly compressed form on the last page of Wittgenstein's *Philosophical Investigations* (Wittgenstein 1958): 'Man learns the concept of the past by remembering.' An elaboration and some defence of the claim are given in Peacocke (1999, ch. 3).

spatial contents, are instance-individuated in the sense of chapter 2 of my book *The Realm of Reason*. But instance-individuation in the case of memory involves causal explanation by conditions obtaining in the past. I would argue again that this is incompatible with their consisting merely in the truth of certain counterfactuals.[13]

In his more recent 'Response', published in 2005, a year after *Truth and the Past*, Dummett gives a revised version of justificationism, intended to avoid the objections to counterfactual explications of what it is for an observable state of affairs to exist at some place-time unoccupied by an observer. In the revised account, the justificationist says that 'a direct justification of a statement that an observable state of affairs obtained at a certain place and time consists of an actual or *possible* observation' (p. 678). Dummett elaborates: 'the justificationist may reasonably take a possible observation to consist in the light-waves, sound-waves, infra-red radiation and other physical phenomena that would enable anyone suitably located to make the observation in question' (p. 679). Light-waves, sound-waves, and infra-red radiation are actual physical phenomena that certainly are not, I agree, mere possibilia.

But can this revised account work without appealing to counterfactuals? Four asteroids can be arranged in a square in cold, dark, silent space without there being any light-waves, sound-waves, or infra-red radiation there. If the revised justificationism tries to avoid this by speaking of what pattern there would be in light-waves, sound-waves, or infra-red radiation if there were such waves or radiation there, it will be appealing to counterfactuals after all. The previous objections to counterfactual explications would apply again. Justificationism must either, implausibly, deny the possibility of four asteroids being arranged in a square in the actual absence of any medium that permits observation of the shape; or it reverts to counterfactual explications again. Dummett says the justificationist 'merely regards physical reality as containing only what there is evidence that it contains—evidence that is not necessarily in our possession' (p. 679). If the evidence that is not necessarily in our possession is construed as possible evidence in the sense quoted, it seems to me a proposition incompatible with current physical theory to say that something can be square only if it is in the presence of light-waves, sound-waves, or infra-red radiation.

---

[13] Dummett does not, or at least in 1997 did not, accept this metaphysics of explanation. See the report of his views in Peacocke (2004: 40). So on this particular point, I should be regarded solely as tracing out the consequences of his views. Construed as an objection, the point relies on further metaphysical theses (for which I tried to argue in Peacocke 2004: 40–9).

The revised justificationist account also invites a question. If we are allowed, as on the revised account, to write into understanding the condition that in unobserved instantiation of an observational property, there is the same sort of possible evidence (in Dummett's special sense) as there is in observed cases, why apply the identity-relation to the evidence, rather than to what it is evidence *for*? Is there any reason that in these cases identity should be intelligible only as applied to the evidence, and not to the states of affairs for which it is evidence? If there is no such restriction on intelligibility, an account of understanding could simply say that understanding involves this appreciation: for an unobserved state of affairs of an observable type to obtain is simply for it to be of the same relevant kind (involving objects of same shape, same texture, same size, etc.) as in observable cases. This is a move in the direction in which I will proceed later. Accounts in this style are not, however, accounts in terms of justification-conditions.

Because I have disagreed so sharply with Dummett's justificationist treatment, I want to note a fundamental issue on which I am not diverging from him. Dummett insists, as he long has, that 'the opposition between justification and truth cannot be resolved until we have decided what form our theory of meaning is to take' (p. 114). Even the formulation in terms of an opposition between justification and truth is something that would have to be rejected if the positive account later in this chapter of the relations between justification and truth are correct. The point of agreement, however, is this: I have opposed justificationism, but I will be opposing it only by outlining another substantive theory of meaning or intentional content for statements about the past and about other places. There is a nexus of internal relations between entitlement, meaning, content, and understanding, and it is only in the context of this system of relations that we can achieve philosophical understanding of any one of its elements.

2. DO PRAGMATIST VIEWS AVOID THIS CRITIQUE?

The justificationist account of Dummett is an example of an account that aims to explain content in terms of what can rationally lead us to make a judgement with that content. In this respect, Dummett's account is grouped with conceptual-role and inferentialist accounts of meaning that focus on the input side, on what can rationally lead to judgement. Would the account do better, and avoid the critique, if it concentrated instead on the rational consequences of judging a given content?

An account of significance in terms of consequences is just what the pragmatists proposed. Charles Peirce gave this early formulation: 'Consider what effects, that might conceivably have practical bearings, we conceive the object of our conception to have. Then, our conception of these effects is our whole conception of the object.' Of the quality of being hard, Peirce wrote, 'The whole conception of this quality, as of every other, lies in its conceived effects.' More specifically, the effects in question must be sensible effects, on Peirce's view: 'Our idea of anything *is* our idea of its sensible effects.'[14] To say the effects must be sensible is not, of course, to say that they must concern experiences: they may concern what it is in the objective world that is experienced. This pragmatist conception was combined with something congenial to the justificationist views we have been considering, the idea that truth is explained in terms of a certain kind of knowability. In an imagined dialogue with an 'Anti-Pragmatist', William James wrote, 'Isn't your truth, after all, simply what any successful knower *would* have to know *in case he existed*?'[15] So does looking not at the grounds of contents, but at their consequences, in the manner the pragmatists propose, offer a way out of the difficulties faced by justificationism?

It does not, for several reasons. First, the point that it is an empirical matter what would be evidence or justification for the content that something holds elsewhere, or at another time, applies equally on the side of consequences. The consequences of its raining in the next valley, or the plays attributed to Shakespeare having been written by someone else, have to be worked out empirically, in light of additional information about the cases. (This applies all the more if it is 'sensible' effects that are in question.) The consequences would not be consequences of the hypothesis about another place or another time by itself. Actually, this is precisely what we should already have expected on other grounds. If there were consequences independently of other empirical hypotheses, there would also be at least non-conclusive evidence independently of other hypotheses, since one form of evidence for a content is that some of its consequences hold. But in general, we should reject the idea that there are consequences here and now of an empirical content about another place or another time that are independent of other empirical hypotheses. That idea involves a failure to appreciate Quine's

---

[14] Peirce (1940: 31).   [15] James (2002: 293).

familiar point. Evidence is in general evidence only for sets of hypotheses, and not for hypotheses one by one. This point applies as strongly on the side of the consequences of a hypothesis as it does on the side of the evidence for a hypothesis.

Another reason the pragmatic treatment does not avoid the problems of the justificationist approach is that some of the specific objections raised do clearly apply to the pragmatic treatment. The interference objection ((3) in the previous section) applies equally to consequences that are specified in counterfactual terms, as the pragmatists' consequences often are. The objections apply in particular to consequences specified as counterfactuals involving the presence of a knower at the place or time in question. When there are counterfactual consequences, in the presence of other empirical conditions, these consequences are explained by the holding of some condition at another time or place. The counterfactual consequences should not be identified with the condition's holding.

These points should not be taken as a blanket rejection of the pragmatists' views. These points are consistent with the idea that some properties are individuated by their causal consequences, a conception that is present in some of the quotations above from Peirce. I also think that there are pragmatist challenges about the importance of the notion of truth in understanding that need to be addressed (see Chapter 2 section 3(3) below). I agree too that we do need to elucidate the connection between understanding and knowing the consequences, in context, of a hypothesis.[16] My point has been that none of this is an account of the understanding of the hypothesis itself. That remains in need of philosophical explanation.

3. A REALISTIC ACCOUNT

We can start by considering a realistic account of observational concepts and their application. It is part of the nature of these concepts that they can be applied on the basis of perceptual experience. A thinker may also

---

[16] The cautious formulation in terms of a 'connection' is used in the second sentence of C. Misak's illuminating account in Misak (2004: 3): '[Pragmatism's] central insight is that there is a connection between knowing the meaning of a hypothesis and knowing what experiential consequences to expect if the hypothesis is true.' If it is only a connection, and not an account of understanding itself, we still need both an account of understanding, and an account of its relation to appreciation of evidence and consequences. This is further discussed in section 4 of the present chapter.

intelligibly, and on occasion correctly, apply the concepts to things or events that he does not perceive at the time of application of the concepts. One component of the realistic account I will be offering deals with application of the observational concept based on perception of the concept's instantiation. The other component deals with judgements involving the concept that do not involve perception of its instantiation on the occasion on which the judgement is made.

Relatively uncontroversial examples of observational concepts include *smooth*, *rough*, *straight*, *square*, *oval*, *stationary*, *moving*, *bent*, to take an arbitrary sample. When one of these concepts is applied on the basis of observation, the thinker takes the representational content of his experience at face value. It thus becomes crucial in specifying the nature of these concepts, and the conditions for their correct application on the basis of observation, to consider the nature of the representational content that is so taken at face value.

In my view, this representational content is objective content in that it is individuated (in part) by specifying how the space around the perceiver must be filled in with matter and light for the experience to be correct. The qualification 'in part' is present because the objects, events, and properties given in perception are also given in a particular way, but these differences in way will not matter for present purposes.[17] Space, ways it is filled in, and the matter and light with which it can be filled in are all mind-independent things. This means that mind-independent correctness conditions are intrinsic to the nature of perceptual experiences, and to the observational concepts that are individuated, in part, by their relations to these experiences. This point is the first component of a realistic account of observational concepts. We can call it "the objective-perceptual component" of the realist's account. The objective-perceptual component is a foundation that is needed for the other elements and theses of a realist's account of these matters. Not everything that is in the content of perceptual experience need be mind-independent—colour is not, on some views—but a vast subset of the contents are, and for them a treatment such as that just outlined is needed.

To say that the representational content of an experience is objective, and to say that the correctness conditions for judgements involving observational concepts are objective, is not to say that anyone who employs observational concepts must himself be exercising some notion of objectivity. A thinker can employ observational concepts without possessing a concept of experience or

---

[17] For more on ways, see Peacocke (2001*a*).

of perception at all. To exercise concepts with objective conditions of correct application is one thing, to have a conception of objectivity is another. Whether or not Dummett's Thesis (E) above about observation is correct in its full strength, part of what he may have intended in it is surely right. A conception of observation as observation is more sophisticated than, and is not implied by, the capacity to observe and make observational judgements about the world.

To say that objective content is independent of possession of a conception of objectivity is not at all, however, to say that possession of observational concepts is independent of the capacity to think of objects, events, or features that are in fact unperceived by the thinker. A subject can think or otherwise represent *There's a large rock behind me* without possessing the concept of perception (and without using a mirror). There is, for reasons of principle, a link between the ability to enjoy experiences with objective representational contents and the ability to represent objects, events, or features that are unperceived by the thinker at the time of the experience. We conceive of the region in which objects, events, and features are represented as occurring in any current perception as a region which is part of a larger space. Normal humans are also able to integrate the contents of their current perception into a cognitive map which maps those regions of space that are currently unperceived by the subject. The map locates objects, events, and features in those currently unperceived regions. Abnormal subjects may lack the ability to integrate the contents of current perceptions into cognitive maps. But they still think of the regions they are currently perceiving as part of a larger space. There will also commonly be subregions of the perceived region, occluded by opaque objects and surfaces, that are not themselves perceived by the subject.

Perhaps we can conceive of a subject, very different from us, located in a space very different from ours, who perceives all regions of the space in which it is located. There would be an upper bound on the distance between points in this space; the subject would have to have sensory surfaces pointing in every direction in the space, or at least surfaces receiving light (or some other medium) from every direction in space; and the objects and events might need to be transparent. Yet even in this distant possibility, there remains a connection between spatial content and the possibility of unperceived existence. For such a subject, that *these* regions (demonstratively given in perception) are all the regions there are is an empirical truth. It needs to be discovered empirically that there is an upper bound on distances between places in this imagined world. It is in the nature of our relation to space and distance that these are empirical issues. Correspondingly, the existence of what is in fact unperceived is always at least in principle something provided for in a conception of a space that one inhabits. This holds even if the subject himself is not exercising the concept of perception.

So much by way of introductory remarks on the first component, the objective-perceptual component, of the realist's account of understanding. The second component of the realist's account explains understanding of what it is for an unperceived thing or event to fall under an observational concept by relating that understanding to the case in which some perceived thing or event falls under that concept. For the concept *oval*, say, the second component of the realist's account states that a thinker's grasp of this concept involves his possession of tacit knowledge of this condition:

> For an arbitrary thing to be oval is for it to be of the same shape as things of this sort

where 'this sort' expresses a recognitional way of thinking of a sort, more specifically in this case a shape. This recognitional capacity is exercised when the thinker is presented in perception with a thing as oval-shaped. It would not be correct to simplify down the tacitly known condition to ' ... is for it to be this way', where 'this way' is the way things are given when perceived to be oval. That shortened condition would be met by an observational shape concept that does not apply to oval things that are either too large or too small to be perceived by us. Our actual shape concept *oval* involves no such restriction, and the condition of sameness of shape (approximate geometrical similarity) in the displayed condition above respects that feature of the concept.

What is said here for the concept *oval* can be generalized, according to the realist, to an arbitrary observational concept, with a suitable substitution for 'same shape'. I call this second element of the realist's account 'the identity-component'. An account of this form is available not only for the observational concepts we currently possess, but also, to take an example, for observational concepts for shapes that we do not currently use, but, given our perceptual capacities, we could easily acquire. The account is not restricted to concepts currently named in our actual language.

The knowledge attributed in this identity-component should be regarded as tacit for several reasons. The content of the knowledge need not be something a thinker consciously accepts, or even would accept if presented to him. Some thinkers may mischaracterize their own understanding. When two philosophers disagree about the nature of observational concepts, at least one of them must be wrong. Their actual common grasp of the concept *oval* may still consist in their common tacit knowledge involved in this identity-component. This tacit knowledge contributes to the actual explanation of their judgements involving the concept *oval* when applied to currently unperceived objects. The tacit knowledge involved in the identity-condition is more specifically a species of the implicit conceptions discussed in Chapter 4, where these notions are further examined.

Another reason that the identity-component involves only tacit knowledge is that its content involves very general notions that need not be possessed at the level of conscious content by everyone who possesses such observational concepts as *oval*. One can conceive of thinkers who acquire specific observational concepts first, and only much later acquire more general concepts such as sameness of shape or sameness of property, applicable equally across observed and unobserved objects. If a thinker only later acquires these more general concepts, it cannot be correct to explain his mastery of the specific observational concepts in a way that would require him to have concepts in his ordinary, non-tacit knowledge that he does not in fact yet possess.

The identity-component aims to explain understanding of a predication of an observational concept of an object or event not currently observed by the thinker in terms of a grasp of truth-conditions. The identity-component specifies a truth-condition for the predication in the content of the tacit knowledge it attributes. This is not an account of understanding in terms of justification, assertibility, consequences, or counterfactuals.

This second component is available to a realist only because of the objective-perceptual account, the first component of the realist's theory of understanding in this domain. For an unperceived thing to be oval is for it to have a mind-independent property. The sort under which a thing is presented as instanced in perception must itself be a mind-independent kind if the identity displayed above is even to be intelligible, let alone true. (The sort must be mind-independent. I am not saying that the subject who has the perceptual experience must thereby have some conception of minds, let alone a conception of mind-dependence.) That the sort presented in perception has this property is just what is stated in the first component of the realist's account. That was the force of the early paragraphs of this section, that the correctness-conditions of perceptual experience concern, *inter alia*, the spatial properties of things in the perceiver's environment. If the first component is correct, the realist is not appealing to unintelligible or illegitimate statements of identity. The correctness-conditions of contents involving the predication of *oval* of currently unperceived objects, if fixed by the identity-component of the realist's account, will thereby and correspondingly concern the mind-independent properties of objects.

For exactly the same reasons that a pleonastic conception of sameness of kinds would not serve Dummett's purposes in section 1 of this chapter, a construal of the quantification over properties as merely substitutional quantification would not serve the realist's purposes in his account. Such a substitutional construal involves taking the proposition

> There exists some shape property that the unobserved object has which is the same as the property things perceived to be oval are thereby perceived to have

as

> There is some predicate 'A' such that a predication of 'A' of the unobserved object is true and 'Things perceived to be oval are thereby perceived to be A' is true.

We are aiming to explain meaning and understanding. If an unobserved object's being oval is explained as its having the same shape property as things perceived to be oval, and that in turn is explained in terms of the truth of some predication of an unobserved object, then we are moving in a circle. The substitutional construal takes for granted appreciation of what it is for a predication of 'A' of the unobserved object to be true. That is what was to be explained.

The second component of the realist's account as given here holds only for observational concepts. The role of the perception-based way of thinking of a sort in the identity that is (according to the realist) tacitly known is specific to observational concepts. Consider the observational concept *elliptical*. This concept is distinct from the shape concept that is given by the equation for an ellipse in geometry with Cartesian coordinates. Someone can think of a shape under its equation specification, and wonder what the graph of that equation looks like. This is not possible for the observational concept, when it is fully grasped.

The identity-component of the realist's account meets six desiderata that emerged from the preceding discussion.

(*a*) By explicitly writing in that for something unperceived to be oval is for it to have the same shape as the perceptibly oval things, it ensures that there is uniformity in what is being predicated of an unperceived and of a perceived object when each is being thought to be oval.

(*b*) The shape property that is being attributed to perceived and unperceived oval things is explanatory of perception of a thing as oval when it is perceived.

(*c*) This realistic account actually, and ironically, restores for Dummett a parallel with the decidable mathematical case that we argued was lacking on the Type One reading of Dummett's account. What makes a predication of *oval* of an object true is an objective property, whether or not the property is perceived to be instantiated. What makes a decidable arithmetical equation true is the existence of a certain kind of proof, whether or not anyone has encountered or thought of such a proof.

(*d*) It is, under the realist's identity-component, a wholly empirical question what, now, would establish that some damp patch on the wall on a building across the street, unobserved by anyone, is currently oval in shape. All that is required for this to be true is that the patch has the same shape as things the thinker can recognize to be oval. If one goes across the street and observes the patch to be oval, that is evidence for the earlier claim only if the patch has not changed in shape. There may be very good evidence that it has not; but that it has not changed is a wholly empirical truth, whose status as such is made intelligible by the identity-component of the realist's account. The same applies *pari passu* to the consequences of the truth of a proposition about some other place-time.

(*e*) This realist's account has no problem with the example of the four asteroids in cold, dark, silent space that I argued earlier constitutes an objection to Dummett's revised justificationist account. These asteroids are still arranged in the same shape as things which are perceived to be square. This is what their falling under the concept *arranged in a square* consists in, under the realist's account. The presence of some medium is not required for this condition to be fulfilled. Hence I differ from Dummett when he writes, in his 'Response', that this realistic account of understanding is 'very similar to that entertained by a justificationist of the type' Dummett himself delineated in his 'Response' (p. 687)—that is, the revised justificationist account in terms of "possible observations", construed as states of physical media. The realistic account and the revised justificationist account differ sharply in what they each regard as intelligible.

(*f*) The two components of the realist's account of grasp of observational concepts can be present without the thinker having any conception of mental states, either his own or others'.

If the arguments against Dummett's conception of observation and observational concepts are correct, there is a generalizable, domain-independent lesson for the realist. Suppose that a mental state is mentioned, as an element of an identity-component in a realist's account of the understanding of some non-local predication. The lesson is then that further conditions, beyond simply the mental state's being conscious, must be mentioned in an account of understanding if such an explication of the non-local case is to succeed. In the case of the realist's account of the grasp of non-local predications of spatial and material concepts, the further conditions allude to the objective representational character of the content of perceptual experience. If the realist failed to mention this further condition, it would be entirely correct to object to him, in a Wittgensteinian spirit (though not to a Wittgensteinian end), that it is no easy thing to conceive of an unperceived object's being square on the basis of one's appreciation of what it is for a perceived thing to be square. Yet one does so appreciate it, all the same. The possibility of one's doing so is entirely dependent upon perception's having an objective representational content, upon which the identity-component of understanding can get a grip. It is because this is so that someone who in one way or another conceives of colour as mind-dependent needs to say more about physical properties underlying colour if he is to make sense of the existence of unperceived coloured things, as he certainly must. Otherwise, the case is not much better than the unacceptable reasoning "You know what it is for a mental event that someone experiences to be a pain; so you know what it is for an unowned event to be a pain". The general requirement of the existence of further conditions in an account of understanding beyond merely the status of a mental state as conscious, if the identity-explication is to succeed, is a requirement that is realized in many different ways in the various domains in which an identity-explication of understanding is plausible. It falls to the realist as a task to explain how this requirement is realized in those various domains. We will be attempting this later in the book, in the case of features of the domain of the mental.

4. HOW EVIDENCE AND TRUTH ARE RELATED

If content is conceived in terms of truth-conditions, rather than justification-conditions, what is the relation between a thinker's grasp of the truth-conditions of a content and his appreciation that something justifies acceptance of that content? If contents are not individuated in terms of what justifies acceptance of them, how do we reach a justification from something that does not involve justification? We know that we do have justifications, empirical justifications, for accepting particular propositions about times and places at which we are not located (for example). Our question is not whether this is so. Our question is what, under the truth-conditional account, makes this possible.

The question about the relations between truth-conditions and conditions of justification is not one that arises only for issues about our understanding of the past and other places. The question arises for any domain in which content is explained in terms of truth-conditions. Correspondingly, any good answer to the question must be generalizable to other domains; or must at least be shown to be an instance of a schema applicable in other domains in which the issue arises. This wholly general question is one that has in fact long been pressed by Dummett. He has written of it as 'a demand upon truth-conditional theories of meaning if they are to qualify as fulfilling what is required of a theory of meaning' that they show 'how what we count as evidence for the truth of a statement can be derived from what we take as the condition for its truth' (p. 115).

'Derived' is much too strong in this statement. As Philip Kitcher remarked to me, it is completely implausible that, in the general case, one can literally derive a statement of what would be evidence for a hypothesis from some specification of its meaning alone. What is evidence for a hypothesis must in the general case depend also on empirical information not derivable from a specification of meaning for the hypothesis, however theoretically rich that specification may be.

A more plausible claim is that, when something is evidence for a hypothesis, there is some explanation, stemming in part from the nature of the meaning of the hypothesis, but drawing also on empirical information, of why it is evidence for the hypothesis. I accept this claim, and the challenge it generates: to say what the explanation is. The intuitive basis of the demand is that it is some feature of the meaning-determined truth-condition of the hypothesis that, in the presence of further empirical information, makes something evidence for the hypothesis. Correspondingly, when we appreciate that something is evidence for a hypothesis, we draw in part on our understanding of that hypothesis. Our task is to explain what it is to do this soundly, on a truth-conditional conception of content and understanding.

In attempting to meet this challenge in the special case of the past, we can start with a simple example. Suppose you look up to the sky, and in the distance see a storm approaching. It is travelling towards you along a certain path. You have some experience of the shape of the paths followed by storms in this area. These circumstances can give you a justification for judging, a little later, "It is now raining in the next village". This justification has nothing to do with whether you would encounter wet roads if you were to travel to the next village. This justification for your belief that it is now raining in the next village is equally good in a hot climate, where you know perfectly well that by the time you travelled to the next village, the roads would be dry from the heat.

This justification for accepting the content "It's now raining in the next village" involves inductive inference. Induction is an inferential transition which, if it starts from empirical premisses, generally yields an empirical conclusion. It is an empirical matter what kinds of paths storms take, and how long they last. The justification, in this example, for believing that it is now raining in the next village is wholly empirical. It could not be reached simply by reflection, however resourceful, simply on the nature of the content "It is now raining in the next village". The input to the induction, its premisses, are cast themselves in spatio-temporal terms. In this particular example, the premisses can be known because the thinker is able to know how it is now at nearby places and at his own location. The crucial point for present purposes is that application of inductive methods, if applied to empirical premisses, can be combined with understanding of predications of one's own and other locations, to yield empirical justifications for beliefs about what is now happening elsewhere.

The same point applies to abductive inference more generally. If what is explained by a good abductive inference is something empirical, abduction will give empirical reasons for believing a particular content. In both the inductive and the abductive case, use of these methods is entirely consistent with a thinker's having no idea what in the physical world might justify acceptance of a particular predication of another place independently of use of inductive or abductive inference. If our understanding is given by grasp of truth-conditions, and this in turn in the case of other places and other times is given in terms of what I called the identity-component in the realist's account, this is plausibly our actual situation.

This yields another irony when considered in relation to some varieties of justificationism. We saw in an earlier section that Dummett's justificationist conceives of his "indirect" methods as ones that establish for the thinker, when successful, what a predication of another place says, namely (for a predication of an observational concept thereof) 'that at that particular location on the spatial map is something of a kind he can recognize when he himself is at the right location' (p. 51). We questioned whether justificationism has a right to this conception. But the present irony is that if what I have said about the empirical character of the evidential relation for thoughts about other places and times is correct, there is no need for a thinker to grasp additional, "indirect" methods as part of the task of grasping the sense of a predication of another place or time. That something is indirect evidence for such a predication can be established using general-purpose inductive or abductive reasoning. If a thinker is capable of such reasoning, and grasps the truth-condition for predications of other places and times, the condition formulated in terms of identity, the thinker needs nothing more to be in a position to appreciate something as evidence for a thought about another time or another place. On the other hand, the notion of identity of kind as between perceived and unperceived cases is virtually empty for a thinker unless he is capable of employing this notion in combination with inductive and abductive reasoning.[18]

The realist's account of predications of other times and places, as I have characterized it, uses a notion of identity of property. The realist must say more about what such identity, and grasp of it, involves. It is attractive at this point to combine the realist's account with Sydney Shoemaker's theory of the identity of properties.[19] Under this account, 'properties are individuated by their causal features—by what contributions they make to the causal powers of the things that have them, and also by how their instantiation can be caused'.[20] It is sometimes an empirical matter which causal powers contribute to the individuation of a property. In finding out, empirically, by the sorts of means we discussed earlier, the causes or effects of rain, we find out what it is for another place or time to be one at which it is raining. Shoemaker's view about property-identity can ratify as rational our actual inductive and abductive practices in making judgements about other places and times. It is a task for realism about understanding and for the metaphysics of properties to explicate this approach further.

---

[18] I have written 'inductive and abductive' in recent paragraphs, but there is a strong case to be made that sound abduction underlies good inductive inference. For a statement of this position, see Harman (1965), and, for a somewhat different rationale supporting the same general thesis, Peacocke (2004, ch. 5: 'Induction').

[19] Shoemaker (1984*a*, 1998).   [20] Shoemaker (1998: 61).

If the use of inductive and abductive methods, applied to empirical premises, can yield empirical justifications for contents whose nature is explained by the identity-component, this reconciliation ought to be available in other domains in which we have the apparent combination of content explained in terms of an identity-component, and in which evidence or justification seems always to be an empirical matter. Almost any description of these areas is going to be somewhat controversial, so here I will just have to plunge in with a statement of the views. A thinker's understanding of attributions of sensations and experiences to others (and arguably to herself in the past) involves an identity-component. The thinker appreciates, on this radically non-Wittgensteinian account, that for someone else to have a pain in her knee, or a tingle in her wrist, is to have something of the same subjective kind as she herself has when she has an experience of each of these respective types. There does also seem always to be an empirical element in the conditions that justify the ascription of a pain sensation, or a tingling sensation, to another person. What physiological conditions, and what central neurophysiological conditions, accompany or realize pain or tingling sensations seems always to be an empirical matter. Which empirical conditions they are that accompany or realize these sensations can be known by inductive and abductive inference, inferences starting from empirical premises about one's own sensations and experiences. It is this combination of the presence of an identity-component in the account of understanding, together with empirical elements in any justification-conditions, that explains the phenomenon that Albritton famously noticed. As he noted, following Alvin Plantinga, it always makes sense to ask 'I wonder how people who are in pain behave nowadays?'[21] There are of course plenty of real problems about how it is that this makes sense. Some of them are addressed in Chapter 5.

A very different kind of domain in which we have the combination of an identity-component in understanding combined with wholly empirical justification-conditions is that of highly theoretical postulation in physics. We can take superstring theory as an example.[22] The current theory postulates that in addition to the three perceptible spatial dimensions, there are also another seven dimensions "curled up", and too small to detect by traditional methods or by perception. There is an identity-component in the account of our understanding of what it is to be one of these additional dimensions.

---

[21] See Albritton (1968).   [22] For an accessible exposition, see Green (2004, esp. chs 12, 13).

They are conceived as things of the same general kind as the familiar three spatial dimensions. A full specification of location in the universe, under this theory, involves specifying location along each of these seven additional dimensions, just as it does for the traditional dimensions. Some physical properties can vary independently along these additional dimensions, just as they can along the four more familiar physical dimensions; and so forth. But the evidence, the justification, for accepting particular propositions about location in any one of the new dimensions is always a wholly empirical matter. It is not given a priori by the nature of our understanding of the existence of these dimensions. The evidence is wholly a posteriori. Abductive inference, with empirical premises as input, provides an explanation of how this is possible. One of the achievements of superstring theory is to explain the families of fundamental particles, and the particular masses and spin properties they have. That electrons, quarks, and gravitons have the particular masses and spin properties they do is a wholly empirical matter. Superstring theory explains the existence of these properties, and the particular families of particles, by the possible energy levels of particular strings in the new dimensions with which these particles are identified. That there are particular kinds of string with particular energy properties is justified by abductive inference from wholly empirical facts. Once again, we reconcile an identity-component in understanding with wholly empirical justification-conditions by means of empirical input to a justifying abductive inference. The fact that understanding is explained in truth-conditional terms is thus reconcilable both with the existence of justifications for propositions about the new dimensions, and with the empirical character of those justifications.

Could the justificationist simply take over the points I have been making, and say that on a more generous construal of justificationism, these points present no problem for that thesis? Empirical justifications are nonetheless justifications; so why should the justificationist not appeal to them? The answer to this question is that the empirical character of the justifications is symptomatic of the fact that the correct account of what is involved in understanding the contents in question does not imply, even in the presence of other a priori theses, that these justifications are justifications. In saying that it is symptomatic, I am relying on the principle that evidential relations involving a content that are a priori can be established as evidential relations simply from the nature of the truth-condition grasped in grasping the content, without reliance on empirical information.[23] It is not open to the justificationist to appeal, for instance, to whatever might, in the presence of other information, justify the content that it is now raining in the next valley, or the content that there are seven additional spatial dimensions. That would be to explain justification-conditions in terms of the content in question, rather than the other way around, which is what the justificationist's thesis requires.

This, it will not have escaped the reader, is exactly the same argument, applied here against justificationism for the statements of superstring theory, as we used in section 1 against the availability to the justificationist of Type Two theories. It is an insistence on non-circularity in the justificationist's specifications of what, by his lights, individuates content and meaning. This issue of non-circularity surfaces repeatedly in the debate between realist and justificationist accounts of content and meaning.

A justificationist may still be tempted to say that understanding the superstring hypothesis that there are eleven dimensions involves appreciating its role in a particular theory, and justification-conditions for the hypothesis can be derived from its role in that theory. This is the move made by Dummett: 'To understand the postulate [that there are eleven dimensions] we must recognize it as part of a whole physical theory, we must know enough of that theory to grasp the role that the postulate plays within it, we must know that the postulate is to be accepted only if the theory is accepted ... ' ('Response', 684). Precisely one of the most striking aspects of superstring theory is that even given the relation of the postulated eleven dimensions to the other properties and relations postulated in the theory, theorists still did not know what would be evidence or justification for the whole theory. They postulated that there are strings and vibrations that explain the familiar families of particles and their confirmed familiar relations. But what would be evidence that there are such strings and vibrations in the hidden dimensions was quite moot for them (and, to the best of my very limited knowledge, still is). Yet the vocabulary of the theory was meaningful, and was understood. Theorists understood superstring theory without having fulfilled what Dummett describes as a 'need to understand the type of abductive argument that can justify its acceptance' ('Response', 684). Of

---

[23] See Peacocke (2004) for a defence of this principle. The principle is not unique to truth-conditional theories of understanding, and could be defended on other theories of content too.

course theorists did seek knowledge of what might confirm such theories. But they did this, it seems to me, already understanding the theory for which they sought such knowledge of possible abductive reasoning. What makes superstring theory empirical is not its relation to possible justifications, but rather simply its subject matter: it is about our space-time, its contents, and what dimensions it has.

It is also implausible that two people mean something different by 'There are eleven dimensions' if they disagree about the nature of the strings in those hidden dimensions, or disagree about what properties of the familiar particles they explain. Yet such a difference of meaning is implied by the claim that understanding of the postulate involves acceptance of a certain physical theory. The arguments against theory-dependence of meaning that were forcibly put by Hilary Putnam seem to me to apply here too.[24] Just as Rutherford and Bohr did not mean something different by 'atom', even though they differed in their theoretical claims about atoms, nor do two superstring theorists mean something different by 'the hidden dimensions', even though they differ about what is located in those dimensions.

A realist's account of the understanding of the hypothesis that there are hidden dimensions appeals to a thinker's tacit knowledge of an identity. The additional, hidden dimensions are magnitudes of the same kind as the familiar spatial dimensions. Location in the universe is not fully specified without specifying values on the hidden dimensions, just as location in three dimensions is not fully specified by giving locations in only two dimensions; and so forth. Similarly, a realist's account of understanding of thought about other places and times that uses an identity-component seeks to explain understanding in terms of the thinker's tacit appreciation of an identity that is required for the correctness of certain kinds of content (a certain sameness of shape in the case of observational shape concepts, and so forth). This style of account of concept-possession is present in some other basic cases, and it should not be regarded as something recherché or unfamiliar. The same phenomenon is found at the level of singular reference. In grasping what it is for an arbitrary object x, perhaps one given under a past-tense mode of presentation, to fall under the singular concept *this F*, where *this F* is a perceptual demonstrative, a thinker tacitly appreciates that x, given under the past-tense mode of presentation, must be identical with the one currently perceptually presented to the thinker. Again, this is a specification of grasp of sense that

---

[24] Putnam (1975*a*).

involves a condition on the world, formulated in terms of identity. Far from being recondite, the phenomenon is ubiquitous in thought. The conditions involved in understanding in these cases can, on this account, be specified only at a level that involves reference to objects, properties, and relations in the world. The phenomenon could not be accommodated by theories that regard talk of reference and truth as a *façon de parler* that plays no fundamental part in the account of intentional content.[25] I return to the discussion of the role of identity in the explanation of understanding in Chapter 5.

The character of the relation between justification and truth in the case of other places and other times bears upon Crispin Wright's discussion, in the early parts of his book *Truth and Objectivity*, of what he calls a variety of minimalism.[26] The variety of minimalism in question is one according to which it is sufficient for something to be a truth predicate that 'it coincides in normative force with warranted assertibility' (even though the predicate is potentially divergent from warranted assertibility in extension; p. 24). For propositions about other times and other places, we have seen that it is an a posteriori matter what warrants their assertion. What warrants such assertions is not determined a priori simply from the meaning of such assertions. If the considerations marshalled so far in this chapter are correct, what makes such a warrant into a warrant has to be explained in terms of truth-conditions, given via an identity of properties under the realistic account I have offered. This means that, for such cases, the doctrine Wright describes cannot really be a form of minimalism. To appreciate the warrants as warrants, a prior grasp of truth-conditions is required. One could not even conform to norms specified in terms of warranted assertibility, for such subject matters, without having some additional grasp of truth-conditions not explained in terms of assertibility.

The applicability of this point is independent of whether the subject matter in question is intuitively realistic in Dummett's sense, that is, admits propositions that could be true without our being able to know that they

---

[25] Since I have been discussing his views so extensively, I note explicitly that Dummett himself has said for many years that reference plays an essential part in an account of understanding. His claims about justificationism should thus be distinguished from those of Brandom, for whom reference and truth play no such fundamental role (see Brandom 1994). My divergence from Dummett is not over whether reference plays an essential part in the philosophical elucidation of understanding, but over what that role is. My discussion is also directed at those who (unlike Dummett) think that justificationism provides an adequate elucidation of understanding that does not involve the notion of reference.

[26] Wright (1992).

are true. The point applies to present-tense predications about other places, even nearby places. Even for these, it is an empirical matter what warrants assertions about them, and our understanding cannot be explained unless we mention a grasp of truth-conditions. The empirical dependence of conditions of warrant upon further truth-conditions is a phenomenon that can be present even when verification-transcendence is not at issue.

This means that one cannot soundly argue from a rejection of verification-transcendent truth to the need for a justificationist theory of meaning. At one point in the final chapter of *Truth and the Past*, entitled 'Truth: Deniers and Defenders', Dummett appears to be arguing in a way that implies that there would be no role for truth-conditions in theories of meaning and understanding that eschew verification-transcendent truth. I quote at length, for the passage is revealing. He writes that justificationist theories of meaning are prompted by the thought

that when we acquire the practice of using language, what we learn is what is taken to justify assertions of different types. We learn what is accepted as entitling us to make those assertions; we learn also whether what justifies us in doing so is conclusive or whether it is defeasible, that is, capable of being overthrown by subsequent counterevidence. We do *not* learn what it is for those assertions to be true independently of any means we have for establishing their truth. How could we? If we are not in a position either to assert or to deny a given proposition, we cannot be shown what nevertheless makes it true or false. So, according to a theory of this kind, to grasp the meaning of a statement is to know what would justify asserting it or denying it. (p. 114)

On the view for which I have been arguing, the conditions for justified assertion that a place that the thinker does not currently occupy or perceive has a certain property are simply justifications for thinking that place has the same property as his current location has to have for it to have the property. If I am allowed to say it one more time, it is an empirical matter what those justifications are. The only general, a priori statement of what those justifications are is an account that uses the materials of the identity-component, and uses it in giving the truth-conditions of assertions about such nearby places. But nothing here involves commitment to a verification-transcendent conception of truth about nearby places. It makes one wonder whether the Dummettian position overlooks certain kinds of rationale for non-justificationist conceptions of meaning.

I make these points only to emphasize the independence of the arguments for anti-justificationism from a commitment to the possibility of verification-transcendent truth. The anti-justificationist arguments get a grip even within the realm of what would commonly be regarded as the decidable within the empirical realm. To emphasize this point is not at all to be committed to the proposition that all truth is in principle verifiable by us, if suitable conditions obtain. Some truths about the physical universe, even truths that we can currently formulate, may be derivable only in theories too difficult mathematically and conceptually for us or any of our successors to grasp. To say that they could be known and grasped by some possible mind is simply to make the notion of a possible mind ride on the back of what is objectively the case, independently of grasp of it, rather than to state any substantive constraint on what could be the case. Even for the restricted case of observational concepts applied to particular place-times, if it holds that any such truth could in principle be known by some human, given suitably placed apparatus and conditions, that those are means of knowing such truths is still an empirical matter. Such knowability cannot help with the theory of understanding.

5. THREE GRADES OF INVOLVEMENT OF TRUTH IN THEORIES OF UNDERSTANDING

On the general relations between justification and truth, we can distinguish (at least) three positions, in order of increasing degree of involvement of truth in an account of justification.

(1) On the first position, there is no involvement at all. This first position holds that we can specify a justification-condition, a pattern of inference, or more generally a conceptual role that individuates a particular content, and can do so without any mention of reference and truth. This first position is occupied by such pure conceptual-role theorists as Gilbert Harman and, more recently, Robert Brandom.[27] It is natural to call it 'Grade 0' in respect of the involvement of truth and reference in justification-conditions. Theorists whose accounts of intentional content are at Grade 0 in respect of their relations to reference and truth are characteristically minimalist or redundancy theorists of truth and reference.

(2) A second position is that it is a substantive, overarching constraint on a theory of concepts and complete intentional contents that judging in

---

[27] Harman (1999*a*); Brandom (1994, 2000).

accordance with content-individuating justification-conditions furthers the goal that only true contents should be accepted. This was the position I occupied in *A Study of Concepts*.[28] It was motivated by the idea that truth is one of the constitutive aims of judgement, and that the constraint this involves cannot be reduced simply to facts about conceptual roles. Theories committed to this second level of involvement of the level of reference in the individuation of content will declare that for any genuine concept, there must be an account of how a reference is determined for the concept, from the justification-conditions mentioned in the possession-condition for the concept. Such an account I called a 'Determination Theory' in *A Study of Concepts*. Alleged concepts for which there is no Determination Theory are not, under this approach, regarded as being genuine concepts at all. It is, however, entirely consistent with this second level of involvement that the specific content-individuating justification-conditions for a particular content be given in terms that do not mention reference and truth at all. The introduction and elimination rules for conjunction, for example, contribute to the individuation of a concept, under this approach, but do not themselves mention reference or truth. There is a Determination Theory for them; but this theory is no part of the justification-conditions themselves, which are as given in the introduction and elimination rules in that particular example. This second position we can classify as having Grade 1 involvement of reference and truth in justification-conditions.

(3) On a third kind of position, justification-conditions for certain kinds of contents are inextricable from reference and truth. On the realist's view as defended earlier in this chapter, understanding an observational predication of another place or time involves tacit knowledge that it is true just in case that place or time has the same property that the thinker's current spatial or temporal location has when it is observed to have the property denoted by the predicate. This characterization could not be replaced with specific justification-conditions that do not mention reference or truth without giving something whose status as a justification is empirical. Knowing of what is in fact an empirical piece of evidence for one of these contents that it is evidence is neither necessary nor sufficient for understanding the predication in question.

Positions of this third kind are content-specific, in contrast with the overarching, entirely general thesis that supports Grade 1 involvement. So this

---

[28] Peacocke (1992).

Grade 2 involvement is in the first instance Grade 2 involvement for a specific concept, such as the concept of another location, or the concept of the sensations of another subject. In principle it would be possible to hold that some concepts are such that a correct theory of them involves Grade 2 involvement, while the correct theory for others involves merely Grade 1 involvement. In fact, in Chapter 2, I will make a case for the stronger claim that every concept is such that the correct theory of it involves Grade 2 involvement.

It is important to consider these distinctions when assessing philosophical claims about meaning, justification, and truth. When faced with a general claim about the relations between justification and truth, we should always ask: which of these grades of involvement are consistent with the claim? Once we distinguish the various grades, how forceful is the claim? An example of the importance of distinguishing the grades is provided by Bernard Williams's discussion, in his last completed book, *Truth and Truthfulness*, in which he disputes Richard Rorty's views that the goal of inquiry is merely justified belief, and that we do not need to mention truth as inquiry's goal.[29] Williams writes, 'A justified belief is one that is arrived at by a method, or supported by considerations, that favour it ... in the specific sense of giving reason to think that it is true.'[30] This formulation cannot be conclusive against the position of Rorty and his supporters on this particular issue. Williams's formulation of the connection between justified belief and truth could, and no doubt would, be accepted by those who hold that there is no more than Grade 0 involvement of truth and reference in justification, and who hold a purely minimalist or redundancy theory of truth. These Grade 0 theorists will still hold that there is a legitimate notion of truth. It is just that, according to them, it plays no essential part at all in a substantive account of intentional content. For example, a Grade 0 theorist may say that judging justified contents comes to no more than judging properly in accordance with his proposed reference-free justification-conditions, or judging contents for which there is reason to think that its proposed reference-free canonical commitments are fulfilled. Such a position will make the quoted thesis from Williams come out true. The Grade 0 theorist can very happily say that a justified belief is one that is arrived at by considerations that give reason to

---

[29] Rorty gives an extended exposition of his position in Rorty (1998). For discussion of my position in relation to Rorty's protest against that idea of truth as an '*additional* norm' (1998: 26), see Ch. 2 sect. 3(3) below.

[30] Williams (2002: 129).

think that it is true. This result is certainly contrary to Williams's intentions; in any case, it shows that the formulation falls short of showing that truth is essential in an account of justification.

The conclusion I draw is that Williams's underlying intentions are right, but those intentions require a different articulation if they are to be properly expressed. To capture a more substantive role for reference and truth in the account of justification, we need to allude to Grade 1 or to Grade 2 involvement of reference and truth. Grade 2 involvement, in particular, of the sort I have argued we find in the cases discussed by Dummett, is something much stronger than many of the more general theses linking justification and truth that, like Williams's formulation, are consistent also with even Grade 0 involvement of truth and reference. When we cannot even specify what would be evidence that something is or was the case at another place or time without invoking sameness of property or event-type as is instantiated in some basic cases, we are then specifying evidential conditions at the level of reference and truth in a way that is incompatible with Rorty's idea that truth plays no essential role in justification-conditions.

6. ANCHORING

In addition to the question we were addressing earlier, of how we attain empirical justification-conditions on the realist's account of understanding, there is the further philosophical question of the nature of the relation between independently specifiable justification-conditions and the individuation of conceptual content on the realist's view. In the case of thought about sensations, and thought about other places and times, certain kinds of predication do have a species of justification that is independently specifiable. The first-person predications have a certain independently specifiable justification in ascriptions of sensation and perceptual experience. Predications about what is the case at this place here have a distinctive justification, at least in the case of observational predications, amongst predications about places. Predications about past times based on personal memory have a distinctive justification amongst predications about other times. We can say that, in this respect, the possession-conditions for concepts of sensation, of places, and of times have a *direct anchoring* in the sense that at least one clause of the statement of the possession-condition relates possession of the concept to a justification-condition that involves a mental state other than judgement.

Concepts of the additional dimensions proposed in superstring theory, by contrast, do not meet this condition. There is no way of thinking of a particular location, specified in the seven additional dimensions, such that perceptual, or any other, knowledge of the place so given has a special role in the thinker's understanding of predications about 7-D places in the way that thoughts of the form *It's raining here* have a special part to play in the grasp of other predications involving the concept *rain*. Nonetheless, the additional dimensions of superstring theory are thought of as having certain relations to the familiar dimensions, our concepts of which do give a special role to the thinker's location. So in addition to the concept of a possession-condition with direct anchoring, we can introduce the idea of a possession-condition that has *linked anchoring*. Linked anchoring has a recursive characterization:

> A possession-condition with linked anchoring either has direct anchoring, or one clause of a statement of the possession-condition relates possession of the concept to a concept that has linked anchoring.

Using these characterizations, I conjecture that the following thesis is true:

> Every concept has a possession-condition with linked anchoring.

I call this last the 'Anchoring Principle'. It implies that there are no unanchored possession-conditions.

Is there a general reason, beyond induction from individual examples of particular concepts, for believing the Anchoring Principle? The most general reason seems to be that if the Anchoring Principle is violated, it is not clear how the thinker could ever have well-founded reasons for believing a thought about the world. As we have seen, although some concepts are not individuated in terms of their justification-conditions, we can by more or less resourceful use of abduction come to have empirical reasons for believing particular contents containing these concepts. The possibility of such abductive inference seems, however, always to rest upon our ability to judge contents that are individuated in terms of their relations to such states as perception, sensation, action-awareness, memory, testimony, reasoning, and calculation. We do not seem to have any model for rational acceptance of an empirical content that does not involve some such states other than judgement. As John McDowell emphasizes, we would not have the required kind of connection with reality itself unless perception and other content-involving states other than judgement are involved in the individuation of some intentional contents.[31] A causal connection of our judgements with reality is not by itself enough. We have to explain how there is a rational connection with reality, a connection secured by reason-giving states that are not themselves judgements.

An insistence on anchoring is in itself, as far as I can see, neutral on whether the representational content of perception is conceptual or not. My own view continues to be that there are strong arguments for saying that the content of perception is partly non-conceptual.[32] But the Anchoring Principle is consistent with the view (not mine) that the contents involved in perceptual states are simultaneously individuated by their role both in perceptual contents and in the contents of judgements, and by the relations of states of both of these sorts to the environment and to other mental states.

The scope of the Anchoring Principle can be delineated partly by emphasizing what it is not. The Anchoring Principle is neither a verificationist principle nor a justificationist principle. The realistic account of understanding of observational spatial contents that I have been defending, an account that is neither verificationist nor justificationist, gives an essential role to perception. Since perception is not a form of judgement, this realistic account respects the Anchoring Principle. Correspondingly, any support enjoyed by the Anchoring Principle should not be taken as an argument in favour of justificationism, nor as an argument in favour of verificationism. A properly formulated realistic account of understanding can and should embrace the Anchoring Principle.

The Anchoring Principle does not deny that you can come to know contents, even contents involving observational properties concerning your immediate environment, in ways other than those specified in the possession-conditions for the concepts in those contents. You can come to know that some object you perceive is oval by testimony, by geometric inference, and in countless other ways, all of which are consistent with the possession-condition for the observational concept *oval* mentioning perceptual experience. Once a possession-condition has determined a property that the concept *oval* picks out, all sorts of ways are ways of coming to know that something has that property. What individuates a certain concept of a property should not be thought of as the sole means of coming to know something as that property, even so thought about. A means of coming to know that

---

[31] McDowell (1994, Lectures I and II).   [32] See Peacocke (2001*a*).

something is oval is ratified as such in part because the means is sufficient to establish that the thing in question has the same property something has to have to fall under the concept *oval*, as determined by that concept's possession-condition.

The Anchoring Principle and the account of observational properties offered that accord with it do not involve any denial of the holism of confirmation. Even in the local case of a judgement *It's raining here*, perceptual evidence can be outweighed by further investigation of one's surroundings. The water dripping on you from above may be determined, on the basis of maps, testimony, and all sorts of other research, to come from a stream flowing near a rock above your head. In that case, it is not rain. But the rationality of rejecting *It's raining* in these circumstances is underwritten by the possession-condition for the concept *rain* itself, and is made rational by that possession-condition. The evidence from maps, testimony, and the rest precisely makes clear, in the imagined example, that the perception of water falling in droplets is not a perception of the same kind of precipitation as is found in the normal cases by which intentional content is fixed (and which, on empirical investigation, turns out to involve atmospheric condensation).

Far from the Anchoring Principle and the holism of confirmation being in tension with one another, they seem to me to have the properties and relations that make possible a happy theoretical marriage between them. Working out what confirms a hypothesis is a rational process. Evidence for a hypothesis may in principle come from all sorts of different sources, but we have to address the question: what makes it evidence for that hypothesis? One answer to that question about making is that it is evidence that confirms, by whatever route, the holding of the truth-condition for that content, the truth-condition determined by the possession-conditions of its constituents. The claims of the truth of that content on the world, beyond its relations to other judgements, are shown by the ultimate anchoring of the possession-conditions of its constituents in world-related states other than judgement.[33] Since those states are individuated by their relations to the world they are about, this is not any form of idealism.

---

[33] A rival approach would define a notion of independence used in the characterization of anchoring in such a way that judgements too are counted as independent, provided they are judgements of contents distinct from the content mentioned in a concept's possession-condition. This approach would not imply that such independent judgements are ultimately related to reason-giving states and events other than judgement. It would permit islands of judgements not ultimately connected to reason-giving states other than judgement.

7. NEXT STEPS

I have argued that our grasp of contents of two kinds, contents about other places and contents about past times, has to be explained in terms that involve essentially truth and reference. In particular, grasp of contents of each of these two kinds involves tacit knowledge of a certain identity, an identity concerning properties, events, and states at the level of reference, not at the level of concepts and thought-contents. Reasons for making judgements about other places and past times can be exhibited as derivative, in the presence of additional information, from grasp of these identity-involving truth-conditions. The question now arises of whether this conception of the role of truth and reference can be generalized.

There are at least two dimensions along which the question of generalization arises. First, does it hold more generally that the truth-conditions for a content, as determined by the reference-conditions of its constituents, contribute to the explanation of what are reasons for judging the content? Does this hypothesis hold for all contents and all their constituents? How does the hypothesis hold in detail for various concepts? Second, does the model that explains understanding of certain predications in terms of tacit knowledge of an identity apply in the domain of concepts of conscious states and events? Can we give a general model of such understanding, and treatments of particular psychological concepts that conform to that model?

These questions about concepts of conscious states and events are addressed in Part II of this book, Chapters 5 through 8. In the next chapter, I address the question of how the hypothesis relating truth- and reference-conditions to reasons for making judgements could hold in general.

2

Reference and Reasons

1. THE MAIN THESIS AND ITS LOCATION

What is the relation between the rule that gives the reference of a concept and the reasons or norms for making judgements that are distinctive of that concept? This is a pivotal issue for our conception of the relations between two dimensions of concepts: their referential dimension on the one hand, and their location in the space of reasons on the other. My claim will be that the rule that gives the reference contributes essentially to the explanation of the norms or reasons specific to the concept.

If such a link between reference and reasons does exist, it bears on a fundamental issue prominently discussed in the past sixty years. Some writers have argued that it is an error to think that reference plays any role at all either in understanding, or in concept-individuation, or in the explanation of norms of rational judgement. These writers are by no means all of one stripe. They include thinkers as radically different from one another as Wilfrid Sellars, Gilbert Harman, one temporal stage of Hilary Putnam, Hartry Field, Ned Block, Robert Brandom, Paul Horwich, and Huw Price.[1] If the reasons and norms distinctive of a concept can be explained only by the rule that determines the reference of the concept, reference does have an essential role to play in concept-individuation and in understanding. More generally, if the hypothesis linking reference and reasons is correct, the norms distinctive of a particular concept cannot be elucidated solely at the level of sense, independently of considerations at the level of reference. As I will discuss

[1] To list them in what is, to the best of my knowledge, temporal order of published expression of this view. See Sellars (1963b,c; 1974); the five essays reprinted in Harman (1999b, pt III: 'Meaning'); Putnam (1978); Field (1977); Block (1986); Horwich (1998), which develops from his earlier published work; Brandom (1994, 2000); Price (1988, forthcoming). Not all who are sceptical of a role for truth and reference in individuating meanings are conceptual-role theorists. For a general scepticism about all substantive, explanatory theories of meaning and intentional content, see Schiffer (1987, 2003).

later, the hypothesis also bears upon what is thought to be a rivalry between use theories of content and meaning on the one hand, and truth-conditional theories on the other.

A full defence of my main thesis would need to contain both a positive part and a negative part. While the positive part would state the case in favour of the thesis, there is also a task of justifying the implied disagreement with those treatments of reference and truth on which rules of reference could not possibly have the explanatory force I claim for them. Such redundancy-inspired accounts of reference and truth have been developed in varying degrees of detail by Sellars, Brandom, Field, and Horwich. Brandom in particular has developed an extended treatment of "refers to" and "is true" which, if correct, would make it impossible for truths about reference and truth to explain anything about understanding and norms.[2] In this chapter, I will concentrate just on the positive part of the task, and simply record my acknowledgement that the negative part must be carried out too. What I am offering here is one contribution to what has emerged as an extended and large-scale debate in our subject about the role of reference and truth in understanding and norms.

By way of further motivation for considering my thesis, I will also be arguing that we can learn more about the nature of the norms distinctive of various specific concepts by examining in detail how they are explained by the rules for the determination of the reference of the concept. We can explain various epistemic phenomena distinctive of particular concepts by drawing on this resource.

Some theorists may react to the hypothesis linking reference and reasons by saying that it follows from what they already accept. I have some sympathy for this reaction; for I would count myself amongst their number. The main thesis itself is a consequence of the conjunction of two views. The first, Fregean, view is that the essence of a concept is given by the fundamental condition for something to be its reference. The fundamental condition for something to be the reference of the concept is what makes the concept the concept it is. The second view is that there are reasons or norms distinctive of a given concept, where these reasons or norms depend upon the nature of the concept. If both these views are correct, it follows that for each concept, there is some condition that gives its reference, and which, since that condition

---

[2] See Brandom (1994, ch. 5). My principal claim in this chapter involves exactly the opposition direction of explanation of understanding and norms from that developed in his stimulating discussion.

gives the essence of the concept, must contribute to the explanation of anything derivative from the nature of the concept, including the norms or reasons distinctive of it. I accept this reasoning. It is, however, one thing to know that something is so; it is another to understand how it can be so. How can the level of reference and norms concerning the level of sense be connected in this way? How can what is often a rich set of norms distinctive of a concept be explained by something as apparently austere as a rule of reference? It is these how-questions that I aim to address here.

The target of an explanation of certain facts about reasons from facts about rules of reference is not a fact about what norms are accepted in certain societies, or what linguistic conventions are in force in some group of thinkers. I am concerned with concepts rather than words, and the reason-relations I aim to explain are timeless and ahistorical. A Fregean more concerned with the relations between thinkers and Thoughts (Frege's *Gedanke*) than was Frege himself would say that these reason-relations pertain to the nature of things in his third realm. The how-question I am addressing seems to me to be of the same general character as certain other how-questions in philosophy. Descartes knew that the meaning of sentences depends on the meaning of the words composing them; the Stoics knew that certain principles of propositional logic are valid; long before Tarski, everyone knew that the sentence 'Snow is white' is true if and only if snow is white. In all these cases, what is required of philosophy is a theory that adequately explains what we already know. In the case of the compositionality of language, we need an acceptable account of the nature of meaning, and specifications of individual meanings, an account that shows how particular sentence-meanings are determined from their component words. In the case of logic, we need an account of what validity is, and what property is preserved in valid transitions, one which allows us to explain why a principle of propositional logic is valid; and so forth.

The methodological parallel between the case of logic and the present project is quite close. We know that certain premises are such that it is never rational both to accept those premises and to reject certain corresponding conclusions containing a given concept. We know that certain mental states give reasons, in certain background conditions, for making certain judgements. Sometimes facts of these sorts are distinctive of a certain concept or class of concepts. So we want to know why they hold; and we want in particular to know how the nature of a concept or of the concepts in a certain set can determine instances of these reason-involving

relations. That is the kind of project I am engaged in here, and I regard
its methodology as continuous with those of the philosophical treatment of
linguistic understanding, logical validity, and a theory of truth. In Strawson's
famous classification, this is 'descriptive' rather than 'revisionary' metaphysics
of content—provided we add immediately that 'non-revisionary' should not
be taken to mean "non-explanatory".[3] To answer the question of how we
should conceive of the relation between reference and reasons is to attain
a more thorough understanding of the relations between thought and the
world, both in general, and in the case of various specific concepts of
philosophical interest.

2. EXPOSITION AND FOUR ARGUMENT-TYPES

The main thesis, whether obvious or not, needs a lot of clarification. It is
a thesis about norms specific to concepts. It is not a thesis about all norms
whatsoever. A first step towards clarification of the thesis is to say what is
meant by 'fundamental rule of reference'. What I mean by the fundamental
rule of reference for a concept is the rule that specifies what makes something
the reference of the concept. Some examples:

> What makes a time the reference of *now* in a thinking is that it is the
> time at which the thinking occurs.

> What makes someone the reference of the first-person concept *I* in a
> thinking is that he or she is the thinker (the producer of that thinking).

> What makes something the reference of a particular perceptual demon-
> strative *that cup*, where the perceptual demonstrative is individuated by
> a particular way W in which something is given in a thinker's percept,
> is that: it is the cup thereby perceived in way W by the thinker.

> What makes something fall within the extension picked out by the
> observational concept *oval* is that it is something of the same shape as
> things are represented to be in the perceptual experiences of things as

---

[3] P. Strawson (1959, introd.).

oval. (This representation will be of the correctness of a non-conceptual content, on my view.)

What makes something fall within the extension of the concept *rain* is that it is an event of the same type that is required for the correctness of a thinker's judgement *It's raining here now*, where the present-tense, local predication of rain is to be further elucidated.

These rules state what relations an object, or extension, or entity of the appropriate category must, as a constitutive matter, stand in to a thinker at a given time to be the reference of the given concept as it occurs in the thinker's thought at that time.

The examples I just gave included both indexical concepts and non-indexical concepts. For the case of indexical concepts, in earlier work I used, in the spirit of Evans's writing, this notation: for any given indexical type Δ, such as the first person-type, the *now*-type, and so forth, there is a corresponding relation R_Δ.[4] R_Δ is the relation in which an arbitrary thing must stand to a thinker at a given time in order to be the reference of a use of an indexical of the type Δ by the thinker at that time. The fundamental rules of reference for the indexical cases just given are such relations R_Δ for the respective types Δ that they treat. For present purposes, it is helpful also to allow a generalization of this notation to the non-indexical case R_C. These will be the cases in which there is no constitutive dependence of the reference of the concept C on features of the thinker's context or identity. In the non-indexical case, as in the indexical case, it is still possible to say what makes something the reference of the concept C as it occurs in a thinker's thinking at a given time. R_C is the relation that, as a constitutive matter, has to hold between a thinker x and some entity Y of the appropriate category, in order for Y to be the reference of x's use of C. In the case of an indexical concept, there is a substantial dependence of the reference of the concept on some relational feature of the particular occasion of use of the concept. There is a dependence of the reference of the concept on who is using it; or on the time of its use; or on the agent of its use; or on the location of its use; or on who or what stands in certain relations to the conscious mental states of the agent at the time of its use; and so forth. In the case of non-indexical concepts,

---

[4] See Peacocke (1981). This is in the spirit of Evans's treatment in Evans (1985*b*). Though Peacocke (1981) differs from Evans on some issues, the positions are at one on the importance of fundamental reference rules.

there is no such substantial variation of reference with such features of the particular occasion of its use. But for both the indexical and the non-indexical cases, there will be a relation which makes something the reference of a given concept on a particular occasion of its use, even if the nature of the relations varies in the two kinds of case.

The condition that makes something the reference of a given concept is not something the thinker herself needs to conceptualize in personal-level thought. It is highly plausible that there can in principle be perceptual-demonstrative thought about her perceived environment by a young child or organism that does not yet have the concepts of experience or perception. This young thinker will employ concepts whose fundamental reference rule mentions perceptual experience, without thereby exercising the concept of perceptual experience. Standing in the relevant relation R_Δ to something makes available Δ-thoughts about that thing. But standing in the relation is something weaker than conceptualizing it as the relation it is. More sophisticated thinkers may be able to reflect on that relation, and such reflection may guide rational thought in those more sophisticated thinkers. All the same, standing in the relation should always be distinguished from thinking about it.

The main thesis of this chapter—that fundamental reference rules contribute to the explanation of norms concerning concepts—is about thought, not about language. The *Oxford English Dictionary* contains only one relevant entry for the *word* "pentagon".[5] But there is clearly more than one concept of this shape. There is, for example, a perceptual concept of the shape. You can come to have a capacity to recognize visually roughly pentagon-shaped things, such as coins of a certain denomination you regularly encounter. Someone can have this perceptual concept without ever having counted the sides of this familiar shape. For such a person, it can be informative that the number of sides in this shape is five.

One consequence of this point is that the fundamental reference rule for a concept F should not be identified with the intuitive notion of what it takes to be F. The notion of what it takes to be F is not sufficiently discriminating to distinguish two different concepts of the same property, or of the same object. The relevant *Oxford English Dictionary* entry for "pentagon" is 'A plane geometrical figure with five angles and five straight sides'. That this specifies what it takes (or at least part of what it takes) to be a pentagon no

---

[5] The online version, as of Apr. 2006; subsequent references are to the same edition.

one should dispute. But since this formulation of what it takes applies equally to what it takes to fall under the perceptual concept of a shape, or under an explicitly defined concept employing the materials in the *OED*, or equally under some specification using Cartesian coordinates, such formulations will not draw enough distinctions to contribute to the explanations of the norms associated with these different concepts.

The same applies to the word "rain". Some dictionaries, including the *Oxford English Dictionary*, give an entry for "rain" which includes the condition that rain is a condensed vapour of the atmosphere. There is certainly a way of thinking of rain, again one tied in part to the perception of rain, under which it is informative, and in no way a priori, that rain is a condensed vapour. It is something that was once discovered empirically. Often, to understand a word, one needs to know only which thing or property it refers to. When this is so, it is entirely legitimate for a dictionary to contain any information that will allow the reader to latch on to the right reference. But when our concern is with the level of concepts and thought, we need to slice more finely.

The main thesis is meant to apply to the explanation of the norms distinctive of a concept only in cases in which the concept does have a fundamental rule of reference. Philosophers have long discussed expressions for which it is incorrect to try to explain the nature of their meaning in terms of contributions to truth-conditions. For example, any such explanation is wrong for a conditional whose meaning is explained in terms of a thinker's or a speaker's subjective conditional probabilities. There are norms for the use of such expressions, norms distinctive of the concept in question, but they have nothing to do with the concept's fundamental reference rule—there are no such fundamental reference rules for such a concept. This restriction on the main thesis (which I will suppress for brevity in the following discussion) by no means makes it a triviality. The main thesis is a quite specific hypothesis about the explanation of norms distinctive of a concept, within the domain of concepts that make a contribution to the truth-conditions of contents in which they feature. It will take hard work to argue for the hypothesis.

There need not be any neglect of the sense–reference distinction in the thesis that the fundamental reference rule for a concept contributes essentially to the explanation of reasons or norms distinctive of that concept. The norms or reasons are characteristically norms or reasons concerning contents involving that concept, norms that apply in specified circumstances in which the thinker may find himself. Now those circumstances may, in one way or another, be mentioned in the fundamental reference rule for a concept.

A thinker may be in the circumstances, or stand in the relations mentioned in, or possess information of a sort mentioned in, the fundamental reference rule for one concept, while not being in the circumstances, nor standing in the relations mentioned in, nor possessing information of a sort mentioned in, the fundamental reference rule for another concept—even if the two concepts refer to the same thing. This is the situation of the two different fundamental reference rules for *Hesperus* and *Phosphorus* in the traditional story. The fundamental reference rule for the former mentions the heavenly body to appear first in the evening. The fundamental reference rule for the latter mentions the last heavenly body to appear in the morning. One of these reference rules, but not the other, contributes to an explanation of why in the morning it can be rational to judge, on the basis of perception, *Phosphorus is shining brightly* but not rational in those same circumstances to judge, on the same basis, *Hesperus is shining brightly*. Because different relations to the same heavenly body are mentioned in the two different reference rules for individual concepts that in fact refer to the same thing, there is no collapse of sense to reference in holding that fundamental reference rules for concepts contribute essentially to the explanation of their normative properties.

It can help at this point to return to some basic characterizations to clarify what is involved in the main thesis of this chapter. Taken in the abstract, with no restrictions on the case whatsoever, an arbitrary reference rule cannot contribute to the explanation of norms, because some such rules may—for example—simply take the form of saying only, of some particular object x, that the reference of a concept is x. Such rules could not contribute to the explanation of the relevant norms, nor uniquely fix (let alone individuate) a concept. 'Concept' as used throughout this book is a notion tied, in the classical Fregean manner, to cognitive significance. Concepts C and D are distinct if it is possible rationally to judge some content containing C without judging the corresponding content containing D. Concepts are constitutively and definitionally tied to rationality in this way. The thesis that a concept so understood is individuated by its fundamental reference rule is a substantive, non-trivial philosophical thesis about such concepts. On this conception, only certain rules will be capable of explaining norms distinctive of concepts. It is these reference rules which, as a substantive matter, individuate certain concepts.

So how in other cases beyond the case of the morning star does a fundamental rule of reference (FRR) for a concept succeed in contributing to the explanation of a norm for it? To begin to answer this question, I introduce a series of argument-types. Each type corresponds to a certain sort of concept. For each type of argument, an instance of that type can explain the existence of a certain norm for a concept of the sort that corresponds to the argument-type.

The first argument-type can be called, for reasons which I hope will become clear, 'the model of Indexical Ascent'.

Argument-Type One: Indexical Ascent

We can take the present-tense concept *now*, and derive one of the general norms for it using this first argument-type. In this derivation we make essential use of the fundamental reference rule for *now*. Here is an instance of the norm in question: an experience that occurs to you at a given time as of its raining at that time entitles you, in our actual circumstances and in the absence of reasons to the contrary, to accept then that it's raining at that same time.

The entitling experience in this formulation occurs at a particular time, but it is also an experience of that particular time. Its content concerns that time, just as a perceptual experience can be an experience of a particular object and the content of the experience will then concern that object. In short, perceptual experience has a *de re* content concerning a particular time.

The norm just formulated concerns the reference of (or in) one constituent of the content of the experience. The norm also concerns the reference of (or in) one constituent of the content of what the thinker accepts. That is why it is a norm at the level of reference, rather than a norm at the level of sense.

The entitlement does not exist in all possible circumstances. If there were a massive time-lag in perception, and the thinker knows or suspects this to be so, then an experience as of its raining at the time at which the experience occurs would not entitle the thinker to judge of that same time that it's raining then.

Generalizing from the property of being a time at which it rains to arbitrary properties F of times, we may say:

(NR1) For any time t, a perceptual experience at a time t as of F holding of t entitles the experiencer, in our actual circumstances and in the absence of reasons to the contrary, to be in this state with respect to t: that of accepting of it then that it's F at that same time; that is, the experience entitles the thinker to stand in this relation to t:

$$\lambda x \lambda \tau [x \text{ accepts at } \tau \text{ that it's F at } \tau].$$

'NR' in the name of this and later principles is to indicate a norm at the level of reference. The present-tense concept is neither used nor mentioned in (NR1). (NR1) is a universal quantification over the times themselves, not ways of thinking of times. Other concepts are tacitly mentioned or quantified over in (NR1). If we were writing this out more strictly, we would indicate the fact that it has to be a concept corresponding to F that features in the content accepted by the thinker. There is no aim of eliminating or reducing concepts in this project. The aim is only that of illuminating some aspects of conceptual content by taking some others for granted. I will similarly use 'NS' in a name to indicate a norm at the level of sense for the target concept in question.

Theorists can and do disagree about the explanation and the status of the principle (NR1). Some say that it holds a priori in the actual world, others that it is empirical. Some say that it holds without restriction on the property F, others that it holds only for a restricted range of properties F. Less contentiously, we can just say: in our actual circumstances, we are in some cases of the occurrence of such an experience entitled to accept at *t* that it's F at that same time. For present purposes, all we need is the truth of some principle of this general character at the level of reference, rather than some particular explanation of its truth or the precise limits of its applicability. Provided some such principle is true, it can contribute to the explanation to be offered in this instance of Argument-Type One, consistently with several different explanations of its truth or its scope.[6]

Whatever may be the philosophical explanation of why (NR1) holds, the core of that explanation will not pivotally concern the present-tense way of thinking. For the explanation, whatever it is, has to be an explanation of why an experience occurring at a time *t* of something's being the case at the time of the experience really makes it more reasonable to think something really is the case at that very same time *t*. Theorists differ on what this explanation is. Some theorists invoke considerations of reliability in the actual and nearby possible worlds. Some invoke additionally considerations having to do with what gives the experience the content it has. Experiences are, on the whole, as of what produces them in everyday circumstances. On each of these approaches, there is a case to be made that the occurrence at *t* of an experience as of its being F at *t* can make it reasonable to think of *t*,

---

[6] Examples of thinkers who formulate norms of which some variant or restricted form of (NR1) will be a consequence are Burge (2003); Field, on the natural reading of his treatment of default reasonableness and its application to perception in Field (2001*c*); and Pryor (2000).

the time itself, that it has the property of being F. Under these approaches, three things are going to be crucial in the explanation of the entitlement to judge: the nature of something's being an experience at *t* as of something's holding at *t*; the experience's relation to the world as it is at *t*; and its relation to a judged content concerning that same time *t*. These three elements and their relations all fundamentally concern times rather than ways of thinking of times.

So, to proceed with the argument: from the fundamental rule of reference for uses of *now*, we also have that if one correctness-condition is fulfilled, so is another:

> (ExRef *now*) Suppose the correctness-condition of what is accepted, when the thinker accepts at *t*, of *t*, that it's F then, is fulfilled: then by the FRR for *now*, the correctness-condition for a thinking of *It's now F* by the thinker at *t* is also fulfilled.

The correctness-condition for a thinking of *It's now F* by the thinker at *t* is simply that it be F at the time of the thinking, namely *t*; and that is implied by the correctness-condition holding for what the thinker accepts in accepting at *t* that it is F at that same time.

It is plausible that entitlement is preserved under transitions involving only the application of fundamental reference rules. Together with that supposition, the norm (NR1) and the proposition (ExRef *now*) jointly imply

> (NS *now*) A perceptual experience at a time *t* as of its being F at *t* entitles the experiencer to judge *It's F now*, in our actual circumstances and in the absence of reasons for doubt.

But this is a norm for the present-tense concept *now*. We have a derivation of a norm for the concept *now* from a norm not mentioning that concept, together with a principle derived from the fundamental reference rule for the concept. ('Accepting', 'judging', and 'thinking' are merely stylistic variants in this reasoning.) A temporal *de re* content of experience is linked, in this argument, to the concept *now* via a conception of entitlement and the fundamental reference rule for *now*.

If we substitute the concept *10.15 a.m.* for the concept *now*, the corresponding argument does not go through. To a first approximation, the fundamental rule of reference for the concept *10.15 a.m.* is that, on any given day, uses of it on that day refer to ten hours and fifteen minutes after the start of the day.[7] The correctness-condition of what is accepted, when the thinker accepts at *t*, of *t*, that it's F then can be fulfilled without the correctness-condition for a thinking of *It's F at 10.15 a.m.* being fulfilled. No further information about the particular time at which one is making the judgement is required for one to be entitled to judge *It's now raining* on the basis of an experience of rain at that time. Further information about the time is required before one is entitled to judge *It's raining at 10.15 a.m.* Being entitled to have, in relation to the time 10.15 a.m., the property

$$\lambda x \lambda \tau \, [x \text{ accepts at } \tau \text{ that it's F at } \tau]$$

is not yet to be entitled to have, in relation to 10.15 a.m., the property

$$\lambda x \lambda \tau \, [x \text{ accepts at } \tau \text{ that it's F at 10.15 a.m.}].$$

This intuitive point about entitlement is underwritten by the apparatus I have been using. The analogue of (ExRef *now*) for the concept *10.15 a.m.*, that is (ExRef *10.15 a.m.*), does not hold. Suppose, of a time that is in fact 10.15 a.m., that the thinker accepts of it that it's F at that time. It does not follow from this and the fundamental reference rule for *10.15 a.m.* that the correctness-condition for a thinking of *It's F at 10.15 a.m.* is also fulfilled. This is so because the holding of the correctness-condition for what is accepted in accepting, *de re*, of what is in fact 10.15 a.m. that it's F at that same time implies nothing about the temporal relation of that time to the start of the day. Yet that is what is required for the correctness-condition of the content *It's F at 10.15 a.m.* to be fulfilled.

Note that there is nothing in the argument so far about knowing these norms, not even (so far) about tacit knowledge of them. There are important phenomena involving knowledge that we need to understand if reference rules do contribute to the explanation of norms at the level of sense, and the explanation may need to draw on knowledge of what we are currently aiming to explain. But at this basic level of explanation of rather primitive norms involving senses, we are not yet using the notion of knowledge of norms at the level of reference.

It matters that the derivation of NS *now* from a principle about entitlement and a reference rule employs a rule of reference that is fundamental. If the derivation proceeded from facts about the reference of a concept that relied

[7] This needs some qualifications that do not affect the force of the argument that follows. Someone who goes to bed early, sleeps deeply, and wakes just before midnight thinking it is 10.15 a.m. is thinking that it is 10.15 a.m. the next day.

on empirical information, or even on a priori information that is highly non-obvious, then the derivation of the norm (NS *now*) could show only that the norm holds when those empirical, or a priori non-obvious, conditions obtain or it is reasonable to rely on their obtaining. Since the norm NS *now* is not so restricted in its applicability, nor do such conditions need to be known to obtain before the norm is known to apply, such explanations would be at best incomplete (and very likely incorrect in the explanatory resources they invoke). If we are relying on the fundamental rule of reference for a concept, on the rule that makes something the reference of the concept, there is no such dependence or restriction.

The reoccurrence of the variable 'τ' in the specification of the property the thinker is entitled to have in relation to the time at which his experience occurs is important. It means that the identity of the time of acceptance with the time that his thought is about is an identity that is registered within his entitlement. It would be possible just to say—and of course to say truly—that an experience at t of F holding at t simply entitles the thinker to accept at t of t that it's F. But that would not register the identity of the latter times within the thinker's own entitlement or conceptions.

The use of identity of variables in specifying the various relations in which a thinker is entitled to stand to a time is crucial for this argument. We could not formulate the argument without it. In the case of language, Kit Fine has argued that we need to enrich standard referential semantics to a form of what he calls relational semantics, in order to do justice to the significance of the identity of variables at their various occurrences.[8] If what I have been saying is correct, the significance of identity of variables across occurrences extends beyond the semantics of language to the theory of thought and epistemic entitlement.

This instance, and any instance, of Argument-Type One involves rising from a norm at the level of things (the times in the first premiss) to a consequential norm concerning senses that present those things. This is the motivation for the label "the model of Indexical Ascent".

We need to be clear about what this instance of Argument-Type One does, and what it does not, imply. The argument is one about explanation in the theory of norms and entitlement. It states that a norm at the level of reference contributes, together with the fundamental reference rule for *now*, to the explanation of a norm at the level of sense. Although the norm at the level of reference concerns a species of *de re* content of experiences and

---

[8] Fine (2003, Lecture 1: 'Variables').

judgements, absolutely nothing here implies that *de re* content is possible without a *de dicto* content that presents the *res* in question. It is a fundamental principle in the theory of intentionality and of sense that there is no thinking of something without thinking of it in some particular way, under some particular mode of presentation. The argument about the explanation of a norm at the level of sense starts from a premiss, (NR1), that characterizes states in terms of their *de re* contents. But the priority of this principle in an explanation of the existence of certain norms does not imply that a thinker could be in such states without also being in states that present the relevant *res* in particular ways. We should distinguish priority in the explanation of norms from priority in the explanation of the possibility of being in *de re* mental states. All I have been arguing is that for the purpose of explaining certain entitlements, the relevant level of characterization of the contents of attitudes involves a *de re* classification of the contents.

It may ease concerns on this score to give a reorganized form of this argu-ment from Indexical Ascent, a reorganized form that starts with a premiss that presumes that perceptual experience has a present-tense content. The reorganized form, like the original form, concludes with a principle about judgements with a present-tense content. In the reorganized form, we start with the principle that at any time t, an experience occurring at t with the present-tense content *It's F now* is an experience at t as of F holding at t. This principle is an instance of what Quine in 'Quantifiers and Propositional Attitudes' called 'exportation'.[9] It involves exportation on the present-tense indexical mode of presentation. At this first line of the argument, we are in effect descending from the level of sense to the level of reference. We are then in a position to apply (NR1), and the argument proceeds as before. This reorga-nized argument will still rely on the principle that a use of *now* in a judgement refers to the time at which that judgement is made. The rule of reference contributes to the explanation of the norm. If we do adopt this reorganized form, then the general type of argument it instantiates should no doubt be renamed "the descent from and subsequent ascent to the indexical level".[10]

Here is a second instance of Argument-Type One, applied to the first-person concept. For any given conscious state-type S, let C(S) be the canonical

---

[9] Quine (1976*a*: 190).

[10] A variant form of the reorganized argument could also be given that is congenial to those who hold that perceptual experience has only a temporally neutral content (*it's raining*, rather than *it's raining now*). Even if the experience itself is so neutral, its occurrence at a particular time still generates entitlements concerning that time.

concept of that state made available to a thinker by his knowing what it is like to be in the state S (as the concept *pain* is such a canonical concept of the state of pain). We have

> (NR2) If a subject *x* has an experience of being in conscious state S, that entitles *x* to be in this state: $\lambda x[x$ accepts *x* is in C(S)].

From the fundamental reference rule for the concept *I*, we have that

> (ExRef *I*) If the correctness-condition for the content accepted by *x* in being in the state $\lambda x[x$ accepts *x* is in C(S)] is fulfilled, then: by the FRR for *I*, the correctness-condition for a thinking of *I'm in C(S)* by *x* is also fulfilled.

This holds because if *x* judges *I'm in C(S)*, he will be the thinker of that thought, and by hypothesis he is also in S, of which C(S) is a canonical concept. So the thought's truth-condition is fulfilled. In inferring to the consequent of (ExRef *I*), we have used only the fundamental reference rule for *I*, together with the specified circumstances of the case (described in *de re* terms) and not any further information.

As before, it is plausible that entitlement is preserved in transitions using only fundamental reference rules. That supposition, together with (NR2) and (ExRef *I*), imply that

> (NS *I*) An experience of being in conscious state S entitles its subject *x* to judge *I am in C(S)*.

Again, we have a norm for the first-person concept derived from norms about things (subjects) and the fundamental reference rule for *I*.

Just as in the present-tense case, an identity of variables in the specification of the entitled state $\lambda x[x$ accepts *x* is in C(S)] secures the point that the identity of the thinker with the subject of the conscious state S is registered within the scope of the thinker's own entitlement.

If we substitute the descriptive concept *the author of the Meditations* for the first-person concept *I*, the corresponding argument does not go through, not even if it is Descartes's own entitlement that is in question. The fundamental reference rule for that descriptive concept is that it refers to the person who uniquely wrote the *Meditations*. Suppose Descartes himself is, for some particular conscious state S, entitled to be in the state

> $\lambda x[x$ accepts *x* is in C(S)].

That does not generate an entitlement to be in the state

$$\lambda x(x \text{ accepts the author of the } Meditations \text{ is in } C(S)).$$

The correctness-condition of what is accepted by someone who is in that second state is by no means ensured, simply by the fundamental reference rule for the descriptive concept *the author of the Meditations* together with what Descartes is accepting in being in the state

$$\lambda x[x \text{ accepts } x \text{ is in } C(S)].$$

We could make the same point for the conceptual content *Descartes is in C(S)*. Descartes's himself being entitled to be in the state

$$\lambda x[x \text{ accepts x is in } C(S)]$$

does not thereby entitle him to be in the state

$$\lambda x[x \text{ accepts Descartes is in } C(S)].$$

Similar remarks also apply as in the present-tense case to those who insist that a subject's experience of being in a conscious state must already involve exercise of a first-person concept. If it should be so, we can once again descend from the level of sense to the level of reference, apply the fundamental reference rule for *I*, and then reascend to explain the correctness of the norm "If *x* is in a conscious state with the content *I am in C(S)*, then he is entitled to judge the first-person content *I am in C(S)*". Only if the first-person concept refers to the thinker of the thought in question can this norm be generally correct.[11]

In both examples of Indexical Ascent, I have been taking it that certain transitions preserve a thinker's entitlement to have a certain property involving acceptance of an intentional content. The transitions I have made use only substitutions based on the fundamental reference rule for a concept. While the transitions on which I have relied may be relatively unproblematic, not just any necessary or even a priori substitution preserves such entitlement. We certainly do need a general explanatory theory of what preserves entitlement and what does not. We can probably legitimately have more confidence, at the moment, that certain transitions preserve entitlement than we have in any one general theory of the preservation of entitlement. It

---

[11] I have largely suppressed the present-tense component in the thought and in what is accepted. If it is made explicit, it can also be treated along the lines of the first instance of Argument-Type One.

would take us in a different direction from the goal of this book to explore theories of the preservation of entitlement. Here and for the moment, I simply acknowledge that the need exists, and rely on the plausibility of the fact that a theory will classify transitions relying only on fundamental reference rules for the concepts involved as transitions that preserve entitlement.

So much by way of examples of the first argument-type. Here now is another argument-type.

Argument-Type Two: Experience and Demonstratives

Instances of Argument-Type Two are ones in which a thinker judges a content involving a singular concept and a predicative concept that are each so related to perception that if the thinker's experience is veridical, then the content will be correct. Take the perceptual-demonstrative judgement *That plate is round*, made on the basis of an experience as of the plate as round. The thinker can be entitled to make that judgement, in the absence of reasons for doubt. The fundamental reference rule for the observational concept *round* will state that things in its extension are of the same shape as things experienced as round, when the thinker's perceptual systems are functioning properly. If those systems are functioning properly, then the perceptual demonstrative *that plate* will refer to a plate that really occupies what in experience it is represented as occupying, to wit, a round region of space; in which case the judgement *That plate is round* will be correct. That is an explanation of the existence of this norm about entitlement to judge on the basis of perceptual experience, an explanation that draws upon the fundamental reference rules for the perceptual demonstrative *that plate* and for the observational concept *round*.

There is no corresponding explanation of any entitlement to judge *that plate has a shape described by the equation* $(x - h)^2 + (y - k)^2 = r^2$, even though the equation picks out the same shape. The fundamental reference rule for the shape concept given by the equation involves mathematical operations, is determined compositionally, and does not directly mention perceptual experience. The observational concept *round* differs from the shape concept involving algebra in all these respects.

This form of argument can be generalized to other observational concepts and perceptual demonstratives, in the presence of suitably corresponding experiences.

Argument-Type Three: Soundness Proofs

Some argument-types that can be used in support of the main thesis of this chapter can be adapted from familiar reasoning from other areas. The reasoning involved in soundness proofs in metalogical theory provides one such example.

The thought-theoretic analogues of soundness proofs in metalogical theory generate corresponding norms. The fundamental rule of reference for the classical concept of alternation is that any Thought of the form $A \lor B$ is true if at least one of A, B is true. From this fundamental rule of reference, it follows that the rule of alternation-introduction ($A/(A \lor B)$) and alternation-elimination ($[A] \ldots C, [B] \ldots C, (A \lor B)/C$) are always truth-preserving. Since judgement aims at truth, we can conclude that one should not accept an instance of the premiss of these rules and remain neutral on the corresponding conclusion. Equally, one should not reject an instance of the conclusion of one of these rules and remain neutral on the corresponding premiss. Such arguments are precisely arguments from fundamental reference rules, in this case reference rules for logical concepts, to norms involving those concepts.

By similar styles of argument, for every logical concept, there will be norms corresponding to the transitions that its fundamental reference rule validates.

I emphasized earlier that we are so far speaking only of reference rules and the norms they help to explain—we have not yet turned to the issue of knowledge of reference rules, and knowledge of norms. All the same, it should be clear that the position I am developing leaves space for the explanation of something that really happens, and which can be puzzling under some other treatments: the fact that thinkers all of whom understand a given logical constant can differ in respect of which primitive principles involving it they find immediately obvious. Two thinkers may both appreciate, in whatever way is required, that an alternation is true if at least one of its constituents is, while differing in respect of how easy they find it to draw certain conclusions from this information, unprompted.

Fundamental reference rules for logical constants could not be explanatory of norms involving those concepts if those reference rules were themselves explanatorily dependent upon the correctness of those norms. That last is the sort of dependence that would exist under any minimalist or redundancy-style treatment that holds that the reference rule for a logical concept is no more than a summary of, or something explanatorily dependent upon, which logical principles are correct for the logical concept in question. This is one of many points at which issues about the correct direction of explanation are directly linked with large-scale issues about the nature of reference and truth. Arguments in favour of the direction of explanation that runs from grasp of contribution to truth-conditions to acceptance of principles, including primitive principles, are resumed in Chapter 4 below.

Argument-Type Four: Evidence and Identity-Principles

In a wide range of cases, what makes something the property an object must have to fall under the concept C is that the property is identical with the property some distinguished object, thought about under concept *d*, must have for the Thought *Cd* to be true. These cases are ones in which intentional content is explained in part in terms of an identity-relation. In the preceding chapter, I argued that concepts of properties of places and times fall under this case. In Chapter 5, I will be arguing that concepts of conscious states should also be assimilated to this model.

Suppose we take properties to be the semantic values of predicative concepts. Then in the cases in question, the fundamental rule of reference for the concept involves an identity-relation. Now consider any example in which there is evidence, for example abductive evidence, that some object *x* has the same property the distinguished object has when *Cd* is true. Then that evidence is also evidence that *x* falls under C too. Many abductive arguments about properties of other places and times, and about the sensations of others, whether highly theoretical or of a more humdrum, everyday sort, fall under this model. In these cases, the role of identity in the fundamental rule of reference contributes to explaining why the evidence is evidence for what it is.

These four argument-types I have selected are intended here simply as examples of a more general phenomenon, the explanation of norms or reasons distinctive of a concept by the fundamental reference rule for the concept. There will be other argument-types besides these. But reflection on these examples does suggest one way of making plausible the thesis that fundamental reference rules play an essential part in the determination of the reasons or norms distinctive of concepts. We can make the thesis plausible by arguing that:

> For each norm distinctive of a concept, there is some argument-type that explains that norm, and which makes essential use of the fundamental reference rule for the concept.

This is not the sort of claim that can be defended in a single chapter, or even a book much longer than the present one. We do not have a list of the totality of sound argument-types of the kind in question (and this may be so for reasons of principle). The thesis can become plausible only by a philosophical argument to the best explanation of a wide range of normative phenomena. We would need to show that the norms, for many different concepts, of many different varieties, are explicable by drawing upon their respective fundamental reference rules.

There is, however, one abstract reason, of equal generality with the thesis itself, that can be offered in its support. Judgement aims at truth (at least), and the norms for a concept seem always to be norms that promote this aim in the case of judgements with certain contents containing the concept. Now the truth or falsity of a judgement turns on the properties and relations of the references of the concepts that feature in the content of the judgement. It is, then, only to be expected that the norms that promote true judgements get a grip at the level of reference.

3. SIGNIFICANCE AND CONSEQUENCES OF THE MAIN THESIS

(1) Can we explain the norms distinctive of particular concepts simply from principles that either employ or refer to those concepts, without alluding to the conditions that determine reference of those concepts? Consider the norm that being in pain gives a thinker a reason to make the first-person judgement *I'm in pain now*. We offered an explanation of this norm from the fundamental reference rules for the concepts in question. What principles involving concepts, but not their references, might provide an alternative explanation? We have such trivial principles as

> For any thinker x, the first person as used by x expresses $[\text{self}]_x$.
> For any time t, the present tense as used at t expresses $[\text{now}]_t$.
> The concept *pain* expresses *pain*.

Here '[self]' subscripted by a term refers to the concept of the first-person type employed by the thinker referred to in the subscripted term; and the same *pari passu* for '[now]'. These displayed principles are all true, of course. But by themselves they do nothing to explain the norm in question. There is no argument, or not one obvious to me, that runs from these principles to the existence of the norm. As far as I can tell, we need to add principles about the way in which the reference of these concepts is determined if we are to explain the norm.

This explanatory gap is not a result of the trivial and a priori status of the displayed principles. It is present equally in a linguistic version of the argument, with empirical premises and an empirical linguistic explanandum. Consider the principles

"pain" expresses in English the concept *pain*.

For any person x, "I" as uttered by x expresses in English $[self]_x$.

For any time t, "now" as uttered at t expresses in English $[now]_t$.

From these principles we cannot, without further information about how the reference of these terms or senses is determined, account for the norm that a thinker's own pain gives her reason to think that the sentence of English "I am in pain now" as uttered by her then is true.

(2) In section 5 of Chapter 1, I distinguished three possible grades of involvement of reference and truth in the individuation of concepts. The strongest kind of involvement, there called Grade 2 involvement, is present when the possession-condition of a specific concept cannot be formulated without speaking of conditions upon the reference of the concept. The argument in Chapter 1 was that Grade 2 involvement exists for concepts whose possession-condition involves an identity-relation. But the considerations marshalled so far in this chapter lend support to the conjecture that *all* concepts exhibit a form of Grade 2 involvement. Even in the old case of the logical concept of conjunction, there is an argument for the view that grasp of this notion involves tacit knowledge of the fundamental reference rule that a conjunction is true iff both its constituents are true. It is an understanding founded on tacit grasp of this contribution to truth-conditions that makes it rational to accept the introduction and elimination rules for conjunction. If this general conjecture about the Grade 2 involvement of all concepts is true, there is not even a restricted subpart of the domain of concepts in which the possession-conditions can be given without mentioning truth and reference.

(3) More generally, if the main thesis of this chapter is correct, the contrast found in many writers, either explicitly or implicitly, between theories of

meaning and concepts that are "use" theories on the one hand and theories of meaning that involve reference and truth on the other is, in certain basic respects, a spurious contrast. I do not mean there are not genuinely competing theories of each of these two kinds—on the contrary, I have spent much time in earlier work, and much space earlier in this book, arguing against pure use theories. My point is rather that if "use" involves norms (as it has to if it is to be adequate in the explanation of meaning and concepts), then explaining why these norms exist will take us back to the level of reference. The later Wittgenstein wrote as if his later views about meaning and understanding would need to involve a thorough rejection of the conception of understanding present in his *Tractatus*. No one today could believe everything in the *Tractatus*. But the idea that understanding is a matter of grasp of truth-conditions, and that grasp of these involves conditions on the reference of the constituents of propositions, is one that, far from being incompatible with the idea that there are norms of use which are distinctive of concepts and meanings, is actually required if we are properly to explain and understand those norms.

This point also tells against an argument much favoured by pragmatists both old and recent. William James repeatedly complained that those of his opponents who require for the truth of a proposition some kind of 'agreement' with reality going beyond the aspects of correct consequences of the sort pragmatists always demanded were asking for something empty. He wrote that when we 'fall back on unnamed forms of agreeing that are expressly denied to be either copyings or leadings or fittings, or any other processes pragmatically definable, the *what* of the "agreement" claimed becomes as unintelligible as the why of it. Neither content nor motive can be imagined for it. It is an absolutely meaningless abstraction.'[12] A century later, Richard Rorty, discussing Crispin Wright, said that there is 'no occasion to look for an *additional* norm' involving truth that goes beyond warranted assertibility if we are trying to characterize the goal of inquiry.[13] In both cases, the arguments of the present book suggest that one cannot even characterize

---

[12] James (2003, Lecture Six, p. 118). At certain points in his late writings, James gives acute formulations of objections to the pragmatist position on truth. He puts these words in the mouth of the 'Anti-Pragmatist' in James (2002, ch. xv: 'A Dialogue'): 'Of course if there be a truth concerning the facts, that truth is what the ideal knower would know. To that extent you can't keep the notion of it and the notion of him separate. But it is not him first and then it; it is it first and then him, in my opinion' (p. 293). Part I of the present book can be seen as a further elaboration of this formulation of an anti-pragmatist position.

[13] Rorty (1998: 26.)

the evidential and warrant relations the pragmatists acknowledge without relying on the notion of truth. The notion of truth is not some transcendent aim going beyond all our normal rational practices in making judgements. Rather, it is a notion that is inextricably involved in a proper characterization of those normal rational practices. In that sense, it is immanent rather than transcendent. If we try to strip away all talk of truth and reference in our characterization of reasons for making judgements of particular contents, we will be left with nothing at all.

(4) It may appear from the exposition so far that concepts, and contents composed from them, have a location in the space of reasons only derivatively, and that this is not something built into their nature. I think such an appearance would be an illusion. It is an overarching constraint on something's being a fundamental reference rule for a concept that, together with other information and conditions, it determine in various circumstances what are good reasons for making certain judgements containing the concept. An alleged fundamental reference rule that uniquely fixes an object, but does not contribute to the determination of reasons in this way, does not succeed in individuating a concept. Consider, for some particular object x, the alleged fundamental reference rule for an alleged singular concept k which states simply that: k refers to x. This proposed rule certainly determines a reference for k. But the rule does not contribute essentially to the determination of reasons in various circumstances for making judgements containing the alleged concept. The additional condition *k is that F (perceptually given)* may contribute to the determination of reasons for making judgements, but then the work is being done by the perceptual demonstrative *that F*. The referential dimension of a concept and its having a location in the space of reasons are coordinate elements in the nature of a concept. Neither can be fully elucidated without invoking the other. This intertwining is the explanation of the Anchoring Principle discussed back in Chapter 1 section 6.

(5) So far we have been arguing that the existence of certain norms distinctive of concepts can be explained by those concepts' fundamental reference rules. Here we have taken the existence of norms for granted, and the task has been to develop an argument about their explanation. But an argument is also possible in the reverse direction, to the existence of norms distinctive of any given concept. The argument runs:

> Every concept (of the sort with which we are concerned) has a fundamental reference rule.

This reference rule will make some judgements rational in certain circumstances (or, better, will make certain considerations rationally bear on their truth).[14]

Hence: for each concept, there will be some reasons or norms distinctive of that concept.

This is a sound argument under the conception I have been promoting. It is an interesting question for further work whether we can say more of interest about the general form of the argument from fundamental reference rules to certain norms or reasons. We should certainly want to know more about what is common to this wide variety of argument-types.

The most pressing task for the defender of the main thesis of this chapter is, however, to make it more plausible in some problem cases, and to describe some of the resources that can be used in its support. One of the main reasons for doubting the thesis is the large apparent gap between the very simple fundamental reference rules at the start of this chapter (section 1)—some of which are only two lines long—and the immensely rich range of normative principles characteristic of certain concepts. Nowhere is this gap likely to seem larger than in the case of the first-person concept. Can we really explain all the normative principles distinctive of the first-person concept by appeal to the simple reference rule that in any thinking containing it, that use in thought refers to the thinker? This test case is the topic of the next chapter.

---

[14] For the arguments in favour of the formulation in parentheses, see Hieronymi (2005). The Hieronymi-style formulation should be preferred at many points throughout this book.

3

The First Person as a Case Study

I now take the first person as the subject matter for a case study of the thesis of the preceding chapter, the thesis that the fundamental reference rule for a concept contributes essentially to the explanation of the norms distinctive of that concept. I have two aims in this exercise. One aim is to suggest some ways in which the extraordinarily rich and philosophically interesting epistemic phenomena exhibited by such an important concept as that of the first person can be explained by its fundamental reference rule. The first person provides a case study in the kind of resources on which one can draw in explaining such phenomena in part by citing a reference rule.

As I suggested at the end of the previous chapter, the first person may at first glance appear to be a salient counter-example to the thesis that fundamental rules of reference for a concept can contribute essentially to the explanation of normative and reason-involving phenomena involving the concept. Articulating the phenomena distinctive of the first person has drawn forth some of the most striking contributions from the greatest philosophers, from Augustine onwards, through Descartes, Kant, and Wittgenstein. It continues to draw forth new contributions from the most distinguished contemporary philosophers, including Shoemaker, Anscombe, and Evans. It must seem to be stretching credulity to suggest that this range of phenomena can be explained merely by drawing upon the simple reference rule that a use of *I* in thought refers to the thinker, the producer of the thinking, together with auxiliary hypotheses. I will nevertheless attempt to show, for a selection of these phenomena, that they can be so explained.

My other aim in taking the first person as a case study is to consider, in this special case, a much more general issue that arises about the individuation of certain concepts. In the case of the first-person, some theorists have pointed to considerations of input in their accounts of the individuation of the first-person concept. They have, like Gareth Evans, emphasized the distinctive states that make it rational to come to accept first-person thoughts.[1] Others, like Robert Brandom, have emphasized the role of the first person in thoughts expressive of intentions, and have suggested this is what is fundamental in the individuation of the concept.[2] Is either of these views right? Is either input or output more fundamental than the other in the individuation of the first-person concept? Or is some third position correct, a position that can explain the role of the first person both on the input and on the output sides?

This issue arises equally for other indexical concepts, for recognitional concepts, and arguably for concepts in general. I will be arguing, as no doubt you can predict, that the reference rule is more fundamental than either the input-oriented or the output-oriented accounts of individuation; and that it can explain phenomena that pose difficulties for those accounts.

The first task is, then, to explain a selection of the epistemic phenomena displayed by the first-person concept by drawing essentially on its fundamental reference rule. I will take two phenomena as targets of this explanatory challenge: the phenomenon of fully self-conscious thought, and the phenomenon of the existence of certain forms of immunity to error through misidentification enjoyed by certain uses of the first person. In both cases, the challenge is to say how the austere resource of the fundamental rule of reference is enough to explain the distinctive normative and reason-involving properties these two phenomena show to be characteristic of the first-person concept.

1. FULLY SELF-CONSCIOUS THOUGHT

A fully self-conscious use of *I* in thought is one in which the thinker knows that he is referring to himself, without drawing on any special information about the case. What do I mean to exclude by the clause 'without drawing on any special information about the case'? Take a thinker, ordinary in other respects, who knows that he is the Chairman of the Company. In thinking to himself, 'It is quite right that the Chairman of the Company be well-paid', he does know that he is thinking about himself. But he is drawing on special information that goes both beyond his grasp of the concepts involved in the thought in question, and beyond what is present in any case of normal

---

[1] Evans (1982, ch. 7: 'Self-Identification').
[2] Brandom (1994, ch. 8 sect. v.2: 'Essentially Indexical Beliefs: The Use of "I" ').

conscious judgement. When each of us knows, in thinking an *I*-thought, that he is thinking about himself, we do not draw on such special additional information about the case that goes beyond what is present in any case of normal conscious judgement, or beyond what is involved in grasp of the concepts in question. It is part of the datum in need of explanation that this knowledge exists without reliance on additional information of the form 'I am the Chairman of the Company', or 'I am the F' for some concept F. Whether or not all uses of *I* are fully self-conscious in this sense, it is clear that a vast multitude of uses of *I* by mature human thinkers are so fully self-conscious.

The fully self-conscious thinker does not have merely the general and *de dicto* knowledge that any of his uses of *I* in thought refer to himself. He knows of his particular judgement *I am F* on a particular occasion that in it, his use of *I* refers to himself. This is *de re* knowledge concerning a particular judgement, a judgement about which he can think demonstratively, as *this judgement* or *this thinking*.

These fully self-conscious uses of *I* also generate a norm. For any fully self-conscious use of *I* in a thought *I am F*, the thinker knows that her thought is true if and only if she herself is F. In the presence of the general norm that one should judge something only if it is true, this implies that the thinker should judge *I am F* only if she herself is F. If the thinker knows the general norm, she is also in a position to know that she should judge *I am F* only if she herself is F.

It is certainly a challenge to explain the existence of fully self-conscious uses of *I*, and the norms they generate, from the austere resource of the fundamental reference rule for *I*. That is the challenge I will attempt to meet.

A helpful starting point in addressing this issue is to examine the upshot of a fruitful disagreement between Elizabeth Anscombe and Gareth Evans.[3] Anscombe argued that we cannot fully characterize the significance of the first-person pronoun simply by saying that it is a word that each person *x* uses to refer to *x*. Her example was that of the 'A'-users. Each person has a letter stamped on the inside of his wrist. It is in fact the same letter 'A' that is stamped inside each person's wrist. 'Reports on one's own actions, which one gives straight off from observation, are made using the name on the wrist' (p. 49). Each person *x* in this imagined community uses 'A' to refer to *x*.

---

[3] Anscombe (1975); Evans (1982, app. to ch. 7, 258–66). Page references in the text refer to these two works.

But, Anscombe insists, 'A' does not have the same significance as the first person, and it need not be true that a user of 'A' knows that he is referring to himself. In the sense in which it is important that users of the first person know that they are referring to themselves, this is a *de se* use of 'themselves'. It is something that goes beyond having an expression or concept which, for each person *x*, refers to *x*.

Anscombe eventually reached the surprising, indeed barely credible, conclusion that ' "I" is neither a name nor another kind of expression whose logical role is to make a reference, *at all*' (p. 60). This conclusion should not be regarded as uncontroversial as the claim that "It" in "It is raining" does not make a reference at all. The position of "It" in "It is raining" is not a quantifiable position. "It" in this occurrence does not even seem to make a reference. When one refers explicitly to a particular place at which it is said to be raining, the term for the place in question follows "It is raining", as in "It is raining at Logan airport". This position is also open to quantification: "It is raining everywhere", "It is raining nowhere". But in the case of, for instance, "I am hungry", the quantifiable position is, by contrast, occupied by the word "I" that Anscombe says does not make a reference at all. "I am hungry" certainly seems to entail "Someone is hungry" and to contradict "No one is hungry". Partly as a result of this, Anscombe's claim that "I" does not refer is hard to accept. It is important, however, that her point about the "A"-users stands independently of her problematic conclusion that "I" does not refer. Her point also stands independently of her view that *de se* thought can be explained only in terms of grasp of the first-person pronoun. However Anscombe intended her example of the 'A'-users to be elaborated in more detail—the matter is not entirely clear, see note 5—it is certainly true that there is a gap between each person *x* knowing that in certain uses he refers to *x* and knowing that he is referring to himself.

Evans objected to Anscombe's diagnosis of the situation. On his view, we do not need to explain the *de se* sense of "referring to oneself" in terms of prior mastery of the first person. Evans's point is that intending to refer to oneself, even in the *de se* sense, is intending to have the property $\lambda x[x$ refers to $x]$.[4] According to Evans, the correct direction of the philosophical explanation of fully self-conscious reference 'goes the other way' from that proposed by Anscombe. Those uses are rather to be explained as ones in which the thinker 'knowingly and intentionally' satisfies $\lambda x[x$ refers to $x]$.

---

[4] Evans (1982: 258 ff.).

While I will eventually be offering a position that is distinct from both of the positions of Anscombe and Evans, what I want to take away from this exchange between them is a more precise formulation of one of the tasks facing an account of first-person thought. The account must explain how it is that a thinker of a first-person thought knows that he is a self-referrer, in the sense that he knows that he has the property $\lambda x[x$ refers to $x]$; or, as we ought more strictly to write, knows that he has the property $\lambda x[x$'s use of I refers to $x]$. So in the context of my project, the question becomes: is the fundamental reference rule for I in that thinking enough, in the presence of other facts common to any ordinary case of thinking, to explain the existence of this knowledge on the part of fully self-conscious users of I?

I offer this explanation of one route by which that knowledge can be achieved, using the fundamental reference rule. Judging something is a mental action, of which a thinker has a distinctive action-awareness. So we start from the point that our normal thinker has an awareness of his mental action, an action-awareness with the content:

(1) I am judging that I am F.

The circumstances of our case are ordinary, and the thinker takes the content of this awareness at face value. That is, he not merely has an awareness as of (1)'s being the case, he endorses the content of the awareness, and judges (1). Our thinker also knows the fundamental reference rule for the first-person concept. That is, he knows

(2) Any use of I in a thinking refers to the thinker of that thinking.

From his knowledge of (1) and (2), and a presumed background knowledge that judging a content is a form of thinking, our thinker knows

(3) I in this judging *I am F* refers to me.

That is, since "me" is just the accusative form of the first person, our thinker knows:

(4) I have the property $\lambda x[x$'s use of I in this judging refers to $x]$.

That is what we were required to show. Here we presume that our thinker knows that in employing a concept in his judgement that refers to something, he is referring to it.

This argument makes essential use of ordinary thinkers' knowledge of the fundamental reference rule for I at line (2). It does not, contrary to the spirit of Anscombe's position, make use of anything stronger, with a *de se* content. Yet we are still able to derive that our thinker knows (4).

This account of how fully self-conscious thought is possible without relying on something richer than the fundamental rule of reference for the first person applies whatever the predicative concept F in the content of the judgement may be. F may be a purely bodily concept, such as *is blonde*, and the argument still goes through. There is no requirement that F be a psychological concept. Since fully self-conscious thought can be present whatever may be the complete content judged that contains the first person, these features of the explanation (1)–(4) respect the extent of the phenomenon.

An analogous version of the argument (1)–(4) would not be available if we substitute *the Chairman of the Company* for *I* throughout in the content of the thinker's thought. The fundamental rule of reference for *the Chairman of the Company* does not, in the presence of the corresponding premises, put the thinker in the position to know "*The Chairman of the Company* refers to me", without special additional information going beyond his grasp of the concepts involved and beyond what is present in any normal case of conscious judgement. For he does not know, without such special additional information, that the Chairman of the Company is the author of his judgement.

The suggestion is sometimes canvassed that fully self-conscious thought really involves a thinking that refers not just to the thinker of the thought, but to that very thinking itself. Under this suggestion, fully self-conscious thinking has a self-referential content. The idea is that fully self-conscious thought would be thought of the form *The thinker of this very thinking is F*. By contrast, the argument formulated in (1)–(4) does not require that the thinking of the content *I am F* be self-referential, that it be a content that somehow involves reference to the thinking of the content.

It is fair to remark that the argument in (1)–(4) does require that in conscious thinking, we have a way of thinking about our judgements that is made available by our action-awareness of making those judgements. We tacitly make use of this in speaking of 'this judging *I am F*' at line (3). The thinker must be in a position to know that this thinking is one of his own thinkings. But this is very different from the judgement's having a self-referential content, a more sophisticated thing that does not need to be present for fully-self conscious thought.

Not only do we not, apparently, need anything stronger than (2) in this argument; (2), or at least (2) as applied to oneself, also seems to contain the minimal information needed to sustain an argument of this type to the conclusion that the use of the relevant concept is self-conscious. If we have a concept or expression E for which the thinker is not in a position to know, just from the identity or meaning of E, that E refers to the author of the utterance or thinking in which it occurs, then this style of argument will not go through.

There is a different way of organizing a sound argument to the conclusion (4). It would start from the thinker's knowledge of the premiss

In my uses of I, I have the property $\lambda x[x$'s use of I refers to $x]$.

How do we get from this premiss to knowledge of one's own uses of I that in using it one is a self-referrer? One needs also to know of the particular use of I in question that it is one of mine. This further knowledge goes beyond the general, a priori, *de dicto* premiss that my uses are mine. It involves *de re* knowledge of a particular use, a particular event. This further knowledge is reached by relying on one's action-awareness. One has an action-awareness that one is judging *I am F* (for some specific F), and this is the source of one's knowledge that the judgement is one's own. So even if we start from the premiss just displayed, we will still need to draw on action-awareness. The resources used in this alternative formulation will also still imply that I am in a position to know that any of my uses of I in a thought refer to its author. For under this formulation, I know that in these uses, I am a self-referrer; and I know from my action-awareness that I am the author of these uses; so I am in a position to know that in these uses I refer to the author of these uses. This offers some support for the claim of the previous paragraph that the information in (2), as applied to oneself, will be implicit in an account of how knowledge of (4) is reached in these normal cases. If we want, as we should, to display a person's knowledge that he is a self-referrer in using I as a consequence of a general grasp of the first-person concept, applicable both to his own and others' uses of the first person, we should generalize the displayed proposition to

If anyone y uses an I-type concept, then in that use y has the property $\lambda x[x$ refers to $x]$.

However Anscombe intended her example to be fleshed out in more detail, the reasoning (1)–(4) vindicates one of her claims. If we try to develop a corresponding version of (1)–(4) for the 'A'-users, the argument stalls. We can suppose an 'A'-user comes to know, just like an I-user,

(1A) I am judging: A is F.

This already may go beyond what Anscombe envisaged in her example, for she sometimes writes as if in her example, it is not merely that uses of 'A' do not express first-person thought, but rather the 'A'-users lack self-consciousness altogether. But let us proceed, since if we cannot even reach (1A), the argument will not get started.

We can suppose the 'A'-user in question also knows the rule for the use of 'A':

> (2A) Any user of 'A' refers to the person on whose inside wrist he sees 'A' inscribed.

From (1A) and (2A) our 'A'-user can come to know

> (3A) A in this judging *A is F* refers to that person on whose wrist that 'A' is inscribed.

Perhaps we could be allowed to rewrite the content of this knowledge

> A in this judging *A is F* refers to A.

But neither (3A) nor this rewriting implies that our thinker knows that, in his judging *A is F*, he is a self-referrer. Knowing (3A) or its rewriting implies only that he knows he is an A-referrer. If he does not know he is A, he cannot infer that he is a self-referrer. If he does have the additional information that he is A, that is coming from some source other than his grasp of the concepts involved or this being an ordinary case of judgement. To repeat, no such additional information was needed in the derivation (1)–(4).[5]

If the content of the action-awareness involved in conscious judgement were not merely of the first-person form *I am judging so-and-so*, but were rather *I, the person on whose wrist 'A' is inscribed, am judging so-and-so*, it would be possible to close the gap in the argument. But it is not. The fact

---

[5] In writing that (2A) gives the rule for the use of 'A', I am picking on just one of two possible readings of Anscombe's article. The other reading attributes the rule that any user of 'A' refers to the person on whose wrist he *usually* sees 'A' inscribed. Different sorts of mistakes are possible under the two readings. Anscombe writes that mistakes are possible (1975: 49), but the context of her example does not resolve the issue between these two readings. The proposition that each user *x* of 'A' refers to *x* has a very different status under these two readings. Under the reading (2A), it is heavily contingent, and not a consequence merely of the rule for 'A' and the circumstances that make it possible. It is more plausibly such a consequence under the alternative reading. But under neither reading can we reach the conclusion that 'A'-users in their normal judgements are in a position, just from the meaning of 'A' and the nature of conscious judgement, to know that they are thereby self-referrers. Under the alternative reading, that conclusion requires the further empirical information that I am the person on whose wrist I usually see 'A' inscribed.

that action-awareness has a first-person content is essential to the argument (1)–(4), and it is not required to have more than a first-person content, in respect of whom it represents as being the agent, for the reasoning (1)–(4) to go through. But an argument starting with (1A)–(3A) could reach the conclusion that 'A'-users could know in normal cases of judgement, without further information, that they are self-referrers only if action-awareness had a different content that it does not in fact possess. (I discuss the first-person content of action-awareness further in Chapter 7.)

Could 'A'-users reach the conclusion that they are referring to themselves by a different route, not relying on the action-awareness? It could be said that each 'A'-user, simply by a legitimate use of disquotation, is in a position to know, when he thinks it, that

(5) *A* in A's thinking refers to A.

From (5) it does indeed follow that each 'A'-user is in a position to know, when he thinks it:

(6) A, in using 'A', is a self-referrer, that is: A has the property $\lambda x[x$'s use of 'A' refers to $x]$.

But this falls short of knowing that *he* has the property $\lambda x[x$'s use of 'A' refers to $x]$. There is no sound move from (5) to (6) without an additional premiss. (6) may represent a distinctive form of A-consciousness, but it is not the same as fully self-conscious first-person thought.

This treatment of the 'A'-users can also be used, by parallel reasoning, to vindicate a point Evans makes about a subject who has an imagined concept *c* of a person. Using the concept *c*, this subject makes spatial judgements with content of the form '*c* stands in such-and-such spatial relation', in similar ways to that in which he comes to make such first-person judgements, and which have similar consequences for action. Evans's point is that this subject, in using the imagined concept *c*, would not thereby 'register the fact that the object he is thinking of is himself' (p. 259), and so would not be engaged in fully self-conscious thinking. For such a concept *c*, similar points would apply to those we just made about Anscombe's 'A'. We could, again, even get as far as the conclusion that *c* in *c*'s thinking refers to c; and hence that c is a self-referrer. And equally again, this falls short of our subject's knowing that he is a self-referrer.[6]

---

[6] It is an important insight of Evans's appendix to his chapter on self-identification (Evans 1982) that we must account for the existence of fully self-conscious thought, and to describe some of the

One moral of this argument seems to be that if we specify a concept of some subject by its characteristic role, we will be able to reach the conclusion that someone using that concept will thereby be thinking of himself as a self-referrer only if we can establish a version of (2) for that concept. That is, we will be able to reach that conclusion about fully self-conscious thought only if anyone using the concept, so picked out, is, in thinking, referring to the author of that thought. It is, to the best of my knowledge, an open question at present whether a non-trivial specification of a role in thought for a concept of a subject (that is, other than "the role determined by the Fundamental Reference Rules") can be shown to entail the corresponding version of (2).

In this section, I have tried to explain the existence of fully self-conscious uses of the first person in cases of ordinary judgement by drawing on the fundamental reference rule for the concept *I*. It also follows, if this explanation is correct, that in uses of the first-person concept with that fundamental reference rule, a normal thinker is in a position to know that any judgement of his of the form *I am F* is true if and only if he himself is F, without special additional information about the case.

I close with three observations on the argument of this section.

(*a*) Just as there is a notion of a fully self-conscious use of the concept *I* in thought, there is an analogous notion of a fully self-conscious use of the pronoun "I" in an utterance. A fully self-conscious use of an expression in an utterance is one in which the utterer is in a position to know that in that use he is referring to himself, without drawing on any special information about the case. As before, 'without drawing on any special information about the case' means: without drawing on any information going beyond his understanding of the expressions involved, and what is present in any normal case of an utterance. Ordinary utterances of the first-person pronoun in human languages by normal speakers, in normal circumstances, are fully self-conscious uses in this sense. A normal utterer of "I" in English, or of "je" in French, or "ich" in German, knows that he is referring to himself, without drawing on any special information about the case.

---

conditions for doing so. But it is also a question whether his own account in the main part of his chapter is not subject to precisely the questions he himself raises about such a mode of presentation *c* characterized by, in some broad sense, a functional role concerning perception and action. He considers, but leaves open, the proposal that a role in psychological self-ascription would close the gap (p. 259). Evans's very brief discussion of this option requires, but does not explain, a connection between psychological ascription to an object that is in fact oneself and thinking about oneself, *de se* ('being a self-thinker'). I believe that this is one of several important passages in *The Varieties of Reference* which would have been substantially reworked had Evans been granted more time.

The fundamental reference rule for the first-person pronoun is that any utterance of it refers to the utterer (more specifically, to the agent of its utterance). From this reference rule, together with an utterer's action-awareness that he is the agent of his utterance, we can explain the phenomenon of fully self-conscious uses of the first-person pronoun. The explanation is simply a transposition of (1)–(4) to the realm of language rather than thought. The utterer has an action-awareness with the content

(1L) I am uttering "I am F".

The utterer takes this action-awareness at face value, and judges (1L). Our utterer also knows

(2L) Any utterance of "I" refers to the author of that utterance.

From (1L) and (2L), our utterer knows

(3L) "I" in this utterance "I am F" refers to me.

That is, our utterer knows

(4L) I have the property $\lambda x[x$'s utterance of "I" refers to $x]$.

So, our utterer's use of "I" is fully self-conscious.[7]

What this argument further shows is that any expression with the fundamental reference rule of the first person will also express the distinctive first-person sense. A speaker will know that his utterances "I am F" are true if and only if he himself is F; others are in a position to know that he knows this; and so on. Theorists who recognize a notion of indexical sense will write, as an axiom for theory of sense for English, this:

(Self) Any utterer x of "I" expresses [self]$_x$ by that utterance.

Here, as elsewhere in the literature, [self] is the first-person type of sense. The particular sense used by a particular person in employing a sense falling under the first-person type is individuated by the pair of the sense-type [self]

---

[7] James Higginbotham remarked to me that we could also argue to such self-ascriptive knowledge from the premiss, formulated in the terms of linguistics, that the rule is for a speaker x to meet the condition that x uses "I" [PRO to refer to x], which is understood to imply that x uses "I" in such a way that: x refers to x.

and the person *x* himself, a pair we can write '[self]$_x$'. What the explanation (1L)–(4L) suggests is that any expression with the fundamental reference rule for the first person will also conform to a sense-specifying axiom like the displayed axiom (Self).

When we explain the principle (Self), rather than state it outright as an axiom, we lose the advantages of theft over honest toil, as Russell once described the benefits of postulation.[8] If we hold that senses are individuated by their fundamental reference rules, we cannot properly avoid this toil. But the toil also has fruits that cannot be gained by theft alone. As I argued in Chapter 2 sections 2 and 3, from the fundamental reference rules for concepts, in combination with other principles, we can derive norms for specific concepts, and for their linguistic expressions, including the first-person concept and its linguistic expression. The resources that explain a principle like (Self) about a sense, or about a type of sense, can also be used to explain features of the sense or type of sense. (Theft will not pay in the long run.)

(*b*) Part of what we derived in this section was, to put it concisely, that an ordinary thinker can know "*I* in my judgements refers to me". When put that way, it is clear that what we have reached here is a version of disquotation for the indexical case within the judgements that are mine. This raises the question of whether we are equally in a position to derive the corresponding versions of similarly restricted disquotational principles for other indexicals from their respective fundamental reference rules. These versions are plausibly true, and known to users who understand the indexical language of other persons. For the linguistic version for the word "now", formulated with sense-types taken as primitive, the content of this knowledge would be given in the axiom

(Now) For any time *t*, an utterance at *t* of "now" expresses [now]$_t$.

A further elaboration of the present approach could do for the present tense and other indexicals and demonstratives what we have done for the first person. It could derive the versions of disquotation that hold for these indexicals from their fundamental reference rules. A starting point for this further elaboration is the fact that a thinker knows both of the following propositions (7) and (8), and so can know the proposition (9) that follows from them by the laws of identity. When one consciously thinks something, one has

---

[8] Russell (1919: 71).

a consciousness of this thinking occurring at that very time. (There is more on conscious thinking in Chapter 7.) That is, the thinker is aware and knows that

(7)   My thinking *F(now)* is occurring now.

In knowing the fundamental rule of reference for *now*, our thinker knows that

(8)   The use of *now* in my thinking *F(now)* refers to its time of occurrence.

Hence our thinker can know, from these resources,

(9)   *now* in my thinking *F(now)* refers to now.

This is the required restricted version of disquotation for *now*. The form of the argument is applicable to arbitrary thinkers thinking arbitrary *now*-thoughts at arbitrary times. Any one of them is in a position to know, by this reasoning, this version of a disquotational principle, and its consequent norms.

(*c*) Action-awareness of one's own judgements plays an indispensable role in the explanation offered in this route by which an ordinary thinker can attain knowledge that *I* in his judgements refers to him. It is not sufficient for reaching that knowledge merely that a thinker have an awareness from the inside that a thinking is occurring, not even a thinking with a first-person content. Consider the schizophrenic subject who suffers the experience labelled 'thought-insertion', and to whom it seems that in having the thoughts occurring to him, he is overhearing someone else's thoughts. The thoughts in respect of which he has such a disturbing consciousness can be first-person thoughts. But this thinker does not even believe, let alone know, that the first person in such thoughts refers to him. He takes those occurrences of the first-person concept in thought to refer to whoever it is who is the agent of the thinkings, an agent he takes to be distinct from himself. Mere consciousness of a first-person thinking from the inside, together with grasp of the concepts from which the content of the thinking is composed, does not suffice for knowledge that the first person in that thinking refers to oneself.[9] The fundamental reference rule for the first person is not merely that any use of the first person in a thinking refers to the subject who has a consciousness from the inside of that thinking.

---

[9] For further discussion of some of the philosophical significance of schizophrenic phenomena, see Ch. 7 sect. 9 below.

This also shows that the phenomenon of self-conscious thought cannot be accounted for simply by mentioning a general grasp of disquotation, or its analogue for thought, and nothing more. The schizophrenic subject suffering from apparent thought-insertion may nevertheless have a good grasp of disquotational principles and their thought-theoretic analogues. He may know that occurrences of the first-person concept in thought express thoughts of a first-person type. Nevertheless, the first-person thoughts that occur to him during an experience of thought-insertion may not be ones of which he judges that the uses of the first person in them refer to him himself. One can fill out the case in such a way that it may even be rational for him to judge that they do not refer to himself. He can rationally judge that he is the subject enjoying the apparently inserted thoughts without judging that he is the reference of *I* as it occurs in them. The cognitive significance of "the subject enjoying this thinking" is distinct from that of "I". If thought-insertion is really possible, these concepts can even have different referents.

The apparently inserted thought might even have a content of the form *The thinker of this very thought is thus-and-so*. It could still be rational for our subject who experiences the apparent insertion not to think that this use of *the thinker of this very thought* refers to himself.

Many of our ordinary thinkings are ones in respect of which we are passive. The thinkings just occur to us. We are in fact their producers, though not through an exercise of mental agency. Each one of us in ordinary cases knows that a use of the first person in such a passive thinking also refers to himself. The source of the entitlement to make such judgements cannot of course involve the exercise of mental agency on the occasion in question. The source of the entitlement seems to be much more similar to the source of the entitlement to rely on non-autobiographical propositional memories. A person is, in ordinary circumstances, entitled to make judgements that rely on his being the producer of his passive thinkings, being the thinker in a form that falls short of conscious mental agency. Such production short of conscious mental agency is still sufficient for occurrences of *I* in these thinkings to refer to himself.

We also need to specify that the production is of the sort characteristic of a mind's production of its own thinkings. In conversation with you, I may intend to and succeed in producing a first-person thinking with a specific content in your mind. The occurrence of the first person in that produced thinking refers to you, not to me. The kind of production required for first-person reference does not go via production of the normal kind in someone else's mind. What is distinctive of the schizophrenic experience of thought-insertion is that it is as if the subject is overhearing someone else's thoughts. The metaphor of overhearing is precisely one in which the thought overheard is not generated by the normal production even of a passive thinking in one's own mind. That what is overheard has the content it does is explained by the operation of someone else's mind, if it really is a case of overhearing.

There are, then, in ordinary cases two sources of knowledge that your uses of *I* in your judgements refer to yourself. One involves knowledge that you are the agent of your judgement. The other, applicable in normal cases to all your thinkings, passive and active, involves knowledge that you are the person thinking them (no one else is the agent producing them). This other, passive, route still conforms to the main thesis of the preceding chapter, that the fundamental reference rule for a concept contributes to the explanation of norms distinctive of the concept. The explanation of the entitlement a normal thinker has for judging that in passive first-person thinkings he is referring to himself involves his right to rely in normal circumstances on his being the producer of his passive thinkings. Given the fundamental reference rule for the first person, that it refers to the producer of the thinking in question (where 'production' is restricted as above), this gives a basis for his entitlement to judge that *I* in his passive thinkings refers to himself. The fundamental reference rule is still an essential element in the explanation, even when that explanation does not proceed via action-awareness.

There are several respects in which judgement is more fundamental than passive thinking. What makes something the first-person concept is its referential character in judgements, not in passive thinkings. Any old contents may passively occur to one (and often do). Passive thinking, since it is not the upshot of rational agency at the conscious personal level, is neither actually nor normatively constrained by considerations of rationality. The conceptual content of passive thinkings has the identity it does by virtue of the role of those concepts (broadly construed here to include referential relations) in active judgements. For something to be the first-person concept in active judgements, its use must be constrained by the thinker's tacit appreciation of its reference rule. Once a conceptual constituent in a thinker's attitudes meets those constraints, it may then feature in all sorts of attitudes that are not the result of mental agency.

A second, related respect in which passive thinkings are less fundamental than judgements is that even when a passive thinking is of a kind that presents its content as correct, it needs a further step on the thinker's part to let that content become, via judgement, the content of one of his beliefs. The content of the passive thinking has to be endorsed, or has to be not endorsed. Since the content presented as true is not the result of rational mental activity aimed at truth, no commitment can or should be made by the thinker to its truth without further examination. Judgement, when done properly, is precisely acceptance based on such rational assessment. Judgement is itself such an endorsement.

Finally, if there were only passive thinkings, and no active judgements, we would not have the picture of the conscious mental life of a rational subject at all. A rational subject is one who, at least to some degree, orders his mental life by an exercise of mental agency in judging and more generally acting for reasons. Passive thinkings can occupy an enormous part of our mental life, but they—and their contents—are part of the mental life of a conscious rational thinker only because the thinker is capable of active judgements.

2. IMMUNITY TO ERROR THROUGH MISIDENTIFICATION RELATIVE TO THE FIRST PERSON

The apparent phenomena of immunity to error through misidentification distinctive of the first-person concept involve knowledge, and thereby involve reasons and norms. If these phenomena are real, and the first person displays distinctive instances of the phenomenon, we would expect the explanation of these instances to draw upon the fundamental reference rule for *I* if our general thesis of Chapter 2, relating reasons and reference, is correct. Do such instances exist? And if so, how are we to give such explanations?

We owe to Shoemaker a pioneering treatment of immunity to error through misidentification, and a statement of its philosophical significance.[10] There are, however, varying characterizations of immunity to error through misidentification, varying characterizations of its extent, differing descriptions of its explanation, and even disputes about whether there are instances of it that are in any special way distinctive of the first person. So we had

---

[10] See Shoemaker (1984*b,c*). Page references in the text are to Shoemaker (1984*b*). It is a further question, not addressed here, whether some variety of the immunities identified by Shoemaker can fully elucidate Wittgenstein's distinction between uses of "I" as subject and uses of "I" as object.

best begin with a clear statement of what is in question. We can start with examples. Suppose circumstances are entirely normal, you are in your study, you are seated in front of a keyboard that you see clearly, and you judge *This keyboard is black*, by taking your perceptual experience of the keyboard at face value. If your judgement is reached that way, in those circumstances, you come to know *This keyboard is black*. It is also not possible, in these normal circumstances, for you to come to know, in that same way, taking your experience at face value, that some keyboard is black, but be mistaken about which keyboard it is that is black. An intuitive elaboration of this claim about impossibility is that in any world w that is normal, and whose nearby worlds are also normal, where normality covers the state of both the environment and your perceptual mechanisms, if you come to know in w in this way of some object that it is black, the object of which you come to know this is the one referred to in your perceptual demonstrative *that keyboard*. We say that in this example your judgement *That keyboard is black* is immune to error through misidentification in respect of the concept *that keyboard* in its first (and only) occurrence in the content judged, when the judgement is reached in that way and is made in those normal circumstances. All these parameters—conceptual constituent, position of its occurrence in the content judged, the way the judgement comes to be made, and the circumstances—matter in this characterization. I sometimes abbreviate 'immune to error through misidentification' to 'IEM'. The generalization of this characterization is:

> A judgement Fa that comes to be made in way W in circumstances C is immune to error through misidentification in respect of the concept a at its occurrence $F(\xi)$ iff W is a way of coming to know that Fa in circumstances C, and it is not possible to come to know in way W in circumstances C of something that it is F but be wrong about whether it is a that is F.

Here the schematic letter 'ξ' is used to indicate the place of occurrence of the concept a. If you judge *It's raining now*, in ordinary circumstances and on the basis of your visual perception as of rain coming down, this judgement is IEM with respect to the constituent *now* at its only occurrence in those normal circumstances. So similarly is the judgement *I am seated* made in ordinary circumstances, on the basis of proprioception, with respect to the first-person concept, again at its only occurrence. So too is *I am in front of a building*, made on the basis of the subject's visual experience as of being in front of a building, in normal circumstances, with respect to the first-person concept, at its only occurrence in that content. This characterization of immunity to error through misidentification focuses on thought, not language. In this it differs from Shoemaker's original formulation in 'Self-Reference and Self-Awareness'. The present characterization is tailored to capture the thought-theoretic phenomena that concern us.[11]

Any case of immunity to error through misidentification is something standing in need of explanation. There must be something about the concepts F, *a*, and the way W and circumstances C, and the requirements on knowledge, that explain why the immunity exists. One should not leap to the conclusion that it is some feature wholly specific to one or more of these items F, *a*, W, and C that is responsible for the immunity. One or more of these items may be of a general type of such a kind that all relevant instances of that kind exhibit the immunity. So in the case of those first-person judgements that, made in the ways we have discussed, are IEM in normal circumstances, we now have to address two questions. First: is the presence of the first person in the content judged crucial to this case of immunity, or does it exist because the first person is an instance of some more general type of concept all of whose members have that immunity? Second: if the phenomenon is specific to the first person, is the best explanation of the immunity the fact that certain ways of coming to know are written primitively into the identity of the first-person concept; or can we explain them from the fundamental reference rule that any use of *I* refers to the thinker of the thought in which it occurs; or is some entirely different feature of *I* responsible for the immunity?

On the first of these two questions, in some of his later reflections following his first paper on the matter, Shoemaker says that in his earlier writings he 'made the mistake of associating' immunity to error through identification with the first person. His later view is that

Although self-reference is typically done with first-person pronouns, it can be done with names, and even with definite descriptions—as when de Gaulle says 'De Gaulle intends ... ' and the chairman of a meeting says 'The Chair recognizes ... ' In such cases these expressions are 'self-referring,' not merely because their reference is in

---

[11] For those approaching this territory from Shoemaker's writings, there are also terminological differences. Where I write of 'ways' of coming to know something, Shoemaker writes of 'circumstances' (1984*a*: 8). I have reserved 'circumstances' as more appropriate for restrictions on worlds and ranges of worlds that Shoemaker considers when he writes of '*de facto* immunity' (p. 46).

fact to the speaker, but also because the speaker intends in using them to refer to himself. (p. 20 n. 3)

Shoemaker later remarks that in such cases, if de Gaulle says 'De Gaulle intends to remove France from NATO', 'his statement is in the relevant sense immune to error through misidentification' (p. 21 n. 5). If what Shoemaker says here holds equally for thought as well as language, then the answer to the first question would apparently be that the fact that a range of judgements with first-person contents are IEM in the ways we have discussed has nothing in particular to do with their having first-person contents. This quotation from Shoemaker may seem very puzzling. I suggest that we can both make sense of why he makes the claim, and also see that it does not have the consequences one might expect, when we reflect on an ambiguity in the characterization of being IEM that I offered.

The characterization might be offered as a specification of what it is for a judgement *Fa* when made by an arbitrary thinker to be IEM with respect to a pair of parameters W, C. So understood, the characterization is not thinker-relative. But the characterization might be understood as involving a thinker-relative notion. It might be understood as specifying, for each thinker *x*, what it is for *x*'s judgement *Fa* to be IEM when *x*'s judgement is made in way W in circumstances C. This characterization leaves open the possibility that one thinker's judgement *Fa* may be so immune while another thinker's judgement of the same content is not so immune.

This second reading allows us to make some sense of Shoemaker's claim, even in its thought-theoretic analogue. In the case in which de Gaulle is *x*, *x*'s own judgement *De Gaulle intends to remove France from NATO*, when made in the normal way we self-ascribe intentions, will always be true in normal circumstances. This holds even if his in fact true belief that he is de Gaulle is ill-founded—perhaps he only believes it on even-numbered dates, and believes on odd-numbered dates that he is Churchill. What this seems to me to show, however, is that the person-relative, second understanding of the characterization of being IEM is not the one we should be using if we are interested in epistemic and referential properties of concepts as such, rather than properties they have only in relation to particular users of those concepts.

When we use the first understanding of the characterization of being IEM, the judgement *De Gaulle intends to remove France from NATO*, when made in the normal way involved in the self-ascription of conscious intentions, and resting on the identity belief *I am de Gaulle*, is not IEM with respect to the component *de Gaulle* in normal circumstances. The thinker who falsely believes that he is de Gaulle, but correctly self-ascribes in the normal way an intention to remove France from NATO is not wrong of himself that he has that intention. Under this first, intended reading of the characterization of being IEM, the cases in which first-person judgements are IEM are much more plausibly specific either to the first person, or to a much more restricted class. What that class is may begin to emerge from the discussion below.

The second question was whether the immunities displayed by certain first-person thoughts in respect of certain ways and circumstances are best explained by a theory that writes certain ways of coming to know certain first-person thoughts into an account of what it is to have the first-person concept, or whether they can equally be explained by the fundamental reference rule that *I* in any thinking refers to the thinker. Evans holds a theory that writes proprioceptive ways of coming to know propositions about the position of one's limbs, for instance, into an account of what it is to have the first-person concept. He writes, in elaboration of his position, 'The immediate bearing of such evidence would have to be part of a functional characterization of what it is to have an "I"-idea.'[12] I hasten to add that it would obviously be wrong to classify Evans as a pure conceptual-role theorist, in the sense of being someone who holds that legitimate conceptual roles are unconstrained by considerations at the level of reference. On the contrary, a functional-role characterization of the first-person concept (or Idea, as he would say) is possible for Evans only because there is a body, an element in the objective order, about which these conceptual roles, when employed in thought in normal circumstances, give information. His is a mixed theory, that allows characterizations of concepts—including the first-person concept—in terms of roles only if certain referential constraints are met. All the same, this role-involving theory is distinct from the theory that the first-person concept is individuated by the fundamental reference rule that I have offered.

On Evans's account, the various cases in which first-person bodily judgements are IEM when based on proprioception and the like, in normal circumstances, are immediate by-products of the functional-role characterization of first-person thought. It is written into the nature of first-person thought that suitable proprioceptive experiences give reasons for judging *I have crossed legs, I am lying down, My arm is above my head*. How is the

---

12 Evans (1982: 224). The 'evidence' he is talking about in this section of his book includes not only proprioception, but also 'our sense of balance, of heat and cold, and of pressure' (p. 220).

rival account of first-person thought, in terms of the fundamental reference rule, to explain the fact that these judgements are, when so made, in normal circumstances, immune to error through misidentification?

Suppose you have a proprioceptive experience as of your legs being crossed. There is nothing out of the ordinary, and no reason to doubt the deliverances of your senses. In these normal circumstances, if you judge

(10) My legs are crossed

then it cannot be the case that although you come to know in this way of someone that his legs are crossed, you are wrong about who it is that has crossed legs. That is, your judgement *My legs are crossed* is IEM with respect to its first-person constituent *I* at its first (and only) occurrence in the content judged, when reached in the specified way, and in normal circumstances. I assume that the Thought expressed by (10) is equivalent to *The legs that belong to me are crossed*, and that "me" is just the accusative form of expression for the first-person concept. Here is an explanation of this immunity that does not draw on the Evans-like, functional-role individuation of the first-person concept. This explanation does not contest the fact that in ordinary circumstances thinkers do make a smooth and entitled transition from having certain proprioceptive experiences to a rational, knowledgeable judgement of contents such as (10). The alternative explanation cites the fact that the following propositions are true in the circumstances of the example. First, we have that in ordinary circumstances, it is true that

(11) This body's legs are crossed

where *this body* is a way of thinking of a body made available by one's experiencing the body from the inside, having proprioception of this body, seeing its limbs as from a position in the body's head, and so forth. It will also be true in normal circumstances that a content

(12) This body is mine

is true when it is evaluated with respect to the time in question, and our subject as the reference of the first person implicit in (12). But from (11) and (12) it follows that

(13) My legs are crossed.

Since (11) and (12) are true in the envisaged circumstances, so will (13) be. Hence it follows that in the envisaged circumstances, it will be my legs that are crossed, not someone else's. So the subject will not be wrong about whose legs are crossed in any of the ordinary circumstances in question, the range of circumstances in which the qualified immunity to error through misidentification exists. That is, the conditions required for immunity to error through misidentification with respect to the way, circumstances, and occurrence of the first person are fulfilled. Here we are relying on a background principle to the effect that for any spatial, material, or any other present-tensed non-psychological concept F, *I am F* is true if *My body is F* is true. This explanation of why the immunity exists does not rely on any premiss to the effect that proprioceptive ways of coming rationally to judge, or to know, contribute to the individuation of the first-person way of thinking.

Now this explanation of such bodily immunities does not, evidently, use the fundamental reference rule for the first person as an explicit premiss. The derivation (11)–(13) and the accompanying justification do not explicitly mention that fundamental reference rule. Does this mean that we have norms and reasons characteristic of the first person that are not explained by its fundamental reference rule? And if there are some that are not so explained, should we not be looking for entirely different explanations of norms, in this case and elsewhere? But in fact it seems to me that although the fundamental reference rule is not used in this explanation (11)–(13), it is presupposed by some of the concepts mentioned in that explanation. It seems to me that we would need to appeal to the fundamental reference rule for the first person in explaining what it is for (12), 'This body is mine', to be true. For a body to be mine is for it to be the established one from which I perceive the world, the body of which I have proprioception, and, for normal humans, the one that responds to my basic attempts to move its limbs. The occurrences of the first person in this account of what it is for a body to be mine must be taken as referring to the thinker of the thoughts "The body from which I perceive the world", "The body of which I have proprioception", and the rest. If these occurrences of "I" were to refer to something that essentially has a bodily location, it would be unintelligible that one might, after one's brain is transferred to a vat and one's body is destroyed, no longer have a body and truly think "I no longer have a body". But this is intelligible. The account of what it is for "This body is mine" to be true must leave room for its intelligibility. The fundamental reference rule for the first person, that any use of *I* in thinking refers to the thinker of that thought, seems to be the most promising way to explain this intelligibility.

This alternative explanation does not involve a commitment to the proposition *I am identical with my body*. At the other end of the spectrum, the explanation also does not involve any commitment to the idea that I might be an immaterial thing. Under the proposed account, in ordinary circumstances (12) holds. There are also more remote cases in which (12) fails. They are the cases of the sort exuberantly expounded in Dennett's 'Where Am I?',[13] in which my brain is remotely connected to sensory and proprioceptive information from some distant body with which it was not previously so connected. The story can be told in such a way that my proprioceptive experiences are in fact evidence not that my, but that someone else's, legs are crossed. These are also cases in which the immunity in question no longer exists. But from none of this does it follow that I am not a material thing. The subject that has all these experiences may consistently with all these possibilities require material realization in a brain or other physical centre. This account certainly does require an ontology of subjects. Subjects can experience, think, remember, engage in mental actions (and, if they have a body, engage in bodily actions too). But these subjects too may be material things.

This explanation of the relevant immunity possessed by (13) does rely on this body's being mine. Is this just to grant Evans's point after all? Does this person's being me simply rely on a conception of myself under which certain ways of coming to know spatial predications of myself must be thought of as primitively written into the nature of the first-person concept (and its reference in my case)? It does not seem that it does. What it is for this person to be me is for this person's body to be the one from which I see and perceive in the other modalities, for this person's body to be the one that moves when I try to move. It is the holding of this condition that makes this person me, or makes this body mine. That, together with the immunity to error through misidentification present for *this body* in the circumstances in question, is enough to explain the first-person immunity for bodily predications. In the phrase *the body from which I see and perceive in other sense modalities*, the reference of *I* continues to be given by the condition that it is the thinker of the thought in which it occurs.

The immunities to error through misidentification of thoughts involving bodily predicates combined with the first person are genuinely significant. I would just locate their significance in a different place than that suggested

---

[13] Dennett (1978*b*).

by Evans. The immunities are significant because they enter a specification of what it is for a body to be mine. For a bodily concept F, in the cases—including their ways and their circumstances—of which Evans says *I am F* is IEM with respect to *I*, what Evans takes to be the reference of *I* is in fact the reference of *my body*. This is so for constitutive reasons. It is the holding of these immunities, when we substitute *my body* for *I*, that makes a body mine. My body is the one of which I gain knowledge in the non-inferential ways specified by Evans. The highly illuminating account of what it is to have a bodily location in the world that is given in Evans's chapter on self-identification is an account of what makes a body mine. It is thereby part of an account of what it is for me to have a location in the objective order.

When we self-ascribe bodily properties in the normal way, in normal circumstances, we do not make an inference from (11) and (12) to (13). The preceding explanation does not say that we make such an inference. The explanation concerns only what is true in the circumstances in question, and these truths are sufficient to explain the impossibility required for the relevant case of immunity to error through misidentification. This then leaves us with the question: what more specifically is the epistemic significance, then, of (11)–(13) if it does not represent an inferential transition made in reaching bodily self-predications? My answer is that an experience of this body's being F entitles me, in normal circumstances, to the first-person judgement *I am F*. This entitlement is founded in the fact that, in normal circumstances, this body is mine.

Since it is only in exotic and highly abnormal circumstances, as when my brain receives input from the eyes and other sense organs in someone else's body, that *This body is mine* could be false, it is surely a fair question to ask how our ordinary conception of ourselves, uninformed by philosophical science fiction, can be expected to pronounce so clearly on counterfactual cases outside the scope of our ordinary experience. Isn't Evans's account superior as a description of our normal first-person thought?

I reply that if the first person has the fundamental reference rule that any use of it in thought refers to the thinker of that thought, then the ordinary concept so individuated does pronounce in a quite specific way on heavily counterfactual cases. This holds even if ordinary users of the first-person concept have not envisaged those cases. On the simple rule that in a thought, a use of *I* refers to the thinker of the thought, it is clear that a thinker in counterfactual circumstances who is enjoying remote perception through another body may truly judge *Though I am seeing and feeling through this body, this body is not mine.* In this thinking *I* refers, as always, to the thinker of the thought, and in the envisaged conditions, the reference of *this body* is not his body.

It may be helpful to compare the situation with the case of perceptual mechanisms that, after working normally, suddenly, by some intervention or accident, come to operate with, say, a fifteen-minute time delay. So in this case, what the perceiver experiences as occurring around him now actually happened fifteen minutes ago. For local objects at least, this situation is quite remote from normal experience, and so it may equally be asked: 'How can our actual concept of the present tense pronounce so specifically on heavily counterfactual cases?' Nevertheless, it does in fact so pronounce. It is unsurprising that it should do so when the fundamental rule of reference for *now* is simply that it refers to the time of occurrence of the thinking in which it occurs. The time-delayed perceiver who knows her situation may truly think *All these [perceptually given] events aren't actually occurring now.* This thought is true, even on the ordinary, unsophisticated concept of the present.

The model of explanation of cases of immunity to error through misidentification built on the truth of (11)–(13) in normal circumstances does not generalize to all first-person cases. The model applies only to those in which the body plays an essential role. In thoughts that locate a subject in relation to other objects and events, the body need not play such a role. In those cases, an explanation along the lines of (11)–(13), with their essential reference to the subject's body, will not serve the purpose. Suppose, for example, that a thinker makes a judgement, on the basis of the scene he visually perceives,

(14) I am in front of a house.

The experience which makes this judgement rational need not involve any perception of his body at all, either by proprioception or by any other means. There is such a thing as what we may call the subject's "point-of-view location", determined simply by the location from which he perceives the world. It is a contingent fact that this coincides with the location of his body, or some part thereof. But, nonetheless, a judgement of (14) when reached in this way still has a qualified form of immunity to error through misidentification. When, in ordinary circumstances, the subject comes rationally to judge (14) in this way, it cannot be that he is right of someone that he is in front of a house, but wrong that it is he himself. What is the explanation of this immunity, given that the model of (11)–(13) does not apply?

The explanation of the immunity in these cases is not that there is, after all, a perceptual means of knowledge of location primitively written into the individuation of the first-person concept. In these visual (and also auditory) cases, the immunity is explicable simply from what is involved in a place being a subject's point-of-view location, together with the fundamental reference rule for I. If the place from which the subject is perceiving is his point-of-view location, then when a subject x has a perception as of being in front of a house, and judges "I am in front of a house", what he judges is true just in case the thinker of that thought—namely x—is in front of a house; which by hypothesis he is. It will be true that it is he, and not someone else, in front of the house in the circumstances under which the immunity to error through misidentification holds. This explanation of the limited immunity does not involve attributing to the first-person way of thinking anything more than the fundamental reference rule. In fact, it parallels in certain respects the explanation we offered in (11)–(13). Just as in that case we said that certain immunities help to constitute what it is for something to be the subject's body, so equally in the present case we say that certain immunities help to constitute what it is for something to be the subject's point-of-view location.

I conclude this section with a brief observation on the immunity to error through misidentification enjoyed by first-person present-tense psychological ascriptions of belief, when these ascriptions are made by a procedure described by Evans, and earlier by Edgley.[14] That procedure involves coming to make the self-ascription *I believe that p* by considering the world, and making the self-ascription just in case one comes to the conclusion, about the world, that p.[15] I equally argue here that the explanation of immunity to error through misidentification of who it is that believes that p also draws upon the fundamental reference rule for the first person. Suppose our thinker considers whether p, and comes, on reflection, to judge that p. Suppose we are concerned with a normal thinker who, as a result of his awareness of making this first-order judgement, comes to think *I believe that p*. Under the fundamental reference rule for the first person I have offered, this self-ascriptive judgement will be true iff the author of this second-order thinking believes that p—which, from the description of the case, he does. So the first-person self-ascriptive judgement will be true in these circumstances. It cannot be in normal circumstances that he comes in this way to believe of someone that he believes that p, but is wrong in thinking that it is he

---

[14] Edgley (1969).   [15] Edgley (1969); Evans (1982, section 7.4: 'Mental Self-Ascription').

that believes it. Nothing more than the fundamental rule of reference for *I*, together with the fact that making a judgement is sufficient for having a belief, and the nature of the normal circumstances with which we are concerned, is needed to explain the legitimacy of this procedure, and to explain the fact that there is no risk of error through misidentification of which person it is that believes that *p*. A parallel argument can be used for some other kinds of psychological self-ascription, including the self-ascription of intentions made, in ordinary circumstances, on the basis of a decision on what to do.

3. CAN A USE OF THE FIRST-PERSON CONCEPT FAIL TO REFER?

The fundamental reference rule for *I*,

(FRR *I*) A use of *I* in a thinking refers to its author

together with the principle

(15) Any thinking has an author

jointly imply that

(16) Any use of *I* in a thinking refers.

That is, they jointly imply that there are no uses of *I* in a thinking that fail to refer.[16]

If the fundamental reference rule for *I* is necessary, and it is also necessary that any thinking has an author, then (16) is also necessary. That is, if (FRR *I*) and (15) are necessary, then it is impossible that there be failures of reference for uses of *I* in a thinking.

It may be said that something different is meant by "reference-failure" for the first-person concept. The point, it may be said, is not that some genuine use of *I* in a thinking fails to refer, but merely that it can seem to a thinker that he is using the first-person concept in thought, but he isn't really, and so fails to refer in a merely apparent use of the first-person concept.

---

[16] The truth of (15) should not be taken as completely obvious. The phenomenon known to psychologists as "anarchic hand" arguably shows that there can be actions without an agent. For some discussion of these cases, see Marcel (2003). If there are analogues of anarchic hand for mental actions, there may be thinkings that do not have a mental agent. The issue merits further research.

It is questionable, however, whether even this version of reference-failure is really a genuine possibility. If it so much as seems to a subject that he is employing the first person, that subject must have the canonical concept of the first-person way of thinking, namely the way of thinking of it that involves thinking of it as the first person. But it is both intuitively plausible, and underwritten by independent theories of canonical concepts, that for any arbitrary concept whatever, one cannot have the canonical concept of that concept without possessing that concept itself. This is so because what makes something the canonical concept of the concept C is that employment of it stands in certain systematic relations to one's employment of the concept C itself. (For further discussion and justification, see Chapter 8 below.) If this is correct, a thinker who has the canonical concept of the first-person concept also possesses the concept of the first person, and so can use it in his thinkings. This point is entirely general, and applies to all canonical concepts of concepts. A thinker equally, for instance, cannot possess the concept *the concept man* unless he possess the concept *man*. If it so much as seems to someone that he is employing the concept *man*, he must really possess the concept *man*. Similarly, if it so much as seems to someone that he is employing the first-person concept, he must possess the first-person concept. If the first person in a thinking cannot fail of reference, it follows that if it so much as seems to someone that he is employing the first-person concept, he also possesses a successfully referring first-person concept.

The fundamental reference rule (FRR *I*) for the first person is, on its face, quite neutral on the correct explication of the notions of thinking, a thinker, reference, and the other notions it employs. However, some theories of these notions imply that reference-failure for uses of *I* really are possible. So—always under the supposition that (15) holds—such theories of the notions used in the statement of the fundamental reference rule for *I* really are incompatible with that rule. Moreover, it seems to me that the intuitive classification of some examples favours the fundamental rule's exclusion of the possibility of reference-failure.

Amongst theories of the first-person concept, we can draw a broad distinction between (*a*) those that require, for a use of the first person to have a reference, that the world cooperate in various ways that are merely contingent, and (*b*) those under which there are no contingencies about the world that must be fulfilled for a use of the first person to have a reference. Both Evans's 1982 theory in his *Varieties of Reference* and a more recent, somewhat similar 2004 theory of John Perry are theories of the first kind.

By the lights of those theories, reference-failure with *I* is possible when the world does not cooperate in the contingent ways required for reference by this concept. Evans recognizes this explicitly. As he formulates the point in summarizing his views: 'The Ideas we have of ourselves, like almost all Ideas we have, rest upon certain empirical presuppositions, and are simply inappropriate to certain describable situations in which these presuppositions are false' (p. 257). He also writes, after presenting his theory of first-person thought, 'I do not see, then, that it is absurd to suppose that there might be a subject of thought who is not in a position to identify himself, and whose attempts at self-identification fail to net any object at all' (p. 253).

Evans has a general theory that relates any way of thinking of something to knowledge of what it is for thoughts containing that way of thinking to be true. He writes, 'our knowledge of what it is for "I am δ_t" to be true, where δ_t is a fundamental identification of a person (conceived of, therefore, as an element of the objective spatial order), consists in our knowledge of what it is for us to be located at a position in space' (p. 223). This formulation draws upon Evans's theory of fundamental Ideas. For any object, there exists what he calls its 'fundamental ground of difference' at a given time. 'This will be a specific answer to the question "What differentiates that object from others?", of the kind appropriate to objects of that sort' (p. 107). To employ a fundamental Idea of an object is to think of it 'as the possessor of the fundamental ground of difference which it in fact possesses' (p. 107). He holds that a fundamental identification of a person is of a kind that 'is also available to someone else' (p. 209), unlike one's first-person identification. So *the person at location l at time t* would be such a fundamental identification δ_t. Evans argued that in turn a person's knowledge of what it is for him to be located at a particular place can be regarded as consisting in his practical capacity to locate himself in space by means of spatial reasoning, based on his perceptions, of the general style 'I perceive such-and-such, such-and-such holds at location *l*, so I'm probably at *l*', 'I was at *l* a moment ago, so moving in this direction I should expect to be a place of such-and-such kind' (p. 223).

It is clear that the subject whose brain has been in a vat for all of its functioning existence, and whose spatial apparent perceptions of an environment are wholly illusory, does not have this practical capacity at all. This subject is not even able to perceive the world outside the vat in which his brain is located. So this subject certainly does not have the ability to self-locate in the objective world. Consistently with the demands of his theory of Ideas and their relation to concepts, in this case the first-person concept,

Evans denies that the permanently envatted subject is able to refer to himself in using the first person in thought (pp. 250–4).

This verdict is not intuitive.[17] While our subject's attempted perceptual demonstratives *this table, that mountain,* and the like will fail to refer if he is permanently envatted, it seems highly plausible that in such thoughts as *I am suffering more from this pain than from that one,* and *If these experiences are all illusory, I wonder if there is some way I can change my situation?,* the use of the concept *I* refers to the envatted subject doing the thinking.

Evans says that even the demonstrative *this pain* will not refer for the permanently envatted subject, because a pain must be 'conceived as the pain of this or that person in the objective order' (p. 253). To meet this criticism by retreating to saying that the subject can think of a pain as *the pain I am now having* fails to meet the objection, Evans says, because his point is precisely that *I* in this description fails to refer. My own view is that this offered reduction of a demonstrative concept *this pain* to a mixed descriptive–indexical concept should be rejected anyway. Moore already forcefully argued, and correctly in my view, that *this colour* does not mean *the colour that is here*.[18] Grasp of the former, in a given context, unlike the latter, requires that the thinker see the colour in question. Proper use of the latter does not. The complex concept *the colour that is here* can be used in thinking, and thinking truly, *There is no such thing as the colour that is here.* The same point applies to demonstrative reference in thought to one's own sensations. The reason that one is able to think about one's own sensations demonstratively is that one stands in a certain relation to them. If each particular sensation is in fact individuated by the person or subject who has it, one will be latching onto a unique sensation, individuated by a unique owner, in standing in the relevant relation to the particular sensation—even if in some sense one does not know who that owner or person is.

On this view, the case is after all analogous to the case in which one genuinely perceives objects and thinks about them demonstratively, without knowing where one is.[19] The envatted subject may equally think about his own thinkings, and about the intentional content of his thinkings. Those contents are things that could be expressed, if our poor subject were properly connected to a body in the world. Our subject can succeed in thinking about

---

[17] As Evans very honestly recognizes (1982: 251).

[18] See the dense but compelling entry under the heading ' "This" and Partial Tautology' in Moore (1962).

[19] Contrary to Evans (1982: 253 n. 71).

things, including himself, that have to meet certain conditions in the world in order to exist, without being able to characterize, in his own thought, what those conditions are.[20]

My position on these issues is, then, a third one distinct both from that of Evans and from that of Anscombe. I am with Evans, and against Anscombe, that uses of *I* in thought (and its corresponding first-person pronoun) do refer. The fact that the first person has a reference is consistent with the fact that in using it, a thinker is in a position to know that he is referring to himself. It is also consistent with the various immunities to error through misidentification expounded by Evans and Shoemaker. Unlike Evans, I hold that these phenomena can be explained by the fundamental reference rule for the first person. Also unlike Evans, I do not think a use of the first person in a thinking can fail of reference. Unlike Anscombe, I do not think that this requires the first person to have some form of Cartesian or other exotic reference.

The three positions can then be summarized thus:

Anscombe:

(A1) Uses of "I" do not refer to anything at all.

(A2) Someone who understands "I" knows that in uttering or thinking it, he is speaking about himself (*de se*); in contrast with the 'A'-users.

(A3) If "I" were to refer, there would be a problem about how each of us knows that he is always referring to the same thing, and a problem of why, apparently, it cannot fail of reference. If "I" were to refer, it would have to refer to a Cartesian ego.

Evans:

(E1) Uses of "I" do refer; they refer to a person with a body, or who once had a body.

(E2) There are explanations of the phenomena of immunity to error through misidentification of various ways of coming to know "I"-thoughts that have to do with the nature of first-person

---

[20] Evans supposes that a position opposed to his that cites the fundamental reference rule for *I* that I have offered must also hold that *I* is synonymous with *the thinker of this thought* (1982: 252). We discussed why fundamental reference rules do not give substitutable synonyms in Ch. 2 sect. 1. They actually never give synonyms in indexical cases.

thought. These explanations are consistent with "I" having a reference.

(E3) The reference of "I" must be conceived of as having both bodily and mental properties.

(E4) A use of "I" in thought can fail of reference.

Peacocke:

(P1) Uses of "I" do refer. (With GE, against EA.)

(P2) There is an explanation of how a thinker knows that in using "I" he is talking about himself, an explanation that is consistent with "I" referring. (For EA's datum, but rejecting her conclusions about what it shows.)

(P3) The rule that any use of "I" in thought refers to the thinker of that thought can by itself be used to explain all the distinctive epistemic phenomena involving the first person. No further account of the sense of "I" is needed. (Against GE.)

(P4) A use of "I" in thought cannot fail of reference. (Against GE, with EA's data, but against her conclusion.)

I now step back from the details of these disputes to make two observations if the programme of explaining the distinctive epistemic and normative characteristics of the first person from its fundamental reference rule can be carried through.

The first observation concerns the theory Robert Nozick develops and entertains in his book *Philosophical Explanations*.[21] Nozick suggests that 'the I is delineated, is synthesized around ... [the] act of reflexive self-referring. An entity is synthesized around the reflective act and it is the "I" of that act' (p. 87). Nozick wrote that only such a theory of a 'synthesized self' can explain why, when we reflexively self-refer, we know it is *ourselves* to whom we refer (p. 90). Many years ago, in *Sense and Content*, I objected to Nozick that this fact can be explained without any particular metaphysics of the self.[22] I stand by the criticism; but what I have just said about the derivability of reason-involving and normative phenomena for the first person suggests a different, and perhaps slightly more sympathetic, way of looking at Nozick's discussion. If the phenomena distinctive of the first person are

---

[21] Nozick (1981). Page references in the text are to this work.   [22] Peacocke (1983: 134–6).

indeed all derivable from the fundamental reference rule for *I*, that it refers to the author of the thinking in which it occurs, then Nozick's project can be seen as a perhaps unduly metaphysical way of carrying through those derivations. A transposition of such derivations to the realm of entities, of something that essentially concerns senses and ways of thinking, would precisely take as the fundamental explanatory resource not the fundamental reference rule, but a metaphysical analogue to the effect that an entity is individuated by its relation to some act of self-reference that it performs. I do not mean that this is intelligible (if the act exists, must not the agent that performs it already exist?). But it is true that the Nozickian project can be seen as a metaphysical hypostatization of a project at the level of norms, reference, and sense that is not only intelligible, but also plausible.

The other observation concerns Evans's famous complaint against David Kaplan and John Perry for their talk of first-person thought being thought 'under the character of "I" ' (where character is a function from contexts to Kaplanian contents in Kaplan's treatment). In his characteristic style, Evans wrote that 'all good Fregeans must live in hope of a yet profounder philosophy'.[23] Evans was certainly right that Frege held that not all modes of presentation employed in thought are descriptive, and that the first-person way of thinking is a straightforward example of a sense that is not descriptive.[24] Evans was also surely right to want an account of self-conscious thought and the immunity phenomena. Yet if the programme of deriving the distinctive epistemic and normative phenomena displayed by the first person from the fundamental reference rule can be carried through, Kaplan and Perry were certainly not looking in entirely the wrong place. The fundamental reference rule for the first-person concept is one form of the transposition to the domain of thought of the character rule for the first-person pronoun formulated by Kaplan (that in any context, "I" refers to the agent of that context). The profounder philosophy is desirable, but if it draws upon a thought-theoretic analogue of the reference rules in Perry and Kaplan, it will, if the present arguments are sound, be in a position to explain the phenomena of which Evans wanted an explanation.

[23] Evans (1985*a*: 321). Evans's immediate target was Perry (1993).
[24] 'Now everyone is presented to himself in a special and primitive way, in which he is presented to no-one else. So, when Dr. Lauben has the thought that he was wounded, he will probably be basing it on this primitive way in which he is presented to himself. And only Dr. Lauben himself can grasp thoughts specified in this way' (Frege 1984*a*: 359). There is no such restriction on the grasp of descriptive thoughts.

4. SOME CONCEPTUAL ROLES ARE DISTINCTIVE BUT NOT FUNDAMENTAL

Something can be a distinctive, important, and even a necessary feature of a concept, without being what individuates a concept. This state of affairs is possible because the distinctive feature in question may be a consequence of something more fundamental, and it is what is more fundamental that individuates the concept. I suggest that this is the state of affairs that actually holds for the first-person concept in respect of its several indisputably important conceptual roles that various philosophers have articulated. What is fundamental is its reference rule, and these conceptual roles are consequential upon that reference rule. Since the reference rule is certainly a necessary feature of the concept, if a particular conceptual role follows from that rule by necessity, then of course the conceptual role will be necessary too. But our concern here is not with necessity, but with what is fundamental and explanatory.

I have already argued one part of this case in discussing the relation between the conceptual roles identified by Evans on the input side, the side of reasons for making first-person judgements. We can very briefly, at this stage of the chapter, make the corresponding point for a suggestion that aims to individuate the first-person concept on the output side, by individuating it in relation to its role in the formation of intentions and the explanation of action. In the course of an illuminating discussion, Robert Brandom writes that 'The central defining uses of "I" are ... its uses in "I shall open the door", as expressing the conclusion of practical deliberation, and therefore as used in the expression of the premises.'[25] I agree that no premises have significance for our practical reasoning and action unless they contain or collectively establish a substantive first-person proposition, and that the conclusion of practical reasoning always involves the first-person concept. Does it follow that this essential feature of the first-person concept is also fundamental?

Consider a parallel case. No collection of propositions has practical significance for how I should try to act now, unless at least one of them has, or unless they collectively imply, a substantive present-tense content. (A similar point could be made for practical significance concerning my current location. Any contents with such immediate practical significance

---

[25] Brandom (1994: 533, from the section on pp. 552–9 on the first person).

must similarly involve the concept *here*.) To use John Perry's example, unless I know that the bear is approaching me now, I do not have information that gives me reason to roll up in a ball now. Knowing that the bear is approaching at 3.30 p.m. has no significance for action unless I know that 3.30 p.m. is now, or unless I know its temporal relation to now. Should we draw the conclusion that this role in action explanation is a central defining feature of the present-tense concept *now*? The immediate reaction to the proposal is that this idea has things back-to-front in the order of philosophical explanation. One needs to know what is happening now, before trying to act in one way rather than another, precisely because *now* refers to the time of one's thinking a thought containing it. The fundamental reference rule for the concept *now* gives a completely satisfying explanation of why you need to know whether the bear is approaching now before you try to roll up in a ball. If the bear is not approaching at the time of your thinking, you have no reason thereby to roll up in a ball at that same time.

I suggest that what I have just asserted to hold for the present-tense concept holds equally for the first-person concept. Propositions have relevance for the formation of intentions only if they bear upon the thinker of one's thoughts, oneself, and this suffices to explain why the premises of practical reasoning must themselves at some point involve the first person. The role of the first person in practical reasoning is distinctive and important. That is consistent with that role being derivative from something more fundamental. In the case of both *I* and *now*, their fundamental reference rules are explanatory of the conceptual roles that are distinctive of them.

We can also draw a distinction between those fundamental reference rules that immediately imply certain conceptual roles relating to perception and action, and those that do so less directly. If the fundamental reference rule for the concept *oval* is that it is true of all and only those things that are the same shape as things perceived in a certain way (given by a non-conceptual content), then it immediately follows that something perceived in that way is oval. The fundamental rules of reference for *I* and *now* do not mention perceptual experience, or action, in this way.

I conclude with a more general hypothesis for further investigation. I have argued, for the illustrative case of the first-person concept, that its fundamental rule of reference, in the presence of agreed background features of the cases, makes rational the various conceptual roles that philosophers have rightly identified as distinctive of it. Judging in accordance with these conceptual roles can be seen, under this approach, as making a rational transition in the circumstances in question. Thinkers are also in a position to appreciate that these roles are rational. Intuitively, we hold that when a thinker appreciates the rationality of one of these roles, his appreciation is explained by his understanding of the notions involved, in particular his grasp of the first person. I suggest that the rationality of the conceptual roles is appreciated as such on the basis of tacit knowledge of the fundamental rules of reference for the concepts in question. When there is understanding-based appreciation of the rationality of a transition that is distinctive of a concept, an essential part of the explanation of this appreciation is the thinker's tacit knowledge of the fundamental reference rule for the concept in question. I conjecture that this is a conception of why the transitions are appreciated as rational that we should apply not only to indexical concepts, but across the board, to rational conceptual transitions in general.

4

Implicit Conceptions

The purpose of this chapter is to elaborate the notion of an implicit conception, to argue for the existence of implicit conceptions, and to present a case for their significance in psychological and philosophical explanations involving the nature of concepts.

An implicit conception is a state of tacit knowledge required for possession of a given concept. Tacit knowledge in general has become, or should have become, well understood from the writings of Noam Chomsky, Martin Davies, and many others.[1] The species of tacit knowledge involved in possession of certain concepts has been less well understood. Saying more about such implicit conceptions is an essential part in carrying out the project of this book. Right back in Chapter 1, I argued that possession of even a basic observational concept involves having an implicit conception whose content involves the identity-relation. This was the 'identity-component' of the realist's account of observational concepts (Chapter 1 section 3). Identity-involving implicit conceptions will also loom large in the treatment of many psychological concepts in Part II of this book. So we need to understand how implicit conceptions work.

To say simply that in some cases, possessing a concept involves having an implicit conception is still to leave open many questions. For example, one type of implicit conception may simply have a content that specifies an inferential (or some other conceptual) role for the concept in question, a role specified without any link to reference or truth. That is, a pure conceptual-role theorist of intentional content may happily, even enthusiastically, embrace the idea that some concepts involve implicit conceptions. So a more specific statement of purpose of this chapter is that it aims to examine further the subclass of cases in which an implicit conception underlying a concept has a certain character: that in which its content specifies, or contributes to

---

[1] From amongst a now very extensive literature: Chomsky (1980, 1986); Davies (1981, chs III and IV; 1987).

the specification of, the reference of the concept in question. This subclass of cases includes the identity-component of the realist's account back in Chapter 1 of this book, for those implicit conceptions contribute to the determination of extension of an observational concept to unperceived cases. It will include any cases in which we need to appeal to tacit knowledge of the fundamental reference rules discussed in Chapter 2. It will also include the identity-components which, I will be arguing in Part II of this book, are involved in the grasp of some central psychological concepts.

It is sufficient for an implicit conception to fall in this target subclass that it contribute to the specification of the reference of the concept in question. The content of the implicit conception may or may not include such notions of reference and truth in providing this contribution to the specification of reference. We will be looking at both cases.[2]

1. IMPLICIT CONCEPTIONS: MOTIVATION AND EXAMPLES

Consider someone who is introduced to a primitive logical axiom, or to a primitive logical rule. This person might be yourself, when you were first taught logic at around the age of 18. Your introduction might be to an axiom schema A → (A or B), or it might be to the inference rule 'From A, a conclusion of the form "A or B" can be inferred'. There is such a phenomenon as a thinker in your situation reflecting, drawing on his understanding of the expressions in the rule, and coming to appreciate that the axiom or rule is valid. What is going on when such reflection takes place?

The example is specified as one in which the axiom or principle is a primitive one. It is not something which is derivable from other axioms or rules. So the movement of thought in which our rational, reflective thinker is engaged cannot be one of straightforward inference. Nor is it a matter of

---

[2] The position expounded in this chapter, a position I developed from 1994 onwards, involves a change from the one I held in *A Study of Concepts* (Peacocke 1992). Several factors influenced the change. One was a growing dissatisfaction with the treatment given in that book of what is involved in accepting primitive axioms and rules. Another was reflection on what is involved in rational acceptance of new principles which do not follow from those a thinker already accepts. A third factor was the attraction of the conception of sense expounded and developed in Burge (2005a). My sense is that there has also been a growing appreciation of how unsatisfactory it is to say that primitive axioms and rules are simply found primitively compelling when the concepts they treat are grasped. For some arguments and examples on this point additional to those in this chapter, see Williamson (2006).

accepting a stipulation involving some newly introduced symbol. The axiom or rule is appreciated, on reflection, as correct when taken as involving the very same words, such as 'or', which an 18-year-old learner of logic, for instance, will have understood for more than fifteen years. Nor is it plausible that our thinker has to draw on memories of his own previous uses of the word 'or' on particular occasions. The logical principle is not about his use of the word. In any case, if he is like me, he will not remember any particular occasions as ones on which he used that very word. All the same, he can still reflect, drawing on his understanding of the word, and come to appreciate that the axiom or principle is valid.

Our thinker's knowledge cannot always be explained as a result of his having explicitly inferred the validity of the axiom or principle from his explicit knowledge of the truth-tables for the connectives involved. This cannot be a fully satisfying explanation for two reasons. First, our thinker can reflect and rationally appreciate the validity of these principles before having been explicitly taught any truth-tables. Second, and crucially, we must also think about rational acceptance of the truth-tables themselves. Each of us, when first presented with the truth-tables for the unproblematic connectives, was able to reflect, and come rationally, on the basis of our understanding of the expressions, to appreciate that the particular truth-table is correct. This is itself a further illustration of the kind of phenomenon we are trying to explain.

No doubt there are various different detailed ways in which reflection may proceed in the original case of the axiom or principle, but one of them is as follows. Like the other variants in which the details differ, the reflection involves a simulation exercise. The thinker imagines—to start with one of the cases—that A is true and B is false. His aim is to address the question of whether the alternation 'A or B' should be regarded as true or false in the imagined circumstances. As in any other simulation exercise, he then exercises a capacity off-line. This capacity is the very same, understanding-based capacity he would be exercising in a real case in which he had the information that A is true and B is false and has to evaluate the alternation 'A or B'. As in the corresponding real case, in the imaginative exercise he goes on to hold that 'A or B' will be true in the imagined circumstances. In coming to hold that 'A or B' is true in the simulated circumstances, our thinker employs only the information about the truth-values, within the simulation, of A and of B, together with his understanding of alternation. He does not draw on any other resources.

Next our thinker proceeds to consider imaginatively another case, say that in which A is true and B is true … As he goes through the cases, he is eventually in a position to accept rationally that there will be no cases in which the antecedent, or premiss, is true, and the consequent, or conclusion, is false for the axiom or inference rule respectively. Thus he comes to accept rationally the axiom or rule as valid. The same procedure and resources will equally allow him to come to accept rationally each line of the truth-table for some connective he understands. When axioms, inference rules, or lines of truth-tables are reached in this way, it seems to me that the resulting judgements constitute knowledge.

In *A Study of Concepts*, I described certain logical axioms and primitive rules as 'primitively compelling'. The problem with that account, as with many other conceptual-role accounts, is that it gives no elucidation of the rationality of accepting primitive axioms and rules. Simply saying that they are non-inferentially accepted is much too undiscriminating. Adding that they are non-inferentially accepted on the basis of the thinker's understanding at least makes clear that understanding plays an explanatory role in the acceptance. It does, though, still fail to describe the nature of the understanding that generates the acceptance, fails to say what 'on the basis of' amounts to here, or to say how the acceptance is rational.

The present account of the reflection gives a clear explanatory priority to the thinker's understanding-based capacity to evaluate particular alternations, such as 'Either he went left or he went right', and particular conjunctions, and other complex statements, on the basis of information about their components. This is a capacity which a thinker can possess and exercise, and normally does do so, prior to having any explicit knowledge of general logical principles or of truth-tables. It is this capacity which is run off-line in the simulation. It is a capacity involved in the very understanding of connectives. Its role in the imaginative exercise makes the case one in which the thinker draws upon his own understanding of the expressions in coming to appreciate, via this reflection, that the axiom or principle is valid.

I suggest further that the thinker's understanding of the connective 'or' involves (and perhaps is even to be identified with) his possession of an implicit conception, a conception with the following content: that any sentence of the form 'A or B' is true if and only if either A is true or B is true. Similarly at the level of thought: a thinker's grasp of the concept of alternation involves (and is perhaps to be identified with) his possession of an implicit conception with the content that any Thought (content) of the form *A or B* is true if and only if either *A* is true or *B* is true. Such implicit conceptions are influential in the thinker's evaluation of alternations given information about the truth-values of their components. The influence is exerted not by the thinker inferring something from the content of the implicit conception. He need not have any explicit knowledge of its content. Rather, his having the implicit conception explains his particular patterns of semantic evaluation of the complex, given information about the truth-values of its constituents. Derivatively, it is this implicit conception which is influential in the simulational part of the reflection which eventually leads him to accept certain primitive axioms and inferential rules involving alternation.

This, then, is a description at the personal level of a way in which a thinker may come rationally to accept a logical principle, a way which is not simply a matter of inferring it from other previously accepted object-language principles. Certain features of this non-inferential but rational means of acceptance need clarification.

(*a*) The very simple description I have given of the rational acceptance of a logical axiom is not meant to enable us to resolve the dispute between classical and constructivist, or any other, interpretation of the logical constants. Nor could it provide such a resolution. The phenomena cited in this simple description of the case are phenomena of a general kind which would equally need to be mentioned in an account of how it is that an ordinary, non-philosophical thinker can come to appreciate that certain axioms are valid, even if a constructivist theory of meaning were correct. The constructivist is likely to elucidate validity of a transition as the transformability of any means of establishing its premises into a means of establishing its conclusion. To work out whether this definition applies to a particular form of transition, the ordinary thinker will have to use simulation to gain knowledge of the ways in which he takes statements of certain forms to be established. Imaginative simulation will be involved in any case in which the thinker is drawing, at least on early occasions, on the understanding he exercises in ordinary, real-world applications. This is something common to classical and to constructivist approaches. Any resolution of the dispute between them must appeal to a quite different body of considerations.

(*b*) The described means of rationally coming to accept a primitive law is a fallible means. A thinker may overlook a combination of truth-values, or may perform the simulation incorrectly. He may fail to run the very same procedure for evaluation off-line as he would exercise on-line. He may misremember information derived from earlier simulations in which he was checking cases. He may use a procedure in imaginatively assessing particular cases which is not just understanding-based, but draws on auxiliary information specific to those particular cases. Much, then, may go wrong. Nonetheless, when the procedure is properly executed, the resulting belief in the logical law has an a priori status. No perceptual state, nor the deliverance of any other causally sensitive faculty for finding out about the world, is playing an essential *justificational* role in the thinker's rational acceptance of the logical law when it is arrived at in this way. This combination of fallible capacities which, when exercised properly, are nevertheless capable of yielding a priori knowledge is something with which we are very familiar in other routes to a priori knowledge.

(*c*) An objector may protest that simulation can never give knowledge of what would be true in the circumstances imagined in the simulation, but can only give knowledge of what the simulating thinker would judge or believe in the imagined circumstances. This, though, seems to me to be false. Simulations, properly executed, can give information about the world, as well (of course) as information about the thinker's mental state in various hypothetical circumstances. Suppose you are asked the question: 'If you walk south down Whitehall, and turn left over Westminster Bridge, when you are on the bridge, what building is slightly to the left of straight ahead of you?' You answer this by imagining yourself following the described route. When, by this means, you reach the conclusion that when on the bridge, the former County Hall would be slightly to the left of straight ahead, this is a means of obtaining information about the world. If they are knowledgeable states which the thinker is drawing upon in performing the simulation, it is also a means of obtaining knowledge about the world. It is important to emphasize that the conditions initially specified to hold in the simulation, both in this spatial example and in our logical case, concern not merely what the subject believes in the simulated circumstances, but what is true in the simulated circumstances.

Of course this spatial example involves sensory imagination, and such experiential imagination does not need to be involved in the simulations I have been considering in the logical case. It is rather a form of suppositional imagining in the logical cases. It is important, though, that even imagining what else would be the case when something is suppositionally imagined to hold still involves simulational capacities. It is a constraint on suppositionally imagining properly, and indeed in reasoning properly from a supposition, that one carry over to the supposed state of affairs the holding of certain transitions that one would be prepared to make in the actual world, in non-suppositional cases. Thus there is a first-personal element which does not simply disappear when we consider non-sensory, merely suppositional imagination.

(*d*) A thinker of a certain frame of mind sometimes classified as neo-Wittgensteinian may wonder whether there is really any objectivity in what is obtained by the simulation procedure as applied in the logical case. It is not the point of this chapter to take on central Wittgensteinian issues, and for present purposes I just note the plausibility of the following biconditional. The results of the simulation, properly carried out, will have the required objectivity if and only if there is objectivity in a thinker's corresponding response to a new case in the real, non-simulational, world. If there is objectivity of the latter, that is if it goes beyond merely an impression of correctness, then the capacity exercised on-line in the real-world cases can be drawn upon in carrying through the simulation.

So much by way of preliminary remarks on the nature of the simulation in this first example. It is not hard to reach, by reflection, principles distinctive of alternation, and in doing so to be appropriately influenced by one's underlying implicit conception. It is not even hard, in that particular example, to make the content of the implicit conception explicit. In other examples, neither of these things is so. There are some cases in which a thinker has an implicit conception, but is unable to make its content explicit. The thinker may even be unable to formulate principles distinctive of the concept his possession of which consists in his possession of that implicit conception.

One of the most spectacular illustrations of this is given by the famous case of Leibniz's and Newton's grappling with the notion of the limit of a series, a notion crucial in the explanation of the differential calculus. It would be a huge injustice to Leibniz and Newton to deny that they had the concept of the limit of a series, or to deny that they had propositional attitudes describable by using the word 'limit' within that-clauses. What they could do was to differentiate particular functions, and they had no difficulty in saying what the limit of a particular series of ratios was. I would say that each of these great thinkers had an implicit conception which explained their application of the phrase 'limit of …' in making judgements about the limits of particular series of ratios. What they could not do, despite repeated pressing by critics and well-wishers, was to make explicit the content of their implicit conceptions. When pressed for explications, Leibniz spoke of values that were infinitely close to one another. This is something we can now make sense of in the theory of infinitesimals, but was quite illegitimate within the ontology of real numbers within which Leibniz was working. Newton spoke of 'limiting values', 'ultimate ratios', and the like, but these were not given a steady explanation. Sometimes the procedures given even seem to require dividing by zero. Newton comes extremely close to a correct explication at one point, but gives that explanation no special salience amongst the others. If their explications were really the best that could be given, it would be hard not to sympathize with Berkeley's critique of the calculus. Even John Bernoulli, in trying to sort the matter out, wrote sentences like this:

> a quantity which is diminished or increased by an infinitely small quantity is neither increased nor decreased.[3]

As is well known, it was not until Bolzano, Cauchy, and arguably even until Weierstrass in the mid-nineteenth century that a completely clear, unproblematic explication of the limit of a series was achieved, the familiar epsilon–delta definition. L is the limit of the function $f(x)$ as x approaches a if for any positive number ε, there is some number δ such that $f(x)$ minus L is less than ε whenever x minus a is less than δ. In this explication there is, famously, no unexplained talk about ultimate ratios, infinitely small values, or anything which even appears to involve dividing by zero. To make an implicit conception explicit can, then, on occasion be a major intellectual achievement.[4]

The case of Leibniz, Newton, and limits also serves to illustrate another point. We do sometimes ascribe attitudes to contents containing a concept to a thinker, even when a thinker has only a partial understanding of the expression for the concept, provided that the thinker defers in his use of the expression to others in the community who understand it better, and provided that the thinker has some minimum level of understanding. That phenomenon has been very well described by Burge.[5] But we ought not to

---

[3] Quoted in Stewart (1996: 77).

[4] Did Newton and Leibniz actually operate with different, but equivalent, implicit definitions of the limit? Newton's informal explications are closer to the Bolzano–Cauchy–Weierstrass definition, while, at first blush, Leibniz's seem like those one would give in the theory of infinitesimals. Hide Ishiguro, however, argues that 'infinitely small' was regarded as contextually defined by Leibniz, and so not thought by him to be referential vocabulary. See Ishiguro (1990, ch. V).

[5] Burge (2007a).

assimilate the example of early uses of the limit concept to cases of deference, for the facts explained by implicit conceptions cannot be explained away by appealing to deference. To whom were Leibniz and Newton supposed to defer? There was no one else who understood the notion better. Nor, one may conjecture from each of their characters, was either of these two gentlemen of a mind to defer to anyone else on these (or any other) matters.

Leibniz's and Newton's use of the limit concept is rather a non-deferential example of what Frege called grasping a definite sense, whilst also failing to grasp it 'sharply'. It is not an example whose philosophical explanation involves social elements. The present chapter is in effect an exploration of what is involved in employing concepts which are not 'sharply grasped', and in which the social–individual divergences are not the crux of the matter. It is striking that this very example of the limit concept occurs in a list in the first section of Frege's *Foundations of Arithmetic*: 'The concepts of function, of continuity, of limit and of infinity have been shown to stand in need of sharper definition.'[6]

The early use of the concept of a limit in Leibniz and Newton is a concrete historical illustration of a state of affairs whose possibility is articulated by Burge. In the course of elaborating Frege's conception of grasp which is not sharp, Burge writes: 'The striking element in Frege's view is his application of this distinction to cases where *the most competent speakers, and indeed the community taken collectively,* could not, even on extended ordinary reflection, articulate the "standard senses" of the terms.'[7] That was precisely the position of Leibniz and Newton in relation to terms for limits. So the Fregean view, Burge's account, and the description I am in the course of developing would all firmly distinguish this phenomenon from that of attributions of concepts legitimized by the existence of deference in the use of expressions.

Some of the intellectual skills required to succeed in making an implicit conception explicit will be skills useful in any enterprise of building an explanation from instances. Choosing the right classification of cases matters. The right classification of cases is a relatively trivial matter for the logical connectives (or at least, it is so once one has settled on a particular kind of semantic theory). It is somewhat less trivial to articulate the implicit conception involved in understanding the word 'chair'. It is definitely non-trivial to make explicit what is involved in being the limit of a series. Equally, skill in appreciating the full range of cases matters too, as failed attempts

[6] Frege (1953, §1).   [7] Burge (2005b: 261).

to define 'chair' which omitted ski-lift chairs showed. So, even though in trying to articulate one's own implicit conceptions, one is trying to articulate what is influencing one in making judgements involving the concept in particular cases, the skills and methodology involved are those pertinent to any abductive investigation. Achieving such an articulation is not simply a matter of passively allowing the content of some implicit conception to float into consciousness from the subpersonal level.

Since it can be hard to make explicit the content of one of one's own implicit conceptions, we should equally not be surprised if thinkers sometimes mischaracterize the content of their implicit conceptions. A thinker's explicit endorsement of an incorrect definition does not mean that he does not have an implicit conception whose content is the correct definition. The attribution of a content to an implicit conception is fundamentally answerable to its role in explaining the thinker's ordinary applications of the concept in question. Classifications of examples by the thinker provide the primary data to which the correctness of an attribution of a particular content to his underlying implicit conception is answerable. Thinkers can be good at classifying cases, and bad at articulating the principles guiding their classifications. Ordinary thinkers, who understand the predicate 'chair' perfectly well, often give an incorrect definition when pressed for one. And if Leibniz and Newton can mischaracterize their own grasp of a concept, how can the rest of us expect never to be in error on such matters?

How wide is the range of concepts and expressions with which implicit conceptions are associated? The examples of implicit conceptions I have offered so far have been associated with logical and mathematical concepts, and have involved definitions. Implicit conceptions involving definition may, though, be found in almost any domain. A significant segment of moral and political thought, for example, consists in making explicit the implicit conceptions and constraints which explain our applications of such notions as fairness, equality, and opportunity. At the other end of the spectrum, I think we need to employ implicit conceptions in characterizing the mastery even of some observational concepts. In mastering the concept *cube*, taken as an observational concept, a thinker must have an implicit conception with a content which includes this: that cubes are closed figures formed from square sides joined at right angles along their edges.

Not all examples will be so trivial. In the case of any philosophically interesting concept, the question of the content of the implicit conception (if any) underlying it will be highly substantive. Answering the question will in such cases involve making some substantive advance in our understanding of the subject matter in question.

The benefits of successfully making explicit the content of some previously merely implicit conception are multiple and various. Since having a merely implicit conception is fundamentally tied to judgements about particular examples, the first benefit of an explicit statement is that of generality. Leibniz and Newton had no difficulty giving the limits of particular series of ratios. What they did not knowledgeably formulate was the general, universally quantified biconditional stating the relation in which a number had to stand to a series to be its limit. The generality brings much in its wake. In particular, it provides a crucial tool needed to prove general theorems about limits.

A second benefit of making the conception explicit, one for which the generality also matters, is the possibility of fully defending the legitimacy of the notion. Only with a general, explicit statement of what it is to be the limit of a series is a theorist in a position to give a fully satisfactory answer to Berkeley's critique of the notion.

A third benefit is one which Frege notes that proofs can also bring: correct definition can help to establish 'the limits to the validity of a proposition' (*Foundations of Arithmetic*, §1 again). In general, proof and definition will do this hand-in-hand. Proofs usually require some definition of the notion in question. Equally, the fruitfulness of the definition can be established only by investigating what can be proved from it.

A fourth benefit, like the second, also has to do with justification. Someone who knows the explicit characterization can give a rationale for his classification of particular examples. This applies both in mathematical and logical cases, and in moral and political examples. Any general constraints on fairness, for instance, which we can discover and formulate with generality will allow us to argue much more forcibly that some particular procedure or arrangement is, or is not, unfair.[8]

If a thinker has an implicit conception, there will be a certain psychological relation in which he stands to a content which specifies the content of that conception. The nature of that psychological relation is something which I will presently be discussing. I do, however, want to distinguish sharply

[8] Here too I am at one with Burge's elaboration of the Fregean position: 'I think that Frege's conception attempts to bridge the gap between actual understanding and actual sense expression by means of a normative concept—that of the deeper foundation or justification for actual understanding and usage' (2005*b*: 261).

between this relation which is under investigation, and at least one familiar notion of tacit or virtual belief. This is the notion of tacit belief which is most trivially illustrated by such examples as an ordinary person's belief that cars are not edible, and perhaps less trivially by an ordinary person's beliefs about an interlocutor with whom he is engaged in a conversation—his rationality, or perhaps some of his higher-order awarenesses. Mark Crimmins seems to me to have made a good case that these examples of tacit belief can be elucidated as ones in which for a person to at-least-tacitly believe that p is for it to be as if the person has an explicit belief in p.[9] In paradigmatic cases, Crimmins says, this elucidation could be paraphrased more specifically by saying that the tacit believer's cognitive dispositions are relevantly as if he has an explicit belief in p.[10] However, the case of Leibniz and Newton having an implicit conception of the correct definition of the limit of a series is a case in which their cognitive dispositions are not relevantly as if they had an explicit belief in the correct definition. For the explicit believer, the correct definition is not news; whereas the Bolzano–Cauchy–Weierstrass definition was certainly news. The point applies even to the modest case of the correct definition of 'chair'.[11]

It follows that the sense of 'limit' as used by Leibniz and Newton—its contribution to cognitive value—is not identical with the correct explicit definition of 'limit'. Burge has made the same point forcefully for a different range of examples.[12]

The distinction between cognitive value and correct explicit definition applies both in cases which have no externalist character, such as the case of limits, and in cases like 'chair', which do. In both kinds of case, it is plausibly the close tie between ordinary employment of the sense and the ability to classify examples correctly which brings with it the distinction between the ordinarily used sense and the more theoretical explicit definition. The close tie with particular examples can be present both in cases where there is external individuation of the concept, and in cases where there is not.

Maybe some substantial restriction on the range of phenomena considered in verifying the 'as if' clause in Crimmins's characterization would capture

[9] Crimmins (1992: 248).   [10] Crimmins (1992: 249).

[11] For further discussion of the example of Leibniz's and Newton's use of the concept *limit* as what Georges Rey calls a 'postulary conception', see Rey (1998) and my reply, Peacocke (1998). There are subtle and intriguing differences between Leibniz's and Newton's accounts that go beyond the immediately obvious differences. For an absorbing account of this apparently perennially interesting history, see Meli (1993).

[12] Burge (2007*b*).

tacit conceptions as a special case of a generic notion of virtual belief.[13] The natural restriction would cut the range of phenomena down to certain canonical applications of the concept for which an implicit conception is being given. In the case of the limit example, we might be restricted to considering the thinker's ability to calculate the limits of particular series. My point at present, however, is that some such substantial restriction is required. There may be a spectrum of tacit and virtual beliefs here, but implicit conceptions are not at the same point along it as many more familiar examples of tacit belief.[14]

2. DEFLATIONARY READINGS REJECTED

What I have said so far can be greeted with varying degrees and kinds of scepticism. One important deflationary reaction is the complaint that the implicit conceptions of which I have spoken are simply projected backwards from the actual inferential and classificatory dispositions of thinkers. The complaint would run thus: in so far as it is legitimate to speak of implicit conceptions at all, they serve simply to summarize the actual classificatory and inferential propensities of those who understand the expressions in question. But, the complaint continues, the implicit conceptions neither explain nor justify anything. Understanding is constituted by the particular inferential and classificatory dispositions, rather than anything which underlies them.

The first consideration I offer in reply is that a person's understanding of an expression may outrun natural generalizations of all the principles he has ever encountered, or could be expected to come up with. A natural illustration of the point is provided by non-standard models of first-order arithmetic, which contain blocks of "non-natural" numbers which follow after all the genuine natural numbers. It seems clear that an ordinary person's understanding of the expression 'whole number' definitely counts non-standard models *as* non-standard. One principle whose truth excludes non-standard models is the ω-rule: in one form, this is the rule that if 'F(0)', 'F(1)', 'F(2)', ... are all provable in the given system, then so is 'All natural numbers are F'. Another such principle is a second-order induction axiom with a quite

---

[13] Crimmins considers a range of grades of 'as if' clauses at (1992: 257).

[14] Near the start of his paper (1992: 241) Crimmins also says that the notion of tacit belief may be needed to explain the relation between thinkers and non-trivial analyses of concepts. The Bolzano–Cauchy–Weierstrass definition is a non-trivial analysis of a concept. It is, then, a question whether it is quite the same standard, or grade of strictness, of 'as if' clause that we need to accommodate both the more trivial examples of tacit belief and the non-trivial analyses.

specific and highly general understanding of the range of the second-order quantifiers. Now ordinary thinkers, who use and understand the expression 'whole number', have no conception of any such principles. Nor, for many hundreds of years, did anyone else. All the same, it seems to me that the ordinary thinker's understanding of the expression 'natural number', and that of everyone more than a century and a half ago, would count the non-standard models as non-standard. That these models of first-order formulations exist would hardly have been striking otherwise. Their designation as non-standard was not simply a matter of stipulation or convention, or a resolution of some indeterminacy.

It is at this point in the discussion that the deflationist about implicit conceptions may be tempted to appeal to counterfactuals. He may suggest that what matters is that our ordinary thinkers would acknowledge these principles as correct on their understanding of 'whole number', were they to be presented with these principles. This seems to me to be a decidedly optimistic view of the person in the street (or many other places) when we imagine that person presented with the ω-rule, or with unrestricted second-order induction. But let us waive that. We will waive it by allowing, more specifically, that there may be some non-question-begging restriction R such that if someone has the ordinary concept of a whole number, and meets this restriction R, then he would acknowledge such principles as the ω-rule, or unrestricted second-order induction, as correct. The important issue here is: does that help the deflationary reading of implicit conceptions?

It seems to me that it does not. Intuitively, a person's prior understanding of the predicate 'is a whole number' *explains* why the counterfactual is true of him. When all is working properly, a person who understands the predicate 'is a whole number' uses that understanding to work out that the ω-rule is correct. The present deflationist is wrongly offering a kind of identification rather than an explanation.

This first deflationist is also vulnerable to a near-ubiquitous problem with counterfactual analyses of categorical notions. We must be able to distinguish between someone who has an understanding of 'is a whole number' in advance, and someone who gains it in the course of his coming to meet the antecedent of the counterfactual. This distinction is incompatible with identifying understanding with something which simply has his satisfaction of the counterfactual as one primitive constituent.

I would say that the counterfactuals, when they are true of a thinker and properly result from his prior understanding of the predicate 'is a whole number', are explained by his possession of a specific implicit conception of the range of that predicate. My own view is that the content of that particular implicit conception should make essential use of primitive recursion with a limiting clause. Its content is given by three primitive principles:

(1) 'is a whole number' is true of 0

(2) 'is a whole number' is true of the successor of anything it is true of; and

(3) nothing falls under 'is a whole number' unless it can be determined to do so on the basis of rules (1) and (2).

Clause (3), on its intuitive understanding, excludes the non-standard models. It is worth noting that no explicit use of the notion of finiteness, or second-order properties, or reference to reasoning by arithmetical induction, occurs in this statement of the implicit conception.

At this point I diverge from Hartry Field, who brings in cosmological considerations to make sense of a determinate notion of finiteness, and to rule out non-standard models.[15] On the position I am advocating, primitive recursion with a limiting clause like (3) is explanatorily more fundamental than the general notion of finiteness. We do not need to rely on any empirical truths about the physical universe to classify the non-standard models as non-standard. It has of course to be part of this position that the modal 'can' which occurs essentially in (3) is not itself to be elucidated in arithmetical terms not governed by an implicit conception—otherwise the problem of non-standard interpretations would be with us again. It is an obligation of the present position to say why the modal approach is to be preferred to second-order characterizations of the natural numbers.[16]

These points may just encourage our deflationist further, to say that a thinker's understanding of 'is a whole number' consists in no more than his willingness to accept as correct an explicit statement of *this* primitive recursion with a limiting clause. But the distinctions of two paragraphs back remain. The implicit conception explains acceptance, when there is rational acceptance based on the thinker's own understanding. This deflationist would also, of course, have to grapple with the problem of the willingness of some thinkers to accept incorrect explications of particular concepts.

This first deflationist view I have been considering may seem like a no-nonsense position, opposed to mysterious views of understanding which

---

[15] Field (1996); see also Field (2001*b*).
[16] For some discussion of related issues, see Hill (1998) and my reply, Peacocke (1998*b*).

transcend the knowable. But in fact nothing in what I have said should encourage the view that implicit conceptions somehow transcend the knowable. There would be a commitment to such transcendence if it were allowed as a possibility that there could be two thinkers whose rational judgements about particular applications of an expression, and about principles involving it, are in actual and counterfactual circumstances identical, and who yet have differing implicit conceptions. Nothing I have said entails that that is a possibility. I have, on the contrary, been emphasizing the role of implicit conceptions in the explanation of particular judgements involving the expression or concept. The upshot is, then, that in so far as we see rejection of this sort of transcendence as desirable, its rejection is not unique to the deflationist. Rejection of transcendence cannot be used in support of the deflationist's view.

So far I have been concentrating on points about explanation; but I also promised a second point in reply to the deflationist's objection that what I say about implicit conceptions is no more than a summary of truths about inferential dispositions. The second point emerges from the question: how is the deflationist to specify the inferential dispositions of which he says that implicit conceptions are not more than a summary? The second point starts from the fact that not any old inferential disposition can be included. Ordinary logical inferences are rational transitions. They are not blind leaps into the dark, inclinations to make transitions in thought which just grip and take over the thinker's rational self.[17] I tried at the start of this chapter to say something about how a thinker's implicit conception can make rational acceptance of even a primitive axiom or inference rule. The phenomenon we highlighted was not merely that our learner of logic is unable to see how a primitive logical law might fail to hold in the actual world. It is rather that he has a quite specific positive means of rationally reaching the view that the particular law in question will always be true. How might our deflationist try to account for the rationality of accepting primitive axioms or inference rules?

He may just say that the rationality of acceptance is explained by the fact that these axioms and inference rules are evidently correct for the truth-functions, or higher-level functions, expressed by logical vocabulary. They are indeed evidently correct; but the point cannot serve the deflationist's purpose, again for two reasons. One reason is that the deflationist had better say *why* these are the correct truth-functions and higher-level functions to associate with the logical expressions. Those specific semantic assignments

---

[17] On this, I am in agreement with Brewer (1995).

are hardly given in advance, and what makes them the correct assignments must have something to do with what is involved in understanding these expressions. The theorist of implicit conceptions will insist that they are the correct assignments because they capture precisely the contribution of the expression to truth-conditions given in the content of the implicit conception associated with the expression by one who understands it.

The other reason the deflationist's purposes are not served by this response is that the rationality of the acceptance of a logical principle must also somehow connect up the truth-function, or higher-level function, which is the semantic value of the expression with the thinker's own understanding. Saying the principles are correct for a certain semantic value does not explain the rationality of accepting the principles unless we make this semantic value something the thinker knows about. How is this connection with the thinker's knowledge to be effected on the deflationist's view? It cannot always be a matter of explicit knowledge of the semantic value. As we noted, the thinker who comes rationally to accept a logical principle does not always have such explicit knowledge. It is also the case that such explicit knowledge seems obtainable by rational reflection on the part of one who understands the expression. If the deflationist tries, at this point, to retreat to the position that the thinker has implicit knowledge of the semantic value, he will thereby be embracing implicit conceptions after all.

The deflationist might respond by taking a different route. He may say that the semantic value of a logical constant is simply fixed as that which makes truth-preserving the axioms and principles the thinker is willing, in some specially primitive way, to accept. This was the line I myself took in some earlier work.[18] It involves what is sometimes called a form of thinker-dependence. On the view proposed, what makes an axiom or principle correct is, as a constitutive matter, dependent upon whether thinkers actually accept it (in some designated, specially primitive way) or not. This is sometimes advertised as a virtue of the view. I think, however, that it makes it impossible to give a satisfactory account of the rationality, the non-blind acceptance, of logical principles and axioms. The rationality of accepting some proposed axiom or principle containing already understood expressions involves aiming at correctness which is, as a constitutive matter, explained independently of acceptance of that particular principle. That sort of independence must be an illusion on a judgement-dependent view of these matters.

---

[18] Peacocke (1987, 1992).

Alternatively, a thinker-dependent view may mention not judgement, but rather how the principle strikes the thinker. How the principle strikes the thinker is quite properly to be distinguished from judgement, for a thinker's judgement may either endorse or overrule how it strikes him. But we still conceive of validity as something which is equally neither constituted nor guaranteed by conditions involving how the principle strikes the thinker. A proposed new logical principle may strike a thinker as correct. But he is not entitled to accept it until he has engaged in rational reflection on it, reflection of the sort we have been discussing. One of the points which distinguishes the logical case from that of colour is that it is not plausible that, before a thinker makes a colour predication of a perceived object, further rational reflection is required, of a thinker who experiences something as a shade of a certain colour, and who has no reason to doubt that environmental and his own perceptual mechanisms are favourable. There is then no blanket objection in what I am saying which would apply to any thinker-dependent treatment of any concept whatsoever. My point is only that we have a conception of validity, and correspondingly of what is required for rational acceptance of logical principles, which makes thinker-dependent treatments of the validity of ordinary (non-metalinguistic) principles inappropriate.

A second, more persistent deflationary objector may still press his case. He may say:

> Everything you explain by appeal to implicit conceptions can be explained by use of inferential dispositions run off-line. For instance, the lines of the truth-table for 'or' can be reached as follows. Our new student of logic treats any sentence A of English as inter-inferable with 'A is true', or, as we may say, he has the disquotational inference for truth. We can consider the thinker's disposition to infer either 'A or B', or its negation, from each of the sets of premises $\{A, B\}, \{A, \sim B\}, \{\sim A, B\}, \{\sim A, \sim B\}$. These inferential dispositions, when exercised off-line, and employed in conjunction with mastery of the disquotational inference, allow him to attain each line of the classical truth-table for alternation. From this he can also infer the validity of the schema $A \rightarrow (A \text{ or } B)$. So we can explain all the phenomena without any appeal to implicit conceptions.[19]

I reply that an inference such as that from the premises $\{\sim A, \sim B\}$ to $\sim(A \text{ or } B)$, is—though no doubt automated for even elementary logicians—

---

[19] I thank Stephen Schiffer for helping me improve on an earlier formulation of this objector's position.

one which our student of logic has to work out to be correct on the basis of his existing understanding of alternation. It seems to me that this working-out must involve use of the concept of truth. It must involve reasoning tantamount to: 'The premisses imply that neither A nor B is true. "A or B" is true, though, only if at least one of A and B is true; so when these premisses hold, "A or B" won't be true, that is "∼(A or B)" will be true.' If this is right, then, even for students who do have the disposition to make the inference from the premisses {∼A, ∼B} to ∼(A or B), that disposition cannot be part of the explanation of their knowledge of the truth-table for alternation. On the contrary, appreciation of the principles which fix the truth-value of an alternation is part of the rational explanation of the student's appreciation of the validity of the transition. I have made the point with a more complicated inference, for the point is perhaps more vivid there. In fact I suspect it applies equally to the rational acceptance of the general schema of alternation-introduction.

In response to this, our second deflationary objector may shift his position slightly. He may say that it suffices for his purposes to consider a conceptual role mentioning metalinguistic transitions involving predications of truth and falsity themselves. It is metalinguistic inferential dispositions which are run off-line, he may say, and which generate the truth-table for 'or'. Given the metalinguistic premiss that A is true and B is false, for instance, the thinker will immediately be willing to infer that 'A or B' is true. I have some incidental doubts about this strategy for other lines of the truth-table. Unlike us experienced (elementary) logicians, I suspect that a transition from the falsity of A and the falsity of B takes a bit of thinking about for an 18-year-old. I suspect he has to reason that if A and B are both false, then neither A nor B is true, that is neither of the conditions at least one of whose truth is required for the truth of 'A or B' holds. But let us waive the incidental doubts. After all, I agree that the corresponding metalinguistic transitions are immediately compelling in the case of conjunction. So what do I say about this second variant of the deflationary objection?

I say that, in moving to the metalinguistic level, it is not presenting a competitor to the theory of implicit conceptions. Finding such a metalinguistic transition as is cited in this objection to be a compelling transition is a manifestation of an implicit conception with the content that any sentence of the form 'A or B' is true iff either A is true or B is true. Our objector may protest, saying, 'Well that's a spurious explanation: the alleged explanans is simply summarizing what needs to be explained.' But I dispute the objector's claim that the attribution of an implicit conception simply summarizes the dispositions to be explained. The explanation makes quite specific commitments. One of these commitments is that what explains the transition is its having a certain form—rather, than, say the Gödel-numbers of its components standing in a certain relation, which is equally something which might be computed.

This last issue is equally one which arises about the implicit conception underlying understanding of the predicate 'chair', and reflection on that case may help to make this part of the reply to the second objector more plausible. Implicit knowledge of the definition of 'chair' can explain a person's applying the word correctly in central cases. To say that a person has a disposition to correct application in central cases is not by itself yet to specify *which* features of chairs in his environment are operative in leading him to apply the term. Saying that the thinker's performance is explained by a specific implicit conception commits one to saying that his performance involves the identification of backs, seats, and the rest—the features mentioned in the content of the implicit conception involved in his understanding.

I myself am very sceptical that there is one set of inference schemata acceptance of instances of which is absolutely constitutive of understanding classical alternation. Some thinkers are better at inferring to alternations, some are better at making inferences from them, some may have a better grasp of the way alternations interact with conditionals, others may find their interactions with negation easier. They may all nevertheless have the same core understanding of alternation and the same implicit conception of its contribution to truth-conditions.

In other parts of the philosophy of mind and language, we have become quite comfortable with the idea that there are states which are not definitionally tied to one kind of manifestation, but which produce their effects only in combination with several other factors. A perceptual state's having a particular spatial content is one such example. Such spatial content may explain all sorts of actions, in combination with other attitudes, abilities, and enabling conditions. It is, though, quite implausible that there is some privileged possible kind of explanandum which is canonical in legitimizing that attribution of a spatial content. Seeing something as at a certain distance and direction from oneself may, in the presence of other attitudes, produce action directed at that position. But it may, as in the case of the prisoner in *The Count of Monte Cristo*, equally produce a certain sequence of winks of any eyelid as a message in code; or may just result in the updating of some mental map on the part of someone incapable of movement at all.

Another example of a psychological state not individuatively tied to just one kind of explanandum is that of a psychologically real grammatical rule. Its psychological reality may explain features of a person's perception of heard utterances; or of his own productions; and the same rule may be real both for one thinker who can understand but not produce, and for another who can produce but not understand. I suggest that this feature, of having explanatory power which is not canonically or definitionally tied to one privileged kind of manifestation, is present also in the state of understanding logical expressions, and in having an implicit conception with a semantic content.

There is yet a third deflationary critic to be considered, one who takes a rather different tack. He will say that we have no need of implicit conceptions. He will say that it suffices, in attaining the correct interpretation, to note that we maximize intelligibility of Newton and Leibniz, for instance, if we attribute to them the concept of the limit of a series.

Now the description 'maximizing intelligibility' is a term of art, but on any natural reading, I doubt whether the reasons offered by this third critic are really incompatible with the existence of implicit conceptions. It cannot be a cosmic coincidence that interpreting Newton and Leibniz as having the concept of the limit of a series counts them as getting the answers to questions about series and gradients right. Interpretations must be counterfactually projectible, or they would be no use in either the explanation or the prediction of thought and action. If the interpretation of an expression which maximizes intelligibility is said to have no implications or commitments for the psychological explanation of why the expression is applied to the cases it is, the charge of cosmic coincidence would, it seems to me, be just. Indeed, I would make the charge even in the humble case of the concept *chair*. If someone is said to be interpretable as meaning *chair* by an expression, and gets its application correct, but is said not to have any tacit knowledge of its definition, then the charge of unexplained coincidence would stick against that view too. The coincidence in question is that of his applying the expression to all and only things which fall under the definition (independently certifiable illusions aside). Extending the coincidence to counterfactual circumstances would only increase the mystery. If, by contrast, the definition, either of 'chair' or of 'limit', is regarded as the content of an implicit conception which is contributing to the psychological explanation of why the expression is applied to the cases it is, there is no coincidence at all.

The astute theorist who says that correct interpretation is to be elucidated in terms of maximizing intelligibility would do better to say the following. When we think through the consequences of maximizing intelligibility, we are forced by the need not to postulate massive cosmic coincidences—one indeed for each thinker and each such concept—to recognize the existence of implicit conceptions. This more astute position is then of course not in conflict with what I have been advocating. It is reaching some of the same conclusions by a (possibly) different route.

It is not always the case that later theory simply articulates a concept which at an earlier time was not fully understood by its users. Sometimes later theoretical developments are refinements, precisifications which resolve earlier indeterminacies. This can happen as much in the physical and other empirical sciences as in the mathematical. Whether an example is one of articulation of a conception which was earlier merely implicit, or is rather one of refinement, has to be examined case by case, and is often a complex and intriguing matter. It would be a brave soul who claims that we have a unique pre-theoretical notion of set. Though the matter needs much argument, it would equally be a brave soul who denies that there was a determinate notion of whole number prior to the theoretical developments of the past hundred years. The theorist of implicit conceptions needs only the recognition that not all cases of theoretical development are resolutions of indeterminacies. I turn now to some further ramifications of the point.

3. THE PHENOMENON OF NEW PRINCIPLES

If we accept the existence of implicit conceptions, what are the consequences for conceptual-role theories of meaning? Conceptual-role theories were proposed by Sellars, Harman, Putnam, Block, Field, Horwich, and Price, amongst others.[20] It is consistent with the existence of implicit conceptions that in at least some cases, some part of the conceptual role of an expression or concept contributes to making the expression have the meaning it does, or contributes to the identity of the concept. I have emphasized the answerability of the content of implicit conceptions to their role in the explanation of particular judgements in particular instances. A concept for which there is a specific type of instance of which it is true that the thinker must be

---

[20] See the references at Ch. 2 n. 1 above.

willing—always rationally, of course—to make certain judgements of such instances—involving certain logical transitions, or certain perceptions, as it might be—then conceptual role will contribute to the individuation of the concept.

If possession of the concept also consists in possession of an implicit conception with a certain content, it will also follow that having the implicit conception explains the concept's having that particular aspect of its conceptual role. Though it would take further detailed argument to establish the point, it would also seem that this explanatory link is in some cases an a priori matter. (It seems to be so in certain logical cases, conjunction-elimination, for instance.) The existence of an a priori connection between the content of the implicit conception and certain of its consequences should not, however, be taken to mean that the implicit conception cannot be genuinely explanatory. The idea that certain states are individuated in ways which connect them a priori with what they are capable of explaining is one we have, quite properly, happily lived with in the philosophy of mind and psychology for many years now. The claim that a thinker's practice with the concepts *chair* or *limit* is explained by his having a certain implicit conception is also one with quite specific import and other explanatory consequences too. In saying that an implicit conception with a certain content explains the practice, we are committing ourselves, for instance in the case of the concept *chair*, to the explanation of particular judgements implicating the thinker's ability to distinguish seats, backs, the relation of support, and something with a certain function for human beings.

Let us label as "purely personal-level conceptual-role theories" those conceptual-role theories of meaning and content which restrict themselves to the role of an expression or concept in such personal-level phenomena as thought, acceptance, or action. One general phenomenon which seems to me to preclude acceptance of purely personal-level conceptual-role theories is that of the rational, justified acceptance of new principles involving a given concept, new in the sense that these principles do not follow from those principles (if any) immediate acceptance of which is required for possession of the concept. I label this "the Phenomenon of New Principles". I am inclined to think that the Phenomenon of New Principles is as decisive an argument against personal-level conceptual-role theories as the phenomenon of understanding sentences one has never encountered before is decisive against theories of meaning which do not proceed compositionally. Rational acceptance of the ω-rule was one example of the Phenomenon. Another, arguably, is the rational acceptance by a 14-year-old of the ordinary principle of arithmetical induction, as correct for the universal quantifier over natural numbers which he has used for several years. We do not even have to go as far as axioms to find examples. Even definitions can provide examples of the phenomenon. For the ordinary user of the concept, the definition of *chair* is something which does not follow from those judgements about instances which he must immediately be able to make if he is to possess the concept *chair*. The same applies once again to the definition of *limit* in relation to Leibniz's and Newton's use of the concept.

The Phenomenon is also displayed by so basic a concept as that of negation. What might a purely personal-level conceptual-role theorist offer as the meaning-determining role for classical negation? He might include the conditions for assertion of the negations of observational sentences. He would need to do more, because negation must be determined for all contents to which it can be applied, whether observational or not. At this point, the purely personal-level conceptual-role theorist is likely to be tempted to reach for and include the classical logical inferential principles for negation: that from $\sim\sim A$ one can infer A, and that if one can derive a contradiction from A, one can infer $\sim A$. Yet again, it seems clear that these classical logical rules for negation (and their instances) are ones whose correctness can be, and needs to be, attained by rational reflection from some prior understanding of negation. The prior understanding is simply possession of the implicit conception that a sentence prefixed with 'It is not the case that' is true just in case the sentence is not true. The same point that appreciation of correctness of the principles is dependent upon a prior understanding of contribution to truth-conditions applies equally to the rules for negation that can be given if one introduces logical rules over an incompatibility-relation, or rules using the Smiley–Rumfitt sentences 'signed' with "yes" or "no".[21] This point does not at all impugn the significance of these treatments for logical investigations. It suggests only that these treatments cannot be transformed in any immediate way into an account of understanding for the logical constants.

In fact in the very special case of negation, it seems to me that possession of the relevant implicit conception does not involve drawing on anything new which was not involved in the understanding of sentences not containing negation. To understand the sentences not containing negation, the thinker must know their truth-conditions; and that is, *ipso facto*, to know their

---

[21] Smiley (1996); Rumfitt (2000).

falsity conditions on a core notion of falsity as incorrectness. As Peter Geach once emphasized, to know the truth-conditions of a sentence is in effect to know the location of the boundary between the cases in which it is true and those in which it is not.[22] There is no such thing as knowing the location of this boundary without possessing knowledge of the falsity-conditions of the sentences. The implicit conception associated with the understanding of negation simply links the expression for negation with these already appreciated falsity-conditions. That this is the subject's implicit conception may be manifested in all sorts of different ways.

This consideration about the relation between understanding a constant and acceptance of a rule containing it is not at all a criticism of these systems considered as significant contributions to logic, nor is it any such criticism of their natural-deduction predecessors. The point is just that the relation of the rules of any of these systems to understanding of the logical constants they treat is not simply that of understanding consisting in acceptance of their rules. On the present position, the goal of giving a correct theory of understanding of the logical constants is not only distinct from the goal of giving a sound logic for those constants. Theories that meet these two goals have also to draw on different resources.

A conceptual-role theorist of meaning and content need not be a purely personal-level conceptual-role theorist. In the case of functionalism, we regularly distinguish, following Block, between analytical functionalism, and 'psychofunctionalism', which takes into account information from an empirical psychology in individuating functional roles.[23] We should make a similar distinction between types of conceptual-role theory. A conceptual-role theory may be a 'psycho-conceptual-role theory'. It may state that what is involved in possessing a particular concept includes the requirement that certain of the thinker's personal-level applications of that concept be explained by subpersonal representational states, ones which could be regarded as realizations of what I would say is an implicit conception. The Phenomenon of New Principles tells only against pure personal-level conceptual-role theories. If I am right, some concepts are such that any conceptual-role theory which treats them adequately must be at least a psycho-conceptual-role theory.

Conceptual-role theorists have not wholly neglected the Phenomenon of New Principles. The sorts of moves they have made to attempt to

---

[22] Geach (1972).   [23] Block (1978).

accommodate it, though, do not seem to me fully to resolve the problem. One move that suggests itself, and which I made in earlier work, is for the theorist to say that a new principle, whose correctness can be rationally appreciated, is fixed by those old principles which are mentioned in the conceptual role in some less direct way than by a consequence-relation.[24] In that earlier work, I spoke of the new principle as being determined as one made correct by, for instance, the strongest semantical assignment that validated some introduction rule mentioned in the conceptual role. In this way, for instance, one can explain why the natural deduction rule of or-elimination is correct, even though it is not found immediately obvious by all those who understand 'or'. Corresponding moves can be made for elimination rules too. This strategy, however, even if it succeeds in fixing the right set of new principles as correct, leaves at least three problems unresolved.

The first problem is that the resources it employs give no credible description of the ordinary thinker, like our new learner of logic, who works out the correctness of a new principle which does not follow from (say) the logical principles he already accepts for a given constant. When you worked out that or-elimination is a valid rule, you did not employ any premiss, or tacit simulation, which committed you to the proposition that the semantical value of a constant is the strongest which validates an introduction rule, or the weakest which validates an elimination rule. You had no such thought or commitment. If we are going to explain the rationality of acceptance of a new principle, we must appeal to something which is plausibly operative with a thinker engaged in rationally accepting it.

The second problem is that in some cases, *all* of the inference rules distinctive of a concept have to be worked out by a thinker. We noted that this was plausibly the case for the natural-deduction rules of negation-introduction and negation-elimination. So in some cases, this strategy does not have the initial materials on which it needs to operate.

The third problem with the strategy of appealing to the strongest semantical assignment which validates an introduction rule is the most fundamental. It is that the strategy gives no rationale for this requirement itself. I do not think it can be founded in considerations of tightness of ascription of contents and semantical values. Suppose, for the sake of giving the view the best chance, we grant that if someone is using an introduction rule correctly, and that if the logical expression is meaningful, there must be some semantical assignment

---

[24] Peacocke (1987).

that validates it. It still does not follow that we must take as the semantic value the strongest such assignment. On the contrary, if we are appealing to considerations of tightness, with only that data, we should consider as semantical assignments only the whole class of those assignments which make valid the introduction rule, rather than the strongest. To select the strongest is actually to go beyond what is justified by the inferential practice.

I conclude, then, that once we acknowledge the full range of phenomena explained by implicit conceptions, including the Phenomenon of New Principles, purely personal-level conceptual roles cannot fully determine meanings, nor fully individuate concepts. For someone who occupies the Fregean standpoint, and regards the examples as evidence of incompletely grasped—but nevertheless determinate—senses, none of this should be surprising. The Phenomenon of New Principles is only to be expected from that standpoint. The new principles which are rationally accepted reflect those aspects of the determinate sense which is already employed in thought, but whose nature needs theoretical thought on the part of its ordinary users if it is to become 'sharply grasped'. Moreover, since the content of the implicit conception specifies a contribution to truth-conditions, this Phenomenon of New Principles is a further example of a feature of thought that can be explained only by an account of content in terms of truth and reference.

In criticizing purely personal-level conceptual-role theories as constitutive theories of understanding and concept-possession, I have not committed myself to the view that meaning can go beyond the full range of correct personal-level conceptual roles for an expression. Equally, a realist about theoretically postulated magnitudes in a physical science should not assert that truths about them go beyond everything determined by possible observational consequences, when we are considering the full range of possible experimental setups. It would, however, also be almost universally agreed that acceptance of this last point does not mean that statements about the theoretically postulated magnitudes can be reduced to those about possible observations. Something analogous seems to me to be true of meaning and concept-possession, and their relation to personal-level conceptual roles. Indeed the very notion of a *correct* conceptual role is precisely one which I have been claiming the conceptual-role theorist cannot fully elucidate. In some cases, what is correct can be explained only by appeal to an underlying implicit conception, with a content concerning contribution to truth-conditions.

I also add a remark for enthusiasts who have followed the debates about conceptual-role theories of meaning and concepts. For some years now I have argued that not every coherent conceptual role determines a meaning or concept. Only those roles which naturally correspond to a certain contribution to truth-conditions do so. This amounts to insistence on the Grade 1 level of involvement of truth and reference in the individuation of intentional content that we discussed back in Chapter 1 section 5. If not every conceptual role determines a meaning, it would hardly be surprising if the specific contribution made to truth-conditions also plays a role in understanding. On the proposal I have been advocating, the content of an implicit conception involved in understanding is given by a rule specifying a contribution to truth- (or satisfaction-) conditions. For conceptual roles for which there is no corresponding contribution to truth- (or satisfaction-) conditions, there is no content available to be the content of any corresponding implicit conception.[25] So conceptual roles which correspond to no contribution to truth-conditions are, under the position I am advocating, not ones for which it is possible for there to be an implicit conception that specifies a contribution to truth-conditions.

4. EXPLANATION BY IMPLICIT CONCEPTIONS

Explanation by implicit conceptions raises a host of queries and doubts. There are doubts about the particular kind of psychological explanation in which they are said to be implicated. There are also more general philosophical doubts about whether implicit conceptions can ever properly be involved in a description of what is involved in possessing a concept or understanding an expression. Let us take first the issue of what kind of psychological explanation an explanation which appeals to implicit conceptions might be.

An explanation by an implicit conception is a species of explanation by a content-involving state, the content being the content of the implicit conception. So the usual features of content-involving explanation apply. An explanation of a judgement involving a particular concept by citing the person's implicit conception is not an explanation of a syntactic state by a syntactic state, not even if both implicit conception and judgement are realized in subpersonal syntactic states. An implicit conception contributes to the explanation of a judgement under its content-involving description

---

[25] Such conceptual roles include the inconsistent ones for Arthur Prior's *tonk* (Prior 1960), and the consistent but semantically unevaluable pseudo-constants, such as those that have an arbitrarily restricted form of, for instance, the elimination rule for alternation (see Peacocke 1993*a*).

as a judgement that *p*, for some particular *p*. The implicit conception does not explain the judgement under a merely syntactic description. Nor could we regard the explanation as one which is covered by a prima facie law relating some syntactic realization of the implicit conception to the occurrence of content-involving judgements. Explanations by content-involving conceptions can be the same across persons who realize contents in different subpersonal systems of representation, different mental "notations" if you will. It is also not at all clear that a "syntax to content" prima facie law would be adequate to explain the knowledgeable status of the resulting judgements.

The model, then, to illustrate it for the simple case of *chair* would run thus. One of the thinker's perceptual systems, say, identifies some object in the environment as having a supporting area and a back, and the subject has the background information that the object is used for sitting on. This information from the perceptual system, together with the background information, is combined, at a subpersonal level, with the content of the implicit conception involved in possession of the concept *chair*. It is computed, from this body of information, that the presented object is a chair. This in turn explains the thinker's willingness to judge that that object, demonstratively given in perception, is a chair. In the case of other concepts, the role just played by the perceptual system will be played by some informational source or other. This source yields a content which, together with the content of the implicit conception underlying the concept and possibly some background information or presupposition, permits computation of a content to the effect that some given object falls under the concept in question. Of course, in both perceptual and non-perceptual cases, we can expect all sorts of short cuts to be used in reaching particular judgements. The full content of the implicit conception need not be on-line in every classification the thinker makes. As Susan Carey emphasized, to say that a concept has a definition is not to say that the constituents of the definition are computationally primitive, nor is it to say that they are developmentally prior.[26] Nor need the content of an implicit conception always take the form of a classical definition, explicit or implicit. It could give the (possibly vague) range of a concept by specifying some prototypes and a required closeness-relation to those prototypes.

All the implicit conceptions I have considered so far have contents which are correct. It is not impossible for there to be an implicit conception with

---

[26] See Carey (1982: 350–1).

an incorrect content. A thinker may misunderstand some word in the public language, in which case the implicit conception may have a false content about the word. False presuppositions about certain kinds of object or event in his environment may also enter the content of his implicit conceptions. Nonetheless, there is a core of cases in which one can expect that the content of the implicit conceptions within that core will be correct. It is very plausible, on grounds having to do with the theory of interpretation and content, that there will be a core of cases in which a thinker will make judgements correctly, and will do so also in a range of counterfactual circumstances. If we accept any theory of content or interpretation on which that is so, then we can expect that any implicit conceptions explaining the applications of the concepts in those judgements will also be largely correct. If the implicit conceptions were not largely correct, the judgements would not be largely correct either.

Having squarely accepted that explanation by implicit conceptions is content-involving explanation, there is still the question of whether the content of the implicit conception is, at the level of subpersonal mental representations, implicitly or explicitly represented. As with other kinds of tacit informational state, what has here been deemed important to an implicit conception is prima facie compatible both with explicit and with implicit representation, at the subpersonal level, of the content of an implicit conception.[27] In the example of the limit of a series, the informational content might be explicitly formulated in a language of thought. There would be some stored formula which states the definition of a limit. But the content of the implicit conception could equally be grounded in the operation of a processor which does not involve, at the subpersonal level, explicit representation of the content of the implicit conception. We can certainly conceive of a processor which takes information about the numerical values approached by a function at a given point, and delivers as output information about the differential at that point. It must be an empirical question which kind of representation is operative in a given thinker.

Whichever way the issue is resolved for a given subject and implicit conception, there is a constraint which a fuller theory ought to satisfy. Thinkers can know that certain general principles hold for some concept for which they have only an implicit conception. Even though a rigorous justification for these principles would need to draw on an explicit statement of that conception, it seems that these principles are known even though the

---

[27] See Davies (1989).

conception is not explicitly known. An example would be the multiplication principle that $(dx/dy).(dy/dz) = dx/dz$. I think Leibniz and Newton knew this general multiplication principle. Again, they did not learn it by being told it by someone else. Though they did not know any adequate explicit definition of a limit, they had sufficient insight into what it must be to realize that this principle is correct. Any theory which characterizes their implicit knowledge as simply serving up the value for the differential of a particular function, and then claiming that such general principles as the one just mentioned are extracted inductively, would be inadequate to the phenomena. Indeed, one does not have to be a Leibniz or a Newton to appreciate that the rate of change of one magnitude with respect to a third magnitude is identical with the rate of change of the first with respect to a second magnitude, multiplied by the rate of change of the second with respect to the third. Perhaps the correct description of the situation is that though they had only an implicit conception of the definition, they did know that limits are instantaneous rates of change of one magnitude (as one loosely writes) with respect to another; and they knew that relative rates of change respect that multiplication principle. This phenomenon, of knowledge of some general principles involving a concept in the absence of knowledge of any explicit definition, is found outside the mathematical and logical cases. It applies in cases from the more interesting moral and political examples, right down to the humble case of the definition of 'chair'.

While we are on the topic of the nature of explanation by implicit conceptions, it may be helpful if I locate the position I have outlined in relation to the well-known theory of the psychology of inference expounded by Philip Johnson-Laird in his book *Mental Models*.[28] What I have said here on implicit conceptions agrees with him on two of the distinctive claims of his approach. Like him, I have held that the validity of logical principles has to be worked out by thinkers on the basis of their prior understanding of the expressions they contain. I am also in agreement with him that this prior understanding takes the form of knowledge of contribution to truth-conditions. Thus Johnson-Laird writes: 'What children learn first are the truth conditions of expressions: they learn the contributions of connectives, quantifiers and other such terms to these truth conditions. And, until they have acquired this knowledge about their language, they are in no position to

---

[28] Johnson-Laird (1983).

make verbal inferences' (p. 144). Some aspects of his theory of mental models could be integrated further with the position I have outlined. However, I do part company with any claim that there is no 'mental logic', that no form of mental reasoning is needed to explain explicit logical inference.[29] There is, on the view I have put forward, inference at one, and possibly two, levels. First, let us recall the example in which we envisaged the subject as working out, via a simulation procedure, at the personal level, the validity of some simple truth-functional principle. There the thinker had to use logical reasoning, for instance in drawing conclusions from the premiss that these were all the truth-values that could be taken by the atomic components. Second, at the subpersonal level, in the explanation envisaged a few paragraphs back of a judgement *That's a chair*, for instance, some form of subpersonal inference is essential. It was employed in moving from the information that the presented object has certain properties together with the content of the implicit conception to the conclusion that the presented object is a chair. Perhaps Johnson-Laird would say, as I think in consistency he should say, that the mental models should be used at that subpersonal level too. But it does become a real question then whether the procedures for constructing and operating on mental models should not be regarded as just the way the system is, subpersonally, encoding various inferential principles. It is true that the inferential principles need not be explicitly represented in a language of thought. (Perhaps that is all Johnson-Laird really wanted to claim about the subpersonal level, in which case our positions would not diverge.) But we noted only a few paragraphs back that absence of explicit representation at the subpersonal level does not mean that there are no psychologically real states which contain the content of those principles. The theory of implicit conceptions which I have started to outline is committed to holding that there are some such psychologically real states whose content is that of the implicit conceptions.

I turn now to two principled objections to the enterprise of employing implicit conceptions in explaining understanding, and will try to indicate the lines of a response to them. The first set of concerns revolves around the 'A(C) form', the non-circularity constraint of *A Study of Concepts*. The other set starts from the views of the later Wittgenstein about meaning and understanding.

---

[29] 'Explicit inferences based on mental models, however, do not need to make use of rules of inference, or any such formal machinery, and in this sense it is not necessary to postulate a logic in the mind' (Johnson-Laird 1983: 131).

What I have said about implicit conceptions is incompatible with adoption of the A(C) form of *A Study of Concepts*, and involves abandonment of that constraint on the philosophical explication of concept-possession. The A(C) requirement on explicating possession of a given concept F was that the concept not feature in the explication, as the concept F, within the scope of attitudes attributed to the thinker. Implicit conceptions of the sort I have been advocating in this chapter violate this principle. I have been advocating implicit conceptions with such contents as 'Any sentence of the form "not-A" is true iff A is not true', and 'Any sentence of the form A ∨ B is true iff either A is true or B is true'. Here the occurrences of 'not' and 'or' on the right-hand side of these biconditionals violates the A(C) restriction when implicit conceptions with these contents are offered as explications of possession of the concepts of negation and alternation. There are various ways in which one might try to qualify the A(C) form to avoid an incompatibility, but I can only report that I have not been able to find any that are well motivated and also cover the ground.

Violations of the A(C) form are unobjectionable in the explication of a concept F because one can use one's own mastery of the concept F to assess what someone with an implicit conception involving F could be expected to think or do in any given state of information. This is why a statement about what is involved in possession of a concept, and which does not respect the A(C) form, is not vacuous. It still makes an assessable claim. Each one of us, in evaluating the claim it makes, draws on his own mastery of the concept F being explicated. One draws on that mastery, and engages in simulations to assess what one would be obliged, or rational, to think or do in any given state of information. With information from these simulations, one is then in a position to assess the claim about possession of the concept in question. It is in just this way that one can evaluate the various claims I have made in this chapter about the content of the implicit conceptions underlying various particular concepts.

Drawing on one's own mastery and using simulations in this way is sharply to be distinguished from making assessments by inference from any theoretical beliefs one may have about the conditions for possession of the concept F. Though of course if one uses the simulations, and draws on one's own mastery of the concept, one will eventually end up with some such theoretical beliefs, the route by which they are attained essentially involves simulation.

We could of course equally proceed this way in assessing what sentences someone would, in various circumstances, be likely to accept on the simple hypothesis that by 'chair' they mean *chair*. We did, though, have given specific motivations in the case of the logical constants for going beyond the disquotational form, and actually introducing semantic notions into the content of the implicit conception. Equally in the case of 'chair' too, there are facts about a thinker's relations to seats, backs, and supporting humans in a seated position which make it important to recognize an implicit conception underlying mastery of the predicate.

To keep this chapter within reasonable bounds, I will not pursue here the many issues involved in adopting a theory of mastery of a concept which cannot be fitted into the A(C) form. A fuller development is needed. It would have to say much more about the constraints on the ascription of content to implicit conceptions, and more too about the nature of explanation by content-involving subpersonal states.[30]

I should also note explicitly that offering, for a given concept F, an implicit conception which violates the A(C) form is consistent with the existence of an A(C)-conforming conceptual role which individuates F. The case of logical conjunction arguably shows the consistency of this combination. Instances of the introduction and elimination rules for conjunction are accepted by one who understands conjunction; but this acceptance is still made rational by the thinker's understanding of the contribution conjunction makes to the truth-conditions of contents in which it occurs, an understanding which involves an implicit conception that employs conjunction in its content. From the standpoint of the present theory, however, this is just a special case from which no general conclusions can be drawn.

A defender of the A(C) form may be inclined to ask the following question. Why cannot we proceed as follows? First, using our own understanding of negation, or alternation, or whatever is the target concept in question, we work out the inferential and transitional patterns distinctive of the target concept. These patterns will in general involve other concepts with which the target concept interacts in valid transitions, and may involve complex principles. Then, this objector continues, we just take this totality of transitional patterns, and say that what is distinctive of the target concept is this: it makes rational that totality. By putting a variable in place of reference to the target concept in the specification of this totality, can we not then attain something which instantiates the A(C) form?

---

[30] For some further consideration of these issues, see Peacocke (1994).

I make three interrelated points in reply. First, the A(C) form was meant to be a form of account of concept-*possession*, or of understanding. It is crucial in this area to distinguish between principles which must be acknowledged for possession of the target concept, and the wider class of correct principles which are rationally held (perhaps even knowable a priori). There are principles and transitions involving a concept which can be rationally endorsed by a thinker, but acknowledgement of which is not required for possession of the concept. That was a point I was pressing in the earlier sections of this chapter. Ignorance, or even rejection, of correct definitions or principles for a concept is consistent with possession of the concept defined. Not everything involving a given concept which can be rationally accepted has to be accepted, even conditionally, by a thinker who possesses the concept.

Second, even if we could, without begging the question, specify circumstances in which the principles it would be rational to hold would in fact be held by a possessor of the given concept, there would still be something unexplained in the proposal. If the target concept makes rational the totality of transitions mentioned by this defender of the A(C) form, there ought to be an answer to the question: *how* does it make these transitions rational? What aspect of possession of the concept makes it rational to accept a primitive principle involving the concept, a principle the thinker had not thought of before? The theorist of implicit conceptions has an answer to this question. The correctness of the new principle follows from the content of the implicit conception which is involved in the thinker's possession of the concept. The implicit conception can influence, for instance via the outcome of simulations, which principles the thinker rationally comes to accept. The defender of the A(C) form does not, it now seems to me, have an answer to these questions about the rational acceptance of new primitive principles.

The third reply to the proposal is that the totality of rational transitions distinctive of a concept is in any case quite open-ended. There is no limit to the valid interactions even of so simple an operator as negation or alternation not only with other logical concepts, but with any other concept, such as that of probability, evidence, arithmetical quantification, observational concepts … or indeed any other new concepts we may introduce. If we ask what unifies this open-ended totality, for instance in the case of negation, it seems to me that there is essentially only one answer we can give. It is that these are all the transitions which we would expect as consequences of possession of an implicit conception with the content that any sentence of the form 'not-A' is true iff A is not true. That is the only way of fully capturing the open-ended class of transitions whose rationality is distinctive of negation. If that is so, the way of capturing the totality is incompatible with, rather than supporting, the A(C) form.

The other issue concerns the relation of implicit conceptions to later Wittgensteinian views on understanding and rule-following. The views I have been presenting are clearly incompatible with some parts of his thought:

(*a*) They are incompatible with his thesis that one's understanding of an expression does not exceed what one can explain.[31] The considerations we developed earlier do seem to me to show that some thinkers' understanding of 'chair', 'limit', and even 'natural number' exceeds what they can in fact explain.

(*b*) The view I have been outlining would also endorse one reading of such a claim as 'Once you have got hold of the rule, you have the route traced out for you'.[32] Wittgenstein rejected that claim, though of course he was considering 'rules' of a sort available to guide a thinker at the reason-giving level in the thinker's intentionally making one application rather than another of the expression in question. Implicit conceptions as understood here are not rules of that sort.

(*c*) Finally, the whole idea of explaining rule-application was apparently anathema to the later Wittgenstein. I am committed to the possibility of content-involving subpersonal computational explanations of thinkers' applications of expressions they understand. Wittgenstein's objections to the possibility of explanation in 'bedrock' cases where, Wittgenstein says, the person has nothing which is his reason for going on the way he does, are addressed either to the reason-giving level of explanation, or, on occasion, to physiological explanations. It would be wrong to assimilate content-involving subpersonal computational explanation to either of those very different cases. I have not myself found anything in Wittgenstein which can be extrapolated to give a sound argument against the possibility of subpersonal computational explanation.

It is equally striking, however, how wide the area of agreement may be between a defender of implicit conceptions and the considerations marshalled in Wittgenstein's arguments about rule-following. That one's reasons for saying that something is the result of adding 2, or is a chair, may in a certain sense give out eventually is entirely compatible with the existence

---

[31] Wittgenstein (1958, §§209 ff.).   [32] Wittgenstein (1978: VI, §31).

of a content-involving computational explanation of why one applies these expressions in the cases one does. The existence of implicit conceptions as understood here is consistent with Wittgenstein's arguments that rule-following in the fundamental cases does not involve consciously consulting anything—as Crispin Wright puts it, there is 'no essential inner epistemology of rule-following'.[33]

There is even a point of positive agreement, rather than mere consistency, between the present view and Wittgenstein's. Wittgenstein insists at various points in his argument that the relation between understanding and correct application is not merely contingent.[34] The way the account of implicit conceptions has been developed here involves a commitment to precisely what Wittgenstein is insisting upon. An implicit conception has as its content a certain condition for falling under the expression it treats. We said that the principles for ascribing content to an implicit conception would ensure that, in certain basic and central applications, an expression associated with that implicit conception would be applied to things satisfying the condition in its content. So indeed the connection between possession of an implicit conception, in cases in which that is the nature of understanding, and correct application, is not merely contingent. Hence we have a point of agreement with Wittgenstein. Indeed once the non-contingency is acknowledged, it even becomes possible for what a thinker finds compelling—the way he goes on—to enter the individuation of a concept, consistently with the theory of implicit conceptions. The content of the implicit conception can be fixed in part by the properties of the cases which the thinker finds it compelling, on the basis of his understanding, that the concept applies.[35] So there is not utter divergence between implicit conceptions and Wittgenstein on rule-following.

It is, though, only fair to add that if one can consistently accept these most recent points about rule-following while rejecting Wittgenstein's claims about the extent and the explanation of understanding, we have to draw

---

[33] Wright (1989: 244).
[34] For instance, in Wittgenstein (1978: VII, §26, p. 328):

But, *if* you have seen this law in it [a series of numbers], that you then continue the series in *this* way—that is no longer an empirical fact.

But how is it not an empirical fact?—for 'seeing *this* in it' was presumably not the same as: continuing it like this.

One can only say that it is not an empirical proposition, by *defining* the step on this level as the one that corresponds to the expression of the rule.

[35] This is a point of contact between the theory of implicit conceptions and the position of *A Study of Concepts* (Peacocke 1992).

a certain conclusion. The conclusion must be that the correctness of these most recent points, about the phenomenology of rule-following and about the non-contingent relation between understanding and application, offer no support for his positions on the explanation of understanding.

5. RATIONALIST ASPECTS

What I have said so far about implicit conceptions, together with the use to which I have put them, has the distinctive flavour of a classical rationalist position. Here, for instance, are six principles which can be supported by appeal to implicit conceptions, and which were held by that paradigm rationalist Leibniz.

> (1) The evidentness of particular axioms is grounded in the understanding of the terms they contain.

In the *New Essays*, Leibniz's protagonist quotes with approval the views of those philosophers who held that axioms 'are evident *ex terminis*—from the terms—as soon as they are understood. That is, they were satisfied that the "force" of their convincingness is grounded in the understanding of the terms.'[36] The description I gave at the start of this chapter of the way in which our logic student comes rationally to accept a logical axiom conforms to the description given by the philosophers with whom Leibniz's protagonist agrees. According to that description, the student's implicit conception is drawn upon in the simulations which lead to rational acceptance of the axiom. In the account given, possession of the appropriate implicit conception was also identified with understanding. So acceptance of the axiom is grounded in understanding. The content of the student's perceptual experience is justificationally irrelevant to his acceptance of the axiom.

> (2) Concerning the Thought expressed by an axiom: finding the axiom evident, when that is properly grounded in the understanding, is a way of coming to know that Thought.

The legitimacy of attributing knowledge when acceptance is reached via the understanding was essential to Leibniz's case against Locke's empiricism.

---

[36] Leibniz (1981, book IV, ch. vii: 'Of the Propositions Which Are Named Maxims or Axioms', p. 406).

Leibniz would hardly have had an anti-empiricist account of knowledge of these axioms if this understanding-based evidentness did not amount to knowledge. I noted early on in this chapter that the reflections which can lead to rational acceptance of an axiom or inference rule plausibly yield knowledge.

The innateness of axioms and inference rules is not, however, something I am advocating. Chomsky, in his book *Cartesian Linguistics*, insisted that the rationalists were right in wanting a psychology which is 'a kind of Platonism without preexistence'.[37] In a similar spirit, I offer implicit conceptions as a rationalist account of understanding and certain kinds of knowledge, but without any commitment to innateness. Implicit conceptions can be acquired.[38] In fact I think there are strands in Leibniz which suggest that what really mattered to him was independent of innateness taken literally. At one point in the *New Essays*, he writes that

quite often a 'consideration of the nature of things' is nothing but the knowledge of the nature of our mind and of these innate ideas, and there is no need to look for them outside oneself. Thus I count as innate any truths which need only such 'consideration' in order to be verified. (p. 84)

The distinctively purely understanding-based 'consideration' can be applied whether or not the understanding is, in the literal sense, innate. Leibniz's here saying that he counts as innate any truth which can be attained by a certain kind of consideration suggests that this part, at least, of the rationalist position may not need to involve literal innateness. The talk of verification in this passage also emphasizes Leibniz's conception of this sort of consideration as a route to truth and knowledge.

Nothing I have said here, however, supports Leibniz's implication that a priori knowledge is really knowledge about the thinker's own mind. The content of a thinker's understanding—the content of his implicit conceptions—can explain a thinker's a priori knowledge without that knowledge being about his understanding. What his understanding makes available is not itself about his understanding. A later rationalist like Frege is clearly, and in Frege's case explicitly, free of any commitment to the idea that a priori knowledge concerns the thinker's own mind. Leibniz's claims on this

---

[37] Chomsky (1966: 63).

[38] Correspondingly, beliefs rationally explained by the possession of an implicit conception may be innate only in C. D. Broad's 'negative sense of internally generated': see Broad (1975: 138).

matter may have been influenced by his other doctrines about the meta-physics of minds, which are not commitments of the position I have been defending.

(3) Logical axioms can be known a priori.

This was the burden of Leibniz's dispute with Locke. We can have an enti-tlement or justification for accepting a logical axiom which is justificationally independent of perceptual experience or sensation, even if experience is an enabling condition for our attaining such an acceptance. The procedure by which, at the start of this chapter, I envisaged someone coming to accept rationally a primitive logical axiom is also one which yields a priori know-ledge. Nothing in that rationale for the subject's belief involves perceptual experience or sensation.

Of course Leibniz had what in our post-Fregean time we would regard as a very rudimentary conception of logic. The logical laws to which, according to him, all a priori truths could be reduced by means of substituting correct definitions were of such forms as 'All A's are A's', or 'All AB's are A's', 'All ABC's are A's', and the like. The 'trifling' character of these axioms was a topic of some discussion in Leibniz's writings. By contrast, someone acquainted with modern logic would be unlikely to characterize all of its axioms as trifling. Yet it seems to me that an understanding-based, non-empirical procedure for attaining knowledge of axioms, even when they are not merely trifling, still lies squarely within the spirit of the rationalists' conception. Moreover, even on his simpler conception of logic, Leibniz still needs to rely on some of the apparatus I have been employing. Correct definitions, to which Leibniz repeatedly appeals in his characterization of demonstrations, are precisely definitions which correctly articulate the implicit conception involved in understanding the term being defined.

To say, as I have, that knowledge of the axioms is grounded in understand-ing of the expressions in them, and is also a priori, is not at all to endorse the Carnapian view that they are true solely in virtue of the meaning of their constituent expressions. On the contrary, the sort of rationale I envisaged a thinker going through at the start of this chapter is one which shows that, for any instance of a logical axiom schema, what it is true in virtue of is its disquoted truth-condition (as indeed would be the case for any other true sentence). I have been trying to develop the present view in a way which respects that point throughout, and which regards the phrase 'true purely in virtue of meaning' as applying to no sentences whatever.[39] For this reason, the views I am developing here are not in the target area of Quine's formidable attack on Carnap's views on truth-purely-in-virtue-of-meaning, particularly in 'Carnap and Logical Truth'.[40] The truth-condition for any sentence containing a logical operator, including primitive logical axioms, is determined in the same uniform way, by application of the clauses of a Tarskian truth-theory. In fact the ways of coming to know these axioms which I have been identifying clearly rely on states whose informational content involves what is stated in the clauses of a truth-theory.

(4) Logical axioms are necessary.

This was a view Leibniz expressed repeatedly, and was another plank of his criticism of Locke. Leibniz thought, rightly in my view, that Locke could explain neither the necessity nor our knowledge of the necessity of the axioms. Indeed Leibniz repeatedly endorses the much stronger claim that for every necessary truth there is a reduction of it to logical axioms by means of substitution of definitions for defined terms.[41] It would take us much too far afield to go into (4), or the stronger claim, in detail. It can be assessed only in the presence of a substantive theory of necessity. For now, let me simply say dogmatically that I think a correct account of the truth-conditions of necessity statements has the consequence that the semantical rules for logical operators hold not only in the actual world, but in any possible world.[42] (Of course a theory must also explain why this is so.) If it is so, then the sorts of rationale I have been considering for primitive logical axioms can be extended to show not only the validity of these axioms, but also their necessity.

(5) Reflection is needed to discover the axioms of logic: it would 'be wrong to think that we can easily read these eternal laws of reason in the soul, as the Praetor's edict can be read on his notice-board, without effort or inquiry'.[43]

---

[39] In this respect at least, my views have not changed since my paper 'How Are A Priori Truths Possible?' (Peacocke 1993*b*).

[40] Quine (1976*b*).

[41] Cf. Leibniz (1969: 646). In Leibniz (1981: 86) Leibniz says of the kind of truths which are innate in his sense, 'among necessary truths no other kind is to be found'.

[42] For a theory of the truth-conditions of statements of necessity which I think can serve this purpose, see Peacocke (1999, ch. 4).

[43] Leibniz (1981: 50).

Leibniz in many places emphasizes that we need to reflect, to attend, if we are to discover logical axioms. I have also emphasized that it can take reflection to appreciate that an axiom or primitive inference rule is correct. If anything, I think Leibniz still overstates their ease of discovery, as in the passage quoted above in which he says they are evident as soon as their terms are understood. He writes as if reflection may be needed to discover the axioms, but that once stated, it will be evident that they are correct. This is too strong. I suspect that if Leibniz had been acquainted with modern logic, he would have withdrawn this point. As far as I can see, nothing in the rationalist conception rules out revision on this point.

> (6) There is an important distinction to be drawn between clear ideas and distinct ideas.

A clear idea, for Leibniz, is one which enables one at least to recognize instances of the concept in question. A clear idea may nevertheless be indistinct, that is, 'I am not able to enumerate separately the characteristics required to distinguish the thing from others, even though such characteristics and distinctions are really in the thing itself and the data which enable us to analyze the notion.'[44] One way to elucidate the distinction between someone whose clear idea is indistinct and someone whose clear idea is distinct is to use the notion of an implicit conception. The thinker with the distinct idea is one who has succeeded in achieving an explicit formulation of the implicit conception which was all he had when he had only an indistinct, though clear, idea.

Beyond this agreement on six particular theses, there is also an underlying sympathy between the approach I have been adopting and the general rationalist conception of knowledge. The views I have been putting forward are at home in a conception of knowledge as rationally or reasonably attained. No doubt, historically, the rationalists overshot in their enthusiasm for this idea. Nonetheless, if there is something in it, it would be a quite unstable position theoretically to hold that it applies to much of our knowledge, but fails to hold when we consider the case of primitive axioms and inference rules. If there are rationality- or reasonability-conditions for knowledge, they must apply in these basic cases too; and in effect I have been trying to argue that they do.

---

[44] Leibniz (1951: 284).

6. CONSEQUENCES: RATIONALITY, JUSTIFICATION, AND UNDERSTANDING

What makes it rational to accept some logical truth of which one has a proof? The considerations canvassed earlier in this chapter suggest that the rationality of accepting it cannot be fully elucidated philosophically just by citing the proof. For what is at the start of this proof? There are two sorts of case to consider. In one type of case, the proof starts with primitive axioms and/or inference rules. The primitive axioms and/or inference rules may be universally quantified, as in Frege's own formulations, or they may be schemata, as in current approaches. But whichever way the starting point of the proof is set out, under this first type of case the starting point of the proof itself does not involve metalinguistic notions. The notion of truth does not occur in the first line of the proof itself. Proofs of this first type we can call *unsupplemented* derivations. Proofs of the second type, by contrast, start with semantic principles, stating the contribution of particular logical connectives to the determination of the truth-conditions of sentences or contents or Thoughts containing them. They will start from such principles that 'Any sentence of the form A ∨ B is true iff either A is false or B is true'. Proofs of this second sort then move from these semantic premises to the logical axioms or primitive inference rules, which the semantics validates. They then proceed as in the unsupplemented case. Proofs of this second kind we call *supplemented* derivations.

Nothing in derivations of the first kind, the unsupplemented derivations, explains the rationality of accepting their starting point, their primitive axioms or inference rules. This state of affairs is especially perplexing for anyone who holds the highly intuitive and (it seems to me) correct view that it is something about the nature of the senses of the expressions in the primitive axioms and inference rules, and correspondingly about the thinker's understanding, that makes it rational to accept them. So we may be tempted to turn to derivations of the second type. Yet it does not seem that they fully explain the rationality of accepting a logical truth, for two reasons. One is that a person can come to recognize the non-semantic axioms as valid, even someone who has no previous explicit knowledge of semantics. It is no doubt partly this point which attracted the classical rationalists to the view that axioms are known independently of other truths. Some prominent logicians, such as Russell, developed logical systems, and knew their axioms, before having been introduced to explicit semantical statements (in his case, by Wittgenstein). The other reason is that the rationality of accepting the semantic axioms is of course itself still unexplained.

The problem is very sharp in Frege himself. Frege held that 'it is part of the concept of an axiom that it can be recognized as true independently of other truths'.[45] In conformity with this, in the formal system of *The Basic Laws of Arithmetic*, we have a system with primitive, non-semantic axioms and inference rules. It was derivations in this system which were supposed to give the 'ultimate justification' for arithmetical propositions. Yet there are many pressures in Frege to want a different position, and these pressures are reflected in the way Frege himself proceeds in *The Basic Laws of Arithmetic*. You might expect someone who holds the quoted rationalist doctrine that axioms can be recognized as true independently of other truths not to derive them from other truths. Yet at every point at which Frege introduces a new primitive axiom or inference rule in the formal language, he actually gives it, in the German, a justification. Indeed a word meaning 'therefore' immediately precedes the statement of the axiom or inference rule. And what precedes the 'therefore' is a statement of the semantic rule—the rule giving the contribution to truth-conditions—of the crucial expressions in the new axiom or inference rule. The very first axiom is introduced by a simple argument that it must always have the truth-value *true*, given the truth rule for the material conditional. Frege writes—I change to a more modern notation for the material conditional and for the variables—

> By §12 [which states which truth-function the conditional '$\rightarrow$' denotes], $(A \rightarrow (B \rightarrow A))$ could be the False only if both A and B were true while A was not the True. This is impossible; therefore $(A \rightarrow (B \rightarrow A))(I)$.[46]

Here '(I)' is Frege's notation for his first axiom. He does something similar for every other axiom and inference rule. This, incidentally, shows that it is false to say, as Ricketts does, that Frege never attempts any informal soundness proofs.[47] These are precisely elements of informal soundness proofs.

Frege's giving an informal soundness proof is not a mere quirk of exposition. It has deep roots in his, and indeed I think in the proper, conception of the relations between sense, justification, and truth. Frege held, like Leibniz, that 'the truth of a logical law is immediately evident from itself, from the sense of the expression'.[48] There ought, if the evidentness of a logical law

---

[45] Frege (1979: 168).   [46] Frege (1964, §18, p. 69).   [47] Ricketts (1996).
[48] Frege (1984b: 405).

depends on the sense, to be some explanation of *how* it depends on the sense. Now Frege famously held that the sense of a sentence is given by its truth-conditions, and the sense of its components by the contribution they make to these truth-conditions. So an explanation of the evidentness of an axiom should start from the contribution made by its components to its truth-conditions. This is precisely how Frege's soundness proofs proceed. Moreover, in proceeding this way, he is giving a justification for thinking that the truth-condition for the axiom is fulfilled. So we are not, after all, lacking at the very foundation the sort of justification which it was the task of the rest of the structure to provide.

Frege did not recognize the tension, given his account of axioms, nor did he resolve it. It is not only a problem for him; it is a problem for us too. Even if we do not accept his characterization of what an axiom is, and so have no problem with a semantic derivation of the truth of an axiom, there is an unresolved issue. Why is it rational to accept the semantic premises? There must be some answer to this. For if a logical derivation is not an example of a justified, rational route to a conclusion, then what is? And how can it be so unless its premises are justified?

I suggest that both the supplemented and the unsupplemented derivations have a role to play in explaining the thinker's justification, and that the way of solving the problem is to distinguish two very different relations a single thinker bears to derivations of each of the two kinds. Every step in the unsupplemented derivation corresponds to some transition explicitly made by a thinker who is inferring some logical truth from the primitive logical axioms. The thinker finds those axioms rationally compelling, and does so by proceeding along the lines we envisaged for our 18-year-old early on in this chapter. Equally, when we consider the supplemented derivation, with its semantic premises, its earliest parts also capture something psychologically real, but they do so in a different way. The semantic premises of the supplemented derivation give the content of those of the thinker's implicit conceptions which are operative in his rationally coming to appreciate that the non-semantic axioms are valid. A statement of the implicit conception associated with understanding a truth-functional connective, for instance, would be a statement which determines its truth-table. When our imagined thinker goes properly through the simulation-involving steps I described at the start of this chapter, he will come to accept as valid the same principles as someone who is explicitly inferring from a statement of the truth-tables. Moreover, the explanation of his doing so will be that his implicit conceptions entail the content stated in those truth-tables. If we regard understanding the logical expression as involving association of the expression with the right implicit conception, we also see on this account how semantic understanding is the source of the thinker's appreciation of the validity of the logical axioms (and primitive rules).

I should add that in making these points, there is no commitment to the possibility of some level of theory at which everything, including all logical transitions, can be justified. Even the mental activities of someone whose thought is captured by the supplemented derivation is still using logic at the very early stages, for instance in moving from information gleaned by simulating the various cases to acceptance that an axiom or inference rule is valid. He will be making such transitions as: if these are possible combinations of truth-values, and there are no others, then this axiom (say) will always be true. We need some form of logic in any theoretical thought. So it seems to be incoherent to suppose that there is some level at which everything can be justified. What this shows is that an $\exists\forall$, an existential-universal, proposition is false: it is false that there is a level at which everything can be justified. That is consistent with a weaker, coherent proposition of $\forall\exists$ form being true: that for every axiom and inference rule, there is some level at which it can be justified. This $\forall\exists$ proposition is much more plausible. It may be a requirement of reason.

I draw two conclusions from these points. The first conclusion is that even in the area of logic, the rationality of accepting a proposition or schema on the basis of one's understanding of the expressions it contains cannot be explained solely in terms of proofs, not even supplemented proofs. For whence does our rational understander obtain his knowledge of the semantic premisses? If he has that knowledge because others have informed him of these premisses, then he is not obtaining his knowledge from his own understanding of the logical vocabulary. It is only if the knowledge is obtained ultimately by the simulation means we outlined that the source of the knowledge is his own understanding of the expressions. Of course he does not have to go through the simulation every time he needs to use a semantic premiss. Knowledge obtained by the simulation can be stored for later use without the thinker having to rehearse its origins, just as knowledge obtained by any other means can be stored without rehearsing *its* origins. But the status of the stored information as knowledge derived from his own understanding rests upon its having been reached by the simulation method.

On this view, then, a full account of the rationality of accepting a logical law, when that derives from the nature of the thinker's own understanding, has to mention implicit conceptions and the way in which reflective simulation provides a means of extracting the informational content of implicit conceptions.

The other conclusion concerns the possibility of explicating Frege's notion of sense in part by appeal to some ideal understander and the axioms which an ideal understander would accept. Probably Frege was attracted to such an explication, and there are aspects of his thought and presentation which square with it. But it does not follow that we (nor that he) should accept that explication in terms of what ideal understanders would accept. The resource to which I have appealed in explaining rational acceptance of the axioms is that of implicit conceptions of the semantic contributions of certain expressions. I have emphasized that these implicit conceptions play a part in ordinary thinkers' evaluations of sentences. They are something possessed by ordinary, and not only idealized, thinkers. In so far as a proposed axiom can be recognized as true, it is recognized on a basis which is rooted in the ordinary, non-idealized understanding of the expressions in the axiom.

7. TRANSITIONAL

To pull the threads together from Part I of this book: we have now argued that only a substantial, realistic theory of concepts in terms of truth-conditions can provide an adequate account of observational concepts and concepts of places and times (Chapter 1); that the role of reference and truth in these accounts can be generalized to a treatment that takes concepts in general to be individuated by their fundamental reference rules (Chapter 2); and that the implicit conceptions involved in these truth-involving accounts can be elucidated and shown to contribute to the explanation of phenomena involved in understanding (Chapter 4). With these theses and the apparatus used to defend them, I turn in Part II of this book to address the question: can this conception of the role of reference and truth be employed to give some philosophical explanation of the nature of our psychological concepts?

PART II

APPLICATIONS TO MENTAL CONCEPTS

5

Conceiving of Conscious States

For a wide range of concepts, a thinker's understanding of what it is for a thing to fall under the concept plausibly involves knowledge of an identity. It involves knowledge that the thing has to have the same property as is exemplified in instantiation of the concept in some distinguished, basic instance. This chapter addresses the question: can we apply this general model of the role of identity in understanding to the case of subjective, conscious states? In particular, can we explain our understanding of what it is for someone else to be in a particular conscious state in terms of our knowledge of the relation of identity which that state bears to some of our own states?

This is a large issue, with many ramifications both within and beyond the philosophy of mind; so let me give a road map for the route I aim to take. We first need to consider the features of explanations of concepts in terms of identity in domains outside the mental. There are substantial constraints on legitimate explanation of concepts in terms of identity. There are also reasons that it is harder to meet these constraints in the case of concepts of conscious states than it is in other cases.

I will go on to suggest a way in which we can overcome the special difficulties of the conscious case, and to try to elaborate the nature both of our understanding of first-person applications of concepts of conscious states, and of our grasp of an identity-relation applied to these states. A positive account of understanding in this area, as in any other, has to dovetail with a credible epistemology of conscious states in oneself and in others. I will offer something under that head, and say how the resulting position steers a middle way distinct from each of the two classic rival positions on conscious states of the later Wittgenstein on the one hand, and of Frege on the other.

1. UNDERSTANDING AND IDENTITY IN OTHER CASES

We can remind ourselves of some of the cases discussed in Chapter 1 in which an explanation of understanding in terms of identity is plausible.

For an observational concept, such as *oval*, to possess the concept is to have tacit knowledge that for an unperceived thing to be oval is for it to be of the same shape as things one perceives to be oval. That a given object is oval is, according to some theorists, something that can be in the non-conceptual content of a perceptual experience. But as far as I can see, this instance of the model of identity in understanding is equally available to theorists who hold that the content of perceptual experience is entirely conceptual. Either kind of theorist can tie a general grasp of what it is for something to be oval to the distinguished case in which something is perceived to be oval.

A second example of the model concerns our understanding of predications of places and times other than our current location and time. It seems that our understanding of what it is for it to be sunny at some arbitrary place-time consists in our tacit knowledge that the place-time has to have the same property as our current place-time has to have for it to be sunny here. (If we were in the mood to be strict, we would with greater accuracy speak of knowledge of what is involved in the truth of an arbitrary predication of a 'here'-thought, wherever it is thought. The knowledge in question involves the demonstrative *here* type, rather than uses of it on a particular occasion.)

These instances of the model of identity in understanding are to be construed as ones in which the grasp of the identity in question is explanatory and constitutive of understanding. The mere truth of this biconditional is trivial:

> It is raining in London iff London has the same property as this place here has when it is raining here.

This biconditional holds as a matter of logic and identity (given the ontology of properties). Correspondingly, mere acceptance of the biconditional by a rational thinker is not by itself something explanatory of the thinker's understanding or grasp of the contents.

The earlier examples of the role of identity in understanding observational concepts, and concepts of other places and times, all aim to say more than these logical truths. Wittgenstein was precisely setting aside these trivialities when he ended *Investigations* §350 with the comment 'one will say that the stove has the same experience as I, *if* one says: it is pain and I am in pain'. Wittgenstein's view was that sameness of experience here is to be explained in terms of my being in pain and something or someone else being in pain. He was right that the important issue is the order of philosophical explanation, not the mere truth of the identity in any case in which I am in pain and some other subject is in pain. The mere truth of the identity can be explained consistently with Wittgenstein's own position on understanding sensation-predications, a position that certainly does not rely on an explanation of meaning in terms of an identity-relation. The position I will develop agrees with Wittgenstein that more is at stake than simply the logical truths themselves, even though the remainder of this chapter opposes Wittgenstein's views on these matters (including the remainder of his text in §350).

There are three important attractions of such identity-involving explanations of concept-possession.

1. The first is that they supply an explanation of uniformity of concepts and meaning across occurrences of a concept or expression in different thoughts or sentences. It is an immediate consequence of the identity-involving explanation of grasp of a concept that one and the same property is predicated both in the distinguished case and in the case understanding of which is explained by grasp of the identity. Other theories, and especially some forms of 'criterial' accounts favoured by some neo-Wittgensteinians, have famously had difficulties in explaining how the same thing is meant in, for instance, first-person and third-person psychological ascriptions. It seems to me a non-negotiable requirement that it be a consequence of a theory of meaning and understanding in the area that uniformity hold. Without it, we would be unable to validate the most basic inferences of identity of state across different predications of a concept, and all that rests upon such identities.

As is particularly evident at this point, and implicit in the preceding pages of this chapter, I am operating with a now widely accepted distinction between concepts and properties.[1] One and the same property may be thought about in indefinitely many ways, in perceptual-demonstrative ways, in recognitional ways, in theoretical ways, in descriptive ways. If we use an

---

[1] Hilary Putnam was one of the first to be clear on the distinction and its applicability to a range of philosophical issues. See Putnam (1975*b*).

ontology of properties, one-place first-level concepts are Fregean modes of presentation of properties. The objects falling under the concept are those possessing the property.

The required uniformity of a concept as applied in first-person and in third-person cases seems to me best formulated at the level of properties. It is necessary, but not sufficient, for a treatment of the concept to respect the concept's uniformity in first- and third-person combinations that, under the account, if a third-person ascription *He's in pain* is correct, then a first-person ascription *I'm in pain* by the attributee will also, under the account, be correct. If that consequence follows only in the presence of information that need be neither known to, nor presupposed by, the users of the concept, this will not be a single, unified concept. It will be analogous to a suggested concept R which is applied on the basis of perception when the object in question is perceptibly red, and applied in other circumstances when the object reflects light in a certain range of wavelengths in given conditions. That suggestion about R would not treat it as a unified concept. The required uniformity seems better formulated as the demand that it follow from the account of the concept itself that it is the same property both in the first person and in the third person (or in the perceived and the non-perceived case for observational concepts). What the nature of the properties in question may be, what forms of relation and theoretical role they are capable of sustaining, will of course be part of the issues needing discussion in any account of particular concepts of those properties.

2. The second attraction of identity-involving accounts is that they respect the Fregean idea that a concept (a sense, in Frege) is determined by the fundamental condition for something to fall under the concept—the condition for being the concept's semantic value. An identity-condition grasped in understanding is something that concerns objects, events, or states at the level of reference. It contributes to the determination of reference, and explains how the concept for which it is given is a way of thinking of a property. This is an advantage of a more theoretical character than the highly intuitive requirement that we explain uniformity. But this more theoretical attraction will speak to anyone for whom it is a non-trivial demand that concepts must have a certain relation to the world. Satisfaction of the demand also arguably helps to explain the epistemic dimension of concepts, in so far as epistemic norms can be explained by the fundamental condition for something to be the reference of a concept (see Chapter 2).

3. For a concept grasp of which is explained in terms of an identity-component, we have an explanation of how it is that a thinker can grasp certain complete contents containing that content without yet knowing what might be independently specifiable evidence for the truth of that content. 'Independently specifiable' here means evidence that is not specified simply by mentioning the content p in question, as in the characterization "evidence in favour of the content p". If existentialists are allowed to summarize their views in the slogan 'Existence precedes Essence', we could summarize this point by saying that for the contents in question, 'Understanding precedes Evidence'. What would be evidence that some tiny array identified in nanotechnology is oval in shape? What would be evidence that some hitherto unexplored underground lake, not all visible from any one angle, is oval in shape? These are entirely empirical matters, and the answer to the questions do not have to be known to someone just because he has the observational concept *oval*. We grasp the content that the array or the lake is oval because we know that for it to be true, the array or the lake has to have the same shape as things we perceive to be oval. For any concept for which Understanding does precede Evidence, the model of tacit grasp of an identity-relation offers an explanation of this feature. Grasping the content in question involves knowledge that a certain identity has to hold for the content to be true. Knowing what would be evidence for or against the holding of this identity is a further matter, requiring empirical evidence and further thought that goes beyond this understanding.

It matters that the point is one concerning specific complete contents. The point I have just been making is, in slightly more formal terms: there exist some concepts C and some complete contents $\Sigma(C)$ containing C such that one can grasp $\Sigma(C)$ without knowing what would be independently specifiable evidence for or against it. This is entirely consistent with the view that: for every concept C (or perhaps for some favoured subclass of concepts C) there exist some complete contents $\Sigma(C)$ such that possessing C requires knowing what would be independently specifiable evidence for or against $\Sigma(C)$. Our grasp of some contents containing a concept can go beyond such independently specifiable evidence and consequences.

With these attractions of sometimes explaining understanding in terms of identity in mind, I turn to address the question of whether your understanding of, for example, what it is for someone else to be in pain consists in your tacit knowledge that another is in pain just in case: that person is in the same state you are in when you are in pain. Since this account of understanding will be the focus of so much of the subsequent discussion, I label it the "Target Account".

2. CONSTRAINTS ON LEGITIMATE EXPLANATIONS IN TERMS OF IDENTITY

Suppose we are attempting to give an explanation of possession of the concept F in terms of grasp of an identity. We say that a thinker's understanding of what it is for an arbitrary thing to be F consists in his grasp of this condition: that for it to be F is for it to be in the same state as some object b when b is F. We can call b's being F the "base case". Then there are three requirements for this explanation of grasp of the concept F to be correct. The identity-condition applied to the base case must meet the following conditions, given here in increasing order of strength:

(*a*) it must be capable of determining a reference for the concept in question;

(*b*) it must give the correct truth-condition for an arbitrary thing to be F; and

(*c*) it must supply the truth-condition in (*b*) unambiguously.

There are clearly cases in which condition (*a*) fails. Suppose someone says that the following is what it is for a number x to be $n/0$, where n is a positive number:

It is for x to stand in the same relation to n and to 0 as:

a number m has to stand in to n and k for m to be n/k, where k is a positive number.

The displayed condition is not capable of determining any number as the reference of the concept $n/0$. For m to be identical with n/k, where k is positive, is for mk to equal n. But this is a relation in which x, n, and 0 cannot stand. Because n is a positive number, there is no number x such that $x0 = n$. So the displayed condition fails to determine a reference for the term or concept $n/0$, where n is positive. The purported explanation of meaning of this term fails requirement (*a*) on explications in terms of identity.

There are several famous points in Wittgenstein's writings at which he objects to explications of understanding of certain specific concepts in terms of identity. Some of these objections can be regarded as based on an insistence that the wholly legitimate requirements (*a*) through (*c*) are fulfilled. The objections take the form of an argument that a particular attempted explication in terms of identity fails one or other of these three conditions.

Wittgenstein objects, for example, to what we have called the Target Account that it is no better than a corresponding identity-based attempt to explain the sense of "It's five o'clock on the sun". One natural reading of his point is that for it to be five o'clock at a given place on the earth at an arbitrary time *t* is for the sun to be at a certain angle in the sky at that place at *t*. Since the sun is never in its own sky, this is a condition that cannot be met by any place ever at the sun. If the condition was meant to pick out a time at a given place on the sun, it fails to do so. The condition does not determine a reference of that sort. Again, when he objects that I cannot imagine someone else's pain on the model of imagining pain in his foot, because that would still be *my* pain, now felt in someone else's foot, that can be seen as an example of appeal to failure of one or the other of requirements (*b*) and (*c*). His objection is that if a truth-condition is determined by the Target Account, it is the wrong one. It does not concern someone else being in pain, as is required. If we regard the correct truth-condition as just one correctness-condition supplied by the Target Account, the very fact that Wittgenstein's point seems to show that it is not the only one is enough to establish that condition (*c*) is not met. The right truth-condition is not unambiguously determined. That, if correct, would already be enough to show that at the very least, the Target Account cannot be the full account of understanding. There must be some further component of the understanding that rules out the unwanted truth-condition.

If an attempted particular explication of concept-possession in terms of grasp of an identity fails because one of these requirements (*a*)–(*c*) is violated, it does not follow that no such explication of the concept is possible. We always have to ask: have we identified the *right* identity-condition?

I will argue that while (*a*)–(*c*) are obviously correct requirements, there are explications of concepts of conscious states in terms of grasp of identity that respect these requirements. They are different explications from those criticized by Wittgenstein; and they have the three advantages over explications that do not involve identity that we noted previously.

3. WHY IS THE SUBJECTIVE CASE DIFFERENT?

Why do explanations in terms of identity work smoothly and successfully in the cases we noted, yet seem to fail for ambiguity or worse in the subjective case? Why are the cases so different? Consider an observational shape concept for purposes of comparison. In the base case for an observational concept like *oval*, the thinker has an experience of something as oval. The thinker's perceptual experience has a content that is itself given in part by reference to a spatial type itself—what I called scenario content in earlier work. The intentional, non-conceptual content already concerns objective, and consequently public, properties and states of affairs. The identity account specifies that for something else to be oval is for it to be of the same shape as is employed in specifying the content of the thinker's experience in the base case. This condition concerns a spatial property itself, and, modulo vagueness, there is nothing indeterminate or ambiguous about whether some object meets that spatial condition at a given time. (Any vagueness is also implicit in the content *a is oval* itself, so that is a desirable feature of the account.) There is no substantial, undesirable indeterminacy of truth-condition in this account.

It will be helpful for future purposes to divide up this account of understanding in the spatial case into three components:

(*a*) In the base case, the thinker can be regarded as employing a recognitional concept C_d of a spatial kind (subscripted with '*d*' for the distinguished case), which intuitively is something like *perceived-by-me-now-to-be-oval*. The concept C_d is not really structured, of course. The hyphenation in the italics is just to indicate the fundamental condition for something to be the concept's reference. C_d is true of an object at a time just in case the object is perceived by the thinker to be oval at that time.

(*b*) C_d also picks out a certain shape property, the shape property P things must have when they fall under this concept C_d. This picking out is not done by some further concept employed by the thinker. The concept C_d is individuated by its connection with perception of things as oval. The shape property itself is used in the individuation of the scenario content of the perceptions that make it rational to apply the concept C_d (and of course too the observational concept we are in the course of elucidating). Correct and rational application of C_d registers the instantiation of a property itself.

(*c*) The thinker's identity-involving understanding of the general concept *oval* is then given by his grasp of the following condition: for something to be oval is for it to have the same shape property P as things must have if they are to fall under the local observational concept C_d in the distinguished, base case. For the avoidance of doubt, as the lawyers say, we can make explicit the logical form of this condition thus:

∃P (P is the shape property things must have to fall under the local observational concept C_d & ∀x (x falls under the concept *oval* iff x has the same shape as things having property P)).

Only an identity at the level of properties will serve the purpose of this account of understanding. This is a point of some significance for the ontological commitments of identity-involving accounts of understanding. Identities at the level of concepts, on the one hand, or at the level of objects and events, on the other, will not serve the purpose.

Take the level of concepts first. At the level of concepts, consider the proposal that grasp consists in appreciation of the fact that for an unperceived object to be oval is for it to fall under the same concept *oval* that is applied by the thinker in a perceptual judgement of an object (perceptually given) that it is oval. This identity is true—but to use it, the thinker must already possess the concept *oval* whose application in the base case is mentioned in the proposed possession-condition. It fails to provide any philosophical explanation of what it is to possess the concept *oval*.

Consider, on the other hand, the level of individual objects and events. Can we say that unperceived instances that fall under the concept *oval* are the same objects as fall under the perceptual-recognitional concept C_d? Evidently not: the unperceived oval things are in general distinct from the perceived oval things. Only the level of properties gives the right kind of bridge to connect the local case—the perceived case, for the concept *oval*—with the non-local case.

What happens when we try to apply this three-component account to the case of the concept *pain*? We encounter a problem. The first two components are unproblematic. In the base case, a thinker employs a recognitional concept which is intuitively something like *pain-experienced-by-me-now*, but is unstructured, exactly as in (*a*) above. The unstructured concept is true at any given time of events that are pains of the thinker at that time. This unstructured concept picks out a certain property P of sensations that is instantiated when this recognitional concept is correctly applied in the base case. It picks out the property not by some further concept or description, but rather by the fact that pain is the property of the sensation to which the thinker is rationally and causally sensitive in his application of the unstructured concept. It is the property to which a thinker is rationally responding when he exercises a recognitional capacity for his own pains. So there is an analogue of (*b*) too.

As in the observational case, it is important that this is formulated at the level of properties. If we tried to build an elaboration of the Target Account solely at the level of concepts, we would have a dilemma structurally quite analogous to that mentioned a few paragraphs back for the case of observational concepts. An unstructured recognitional concept true at any time only of pains experienced by me at that time will, in the nature of the case, be inapplicable to the pains of others. No identity-condition using this concept will satisfactorily explain understanding of pain in others, since this concept does not apply to the pain of others. On the other hand, if we were restricted to the level of concepts in elucidating a Target Account, and tried instead to use the general concept *pain* as possessed by the subject in the base case, we would be presupposing what was to be elucidated, to wit, the subject's grasp of a concept of pain applicable to pains other than his own. The level of properties is as important in the case of concepts of conscious states as it is in the case of observational concepts.

It is, however, the third component that is problematic if we try to apply this three-component account naively. Can we say that the thinker's identity-involving understanding of the general concept *pain* is that for something to fall under it is for some event involving an arbitrary body, and bodily location, at some arbitrary time, to have the same property as is picked out by the unstructured local concept that corresponds in the way indicated to *pain-experienced-by-me-now*? The problem is that this does not distinguish between two radically different cases.

The first is the case in which you have pain in another body, at that bodily location, at another time. This first case subdivides into that in which that body is your only body; and that in which, if it is possible, you have your actual body, but are also capable, by some setup, of feeling pain in another body too. In either of these subdivisions, the pain is yours.

The second case is that in which someone else has pain in that body, at that bodily location, at the time in question.

The three-component exposition of identity-involving understanding has failed to distinguish these two cases. Because that exposition is consistent with only the former case being the proposed condition for an arbitrary event to be a pain-event, a case in which the pain is still yours, the account is wrong.

This point applies quite generally, whether we conceive of pain as a partially or fully intentional state, conceptualized or not conceptualized, or conceive of it as merely a sensational property of individual events. Whether it is a simple sensational property that is in question, or a more or less complex intentional property, to say that that property is instantiated at a given time, by someone with a given body, with the pain apparently or really located at a particular place in that body, still leaves open whether the subject of the pain is you or is someone else. That is why there is ambiguity in the subjective case even though there is determinacy in the observational case.

Imagining the same state in someone else's body—a pain in someone else's foot—is the wrong identity to which to appeal in an account of understanding of attributions of conscious states to others, as Wittgenstein rightly said or implied (*Philosophical Investigations* §302). The present point about ambiguity can be used in support of the idea that the faculty of imagination cannot itself be used to explain our understanding of what it is for something to be a pain, when pain is something that many different subjects may have. Discussions of imagination have emphasized the distinction between what is in the content of the image when one imagines, and what is merely suppositionally imagined to be the case, and is not part of the image itself.[2] When I imagine Philosophy Hall from the outside, some of its perceptible features are represented in my mental image. I also imagine that the building has rooms and walls inside it, and is not an empty shell. But these imaginings about the inside of the building are merely suppositional imaginings, and are not in the content of the mental image itself. (The same mental image could be present when I am just imaging the façade of the building.) When I imagine from the inside pain in a different body from my own, what is given in the mental image of the pain from the inside is still a first-person content such as *this elbow is hurting me*. It may be that what I suppositionally imagine is that I am someone else, not CP. Since what is distinctive of imagination is the image, and its content is first-personal, its content is giving me no leverage at all on the possibility that a third-person

---

[2] See Peacocke (1985).

pain-ascription may be true. The suppositional content of an imagining, on the other hand, we know is something that may not even be possibly true. It follows that imagination is not a resource that can be used in the explanation of grasp of concepts of others' conscious states.[3]

If we think that the Target Account still has something to be said for it, it follows that we must develop an identity-involving model for the case of conscious states that takes account of this difference from the observational and other cases. We need to step back and consider what makes identity-explanations of concepts work in the cases in which they do work.

It is a single, unified space which makes intelligible the idea of something elsewhere being the same shape as something you currently perceive. We have taken that conception for granted in expounding the identity-involving conception in the observational and in other cases in which it works relatively straightforwardly. It is a single, unified space that prevents there being any ambiguity or indeterminacy of a fatal sort in the identity-account of concepts like *oval*. There is no such thing as a thinker perceiving something to be in an oval-shaped region of space independently of that region's being part of a single, unified larger space. What makes the content of the thinker's experiences spatial is that their content can contribute to his conception of the layout of things and events in the larger space of which the region he perceives is part. Experiences are intelligible as having representational content concerning space only if they are capable of playing that role in the thinker's psychology. Correspondingly, there is no such thing as a concept *oval in my perceived space* that picks out a different shape from *oval (and of the right size)* period. This is why there is no analogue in the spatial case of the ambiguity that we have been identifying in the naive development of the identity-involving model for thought about conscious states. The point is not merely that the spatial property that is perceived to be instantiated is already mind-independent and subject-independent. The point is rather that this independence is already involved in various ways in the content of experience itself: scenario content itself involves it. But there is, apparently, nothing in a subject's own pains, or what is involved in having such experiences, that involves or grounds the possibility of other subjects having such experiences.

---

[3] For remarks on the application of the distinction between what is in the image and what is S-imagined to our understanding of other minds, see Peacocke (1985). The points of this paragraph may involve a minor difference from Thomas Nagel, who in *The View from Nowhere* (Nagel 1986: 21) appears to give a central role to imagination in understanding the attribution of conscious states to others like us.

We need then to look more closely at the analogue of space in the problematic case of conscious states.

It is the conception of multiple subjects of experience that makes intelligible the idea of there existing conscious states and events other than your own.[4]

There is a metaphysical interdependence between conscious states and their subjects. This metaphysical interdependence is captured in two principles that aim to state what makes something conscious, and what makes something a subject:

> (E) Conscious states are states such that there is something it is like to be in that state, more specifically something it is like for the subject of that state.
>
> (S) Subjects are things capable of being in conscious states.

The latter dependence of mental states and events on subjects was famously and sharply formulated by Frege: 'Secondly: ideas are something we have. ... Thirdly: ideas need an owner. Things of the outer world are on the contrary independent.'[5]

Precisely because of this metaphysical duality, this interdependence, of experience and subjects, we have to treat two identities simultaneously in explaining the role of identity in a thinker's understanding of conscious states and of multiple conscious subjects. We have to treat grasp of conscious states and grasp of a potential multiplicity of subjects in a single principle, a principle that treats them as interlocking notions. We can say:

> For x, distinct from me, to be in pain, is both:
>
> for x to be something of the same kind as me (a subject); and is also
>
> for x to be in the same state I'm in when I'm in pain.

We can call this the "Interlocking Account". Under the Interlocking Account, subjects are conceived of as things of the same kind as me. This is why 'I'm a subject' is not informative. Under this account, there is a first-person element

---

[4] Compare the discussion in Nagel (1986, ch. 2, sect. 'Other Minds', p. 20): 'The first stage of objectification of the mental is for each of us to be able to grasp the idea of all human perspectives, including his own, without depriving them of their character as perspectives. It is the analogue for minds of a centerless conception of space for physical objects, in which no point has a privileged position.' Modulo the apparent divergence over the role of imagination recorded in the preceding footnote, the position I develop in this chapter can be regarded as a detailed elaboration of a realism about the mental, and of the corresponding nature of thought about it, which, if correct, substantiates the general character Nagel attributes to them.

[5] Frege (1977: 14). See also Galen Strawson's discussion in G. Strawson (1994: 129–34).

in the notion of being a subject, as well as in canonical concepts of conscious states.

A way to avoid the problematic ambiguity that bedevilled the naive application of the identity model to the case of thought about conscious states is for the understanding-condition to mention difference of subject also. It does not suffice for the understanding-condition to deal only with subjective kinds of experience, body, and bodily location. Under the Interlocking Account, we specify other-attribution as the case in which we have: same state, another subject, where the subject is thought of as a thing of the same kind as oneself.

Those who accept the Interlocking Account will say that there is a non sequitur to be avoided here, that of moving from the correct point

(1) that conceiving of pain in another's leg is not the same as conceiving of another person's being in pain

to the conclusion that

(2) identity is not involved in the understanding of another's being in pain.

On the Interlocking View, conceiving of another person's being in pain is conceiving of the case: same state as one experiences when one experiences pain in a leg, but with instantiation of this state in a subject distinct from oneself. By contrast, simply conceiving of pain in another's leg at best leaves open whether the subject of the pain is oneself or someone else. So (1) is true on the Interlocking View. But identity evidently still plays a central and ineliminable role in this account of understanding, so (2) is false on the Interlocking View. Those who do make the fallacious transition from (1) to (2) may go on to conclude that some kind of criterial or other model of understanding is required. One wonders whether Wittgenstein, even if he did not actually make the transition from (1) to (2), nevertheless intended (1) to be evidence for his view. In any case, the genuine insight that (1) is true should not be used as support for the view that identity is not involved in understanding what it is for another person to be in pain.

4. ATTRACTIONS OF THE INTERLOCKING ACCOUNT

In its use of an identity-relation, the Interlocking Account inherits the attractions of any identity-involving account. An explanation of the uniformity of sense in the predicates of first- and third-person predications, and the required connection with the level of reference, were the first two of these attractions. The third, 'Understanding precedes Evidence', also seems to apply to conscious states. Simply from grasping what it is for another to be in pain, one does indeed not thereby know what would be evidence that someone else is in pain. It is this that makes intelligible the Plantinga–Albritton question: "I wonder what people do these days when they're in pain?"[6] The proponent of this Interlocking Account will, then, be in disagreement with Dummett when he writes that understanding "John is in pain" involves

knowing that pain-behaviour, or the presence of an ordinarily painful stimulus, is normally a sufficient ground for an ascription of pain, but one that can be rebutted, in the former case by the clues that betray the shammer or by subsequent disclaimer; learning the symptoms of inhibiting the natural manifestation of pain, and the limits beyond which this is impossible; knowing the usual connection between pain and bodily conditions, and the sort of cases in which the connection may be broken; and so on.[7]

You can understand "John is in pain" without knowing any of these things, provided that 'pain-behaviour' is characterized independently of the notion of pain (if it is not, there is no full account of understanding here). The conditions Dummett cites here are all empirical information about the conditions under which third-person ascriptions are true, but they are not constitutive of, nor required for, understanding of "pain". In short, the principle 'Understanding precedes Evidence' applies here too under the Interlocking Account.

It is also, incidentally, not plausible that the conditions Dummett cites are sufficient for grasping third-person predications of the concept *pain*. Consider a subject who suffers from CIPA, which involves a congenital insensitivity to conditions that in normal subjects cause pain. This subject never feels pain, and does not know what it would be like to experience pain. He could nevertheless know the empirical facts listed by Dummett. He would not have a full grasp of what it is for someone else to be in pain, any more than the colour-blind subject fully understands colour vocabulary.

To say that your understanding of another's being in pain is that he is in the same state you are in when you are in pain is not to imply that he could be in pain only if you exist. The Interlocking Account gives a way of latching onto a property, that of being in pain. In evaluating a content containing the

[6] See Albritton (1968).   [7] Dummett (1978*a*, p. xxxv).

concept *pain* with respect to some non-actual state of affairs *w*, we consider which things in *w* have the property of being in pain, rather than which things in *w* stand in the relation to you that make available a distinctive way of thinking of the property. As David Kaplan would say, in evaluating a sentence '*a* is in pain' with respect to another possible world, we carry with us the property P of being in pain, and evaluate the sentence as true with respect to that other world according as the referent of '*a*' with respect to that other world has the property P in that world. We do not have to consider what in that other world falls under a particular mode of presentation of P; we have only to consider what has, in that world, the property P itself of being in pain. The challenges posed by the Interlocking Account have to do with understanding, rather than the modal.

The component of the Interlocking Account that speaks of identity of state is essential to determining the property of pain as the property picked out by the concept *pain*, and correspondingly as the property picked out by the word "pain" in the linguistic case. If a thinker sincerely utters "I'm W" in rational response to his own pain, that is consistent with three quite different hypotheses about the meaning of the predicate W:

(*a*) it may mean something that is true of himself when he is in pain, and is false of anyone else (the self-restriction case);

(*b*) it may mean something that is true of the thinker himself when he is in pain, and it is left completely unsettled whether it can be true of anyone else (the case of indeterminacy);

(*c*) it may mean the same as our predicate "is in pain", and so can be true of others (the case of genuine other-ascription).

Each of (*a*)–(*c*) is consistent with the thinker's self-ascription "I'm W" being causally and rationally explained by one of his sensations having the property of being a pain. The generality of the property of being a pain does not by itself resolve the matter at the level of concepts and meaning of which of (*a*) through (*c*) is correct. That issue is resolved only by the content of the tacit knowledge involved in understanding the predicate W. In the self-restriction case, (*a*), understanding involves tacit knowledge that W, as uttered by oneself, is true only of oneself and not of anyone else. In the case of indeterminacy, there is no knowledge of conditions under which W is true of anyone distinct from oneself. In the case of genuine other-ascription, understanding W involves tacit knowledge that W is true of a subject *x* distinct from oneself just in case *x* is in the same subjective state one is in oneself that makes it rational to accept "I'm W". This point that an identity-component in understanding is needed to fix the correct property as reference of a predicate is not at all restricted to concepts of conscious psychological states. It applies equally to the observational concepts we considered earlier. A word U that is rationally applied in response to perceptions of things as oval might apply only to things that are perceived as oval; or it might be indeterminate whether U applies to things that are too small, too large, or made of the wrong kind of stuff (e.g. dark matter) to be perceived as oval; or U might mean the same as our 'oval'. Again, the issue is resolved only by the nature of the identity-component, if any, involved in understanding U.

Someone may object to the Interlocking Account that it can work only if identity of state between different subjects is given some further elaboration, in terms of functional role, or at least something else. I disagree. There cannot be any such abstract general requirement that identity should be reduced to something else. I argued back in Chapter 1 that tacit knowledge of identity of, for example, shape is a component of our grasp of spatial observational concepts. Attempts to elucidate the holding of identity of shape between observed and unobserved objects in terms of justification-conditions were not correct. No such analysis, or any other, is required. Identity of shape is a notion in good standing, and as such is graspable by a thinker capable of spatial perception and with a conception of the space in which he is located, without any need for a reduction to something else. I would say the same about identity of conscious states between different subjects. Identity of state is a notion in good standing, and as such is graspable by a thinker capable of being in conscious states and with a conception of multiple subjects of experience, without any need for a reduction to something else.

There is a background presupposition in these remarks of a certain irreducible realism about the spatial and material properties picked out in the observational case, and a corresponding realism about the mental properties picked out in the psychological case. If there really are spatial and material properties in their own right, and there exists a space in which objects possessing them are located, and if a thinker is related to a property in the distinctive way he is when he perceives it to be instantiated, then thoughts about whether that same property is instantiated in objects in other places must make sense. The same applies, *pari passu*, in the mental case. If the states of either domain had to be reduced to something else, then grasp of identity would involve grasp of identity of the reducing condition in question. Correspondingly more would be required for mastery of the conception of an objective world, and a world of many mental subjects. But I doubt that any such reduction is required, in either case.

What is true is that when the Interlocking Account speaks of 'same state I'm in when I'm in pain', sameness of state here must mean: same conscious state. There are physiological states I am in when I am in pain, but sameness of those physiological states is not what I mean when I think someone else is in pain. This is one of many points in this book, and in much other contemporary work in the philosophy of mind and thought, at which we simply use the notion of consciousness, and some representation of it, without at all having a full understanding of what it involves. More generally, when an account of understanding involves tacit knowledge of an identity, the property or state whose identity is mentioned will be a property or state of a certain kind. In the case we have just been discussing, it is identity of conscious state; in the case of observational shape concepts, it is identity of shape property; and so forth. This should not be at all surprising if we accept a natural generalization of principle concerning identity that David Wiggins identified and labels 'D': that x is identical with y iff there is some sortal F such that x is the same F as y.[8] The generalization of this principle to all categories, including properties, seems to me equally plausible. P is the same property as Q iff there is some substantive kind K such that P is the same property of kind K as Q. Grasp of identity of objects of a given sort involves some tacit appreciation that they have a sortal kind. Similarly, grasp of identity of properties of a given sort involves some tacit appreciation of their possession of a substantive kind. This is another point at which a theory of understanding and a metaphysics of the objects and entities thought about intersect.

The first person plays a double role in the Interlocking Account, a role not played by any other way of thinking of a person or a subject. It enters the base case both for the concept of a subject and for the concept of a given conscious state. The Interlocking Account gives a legitimate undergirding to the intuitive claim that one knows from one's own case what it is for someone else to be in pain, or in some other given conscious state. It gives a corresponding undergirding for the intuitive claim that one knows from one's own case what it is to be a subject. In abstract structure and in their source, these claims should be thought of as no more problematic in principle than the idea that one knows from perceptual experience what it is for something to fall under an observational concept; or knows what it is for it to be raining

---

[8] Wiggins (2001: 56 ff.).

from the case in which it is raining at one's own location. Knowing what it is from one's own case has a special place in the account of concepts of subjects and conscious states just because the first person features in the base case in concepts of conscious states. The distinctive characteristics of the base case always have consequences for the nature of any concept which is individuated by tacit knowledge of an identity-condition applied to a base case. This is not to deny that the phenomenon of knowing from one's own case raises special epistemological issues (to which we will turn in section 5 of this chapter). It is only to emphasize that the source of the phenomenon, if it exists, is not something without precedent and without a more general explanation.

There may well remain a residual worry about this account, to the effect that there is something impossible in the attempt to extract a general understanding of the concept of pain from one's own case. 'How could *this* property be experienced by anyone else?' the doubter may think. This need not be a confused thought about mental particulars, which are indeed individuated by the subject who is enjoying (or suffering) them. It may rather be a thought referring to the conscious property of pain he is experiencing, a type of event. Is there anything right in this thought, and if so, what is it, and what does it show?

What is right in the thought—or at least in a nearby thought—is this. The state of affairs that obtains when he is in pain is a state of affairs that is experienced by him in a way that no one else can experience it. This truth does not imply that the property he has, when such states of affairs obtain, cannot be experienced in exactly the same way by others when they have that property. It can be and is so experienced. It is fallacious to move from a truth about how a state of affairs involving oneself could be presented to others to a conclusion about the impossibility of the property involved in that state of affairs being instantiated by others. Precisely what one has once one possesses the conception of oneself as one subject amongst others is a conception of oneself as having conscious properties that other subjects may also have.

It may be of interest to compare this reaction to the person who says 'How could *this* property be experienced by anyone else?' with Wittgenstein's reaction to the person he envisages who says the almost synonymous 'But surely another person can't have THIS pain!' (*Philosophical Investigations* §253). Wittgenstein's reaction is: 'The answer to this is that one does not define a criterion of identity by emphatic stressing of the word 'this'. Rather, what the emphasis does is to suggest the case in which we are conversant with such a criterion of identity, but have to be reminded of it' (§253).

The reply I offered differs from Wittgenstein's in two respects: it found something true (though by no means a full justification) underlying the remark; and the positive response does not invoke the notion of a criterion of identity. Theories that invoke grasp of identity itself, of the sort I have been advocating in this chapter, and earlier for the observational case, are distinct from theories that rely on some 'criterion of identity'. Here I just note this as a marker. Later, in section 5 of this chapter, I will be arguing that properties, and identity of properties, themselves can play part of the controlling and constitutive role played by the notion of a criterion of identity in Wittgenstein's position, in so far as we really have an understanding of his position.

There are at this point two fundamental tasks for the Interlocking Account. We have so far taken for granted several notions that need some philosophical elaboration. If the Interlocking Account is to be acceptable, we ought

(A) to explain what it is to think of oneself as a subject; and

(B) to explain what it is to have the conception of a possible range of subjects, one of which is oneself.

I attempt some preliminary elucidation of each of these in turn.

(A) Subject-Involving Thought

There is a form of thinking of oneself as a subject which does not involve already having the general concept of a subject of conscious states—the concept whose possession we aim to elucidate—nor even some restriction of the general concept of a subject, such as *person* or *friend*. This form of thinking can be described as subject-involving thought. Intuitively, it is thought about oneself that, in its nature, is thought about a subject of conscious states. We have something here which is intermediate between merely referring to something which is in fact a subject—as in "the thing mentioned on page 17 of such-and-such book"—and possession of the general concept of a subject.

It is a substantive, non-definitional, but highly plausible thesis that subject-involving thought about oneself is thought that essentially employs the first-person concept. Why should this be so? Any answer to this question is committed to taking a stand on which theory, or at least which subset of theories, of the first-person concept is correct. I will just state a view without here giving arguments against rival theories. In my view, the first-person concept is, like any other, individuated by the fundamental rule that determines its reference on a given occasion of use. For the first person, the rule is that any particular use of the first-person concept in a thought refers to the thinker of the thought. Since the thinker of a thought is certainly a subject, this explains why any use of the first person in thought refers, by the nature of the concept, to a subject.

This fundamental reference rule also explains why the Thought *I am F* differs from the Thought *This body is F*. The reference of *this body* is not required by its sense to be a subject. Even if a case can be made that in certain special circumstances it is a subject, it is not guaranteed in all circumstances to be the same subject as actually thinks the thought *I am F*.

To say that the fundamental rule for the reference of *I* in a thought is that it refers to the thinker of the thought is not at all to imply that *I* is equivalent to something like the complex descriptive-cum-demonstrative *the thinker of this thought*. The fundamental rule for a use of the perceptual demonstrative *that F* tied to a certain perception is that it refers to the F given in that perception. It by no means follows that the perceptual demonstrative *that F* is equivalent to *the F perceived in this perception*. It is definitely not so equivalent. Both the reference rule for the first-person concept, and the reference rule for perceptual demonstratives, should rather be considered as specifying what relation an object has to bear to the use of the relevant concept in order to be its reference.[9]

The two points we need to carry forward from this discussion are that subject-involving thought—thought that by its nature involves a subject as its reference—is possible without yet involving the general concept of a subject (or restrictions thereof); and that such thought is first-person thought.

(B) Having a Conception of a Range of Subjects

Here is what I call the "thin" account of what it is to have the conception of a range of subjects that includes oneself:

> A range of subjects is conceived of as a range of things of the same kind as me, standing in the same kinds of relations to the world, events, objects, and actions as are required for me to exist.

The first person as it occurs in this specification of the content of the conception can be construed as minimal subject-involving thought of the

---

[9] See the discussion in Ch. 2 sect. 1 above.

sort we have just been discussing. If minimal subject-involving thought does exist, then the use of the first person in this thin account need not already presuppose that the thinker has a conception of many subjects. It requires only subject-involving thought. If, for one reason or another, you are sceptical of the existence of an intermediate level of minimal subject-involving thought, you could still consistently accept this thin account. You would just be committed to a more holistic understanding of the specification of the content of the thin account, an understanding according to which the first person and the conception of a range of subjects are explained simultaneously.

The thin account has these consequences.

(*a*) As we noted, the thin account explains why the Thought *I am a subject* is uninformative. Subjects in general are thought of as things of the same kind as me. What that kind is may need further investigation by the thinker: its nature need not be immediately obvious simply from the general concept of a subject, or the ability to have subject-involving thoughts about oneself.

(*b*) The thin account permits other subjects to look unlike and to be very unlike me. It suffices, under the thin account, that they stand to the world in the same kinds of relations that make me a subject. That an octopus or a stingray should potentially be a subject is straightforward on this view. Organisms that are very different from humans are not, under this account, required to be subjects in some merely derivative or courtesy sense.

(*c*) Similarly, under the thin account, another subject's actions may look and be quite different from one's own; and it may perceive quite different events, properties, relations, and magnitudes in the environment than are perceived by me. I may not even know about the events, properties, and the rest that it perceives. This and the preceding consequence are respects in which this account of the conception of many subjects can be described as thin.

It is, arguably, a general thesis in metaphysics that any real event in time, and any spatio-temporal object's having a property or standing in a relation, will in some circumstances have causal effects. This principle applies as much to mental events and mental properties and relations as it does to the non-mental realm. If the principle is correct, then the mental events and states of other subjects will in some circumstances have effects. It follows that they can then potentially be thought about in a third-person way. What these third-person ways are may need to be worked out. A further respect in which the present account is thin is, then, that it does not require, for a conception of a range of subjects, that one know what these third-person ways of thinking of others' mental states are simply in order to have the conception.

Mature, normal humans in fact have an extensive range of third-personal ways in which they can think of others' mental states, ways of thinking made available by their ability to perceive another as sad, to see a facial expression as one of anger, to perceive a wince as an expression of pain, to see someone as looking at an object in the common environment. Such perceptual abilities are enormously important in our lives. They facilitate our ability to know about others' mental states. They make possible all sorts of close interpersonal relations. They provide a special way into possession of the conception of many subjects ('*He's* a subject', '*You* are a subject' may play a special role in the way we reach and master the conception). These perceptual abilities, their nature and ramifications, deserve much more attention than they have received hitherto from the philosophical community. But the ability to be in such states involving perception of expressions of others' mental states is not, according to the thin account, actually required for possession of the conception of a range of subjects, however poorer we would be without the ability to enjoy such states.

There is yet a further respect in which this account is thin. Prima facie, the earlier account of thinking of oneself as a subject is one a thinker can satisfy without yet meeting these conditions for having the general conception of a range of subjects. If this is correct, it further highlights the importance of not identifying the property of thinking of oneself as a subject with the property of employing the general concept *subject* and applying it to oneself. Judging contents about oneself that, of their very nature as contents, require one to be a subject is not yet to have the general concept *subject*.

5. TACIT KNOWLEDGE, AND EXTERNALISM ABOUT THE INTERNAL

Tacit knowledge of the identity in the Target Account is, like any other case of tacit knowledge, essentially an explanatory state. This tacit knowledge explains properties and relations of events and states, and classes thereof, which would not otherwise be explained. Attribution of tacit knowledge is justified if there is reason to think that there are such properties and relations that would not otherwise be explained. Tacit knowledge of a definition of a concept can explain a thinker's application of the concept in actual and counterfactual circumstances, applications that could not be equally well explained without it (see Chapter 4). Tacit knowledge of a grammatical rule can explain why all the sentences a subject finds to be grammatical have a certain common property; and so forth.[10]

This account applies straightforwardly to tacit knowledge of the identities involved in understanding, including the identity in the Target Account. Tacit knowledge of an identity, in the case in which it really is involved in the grasp of a concept, can, when combined with the thinker's other beliefs and hypotheses, explain why the thinker applies that concept, or rejects its application, in various actual and counterfactual circumstances. The thinker's application of the concept, outright or in the course of one or another kind of inference, involves his tacitly drawing on the information in the content of the knowledge.

Precisely because it is an empirical matter what would be evidence that another place, or another time, or another person, has certain kinds of property, there is correspondingly no specific, independently characterized kind of evidence about other places, times, and persons that a thinker must be sensitive to in grasping such contents about other places, times, and persons. The only characterization of the evidence to which a thinker must be sensitive is given parasitically on the identities themselves. It is evidence that the other place, time, or person has the same property as here, or as now, or as the subject himself possesses, when these respective objects have the property in question.

The presence of tacit knowledge of an identity in understanding contributes to the explanation of a thinker's judgements, or pattern of judgements, only in the presence of various other states. In this, tacit knowledge of identities in understanding resembles virtually every other interesting case of tacit knowledge. Tacit knowledge of a particular syntactic or semantic rule explains facts about the thinker's appreciation of language only in the presence of his tacit knowledge of other syntactic or semantic facts. This is not intrinsically more problematic than any other case of explanation by theoretical truths in an empirical science. It means that the evidence for the attribution of any specific piece of tacit knowledge is, in the nature of the case and not merely contingently, holistic. Two states of tacit knowledge that differ in their content—for instance, in respect of the property in the base case to

---

10 For further discussion, see Chomsky (1980, 1986); Davies (1981, chs iii and iv; 1987).

which identity is applied, or in the relation applied to the base case—will in some circumstances or other have different explanatory consequences. The different states will have those different consequences only in the presence of additional conditions.

These points apply to all cases of identities that are involved in understanding. But the identity involved in the target case of subjective states is also of special significance for positions that have been held in the philosophy of mind. The identity-condition involved in understanding that another person is in pain implies that the state the other has to be in for that content to be true is identical with the state one is in oneself when one is in pain. I have emphasized that on the account I am defending, this identity is not a mere *façon de parler* for some other condition that does not involve identity. Since a thinker refers to a certain kind of mental state in attributing pain to another, it follows that if the Target Account is correct, when a thinker judges *I'm in pain* he must also be referring to the same mental state. A non-referential view of thought and language about one's own pain and other conscious states and events is not an option under the Target Account. The question then arises: how are we to conceive of thought about pain and other subjective states in the first-person case if we are committed to a referential account of such thought?

What makes a thinker's thought involve the concept *pain* is in part that his application of the concept is causally and rationally sensitive to the occurrence of pain itself in him. That is the very close connection between the concept *pain* and the property of being a pain that exists on the present account. We have here what we can call, without genuine paradox, 'Externalism about the Internal'. There is no paradox, because the point of the doctrine can be formulated thus. In the case of thought about the external world, if we draw a boundary around the body, it has become clear both from multiple examples, and from theoretical considerations about explanation and rationality, that mental states with content do not supervene only on what is going on inside that boundary. A precisely corresponding point applies even to mental states like pain. A thinker's judgements involving the concept *pain* possess that conceptual content only because they stand in certain relations to pains themselves (or to recognitional capacities whose nature is to be explained in relation to pains themselves). Though the concept *pain* is not an observational concept, and a perceptual model should not be applied to it, nonetheless *pain* is a concept individuated in part by the relations of certain judgements involving it to instances of that very concept. The concept is analogous in this respect to experiences that are instance-individuated, in the sense of *The Realm of Reason*.[11] If we draw an imaginary boundary around those of the subject's brain states that involve his exercise of concepts, but leave outside the boundary which of his subjective mental states rationally cause these exercises, the intentional content of his mental states will not supervene on what is inside this imaginary boundary. In this sense, to mimic Evans on a different point, idealism is false even as a theory of thought about the mind itself, and even in its most subjective aspects.[12] Even for the thoroughly subjective, how something is thought about is not independent of what it really is that is thought about.

It is not only a fact about the concept *pain*, but a fact about the nature of the state of being in pain itself, that gives the first person a special status in grasp of the concept *pain*. Because there is something it is like to be in pain, and because conscious states can give reasons for making judgements, there is a distinctive way of thinking about the state of being in pain available to those who know what it is like to be in pain. This is an instance of a more general phenomenon familiar from many other cases. Quite generally, a subject can think of an object, event, or state in a distinctive way because he stands in a certain corresponding conscious relation to that object, event, or state. Each subject stands in a certain conscious relation to his own pains, a relation in which he does not stand to anyone else's pains. It is this relation that makes it possible for a thinker to think of his own pains as pains.

Under this treatment, an event's having the property of being a pain contributes to the causal and rational explanation of a thinker's self-application of the concept *pain*. The objectivity and constancy of the thinker's use of the concept *pain* does not, on this view, come merely from the subject's thinking that he is applying it correctly. The objectivity comes from his first-person present-tense use being keyed to whether an event really is a pain or not.

Suppose, in the spirit of a famous paragraph of Wittgenstein's *Philosophical Investigations* (§258) that the thinker's concept *pain* is expressed in a symbol 'S' and suppose too that the question arises of whether our thinker has, unbeknownst to himself, misremembered what this symbol means. On the present view, the distinction between the case in which there is undetected misremembering and the case in which there is correct remembering is

---

11 Peacocke (2004); and, for an independent statement of similar views, see Burge (2003).
12 Evans (1982: 256): 'Therefore we are not Idealists about ourselves.'

simply that between the case in which his use of the symbol 'S' was not in the past explained by an event's being a pain, and that in which it is still so explained.

The distinction between correct use and merely apparently correct use is here elucidated consistently with others being able to know, on occasion, that our subject is in pain. There is no commitment to privacy in this view. Nor is there any implied need for the thinker to have a further 'criterion' for whether he is in pain.

I do not at all mean to imply that the model of judgements made rationally in response to the instantiation of a property, and caused by that property, provides a full answer to the rule-following considerations. A full answer to the rule-following considerations must explicate the notion of a thinker's making a judgement rationally in the light of his understanding of the concepts involved. Such an explication must use resources beyond those outlined here. My point at present is only that, even if it is far from the whole story, the notion of a judgement being causally explained by one property rather than another is an essential component of an answer to the rule-following considerations.

This form of Externalism about the Internal does not, or does not obviously, tie first-person present-tense ascriptions of pain to any particular bodily expression of the sensation by the thinker. Bodily expression may change, or even become non-existent, consistently with the thinker's first-person present-tense applications being explained by an event's being a pain event. When a person suffering intense pain takes morphine, the initial effect of the drug is not that the pain disappears. The pain can continue to exist, but the patient no longer minds it.[13] In these circumstances, the patient is not disposed to any particular bodily expression of his pain. His bodily expressions will certainly be quite different from those to which he was disposed prior to taking the morphine. But his use of the concept *pain* is still keyed to instances in him of the property of being a pain.

Wittgenstein wrote, 'if I assume the abrogation of the normal language-game with the expression of a sensation, I need a criterion of identity for the sensation; and then the possibility of error also exists' (end of §288 in the *Investigations*). I would dispute both of these claims. No criterion of identity, beyond sensitivity to instances of the property of pain, is required in the morphine cases. Yet there is still an explanation under the present approach of

---

[13] The importance of these cases was emphasized by Dennett (1978*a*: 208–11).

the impossibility of error of the sort Wittgenstein has in mind. If having the concept *pain* requires one to judge that one is in pain in the presence of one of one's own pain-events, then in central cases it will indeed not be possible for a subject with the concept *pain* coherently to think, in Wittgenstein's words, 'Oh, I know what "pain" means; what I don't know is whether *this*, that I have now, is pain' (also §288).

How then might a neo-Wittgensteinian respond to the account I have offered? Crispin Wright suggested to me that the response would be that there simply is no property of being in pain that has all the characteristics needed by the Interlocking Account.[14] Under this response, it is legitimate to speak of the property of being a pain, but this property of a mental event must be regarded as a construct out of human conceptual reactions and expressive capacities, in a way that is incompatible with its being causally and rationally explanatory of thinkers' first-person judgements that they are in pain.

Pain is a property that can be instantiated by events in the life of an octopus, a dolphin, or a whale. The neo-Wittgensteinian account of the property of being a pain needs to accommodate this fact. How can it capture the application of the property in non-human cases? No doubt it is in fact sufficient for a creature of another species to be in pain if its brain is in the same relevant neurophysiological state as that of a human who is in pain. But what entitles the neo-Wittgensteinian to accept that principle about neurophysiological states? What captures the cases in which the underlying physiological states are realizations of pain? The neo-Wittgensteinian is regarding the property of being in pain as a construct out of human conceptual reactions and expressive dispositions. But the dolphin and the octopus have no such distinctively human reactions and expressive dispositions. No neurophysiological state of a dolphin is the realizing state for a role that involves what is distinctively human.

Could our neo-Wittgensteinian say that a role in human conceptual and expressive life allows us to fix on the conscious mental property of being in pain, but add that what is involved here is just a kind of reference-fixing, so that the very same conscious property could be instantiated by creatures for which it does not have that role? That seems like an unstable middle position. If there is such a real conscious property that has a nature independently of human conceptual reactions and expressions, then that property can play a

---

[14] Personal conversation.

causal role in making first-person judgements rational. It could then after all have the role it is assigned in the Interlocking Account.

There are many variant epicycles on a neo-Wittgensteinian position that could be formulated at this point. The variants known to me seem to be vulnerable to problems of the kind already discussed. I myself doubt that there is a neo-Wittgensteinian treatment of the property of being in pain that both classifies all the cases correctly, and is also a genuine alternative to the Interlocking Account.

6. IS THIS THE MYTH OF THE GIVEN?

Is the treatment I have offered of the first-person case open to the objection that it is an instance of the objectionable and refuted Myth of the Given? The Myth has been given various formulations in the literature, and these formulations are sometimes dependent upon acceptance of ancillary controversial theses. The central idea is that there cannot be a state that both justifies you in making a judgement with a certain content, and yet is also a state that lacks representational content.

It is an additional thesis, incorporated into the formulation of the Myth of the Given in Sellars, McDowell, and Brandom, that all representational content is conceptual content.[15] If that additional thesis is accepted, then the Myth can be formulated as the idea that there can exist states that justify making a judgement with a certain content, where the justifying states lack conceptual content. But even without acceptance of that additional thesis, the Myth can still be formulated. There are still good reasons for thinking that the Myth is indeed a myth, and that the errors highlighted by identifying it as such have been committed in some parts of twentieth-century epistemology.

Part of the core idea behind the identification of the Myth, an idea one can accept even if one believes in non-conceptual representational content, is that a state cannot give reasons for making a judgement about the world beyond that state unless the state has representational content. To make such a judgement on the basis of such an alleged state would not be an exercise of rationality. Such states, as McDowell puts it, would give us 'exculpations where we wanted justifications'.[16] To move to a judgement about the world

---

[15] See Sellars (1997); Brandom (1997); McDowell (1994).   [16] McDowell (1994: 8).

because one is in a state that does not represent anything about the world beyond that state as being the case is simply to make an irrational leap into the dark. I accept this point, in the qualified formulation given here. I also accept its importance.

So does the treatment of first-person ascription of conscious states given here conflict even with this qualified formulation? To assess this, we first have to consider whether the conscious states in question do have representational content with a pertinent correctness-condition. Some obviously do, and I will return to them: but let us take first a case where it is less plausible that they do (though there are certainly some who hold that they do[17]). I myself hold that when a subject s is in pain apparently in a part of his body, a perspicuous representation of this fact is given simply by the condition

$$\text{Pain}(e, s, t, \beta).$$

This says that token event e is a pain of subject s occurring at time t in apparent body-part β. β is in italics because it is a singular intentional component. A subject can be in pain in a phantom limb. β is a way it seems some bodily part is given in the subject's experience. Everyone should agree that this component of an experience of pain exists. Your pain-experience does represent you as having the bodily part in which the pain seems to occur. So it is wrong to say that pain-experiences have no representational content whatever. But it is clear that this particular component is quite inadequate to avoiding the Myth of the Given as squarely as one would in the case of perceptual experience of the outer world. The content of the pain-experience cannot be just that one has a bodily part of a certain kind. On the treatment captured by the displayed condition, pain is a relational property of an event. The event e does not represent oneself as being in pain. The pain-event e itself will have many other properties too, some of them intrinsic to the conscious experience itself.

So this conception of pain seems squarely within the target area at which the objections framed in terms of the Myth of the Given are aimed. Yet it is very hard to see how a thinker s making a judgement that he is in pain, because and for the reason that $\text{Pain}(e, s, t, \beta)$ holds for suitable e, t, and β, is just making an irrational leap in the dark. Our thinker is judging no more than that he is in a state, and his reason (non-inferential) is his being in that very

---

17 For instance, Tye (1997).

state. The state seems to be the best possible justification for his judgement, rather than an exculpation for making it. If the judgement concerned the world other than his state, there would indeed be a problem. But it does not. We can even, if we so wish, insist that our thinker is rationally responding to the fact that Pain(e, s, t, β). In this respect, his mind is embracing the (mental) world he is thinking about. His judgement, under this account, does not fall short of knowledge.

It is true that some formulations of the Myth of the Given seem drafted in such a way as to preclude even justification of such mental self-knowledge by the mental states thought about. Any formulation of the Myth that requires any reason-giving state to have a conceptual content will certainly preclude an account under which an occurrence of pain itself, understood as not having conceptual content, can justify a self-ascription of pain. But from the point of the argument of the preceding paragraph, these formulations do not inherit the argumentative force of the consideration that rational judgement cannot be a blind leap in the dark. Self-ascription of pain because one experiences a pain-event is not a blind leap in the dark.

McDowell offers a treatment under which pain-experiences do have a representational content concerning mental states. He writes that pain 'is an awareness of the circumstance that the subject is in pain'.[18] As many have pointed out, it is very implausible that any creature that experiences pain also has to have the concept of pain. If McDowell's phrase 'circumstance that the subject is in pain' is meant to identify a conceptual content the sufferer from pain must grasp, the account is too strong. We might attempt to save the position, albeit in a non-McDowellian fashion, by saying that the content here is at the level of reference, perhaps a Russellian proposition or, again, a fact. I myself think that even this is too sophisticated. An animal that is in pain has an experience as of part of its body hurting. It seems to me that an animal, or even a child, does not even have to have an ontology of subjects who are in pain. A creature that thinks just about material objects, has mental states but does not think about mental states, can be in pain. This creature may think about its own body, and other bodies, and its body's place in the world. All of this can exist, and so can the pain, without our creature thinking about subjects.

What of first-person ascription of mental states for which 'esse est percipi' is not true, for which illusions of being in the state are possible? I do want to

---

[18] McDowell (1994: 88).

apply the present model of first-person psychological self-ascription to these too. For example, a thinker's making the transition from his

> seeing that *p*

to the self-ascriptive judgement

> I see that *p*

seems to me to be part of what is involved in having the concept *seeing that p*. (For further discussion, see Chapter 6.) Making this transition is a way of coming to know that one sees that *p*. Similarly, a thinker's having an

> action-awareness of his φ-ing

can rationally lead him to judge, and to know

> I am φ-ing.

(This is also further discussed in Chapters 6 and 7.) In both these transitions, fact-involving states—seeing that *p*, having an action-awareness that one is φ-ing—are the reason-giving, justifying states. Precisely because they are fact-involving, the justifying state does not fall short of the content of the judgement that is justified. Again, the justified judgement is not a blind leap. A thinker may of course mistakenly think he is in one of these justifying states when in fact he is not. But this is no more an objection to his having justification, and attaining knowledge, in favourable cases than it would be in the analogous cases of perceptual experience.

Here too we can, if we want, endorse a version of the mind embracing the very fact in question. A state can be factive even if its representational content is non-conceptual. A perceptual state with what in *A Study of Concepts* I called 'scenario content' can represent the layout of the world as being a certain way. For the state to be genuine perception, the world around the perceiver must really be that (non-conceptually individuated) way. If a subject has a non-conceptual awareness of itself as performing certain actions, either bodily or mental, that awareness too is factive, and requires that the subject really be performing those actions. Such factive states, as rationalizing states, permit the judgements they make rational to have justifications that reach out into the way the world is.

In all of these cases, I have endorsed a treatment of first-person self-ascriptions without regarding the states or events that justify the self-ascriptions as perceived. There does not need to be a further level of perception of the pain, or perception of the seeing, or perception of the action-awareness, for this first-person account to work. It suffices that the first-level mental states themselves are states of consciousness. That is also necessary, if the states and events are, from the thinker's own point of view, to make judgements about those mental states rational.

7. KNOWLEDGE OF OTHERS' CONSCIOUS STATES

How do we have knowledge of others' conscious states if the Target Account is correct? There is a challenge here distinct from the usual forms of scepticism. Very often, we know that someone else is in pain, say, because the other person's bodily events express that pain, most notably in their facial expression. We see the other person's facial expression as that of someone who is in pain. How do we reconcile the fact that this is a means of coming to know with the correctness of the Target Account? This is a challenge, because if the Target Account is correct, perceiving from someone's facial expression that they are in pain is not something written into grasp of *That person is in pain* as a means of coming to know that content. The understanding is just given by the identity-condition in the Target Account. Moreover, it seems intuitively that someone could have the concept of pain without having the capacity to see someone else's facial expression as one of pain. Lacking that capacity, such a thinker can still know what it is for the other person to be in pain. This thinker is in the same position in relation to other persons as we are in relation to very different species. We know what it is for organisms of very different species from us to be in pain, even though we may have no idea of what would be a natural expression of pain in that species. There is no plausibility in the suggestion that we do not mean the same by the concept of pain when applied to members of these other species as we do when we apply it to humans. Nor would it be plausible, for a notion of sense that is tied to cognitive significance, to say that the thinker who cannot perceive facial expressions as expressions of pain must have a different concept of pain from our own.

This is one of several respects in which the relation between an observational concept, such as *round*, and the perceptions which immediately justify its application, differs from the relation between a perceptual experience of a facial expression as being one of pain, and the concept *pain*. Someone who is not capable of any perceptual experience of something as round, in any sense modality, does not have the concept *round* that is an observational concept. He may have some geometric concept of it, given by some equation; but that will be a different concept of the same property by the Fregean criterion of cognitive significance. When an object is thought of as falling under the observational concept *round*, it is tacitly conceived of as having the same shape as things perceived to be round. This is a conception that is simply unavailable to a thinker incapable of perceiving things as round (more strictly, to a thinker who does not know what it would be like to perceive something as round). But in the case of the concept *pain*, the Target Account does precisely give a thinker who does not know what it would be like to see something as an expression of pain a way of conceiving what it would be for another person to be in pain. So experiences of expressions of pain as such do not stand in the same relation to the concept *pain* as experiences of things as round stand to the observational concept *round*.

We can distinguish a general challenge and a specific challenge presented by perceptual experiences of another's facial expression as one of pain. The general challenge is to say how these experiences provide a means of coming to know that another person is in pain, consistently with the Target Account. That challenge is general because it arises for anyone who thinks that perceiving such expressions is a way of coming to acquire the relevant knowledge, and who also accepts the Target Account.

For those whose epistemology is of a more rationalist stripe, and who reject pure reliabilism in epistemology, there is also a more specific, local challenge. Must acknowledgement of perception of facial expression as a means of coming to know of another's conscious states be some kind of concession to reliabilism? If not, why not? We have already said that the relation between perception of facial expression and the concept *pain* is not the relation characteristic of observational concepts. It follows that whatever the rationalist treatment of observational knowledge, it is not something applicable to knowledge of others' conscious states. If the content of an experience of another person's facial expression as one of pain is relevant to our entitlement to judge that the other is in pain, why is it so? We know that the basis of the entitlement cannot be the presence of that type of perception in the possession-condition for the concept *pain*: for it is not mentioned in that possession-condition. Does the case show that any rationalist conception of knowledge and entitlement in this area has to be abandoned?

I argue that there is a different, third, way in which an experience as of another's bodily or facial expression of pain can be epistemologically crucial in leading to knowledge without that experience-type being mentioned in the possession-condition for the concept *pain*, and without a reversion to pure reliabilism. The starting point for the argument is a consideration of some of the properties of a visual experience, say, of another's bodily or facial expression as one of pain. In having such an experience, one sees the other's action as of a type that one could make oneself. Asked to perform such an action oneself, when all is working properly no inference or further background information is needed before simply making the action oneself. The causal basis of this ability is no doubt the set of 'mirror' neurons identified by Rizzolati, Gallese, and their colleagues.[19] But the striking properties of the experience do not involve merely a mirroring of the action and its intentionality. At the level of phenomenology, one also sees the other subject's action as one that would in oneself be an expression of pain.

The fact that the actions or movements of one creature are seen by a second as expressions of a mental state which would produce the same expressions in himself is a highly complex state of affairs. The occurrence of such states of affairs calls for explanation. Very likely the best explanation of the occurrence of such states of affairs is that the actions and movements in question really are expressions of pain, say, and their being perceived as such by a second conspecific is an instance of a kind of situation that is self-perpetuating in a species. It is as adaptive to be right, on the whole, about the mental states of one's conspecifics as it is adaptive for one's perceptual experiences about the non-mental world to be by-and-large correct. There will be selection of mechanisms, both individual and social, that perpetuate such correct perception.

This means that one of the forms of argument I developed in *The Realm of Reason* is applicable to the experience of another's action or movement as an expression of pain. You are default-entitled to judge that a condition obtains when it holds in the easiest, most likely way that such experiences come about (and where the status of a condition as such does not depend on a posteriori argument about the detailed nature of the mechanism).

In the case of genuinely observational concepts, I argued in *The Realm of Reason*, the experiences that entitle the thinker to apply those concepts have the content they do in part in virtue of interactions between things actually falling under those contents and the experiences produced by their so falling. Tyler Burge developed the same point.[20] I described such experiences as having 'instance-individuated' contents. An experience of the facial or other

---

[19] Rizzolati et al. (1996); Gallese et al. (2004). The phenomenon is crucial to the perception of depictions and sculpture: see Freedberg and Gallese (2007).
[20] Burge (2003).

bodily movements of another person as expressions of pain does not have an instance-individuated content. Its content is not directly inherited in part from its causation by pain itself. But nonetheless, the simplest, most likely explanation of the occurrence of such an experience does involve interaction between the experiencer and conspecifics who really have the conscious states the experience represents the conspecific as undergoing. This is offered as what I called a Level-3 explanation of entitlement in *The Realm of Reason*, explanations which explain why certain general truths about the entitlement-relation hold. The particular explanation offered here supports only defeasible entitlement. Experiences as of another's action expressing pain can, and sometimes do, have other causal origins. The entitlement to take them at face value is merely prima facie; and it is a good feature of this explanation that it extends only as far as prima facie entitlement.

The explanation is not purely reliabilist. It is rational to make judgements that will be true in the easiest circumstances in which one's actual experiences can come about, and that it is so seems to be an a priori matter. The explanation also turns on the content of the intentional state. It thus conforms to a claim of *The Realm of Reason*, to the effect that all entitlement depends on the nature of the content of the states involved in the entitlement in question. In this way it aims to meet the more specific, local challenge to the rationalist position.

What the argument shows, if sound, is that there are ways in which the content of an entitling state can be crucial to the entitlement to make a judgement without that state entering the possession-condition for any of the concepts in the content of the judgement in question. All the same, in the case in which the experiences as of expressions of pain have come about in the easiest way, the other person will be in pain. Hence he will be in the same state as the subject is in himself when he is in pain; and so the correctness-condition implied by the Target Account of understanding for "The other person is in pain" will be fulfilled.

There may be some doubt as to whether this account really supplies all we need for knowledge that someone else is in pain. In particular, its reliance on the knower and the other person being members of the same species in the case in which one experiences another's action as an expression of pain may seem to be something not found in other cases of knowledge. But it seems to me that knowledge of other aspects of another person, besides knowledge of their conscious states, also relies on identity of underlying mental structures. A clear case, outside the domain of thought about conscious states, is perceiving, and coming to know, that the sentence uttered by another person has a certain syntactic structure. We hear the sentence as having one structure rather than another. We know from the work of Chomsky and of those influenced by him that this knowledge of the structure is substantially underdetermined by the evidence to which we are exposed early in life. An innate endowment common to all humans selects one grammar for a particular language rather than another on the basis of a small sample of evidence. Yet we do know what someone else means when he utters a sentence we have never heard before. This knowledge is partially dependent upon our appreciation of the sentence as having one syntactic structure rather than another; and this appreciation is in turn undergirded by our common grammatical endowment we share with our conspecifics. An account of our knowledge of what someone else is saying, and of the role of our perceptual impression of syntactic structure in that knowledge, has at some point to draw on the fact that we are of the same species, with a common grammatical endowment. This parallels the reliance on shared mental structures in the preceding account of what makes possible knowledge that another human is in pain.

If an intelligent alien seemed to learn our language, and agreed with us on the syntactic construal of sentences hitherto encountered, but suddenly diverged in his construal of a new sentence, we could discover that fact. It would not be something unknowable. If some new being apparently used the word "pain" in the same circumstances as us, but actually meant something different by it, could we discover that fact? It seems clear that such a discovery is possible only if there is supervenience of the mental on the physical facts about this new being (including his complex environmental relations). If supervenience failed, not even the most detailed knowledge of the subject's brain states would give us knowledge of what sensations he is experiencing; and so knowledge of what this being means by the word "pain" would remain inaccessible. There is, then, a tacit commitment to some form of supervenience thesis in the position I have been endorsing. This is one of several points at which the account of understanding in this book involves commitments in metaphysics. If a supervenience thesis of the mental on the physical is true, we certainly do not have at present a full understanding of why it is true, why mental properties supervene on the particular properties they do, and why such a thesis is necessary (if it is necessary). It follows that full understanding of understanding would require a grasp of issues about which we are at present ignorant. Here I am just pointing out the commitments and interconnections of the present account of understanding and a corresponding epistemology for the concept *pain*.

Not every case in which we come to know that someone else is in pain by interaction with that person is one in which we have an experience of some action or movement of his as an expression of pain. Sometimes we know that certain kinds of injury, damage, or relations to other objects and events are painful to the subject without the perception of such states of affairs involving experience of an expression of pain. Under the Target Account, there is no obstacle to using some form of the classical argument from analogy to explain our knowledge in some of these cases. If the Target Account of understanding is correct, uses of the traditional argument from analogy can be legitimate cases of inductive or abductive reasoning, depending on the details of the application. The argument from analogy can never, however, provide an account of what it is to understand the proposition that someone else is in pain. Use of the argument from analogy presupposes that understanding.

Nor is it an option to say that for someone else to be in pain is for there to be such a proper use of the argument from analogy to the conclusion that the other person is in pain. That would be incompatible with our appreciation that abductive and inductive arguments are never conclusive. The fact that they are never conclusive, however strong, is an immediate consequence of—and is thus explained by—the Target Account. However strong the inductive and abductive arguments, their premises never establish completely conclusively (in the manner of deductive arguments) that the other person is in pain. They never do so, because your understanding of what it is for the other to be in pain is that it is for her to be in the same state you are in when you are in pain. That is never conclusively established by the inductive and abductive arguments. But arguments from analogy can be used, non-conclusively, to explain our knowledge in some cases, consistently with the correctness of the Target Account.

So much for one form of epistemology available to the neo-rationalist that would reconcile our actual ways of coming to know of others' conscious states with the Target Account of our understanding of what it is for them to be in those states. The Target Account is of course not the exclusive property of neo-rationalist treatments of concepts. It is neutral on rationalist issues, and can consistently be held by pure reliabilists and by many other positions in epistemology. A pure reliabilist in epistemology could consistently adopt the Target Account of understanding. The reliable mechanism of belief-formation would, for him, be enough for a thinker to come to know the holding of the condition that another is in pain. The knower's understanding of that condition can still be given by the Target Account.

Another position in epistemology consistent with the Target Account of understanding would be one which emphasizes the factive, and knowledge-sustaining, character of the mental state of seeing that the other person is in pain. On some views, a subject's being in this state is enough to explain how he acquires knowledge that the other person is in pain. No further account of how an experience as of the other's being in pain default-entitles one to the judgement that he is in pain is needed, on this view. Someone with these epistemological views could still hold, and accept for the reasons given earlier, the Target Account of the thinker's understanding of what it is for the other person to be in pain. The factive, knowledge-sustaining states are just one way of coming to know that the condition identified in the Target Account obtains.

This is not the place to discuss which one of these epistemological views is to be preferred, an issue primarily in epistemology rather than the theory of understanding. All I want to emphasize here is that the fate of the Target Account is not tied to a neo-rationalist view of entitlement. Its attractive features are available on several different epistemological views. It is available, without revisionism, to any epistemology that can offer an adequate account of how, under the terms of that epistemology, the correctness-condition for "That person is in pain", as identified by the Target Account, can be known by the person who understands that condition.

8. COMMUNICABILITY: BETWEEN FREGE AND WITTGENSTEIN

There has in many prominent writers been some tacit or explicit acceptance of the idea that if identity were to feature in our understanding of thoughts about conscious states in the way the Target Account proposes, that would imply the possibility of a private language for conscious states, a language that only one person could understand. My position is just the opposite. The Target Account, as an explication of understanding, helps to explain how communication between different subjects about their respective conscious states is possible at all.[21]

---

[21] A very straightforward endorsement of a link between what I have called the Target Account and commitment to the possibility of a private language is made in Dummett (1978a, preface).

If you and I both have experiences of pain, and each of us understands what it is for another to be in pain in the terms given in the Target and Interlocking Accounts, it follows that we have the same understanding of what it is for the other to be in pain. Is it a good objection to this that our samples of pain are numerically distinct, and so our concepts must be distinct? If that were a good objection, one would have to say that you and I have distinct concepts of a tomato if we learn it from different instances; and this seems far too strong. There are plenty of metaphysical differences between tomatoes and mental events, but actual distinctness of samples that have been the basis of different thinkers' mastery of the concept is much too weak a basis to sustain distinctness of concept. The two thinkers can still be latching on to the same property; and that is exactly what I have been arguing that two thinkers can each do with the concept *pain*. It is identity of property that is important here, not identity of instances.

The fact that an account entails that distinct thinkers have the same concept of pain does not of course absolve it of the charge of privacy. If we are to explain why concepts of conscious states are not private concepts, we have to show how distinct thinkers not only share the same concept, but can also know that they do. Understanding and privacy are epistemological notions, and do not turn solely on identity of concept. Understanding another's utterance involves knowing what is being said. That is why it was important, in the preceding section 6, to argue that the Target Account is consistent with the knowability of the Thought that another is in pain. If you can know that someone else is in pain, you can be in a position to know whether he means pain by "pain". It is highly plausible that if you cannot know whether another person is in pain, you also will be unable to know whether some word of his means *pain*. Your attempts to know what he means will in those circumstances be vulnerable to what I called 'switching' arguments, that many different assignments of these allegedly private states as the references of his words will equally be consistent with all your evidence, however extensive.[22] At this point, I am in agreement with the spirit, and even the letter, of some of the later Wittgenstein's remarks.

After attributing to Peter Strawson acceptance of what is essentially the Target Account, Dummett writes, 'Strawson here unblushingly rejects that whole polemic of Wittgenstein's that has come to be known as "the private-language" argument' (p. xxxii). Actually we know from Strawson's other writings that he has doubts about the polemic anyway (and without blushing—see Strawson 1954). My point is that the Target Account does not involve a commitment to the kind of privacy against the possibility of which Wittgenstein was arguing.

[22] Peacocke (1988).

The position I am advocating is then intermediate between that of Frege and Wittgenstein on sensation concepts. It seems they both held that any explication of concepts of conscious states that involves recognition of state-type and use of an identity-relation would lead to incommunicability, privacy, and to no more than an individual understanding of expressions falling short of genuinely shared, public meaning. Frege concluded that some aspects of experience are incommunicable. As he concisely wrote, 'What is purely intuitable is not communicable.'[23] Wittgenstein concluded that the model of recognition and identity must be wrong, at least for the case of conscious states. I am proposing a middle way. The model of recognition and grasp of identity is right even in the case of concepts of conscious states; but it does not lead to privacy of meaning and incommunicability. To set out the positions in tabular form:

	Frege	Wittgen-stein	Present Account
Understanding involves identity and Target Account	Yes	No	Yes
Private language is possible	Yes	No	No

9. CONCLUSIONS AND SIGNIFICANCE

If the Target Account gives a correct account of our ability to think about conscious states, it should not be surprising that we can make major errors of theory about our conscious states, consistently with our still thinking about them. What makes our thought thought about pain, or about visual experience, or about mental calculation, has nothing to do with any kind of theory we may have about any of those states or events. Albritton and Putnam emphasized that we may be bizarrely wrong about the nature of pencils, or other things in our environment, while still

---

[23] Frege (1953, §26, p. 35); and 'Often ... a colour word does not signify our subjective sensation, which we cannot know to agree with anyone else's ... ' (§26, p. 36). By the time, many years later, that he wrote 'Thoughts', Frege did not think that it even makes sense to say that different persons' sense-impressions are subjectively the same: 'For when the word "red" is meant not to state a property of things but to characterize sense-impressions belonging to my consciousness, it is only applicable within the realm of my consciousness' (Frege 1977: 14–15).

thinking about them.[24] The same goes for conscious mental events and states. Many people naively think we withdraw our hand from very hot radiators because of the pain caused. Yet we know it is a reflex, and we know that the causal line that ends up with the withdrawal of the hand does not involve the pain at all (which can occur after the hand's withdrawal has already begun). This should not make us think that those who do not know it is a reflex are not thinking about pain. The same goes for grander theories involving pain and other conscious states. Our thought about conscious states and events is not thought about whatever plays such-and-such role in a theory, whatever kind of theory might be proffered to play this part.

The other, much more general, conclusion concerns the role of reference in the theory of understanding and concept-possession. The account of understanding concepts for conscious states and events offered here can be seen as attributing to the thinker tacit knowledge of the rule that *pain* is true of those events that feel to one a certain way now, and of those events at other times and in other subjects that are events of the same (subjective) kind as those that feel that way. The understanding involves knowledge of an identity of properties, something at the level of reference, not sense or concepts. I have tried to show how some of the epistemic and cognitive aspects of concepts of conscious states can be explained in accordance with tacit knowledge of this reference rule. The preceding discussion can therefore be seen as putting together one part of the jigsaw we need to complete if we are to argue successfully that the epistemic properties of an arbitrary concept are explicable from properties of its fundamental reference rule. If the pieces have been put together properly for the case of concepts of conscious states, they offer support for that general thesis about the relation between concepts and their reference-relations.

---

[24] The example is attributed to Albritton in Putnam (1975c: 242–5). The case is in the spirit of the examples in Putnam's earlier (1962) 'It Ain't Necessarily So' (Putnam 1975d).

6

'Another I': Representing Perception and Action

What is it for a thinker to possess the concept of perceptual experience? What is it to be able to think of seeings, hearings, and touchings, and to be able to think of experiences that are subjectively like seeings, hearings, and touchings?

This question is of philosophical interest for multiple reasons in addition to the agenda of Part II of this book. To understand, explain, and predict the thought and action of others, you must know what they perceive. This requires you to possess the concept of perception, or at least to represent in some form that the other person perceives. Each of us every day rests his life on his correct application of the concept of perception. When you cross the road, or drive, your future depends on your ability to know that someone else sees you.

The concept of perception is also crucial to more first-personal projects of thought. To assess critically the way you reach your own judgments, to revise and improve your methods of reaching beliefs, requires you to be capable of thinking of the perceptual experiences that led you to make or withhold various judgements. You can do this only if you are capable of thinking of your own perceptions.

The question of what it is to possess the concept of perception is also of interest to the philosophy of mind more generally. Perception is one of the mind's states that relate it most directly to the non-mental world. Can a good treatment of possession of the concept of perception provide a model for possession of concepts of other mental states with distinctively close relations to the world? Do features of a good treatment generalize? And do they permit us to make sense of the striking empirical phenomena displayed by children's acquisition of the concept of perception? These are some of the questions I will be attempting to address.

A perceiving thinker who has the capacity to appreciate that others also perceive is on the way to thinking of others as subjects like himself—to thinking of another person as 'another I', in Zeno's phrase. 'Another I' was reportedly Zeno's answer to the question 'What is a friend?' If we strip the notion of thinking of someone as 'another I' of the elements of identification and sympathy that Zeno no doubt intended, Zeno's phrase captures perfectly what is involved in thinking of another as a subject like oneself. It is a real challenge to say what is involved in such thinking. I will try to indicate in the course of this chapter points at which the approach aims to contribute to meeting that challenge in more detail than the somewhat abstract account of the conception of many subjects I developed in Chapter 5.

I start by considering the first-person case, that in which a thinker judges that he himself sees. The philosophical theory of self-ascription is a domain in which Gareth Evans made original, important, and influential contributions, notably on the self-ascription of belief.[1] Evans showed how treatments that are in various respects outward-looking do not merely accommodate the distinctive epistemic features of first-person thought. An outward-looking treatment is actually required if we are to do justice to those distinctive epistemic features. While Evans's own remarks on the different topic of the self-ascription of experience are briefer than his remarks on the self-ascription of belief, and though I shall be offering an alternative account, I hope that what I present here respects the generally outward-looking reorientation that he recommended.

After proposing a treatment of the first-person case, and some of its epistemic and metaphysical ramifications (sections 1–2), I go on to compare it with Evans's account (section 3). From that I move to discuss the relation between first-person and third-person ascription, and the explanation of some developmental phenomena (section 4). I conclude with a discussion of the extension of the model presented to the self-ascription and other-ascription of action and intentionality (section 5).

1. THE CORE RULE

Aristotle held that it is by sight that you perceive that you see.[2] The heart of Aristotle's idea seems to me right, provided that we understand it as follows: it is by sight that you know that you see. Suppose you see that

That desk is covered with papers.

---

[1] Evans (1982: 225–6).
[2] *On the Soul* 3.2, 425^{b}12–17, passage starting 'Since we perceive that we are seeing and hearing…' (Aristotle 1995).

This visual knowledge about the world gives you a good reason to make the self-ascriptive judgement

I see that that desk is covered with papers.

This is a transition you are entitled to make, from a conscious state you enjoy to a judgement. If a thinker comes to judge, by this means, that he sees that that desk is covered with papers, his judgement can thereby be knowledge. 'By this means' here is intended to include the fulfilment of the following conditions: the thinker's visual experience is part of the causal explanation of the self-ascription of seeing; the visual experience is also his reason for making the self-ascription; and it is specifically the content of the visual experience that is the thinker's reason for making the self-ascription, rather than some inference from what is seen to be the case. A thinker is not making a self-ascription by the intended means when, for instance, on reading the newspaper he says sincerely "I see the Mets lost last night's game", nor when seeing his friend driving a Mercedes, he says, sincerely, "I see you are driving a German car". What he sees to be the case in these examples is certain sentences with the meaning that the Mets lost, and that his friend is driving a Mercedes. These are the seeings he can self-ascribe by the means in question.

This is the starting point of a general model of self-ascriptive knowledge of one's own perceptual states. Because the thinker sees that

p

he moves, rationally, to the judgement

I see that p

and thereby gains knowledge that he so sees. If a thinker comes to judge that he sees that p in this way, and does so by the means specified in the preceding paragraph, then he is following what I call the Core Rule. More specifically, it is the Core Rule for vision, for the case of seeing-that. One can equally formulate the Core Rule for other sense modalities. Here sense modalities are regarded as individuated by their phenomenology, rather than by the identity of the sense organs whose states cause perceptions in the modality.

Following the Core Rule for seeing does not require the thinker to have the concept of seeing-that in advance. It just requires a differential sensitivity to the cases in which one sees that something is the case, as opposed to perceiving it in some other modality, or knowing it not through the senses at all. A thinker may also be in error about whether a state is a seeing-that. But in a case in which he seems to be seeing that something is the case, he is entitled, absent reasons for doubt, to make the transition to a self-ascription of a seeing. Here, as in the case of entitlement to perceptual beliefs, I would argue that the factive entitling state is more fundamental in explaining the nature of the entitlement relation than is the non-factive state of having an experience as of seeing that p.[3]

It would be a misunderstanding of the Core Rule to think that following it involves making a transition from a belief or judgement that one is seeing. Rather, following the Core Rule involves making a transition from a seeing-that itself. Since the conclusion of the Core Rule is that one sees that p, that misunderstanding of the Core Rule would construe it as making a transition from one content to the same content again. It would also be a transition from a state that presupposes that the thinker already has the concept of seeing.

The state of seeing that p is not merely factive. To be in the state also requires that the person who enjoys that state knows that p.[4] This means that circumstances in which a subject doubts the deliverances of his visual experiences are not counter-examples to the Core Rule, for they are not circumstances in which the subject sees that p. It is, however, possible to identify a variant notion of seeing something x to be F which is factive, but which implies neither knowledge that p nor belief that p on the part of the subject. The possession-condition for this notion would have to involve something with more complex input conditions than the Core Rule has. Someone can be in such a state of seeing something x to be F, without accepting that x is F, and hence without self-ascribing such a factive state of seeing. The possession-condition for this notion would have to ensure a restriction to the cases in which the subject does take his perception at face value. It would also have to ensure that the notion of seeing x to be F can be correctly self-applied even when the subject does not think it can be.[5]

One can also formulate a Core Rule for seeing an object, as opposed to seeing-that. Suppose our subject x sees object o, under mode of presentation m. Then he is entitled to judge

I see m.

---

[3] For some reasons in support of this position, see Peacocke (2004, ch. 4 sect. 1(*d*)).
[4] Here I am in agreement with Timothy Williamson (2002: 37–8).
[5] The remarks in this paragraph result from reflection on some helpful comments from Susanna Siegel.

Here of course the mode of presentation *m* is employed in our subject *x*'s thought, rather than mentioned. The resulting judgement is about the object presented under *m*, namely the object perceived, rather than being about *m*. *m* might be expressed linguistically by the phrase "that door over there", accompanied by a pointing gesture. A full characterization of *m* would specify the egocentrically identified apparent location of the perceived object in relation to the subject, and the way in which the object is perceived. In both this most recent case of object-seeing, and the preceding case of seeing-that, it is the subject's seeing, of the respective kinds, that makes rational the subject's judgement about his seeing.

What I have given so far can be described as the positive part of the Core Rule. There is also a negative part, having to do with the conditions under which a thinker is entitled to judge that he does not see that *p*. If a subject is not in a position to judge, knowledgeably, that *p*, simply by virtue of what he sees to be the case, then he certainly does not see that *p*, and no further information is needed to establish that he does not see that *p*. If a thinker does not see that *p*, then he is entitled to judge

$$\sim(\text{I see that } p).$$

I call this the negative component of the Core Rule.

Here there is a difference between the concept of seeing-that, and an observational concept. No such negative clause as we have just given for the case of seeing-that holds for an observational concept. From the fact that some speck or tiny dot, for instance, is not experienced by the subject as square, even when it is being observed, it does not follow that it is not square. Its shape may just be too small to see, or be perceived in any other of the subject's sense modalities. This difference is one of the marks which distinguishes possession of an objective concept of things in the world from possession of a psychological concept like seeing-that.

I suggest that following the Core Rule for any given sense modality is part of (one clause of) the possession-condition for the concept of perceptual experience in that modality. To possess the concept of visual experience, the thinker must be following the Core Rule for vision; and so forth.

The Core Rule is not, and could not be, an exhaustive account of what it is to be able to judge the content "I see that *p*". That content contains the first person, and the present tense, which also have a life outside judgements of "I see that *p*". The Core Rule is just one piece of a jigsaw. Other pieces of the jigsaw are required to have a full picture of mastery of "I see that p". The other pieces would be accounts of mastery of the other conceptual constituents of "I see that p". It is a more general task in the philosophy of mind to describe these other pieces correctly, and to show how they interlock to form a full picture of mastery of "I see that p".

I further suggest that what I shall call the "Extended Core Rule" for vision is a component of the possession-condition for the concept of visual experience, considered as applicable both in perceptual and in the illusory, or more strictly non-perceptual, case. The Extended Core Rule, in the case of vision, states that if the thinker is in a state that is subjectively as if he sees that p (at least in respect of his visual experience), or subjectively as if he sees an object given under mode of presentation m (in respect of his visual experience), then he is entitled to judge

I have a visual experience as of p's being the case

or

I have a visual experience as of m

respectively. A subject's judgement of such a content, made for the reason that he is in the entitling state, can in ordinary circumstances be knowledge.

'Subjectively similar in respect of his visual experience' should not be taken as equivalent to 'producing the same dispositions to judgement'. What a subject is disposed to judge need not be part of the content of his perceptual experience (nor need any non-conceptual content to which the content of the judgement is constitutively tied). I cannot make the point better than does an entertaining example of Edward Craig's.

Let us suppose that I have an elderly acquaintance whom, perhaps because of his large moustache and upright bearing, I find myself constantly thinking of as a retired colonel. I do not believe him to be such, since I have every reason to think that he has never had anything to do with the army, but on the other hand it is not just that I keep imagining him as a retired colonel. … For instance, in spite of my knowledge of his real background, I have a strange feeling that I would not be surprised if he were suddenly to start telling me the story of some campaign or other. And on an occasion when we were watching a television documentary about the Second World War together I suddenly found that I had slipped unawares into treating him as if he were an expert on tactics, and had confidently put to him a fairly technical question about the manoeuvrability of tanks. Or again, I once felt momentarily embarrassed when a third person, in his presence, made a disparaging remark about military academies, although I knew 'the colonel' to have no particular feelings about such institutions.[6]

Craig is here describing a disposition to believe. It is also true in this example—or the example could easily be elaborated in such a way—that if the subject did not have the information that the man is not a colonel, he would believe on the basis of his perception that the man is a colonel. Nonetheless, the subject's experience even in this example does not itself represent the man as a colonel. It represents him only as having a moustache and upright bearing. Two subjects could each be perceiving this man with a moustache, and perceive him visually in the same way, even though one of them has the particular dispositions to believe that Craig describes and the other does not. The man need not look any different when our subject loses the disposition to believe that the man with the moustache is a colonel. The description "he looks like a colonel" is fine, but this means: he is seen to have properties that are thought to be characteristic of colonels. Some inclinations to judge may also be conscious—as they are in Craig's example—but we should always distinguish the phenomenology of conscious thinking from that of perceptual experience. (There is more on the phenomenology of conscious thought in Chapter 7.) In making these remarks, I should add that I do not mean that only spatial and material properties and relations can enter the content of visual experience itself. Visual experience may be of one event causing a second, may be an experience of a face that is expressing anger, may be an experience of another's bodily movement as an action. While it is important to distinguish the content of experience from the content of other mental states and events such as judgement, that does not mean we should have an impoverished conception of the range of contents that experience may enjoy.

The Extended Core Rule will, perhaps surprisingly, not cover all cases in which someone is entitled to self-ascribe an experience with a given content. Consider an experience as of looking at the 'impossible' object constructed by Penrose. This is a triangular 3D model, similar to prototypes drawn by Escher, which when viewed from a certain angle gives an experience in which corner A seems to be closer to the viewer than corner B, corner B seems to be closer than corner C, and yet corner C seems to be closer than corner A.[7] (It is

---

[6] Craig (1976: 16–17). Craig in fact uses the example to support a different point.
[7] For photographs of Penrose's 'impossible object', see Gregory (1974: 369; and also 1970: 54–7).

not really so, of course.) Now a thinker cannot soundly reach a self-ascription of this experience by relying on an experience subjectively of the same kind as an experience in which he sees that this content holds. Since the content is inconsistent, there are no such genuine seeings that it holds, nor could there be. Hence there are no experiences that are subjectively similar to such genuine seeings.

One way to attribute the correct content to the experience, e, of seeing the model is as follows. (I do not claim it is the only solution to the problem; there may well be others.) e is subjectively similar to genuine seeing e' that A is closer than B; it is subjectively similar to a genuine seeing e'' in which it is seen that B is closer than C; and it is subjectively similar to a genuine seeing e''' in which it is seen that C is closer than A. The content of e is thus determined by its subjective similarity-relations to several genuine seeings, and not all of these seeings can be identical with one another. We call this "the multiple similarity" solution to the problem. We will henceforth take the Extended Core Rule to employ a notion of subjective similarity for an experience that allows such similarity to be determined by multiple similarities to different genuine seeings.

There are many attractive consequences of incorporating the Core Rule into the possession-condition for the concept of experience.

(*a*) It explains and justifies the sense in which one's own perceptions are not given to one in any mode other than is made available simply by the ability to have the perception itself. A fortiori, the perception is not given in some further perceptual mode. Despite some divergences to be noted later, this is a point on which I am in agreement with Gareth Evans when, in *The Varieties of Reference*, he writes: '[The subject's] internal state cannot in any sense become an *object* to him. (He is *in* it.)'[8]

Evans's remark is a little Delphic, but it has a natural elucidation. Whenever we perceive some spatial, material object or event, we perceive it in some sense modality. When something is perceived in some sense modality, it becomes an object to the subject. The modality in which one perceives some particular chair—be it by sight, or touch—is not in any way a priori determined by the object or the event itself. In the case of a particular perception, however, there is a way in which the perception is given in thought that does not involve any sense modality not fixed by the event itself. The mode in which

---

[8] Evans (1982: 227).

the perceptual experience is given to the thinker who enjoys the experience is a priori determined by the perception itself. No further sense modality is involved. I refer to this feature of thought about perception as its unadorned character.

What is the explanation of the difference between the unadorned character of a subject's thought about his own perceptions, and the adorned character of his perceptual thought about spatial, material objects and events? The explanation is that perceptual experience is itself a conscious state that can thereby function as a reason for the thinker to make judgements. It can enter the possession-condition for concepts in a way that spatial, material objects, events, or states of affairs in themselves, not considered as given in any particular sense modality, cannot.

(*b*) Incorporating the Core Rule into the possession-condition is the first step towards capturing the respect in which the concept of perception is first-personal. If the Core Rule is part of the possession-condition for the concept of perception, then there is a clause dealing specifically with first-person application in the possession-condition.

It is important to formulate sharply the sense in which the concept of perception is first-personal, if the Core Rule is correct. Quite generally, it is not sufficient for a concept F to be first-personal that there is a special way of coming to know that one is F oneself. There is a special way, in ordinary circumstances, of coming to know that one is touching one's own toes, but the general concept *x is touching x's toes* is not one that involves the first person in any deep way. One's knowledge of what it is for an arbitrary thing to be touching its toes does not in itself have specific connections with the first person. The deeper sense in which the first person is involved in the general concept of seeing something to be so is that one's knowledge of what it is for an arbitrary thing to have that property makes reference in one way or another to what is involved in first-person ascription of that property (unlike one's grasp of *x is touching x's toes*).

I say 'makes reference in one way or another', because there is more than one way in which there can be such a connection to first-person ascriptions. One way is that discussed in the preceding chapter, and criticized by Wittgenstein: the idea that your conception of what is involved in another person's having a certain sensation is that they are having the same type of experience as you when you are in pain, that is, when you can truly self-ascribe the concept *pain*. But that is not the only way in which there can be a special connection between the understanding of the general property and the first person, and I shall describe another way a few paragraphs hence.

For enthusiasts of the study of first-person thought, I note also that the occurrence of the first person in "I see that p" when it is reached in this way is representationally independent, in the sense I used in *Being Known*.[9] That is, when the thinker is following the Core Rule, his reason for judging as he does is not that he is in some state with the representational content "I see that p", which he then takes at face value. His reason is simply his being in the state of seeing that p.

(*c*) The clause containing the Core Rule can explain why self-ascriptions of perception made in this way are rational, and can yield knowledge. Any context in which a thinker follows the Core Rule for, say, the visual case, will be a context with respect to which the self-ascription "I see that p" will also be true. This generalization holds because the concept self-ascribed by the use of this Rule requires for the correctness of this application precisely that the subject be in the state that he is in fact in when he meets the input-condition for the application of this Rule, namely that he sees that p. Self-ascriptions of seeings made by following the Core Rule are correct because of the nature of the concepts and states involved in it.[10] The entitlement to make a self-ascription of a seeing in the given circumstances also correspondingly respects the general principle that corresponding to every entitlement, there is an objective norm of correctness.

(*d*) All experiences with representational content, whether genuine perceptions or hallucinations, are, in respect of the sense modalities in which they occur, subjectively as if they are perceptions. (This is why there is such thing as taking perceptual experience at face value in the first place.) Not only is this a feature of the subjective experiences themselves; it is also a feature that seems to be immediately obvious to us when we think of perceptual experience as perceptual experience. If our account of possession of the concept of perceptual experience incorporates the Core Rule and the Extended Core Rule, we can explain this fact. The Extended Core Rule implies that anything that is thought of as a perceptual experience is thought of as the same, subjectively, as an experience in which one genuinely perceives

---

[9] Peacocke (1999: 266–74).

[10] That is, the Core Rule respects what I called 'the second principle of rationalism', in Peacocke (2004, ch. 2). See further in that book, and Peacocke (1992, ch. 6, p. 157) for further discussion of the links between possession-conditions, the rationality of a transition in thought, and attaining knowledge.

something to be the case. Incorporating the Extended Core Rule and the Core Rule into the account of possession of the concept of perceptual experience explains our appreciation of the primacy of the genuinely perceptual case in the phenomenology of perceptual experience. This primacy of the fully veridical case must be present in any other domain to which the Core Rule and Extended Core Rule generalize.[11]

(*e*) Incorporating the Core Rule into the possession-condition for the concept of seeing plausibly implies that one cannot fully possess the concept of seeing unless one knows what it is like to see. A plausible account of knowing what it is like to be in a given kind of conscious state is that one possesses a capacity to recognize that one is in that state, on the basis of being in that state. But this is precisely what one does in following the Core Rule.

If grasp of the Core Rule is required for full understanding of the concept *seeing that p*, for a given *p*, then someone who does not know which kinds of seeings would entitle her to self-ascribe "I see that that light is red" does not have a full grasp of the concept of seeing something to be red. 'Knowing which kinds of seeing' here requires knowing how the light would have to be seen for the Core Rule to be applicable. This is a form of knowledge that involves a recognitional capacity, the capacity to recognize the colour when it is demonstratively given in perception. Lack of this recognitional capacity, and ignorance about which kinds of seeings license the application of the Core Rule, is precisely the situation of Frank Jackson's Mary, when she is confined to her black-and-white room, and is in receipt of information about the world only through black-and-white books and black-and-white television.[12] The account I am offering supports Jackson's claim that 'after Mary sees her first ripe tomato, she will realize how impoverished her conception of the mental life of *others* has been *all along*'.[13] Ordinary practices in the ascription of attitudes license us to say that Mary, when confined to the black-and-white room, does know that others outside the room see things to be red—the lecturers on her television set will have told her so, in those very words. But there is a strong pre-theoretical intuition that she does not fully understand what this means. That pre-theoretical intuition is vindicated if grasp of the Core Rule is required for full understanding of predications of the concept *seeing that that light is red*.

---

[11] I would argue that this feature is present for the generalization given in sect. 5 below.
[12] Jackson (1986).   [13] Jackson (1986: 292).

(*f*) Perceiving that *p* is certainly an externally individuated state, for many reasons. For the perceptual state to have the intentional content *p* is for it to be of a kind that stands in certain complex environmental relations to what it represents as being the case. In addition, on a particular occasion, whether someone is perceiving that *p* depends on their relations to external states of affairs on that particular occasion. Further still, perceiving that *p* is a form of knowing that *p*, and whether one knows something depends in part on what could easily have been the case (on what happens in nearby possible worlds, as one says). What could easily have been the case is something that depends on multiple conditions concerning matters far outside the perceiver's head. If, as I am suggesting, the concept *x perceives that p* is individuated by its connections with the externally individuated relation of perceiving that *p*, then it follows that the concept is also externally individuated. So this is another case in which not only the intentional content of a state is externally individuated, but so is the psychological relation to the intentional content.

More specifically, on the present treatment the concept of perception is what I have called 'instance-individuated', in the sense I discussed in *The Realm of Reason*.[14] Although a possession-condition for the concept of perception that incorporates the Core Rule emphatically does not treat it as an observational concept, it does share one feature with observational concepts. It entails that in order to possess the concept, the thinker must be willing to apply the concept in response to instances of the concept. Some psychological concepts, as well as observational concepts, have this property. This is another example of externalism about the internal that we noted in Chapter 5 section 5. This internal externalism is consistent with the unadorned character of a subject's thought about his own perceptions.

(*g*) As Mark Crimmins noted to me, a thinker can employ the Core Rule for seeing without having much idea at all of how sight works, either of its neurophysiological and computational bases, or of light as the environmental medium of transmission of the information of visual information.[15] This attractive feature will be present in some of the later applications of the Core Rule.

(*h*) The Core Rule vindicates the Aristotelian-like doctrine that it is by sight that you know that you see. It does this without any regress in the

---

[14] In Peacocke (2004, chs 2–4).   [15] Personal communication, 2003.

content of seeing, and without any attribution of reflexivity in the content of the seeing.[16]

The Core Rule also has some implications for the theory of epistemic entitlement and norms. If the Core Rule is part of the possession-condition for the concept of perceptual experience, then the most fundamental way of coming to know that, for instance, one is seeing something is by first making a perceptually based judgement about the non-mental world beyond oneself. For this reason, one can classify this position on self-ascription of experience as an 'Outside-In' theory.

It follows that it cannot be correct to say that our basic means of knowing by perception about the external world is first by knowing that we see something, or see something to be the case. Under the present approach, that is precisely the reverse of the correct order of epistemic entitlement.

The second implication of the position for epistemic entitlement concerns the transmission of warrant. It is sometimes said that warrant cannot be transmitted from an observational judgement that p made on the basis of visual perception to the conclusion "I see that p". On the present position, warrant is transmitted in that transition. In fact the paradigm of entitlement is when a judgement is made in accordance with the possession-condition for some concept in the content of the judgement, and the truth-preservingness of this transition follows from the nature of the concepts and contents involved in the transition. (This was the thesis of chapters 1 and 2 of *The Realm of Reason*.) If that property is not sufficient for entitlement, it is questionable whether anything ever is. But it is, on the present approach, that property that is present when one judges "I see that p" on the basis of seeing that p.

This is of course not to imply that we have here any kind of answer to scepticism about perception. The sceptic is questioning whether we are really ever entitled to take perception at face value. According to him, we never really get as far as the first line of the transition in the Core Rule. If we cannot know that p perceptually, we never see that p, since seeing that p implies knowing that p. But if we do get as far as that, there is nothing erroneous or unwarranted in making the transition to "I see that p".

---

[16] For extensive discussion of issues of regress and reflexivity, and historical references, see Caston (2002). I believe the Core Rule meets many of the desiderata Caston formulates, and ought to be considered either as a possible interpretation of Aristotle, or as a thesis doing justice to his best insights on this matter.

It is a corollary of these points that it cannot be a correct account of what entitles one to make an observational judgement with the content that *p* about the non-mental world that one has first to be entitled to judge that one perceives that *p*. If the present view is correct, exactly the reverse order of entitlement holds. This is a corollary that should constrain discussions of the nature of perceptual entitlement.[17]

The Core Rule, in its two parts, together with the Extended Core Rule, can be compared with a competing rule, one we might call an "Inside-In" Rule. This 'Inside-In' Rule states, as a primitive rule, that when a thinker has a visual experience as of its being the case that *p*, he can judge 'I have a visual experience as of *p*'s being the case'; and similarly for other modalities. Why should we not use the Inside-In Rule in giving a possession-condition for the concepts of experience and perception?

It can hardly be objected that the Inside-In Rule is incorrect. On the contrary, what it proposes as primitive is a consequence of the Core Rule plus the Extended Rule. If someone has a visual experience as of *p*'s being the case, then he is in a state that is subjectively similar to the state he is in when he can apply the Core Rule. Hence, by the Extended Core Rule, he can judge 'I have a visual experience as of *p*'s being the case'. The question is not, then, of whether the Inside-In Rule is correct, but rather: is the Inside-In Rule fundamental, or is it merely consequential?

If the Inside-In Rule is consequential, what is the rule for self-ascribing seeings? If seeings are fundamentally conceived of as visual experiences that additionally stand in the right kind of relation to environmental states, the question arises of what kind of grounds a thinker can have for thinking that he stands in the right kind of relation. What, for example, under this approach would give the thinker rational grounds for self-ascribing a seeing in quite ordinary circumstances in which he really does see? The obvious answer to this question is that we know that the visual experience stands in the right relations to be a seeing when indeed we see, so we can self-ascribe a seeing. That is quite right; but it evidently relies on the Core Rule, rather than on the Inside-In Rule together with additional materials. I conjecture that if we try to take as fundamental in the order of explanation of understanding a neutral notion of visual experience, whose content may or may not be

---

[17] The point bears on the diagnosis of what is wrong with Moore's 'Proof of an External World' (Moore 1993). If the arguments of the text above are sound, what is wrong with Moore's 'Proof' cannot be that in making the perceptual judgement 'Here is a hand', he is already relying on the proposition that he is perceiving. For further discussion, see Peacocke (2004, ch. 4 sect. 1(*c*)).

correct, and try to build up to mastery of a notion of genuine perception by additional conditions, without using the Core Rule, we will never reach our intended destination in a way that makes sense of ordinary self-ascription. We have to take the genuinely perceptual case as fundamental both in the explanation of understanding, and in the account of the nature of perceptual states themselves.

2. MODAL STATUS AND ITS SIGNIFICANCE

We should distinguish the following two kinds of transition. First, there is a transition from

seeing that p

to the judgement

I see that p.

When someone makes a transition because it is of the displayed form, the fact that he is in the state of seeing that p is part of the explanation of his moving to the judgement that he sees that p. In a second kind of transition, the thinker moves from an accepted content

p

where p is one made available by his seeing—perhaps because it contains a visual perceptual demonstrative such as *that desk*—to the judgement

I see that p.

Transitions of this second kind are not metaphysically necessary. It is metaphysically possible that that desk (actually given in perception) is covered with papers and you do not see that it is covered with papers. In some other possible circumstances, that desk is covered with papers and you are facing away from it, or you are not in the room at all, or your eyes are closed. Not only is this possible: on your ordinary understanding of the notions involved, you also have some appreciation that it is possible. This appreciation is reflected in—amongst other things—your assessment of the truth-values of counterfactuals. We accept as true the counterfactual 'If you had not entered the study, you would not have seen that that desk is covered with papers, but it would still have been covered with papers'. The most we can say about transitions of the second kind is that in any context in which the premiss is seen to be true, the conclusion will also be true. That is, the transition meets a condition that is a variant of Kaplan's notion of logical validity in the logic of demonstratives.[18] But this is well known to fall short of metaphysical necessity.

The fact that transitions of the second kind are not metaphysically necessary raises a question about the concept of seeing. In what features of the concept is this possibility founded? Can the possession-condition for the concept of seeing explain the possibility? What does the explanation show about other treatments of the concept of seeing?

If we consider just the thought-contents involved, the possibility of modal divergence between *That desk is covered with papers* and *I see that that desk is covered with papers* is quite unsurprising. *That desk is covered with papers* has a categorical truth-condition, which is fulfilled with respect to some arbitrary possible state of affairs *s* provided that it holds, with respect to *s*, that that same desk has the categorical property of being covered with papers. For *I see that that desk is covered with papers,* as thought by you, to hold with respect to *s*, it has to hold with respect to *s* that you stand in the same psychological relation to the content *that desk is covered with papers* as you do when in the actual world you see that that desk is covered with papers.[19] It seems clear that nothing rules out that *s* meets the first condition without meeting the second. The fact that this can be the case is part of our conception of objectivity of the world we perceive, and of our conception of the mind-dependence of perception.

The reason there is a special problem in accounting for these modal truths about the concept of perception is that the concept is a member of a family for which the possession-condition is given by reference to a psychological state that makes application of the concept rational, a family for which there is, thereby, also what it is natural to call a "cantilevering" problem. The concept of seeing, other concepts of perception, concepts of sensation, and observational concepts of material objects and events are each concepts that, in very different ways, all have possession-conditions that mention a psychological state that makes application of the concept reasonable. What makes a concept an observational one is that a certain perceptual experience gives reason for applying the concept to a perceptually given object. What

---

[18] Kaplan (1989).
[19] This is an application of the Modal Extension Principle I developed in the treatment of necessity in Peacocke (1999, ch. 4: 'Necessity').

makes a concept a concept of sensation is that certain sensations themselves give reason for self-ascribing the concept of sensation; and so forth. (These facts about reasons for applying the concept are all derivative from the fundamental reference rule for the concept, if Chapter 2 is correct.) Now in all of these cases, the psychological states that give reason for applying the concepts give reason only for making a judgement that contains a particular favoured kind of mode of presentation of the object to which the concept applies. The particular favoured kind of mode of presentation, or way of thinking, in question is that of the first person for concepts of perception and sensation. The particular favoured kind of mode of presentation in the case of observational concepts is that of perceptual modes of presentation of objects and events. But the concept in question applies to objects not given in the favoured way. People other than oneself can see, perceive in other modalities, and have sensations. Objects other than those perceptually presented to the thinker can have observational properties. And in other possible states of affairs, there are determinate truths about the extension of all of these concepts, even though of course a rational response to a psychological state (or to its absence) in the application of one of these concepts can in the nature of the case only be a rational response to an actual psychological state (or an actual absence). So in all of these cases, it is a task for a philosophical theory of concepts to explain how the concept applies beyond those cases that are given in the favoured ways. This is what I mean by the cantilevering problem.

I suggest that the cantilevering we need in the case of the concept of seeing to the modal cases is supplied by a piece of tacit knowledge that involves grasp of a sameness relation, along the lines we discussed in Chapters 1 and 4. Someone who possesses the concept of seeing tacitly knows that for it to be true with respect to a given possible situation that he sees that p, he must be in the same psychological state as he is when he reaches the judgement "I see that p" by following the Core Rule in the actual world. He will not be in the same psychological state in a possible state of affairs in which, though that desk is covered with papers, he is not in the same room, and does not see the desk at all. The presence of an element of tacit knowledge involving a sameness relation is not at all unique to the possession-condition for the concept of seeing, or to other concepts of perceptual states. We argued in Chapter 1 that it exists too for observational concepts.

The resulting position presents a further challenge to a claim that seems to be present in the writings of the later Wittgenstein, beyond the challenge developed in Chapter 5. I argued there against Wittgenstein's idea that grasp of identity of state is to be explained in terms of the truth of two predications of the state in question. The present point about the concept of seeing goes beyond those claims. For what is striking in the present case of the concept of seeing is the need to invoke grasp of an identity-relation in an account of possession of the concept even for *first*-person ascriptions, when we consider embeddings in modals and counterfactuals. When we consider the occurrence of first-person predications of seeing in counterfactuals and in other modals, our understanding of first-person predications of seeings is not free of any tacit use of the notion of sameness of conscious state. It is not an identity-free level of predication that could be used to explain thought about identity of conscious states. To suggest that our understanding of identity of state across actual and possible situations can be explained, on Wittgensteinian lines, in terms of identity of true predications in the actual and merely possible cases would simply leave unexplained our understanding of what it is for the first-person predication to be true in the merely possible state of affairs.[20]

The identity-involving account of possession of the concept of seeing contrasts very sharply with any account which states that having the concept of seeing involves some knowledge, whether explicit or tacit, of the role of seeing in a thinker's psychology. Some central parts of what ordinary thinkers accept, either explicitly or tacitly, about the role of seeing in a thinker's psychology is false. Uninformed ordinary thinkers, and quite sophisticated but scientifically uninformed persons, will say that visual experience explains the intentional movements of a person's body when acting. Their ascriptions of seeings based on their observations of the actions of others also warrant the ascription of the tacit belief that intentional actions on things in the subject's environment is guided by visual experience. But in fact we know

---

[20] This additional element of tacit knowledge involved in grasping "I see that *p*" should affect our conception of how the relation of seeing is fixed as the reference of the concept of seeing. The relation of seeing (seeing-that), between a thinker and a content, is not the unique relation R that makes always truth-preserving in the actual world the transition from the thinker's seeing that *p* to the content (with our thinker as reference of "I") I R that *p*. Consider the unintended relation R* such that I R* that *p* holds in the actual world iff in the actual world I see that *p*, and I R* that *p* holds in some other possible world *w* just in case *p* holds in *w*. This gives incorrect modal evaluations, as we just discussed. Such unintended relations are ruled out by the requirement that the relation of seeing is one that is the same psychological relation as holds between the subject and the content when the thinker is following the Core Rule. The deviant candidate R* does not meet this condition: it is really a property of contents, fixed in the actual world indeed by a psychological relation to a thinker, but it is not that psychological relation that determines the application of the property in all possible cases.

that any such belief is false. Concurrent intentional action on things in the environment is caused by information supplied by the older, dorsal route in the brain, a route that does not involve perceptual consciousness (and is, unsurprisingly, faster than the conscious visual route).[21] Does this mean that the ordinary person's concept of seeing therefore has no application to others, or applies to the wrong states? It would mean that if the reference of the concept were fixed by a role the state of seeing is thought to have. But in fact the reference is not fixed that way, and there is no difficulty in the idea that it comes as a surprise that seeings do not really have the role we thought they have. You are still thinking about seeings when you make this discovery, because the seeings in others are states of the same subjective kind as you have when you really see. The surprise is that those states in others do not have the role you might have thought they do. Reference is no more fixed by descriptive role for psychological concepts than it is for other natural kind concepts. Our close relation to our own psychological states, together with our tacit grasp of an identity-relation, allows us to think of seeings, and other conscious psychological states, in a distinctive way that makes it an empirical discovery what the further explanatory role of seeing may or may not be. This point is the analogue for the concept of seeing that we made for the concept of pain back in Chapter 5 section 9. I will be arguing in Chapter 8 that there is even an analogue of the point for the case of concepts and meaning too.

3. COMPARISONS

Evans gives a different account of how a thinker can attribute a content to his perceptual experience. In *The Varieties of Reference*,[22] he writes: 'He [the subject] goes through exactly the same procedure as he would go through if he were trying to make a judgement about how it is at this place now, but excluding any knowledge he has *of an extraneous kind*. (That is, he seeks to determine what he would judge if he did not have such extraneous information.)' (p. 227). Evans's idea is that if the subject, using this procedure, determines that he would judge that *p* under these conditions, then he can ascribe the content *p* to his perceptual experience.

---

[21] Milner and Goodale (1995); Goodale and Milner (2004).
[22] Evans (1982). Page references in the text are to this work.

To explain what he means by 'extraneous information', Evans mentions an example of Dummett's.[23] If you see a pile of newspapers at the Smiths' front door, you may judge "I see the Smiths forgot to cancel their newspapers". But, under Evans's approach, the content *the Smiths forgot to cancel their newspapers* is not to be counted as part of the content to be ascribed to your experience, because it is 'extraneous'. Also, if you know that your visual experience is an illusion, that knowledge is also extraneous information that is to be excluded in assessing what you would judge when you apply Evans's criterion (228 n. 39).

It seems to me that the condition Evans formulates is not necessary for an experience to have a given content. Something can be in the content of a given experience without the subject being willing to make the corresponding judgement Evans mentions. Several different kinds of example show this.

Consider recognitional concepts of individuals. A person can have the capacity to recognize the former Iraqi dictator Saddam Hussein. When he sees Saddam, his visual experience has a content specified in part by using that recognitional concept: it seems to him that Saddam, so thought of, is in front of him. Other things equal, he will take such visual experiences at face value, and judge that Saddam is in front of him. But his willingness to do so rests, and rationally rests, on his belief that there is only one person, at least in this part of the world, who looks that way. This seemingly extraneous belief is in fact essential for our subject to be willing to move from the experience to the judgement that Saddam is in front of him. When our subject comes to learn that Saddam actually employs three lookalikes, he will not move from the experience to the judgement that Saddam is in front of him. But his visual experience will continue to have that content all the same. So it seems that Evans's condition is not necessary.

Perhaps Evans could add the requirement that the judgement he mentions can rely on information if that information is necessary if the subject is to be willing to employ the concept in judgements at all. That would save the Saddam example, but it would not help with others.

Suppose you hear the sounds "Peter leaped". It is in the representational content of your experience that someone said that Peter leaped (its sense, not merely the sound and phonemes). But, we can suppose, it is only because you take yourself to be amongst English speakers that you also judge that the

---

23 Dummett (1976: 95).

speaker said that Peter leaped. If you took yourself to be amongst German speakers, you would judge not that someone has said that Peter had made a certain kind of jump, but rather that someone had said that Peter is in love ("Peter liebt"). So Evans's procedure fails to attribute to the experience the content that someone said that Peter leaped.

This is not a problem for the Core Rule, for in such examples a person can certainly hear that someone has said that Peter leaped, and move from that to a self-ascription of such a hearing. He can do this independently of whether he needs additional information before endorsing the content of the experience in a judgement.

There is a range of other examples of a similar sort. If you can see something as a car, a computer, or a phone, it is only because of your background knowledge of the function of these perceptually recognizable objects that we judge that the seen things are cars, or phones, and so forth. If this background knowledge were not there, some of us would not make the judgement that it is a car, or phone, or computer that is in front of us.

A hard line with these examples would be to take the unintuitive line that you do not really see the object as a computer, say, but only as something of a certain size and shape. But not all examples can be handled by such a hard line. The example of "Peter leaped" cannot. It would be a huge misrepresentation of our auditory experience to say that we do not really hear words as having certain senses.

There is a third kind of case demonstrating the non-necessity of Evans's conditions. In cases of this third kind, the content of the experience is so outlandish that we would never judge it to hold, given our background knowledge. A competent magician can make it look as if three pigeons have just come out of his jacket sleeve. We do not judge that they were there. If it is said that we must exclude knowledge of how physical objects behave, or what sorts are around us, we will thereby exclude all sorts of features of our visual experience. We see an occluded object as having a certain shape, as continuing in a certain way behind the occluding object; and our willingness to take these experiences at face value relies on our background information. Another example is provided by such experiences as that of the rising, but apparently curving, zigzag jet of water in the display that is, or used to be (*circa* 1983–4), in the Exploratorium in San Francisco (see Fig. 1). The effect was produced by a rising jet of water that was in fact continuously moving back and forth across the arc of a circle, but under carefully timed,

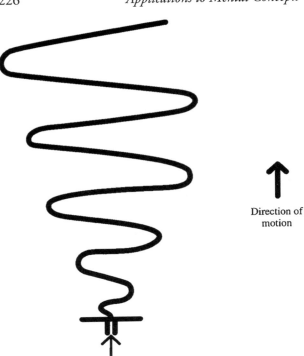

Direction of
motion

and unnoticed, stroboscopic lighting that produced the visual effect of an unsupported continuous jet of water in the zigzag shape. The experience of this striking display was undoubtedly of the curving, zigzagging jet of water. We are going to get the right answer from Evans's procedure only if we ask such questions as "What would I judge if I did not think that the laws of motion did not hold?" It is impossible to believe that such barely assessable questions have to be answered before we can pronounce on the question of the content of our perceptual experience in looking at such a display.[24]

I conclude from this range of cases that it is one thing for a judgement to have a certain content in the circumstances described by Evans, and it is another for the experience to have the same content, even though there is sometimes overlap between the two. There would be complete coincidence

---

[24] Could Evans solve this problem by appealing to multiple-similarity relations, just as I myself did in an earlier section? One needs to capture that the jet is going around curves, for this is given in the experience itself. That it is so perceived is not captured by similarities to other genuine seeings overlapping in contents.

if 'extraneous information' meant any content that is not in the content of the perceptual experience: but that would be a very different procedure and criterion from that which Evans suggested. That different procedure would not be genuinely circumstance-dependent, in the way Evans's procedure is. For example, if one just requires someone to judge only what is in the content of the perceptual experience, one would not need Evans's instruction that if one knows one's experience is illusory, one should prescind from that information. Just requiring sensitivity to the content of the experience would be enough, whether it is a genuine perception or not. That alternative approach would not also preserve the primacy of the genuinely perceptual case in the self-ascription of experiential content, an attractive and important feature of Evans's approach.

Evans's approach is not the only treatment to preserve the primacy of the genuinely perceptual case. The possession-condition that incorporates the Core Rule and the Extended Core Rule also attributes explanatory primacy to the genuinely perceptual case. It does so in two respects. The genuinely perceptual states of seeing-that, feeling-that, hearing-that, and the rest are the initial states from which transitions are made in the Core Rule when the thinker makes a self-ascription of an experience. The treatment of thought about illusions as states that are subjectively similar to genuine perceptions also gives an explanatory primacy to the genuinely perceptual case.

I argued that Evans's counterfactual condition about what a subject would judge in certain circumstances is not a necessary condition for an experience to have a particular content. Correspondingly it should not be mentioned in a correct procedure for self-ascribing perceptual experience. I do not at all mean to imply, however, that we should after all say that what the subject would judge using extraneous information really is part of the content of the perceptual experience. That is not true. I have been distinguishing throughout between the content of experience and the content of judgement. The Core Rule gives a procedure for self-ascribing experience without reliance on any attempted reduction of the content of experience to counterfactuals about what the subject would judge in certain circumstances. Experience has a content in its own right, without the need for any such reduction.

Why did Evans adopt his account of the self-ascription of experience, with its circumstance-dependent character? Despite the differences he notes between the two, he was likely partly tempted by the partial parallel with his treatment of the self-ascription of belief (pp. 225–6). In the case of belief, he suggests, a thinker can employ the procedure of asking himself a question about the world, whether *p* holds, and then self-ascribing the belief that *p* just in case his answer is affirmative. In both the case of belief and the case of perception, the self-ascription of a psychological state is said to be dependent upon what, in certain circumstances, one thinks about the world. But beyond this parallel between the two cases under his own view of them, I conjecture that there was a further reason for Evans's (arguably uncritical) adoption of his circumstance-dependent account of the self-ascription of experience. The reason lies in his account of experience itself. In a passage that has achieved some notoriety, Evans wrote in *The Varieties of Reference* that

we arrive at conscious perceptual experience when sensory input ... also serves as the input to a *thinking, concept-applying and reasoning system*; so that the subject's thoughts, plans and deliberations are also systematically dependent on the informational properties of the input. When there is such a further link, we can say that the person, rather than just some part of his brain, receives and possesses the information. (p. 158)

On this conception of experience, what makes something the content of an *experience* must be its relations to thought and concept-application. Under such an approach, what is the most obvious resource to use in specifying how a state must be related to 'the concept-applying system' if it is to be an experience with a given representational content? The most obvious resource is to say the content of the experience is determined by the content of the judgement the thinker would make when enjoying the experience, and when prescinding from other extraneous considerations. As we have seen, this does not work. But it has to be some resource of this sort, involving relations to states with conceptual content, if, like Evans, one does not think that there is a notion of the representational content of experience available independently (in respect of philosophical explanation) of relations to states with conceptual content.

In my judgement, the idea that the very same state that can occur in a creature that does not possess concepts and which is not in fact an experience can itself nevertheless be an experience in a genuinely concept-using creature is an idea that has no legitimate attractions. Far from supporting the thesis that the same perceptual experiences can occur in more primitive animals, the idea is incompatible with that thesis. (For what it is worth, I suspect that Evans would have dropped the idea had he lived longer, and been able to revise *The Varieties of Reference*.) The most primitive conceptual contents of thought are individuated by their relations to a system of perceptual states whose content is autonomous in relation to the level of conceptual content. Those perceptual states must indeed make a contribution to their subject's conception of the layout of the world around him. But all this can happen at a level of non-conceptual content that is far more primitive than the level of conceptual content individuated in terms of rationality and judgements.[25]

4. THE POSSESSION-CONDITION AND SOME EMPIRICAL PHENOMENA

What should be the relation between the possession-condition for a concept and empirical psychological phenomena involving possession of that concept? The relation between the two is complex and multifaceted. Here I want to emphasize one of the tasks of a theory of possession-conditions that is particularly pertinent to issues surrounding possession of the concept of perception.[26]

A statement of a possession-condition for a concept is responsible in the first instance to the epistemic phenomena involving possession of that concept. These phenomena involve the rationality or irrationality, in given circumstances, of judging certain contents containing that concept. The fact that it can be rational, and correct, to apply an observational concept to an object even when the object is not perceived must be explained by the possession-condition for the observational concept. The fact that we can rationally come to accept new axioms for some logical or mathematical concept, axioms that are not implied by what we previously accepted, also has to be explained by the possession-conditions for the logical or mathematical concepts in question. Frege constrained the notion of a *Sinn* by considerations of informativeness. If the identity of a *Sinn*, or a concept in our terms, is answerable to Frege's informativeness condition, and a possession-condition individuates a concept, then these tasks of a theory of possession-conditions are demanded simply by the nature of the subject matter of a theory of possession-conditions.

---

[25] For further discussion, see Peacocke (2001*a*). I have not always held the views just stated in the text. For further discussion of the issues, see Peacocke (2003*a*). For further discussion of non-conceptual content in animal perception, see Burge (2003). The whole of the above discussion could also be adjusted to take account of the distinction between conceptual and non-conceptual content, without fundamental change to the essential elements of the account.

[26] For discussion of other issues concerning the relation between a philosophical theory of concepts and empirical psychological phenomena involving concepts, see Peacocke (2001*b*).

These explanatory tasks are philosophical, and have a relatively a priori character. The rationality or otherwise of judging something in given circumstances is a relatively a priori matter. So these tasks have the characteristic epistemic status of much of philosophy that aims to be explanatory. The task is to explain a set of a priori truths—truths about what is informative in given circumstances, truths about what contents involving a given concept it is rational to judge in those circumstances—from more fundamental principles that individuate the concept in question.

Some of the phenomena displayed by possession of a given concept by actual human thinkers are, however, empirical phenomena that could not be excogitated simply from the a priori nature of the concept. If these phenomena are special to the concept in question, the possession-condition for the concept can contribute to an explanation of how these phenomena are possible. One way such an explanation might run is illustrated by a treatment I will offer of some empirical phenomena involving possession of the concept of perception.

All of the following phenomena are displayed by children employing the concept of perception, and are well attested by psychological research. Many of these phenomena will be familiar to any parent.

(*a*) Toddlers between the ages of 24 and 30 months do not appreciate that they can see something that someone on the other side of an opaque screen cannot see.[27] Asked to hide a toy from another person, who is on the other side of the screen, a child of this age will often put the toy in a position in which the child himself cannot see it, on the other side of the screen where the other person can see it. These are what Hughes has called 'projective' errors, and Flavell calls 'Level 1' errors.[28]

(*b*) In playing hide-and-seek, a child of this age will be willing to hide under a table, in a location in which it is evident to any adult that the child can be seen in the room, even though the child himself cannot see the rest of the room. We can call this phenomenon "incompetent hide-and-seek". Incompetent hide-and-seek is plausibly an instance of the same inability displayed in projective errors. It is the special case in which there is failure to grasp the conditions under which the seeker sees something.

(*c*) Somewhat older children, who do not make these errors, nonetheless make a different error. In a situation in which one of these older children

---

[27] For an engaging overview, see Gopnik et al. (1999: 40–1, and the literature cited there).
[28] See Masangkay et al. (1974); Yaniv and Shatz (1988).

sees an object, and appreciates that someone else also sees the same object, they nevertheless fail to appreciate that the other person will see a different side of the object than they themselves see—even though they know that the object is different on its two sides.[29] Hughes calls these 'perspective errors', and Flavell calls them 'Level 2' errors.

(*d*) Ordinary 3- to 4-year-olds are ignorant of the sources of their own and others' knowledge in the following respect. Suppose one child sees a second child look into a box. The first child denies that the second child knows what is in the box, even though he himself (i) looked in the box, (ii) came thereby to know what was in the box, and (iii) knows that he knew what was in the box. The explanation for the possibility of this state of affairs is that the first child does not know how he himself came to know what is in the box, even though he does have the concept of seeing. We can call this phenomenon "Ignorance of Sources".[30]

These phenomena (*a*)–(*d*) are all empirical phenomena involving the concept of seeing. We can explain how they are possible by drawing on the possession-condition for the concept of seeing. They can all be explained by drawing on the Core Rule, in both its positive and negative parts. I propose what I call the "Same Rule Hypothesis":

> the child, in attributing seeings to others, applies the same Core Rule to others as he does in self-ascribing experiences, but does so taking as input to the Rule not another's seeing-that *p*, but his own.

That is, the child moves from his own

> seeing that *p*

to

> the other person sees that *p*.

A natural extension and partner of the Same Rule Hypothesis for the negative case is that: the child uses the same procedure in judging that the other person does not see as she uses in judging that she herself does not see.

In the rather primitive and special case in which a thinker's only conception of what is involved in another person's seeing is that it is a state attributable

---

[29] See Masangkay et al. (1974).
[30] See Gopnik et al. (2001: 46–7, and the references therein); and especially Wimmer et al. (1988).

by applying the Core Rule in the case of others, in the way just described, then the Same Rule Hypothesis is an example, as promised earlier, of one of the other ways in which one's grasp of a general property can be essentially first-personal without being of the sort Wittgenstein criticized. The thinker has some understanding of what it is for another to have some property because he knows that it can be attributed by applying the same rule for others as he employs in making self-attributions.

The Same Rule Hypothesis can contribute to the explanation of each of the phenomena (*a*)–(*d*).

The Same Rule Hypothesis explains the 'projective' errors in (*a*). If a child uses these procedures, he will judge that another person sees something, or sees something to be the case, precisely when he himself sees it, or sees something to be the case. Equally, if the child uses the negative part of the Core Rule in the same way, he will judge that the other does not see something in exactly the same conditions as he does not see something.

The Same Rule Hypothesis also explains the phenomenon of Incompetent Hide-and-Seek. If our child judges, using the Core Rule, that he does not see anyone in the room, then if he uses the same Rule in the way indicated to make judgements about the visual experience of the other player in the game, he will judge that the seeker equally does not see anyone in the room.

Perspectival errors can be explained using the same resource. Suppose the child sees one side of an object, and applies the Core Rule to judge that he himself sees that side. Applying the same rule in other-ascription then would yield the result that he ascribes to the other a view of that same side.

Under this approach, increasing knowledge about the conditions under which others see, and what features of an object they see, is attained by the child's coming to qualify the conditions under which the Core Rule can be applied in other-ascription in this naive way. The Core Rule works in other-ascription of seeings only for someone in roughly the same location as oneself, in the same conditions, with unobstructed sight. Eventually, for full knowledge, the child must have correct information about the empirical conditions under which others are in the same state as he is when he himself sees. The naive applications of the Core Rule in other-ascriptions are progressively qualified by conditions on the other's relations to the objects and states of affairs perceived, qualifications that must be fulfilled if the other is to be in the same state as when he sees. The very qualifications on the use of the Core Rule in other-ascription also, incidentally, give a special role to the first person. The conditions under which the subject himself does not see will be used in formulating the conditions under which the Core Rule is to be qualified in its use in ascriptions to others.

The account just offered should be distinguished from a theory according to which the child progressively refines a functional characterization of the role of seeing in others (in combination with the Core Rule for first-person applications). I emphasized at the end of section 2 above that the account in this chapter of the concept of seeing is not a functional-role account. What is progressively refined as the child learns the conditions under which the other sees is not a functional-role characterization of a state. What is progressively refined is rather the empirical characterization of the conditions under which the other is in the same state as he is, when he himself sees. The Same Rule Hypothesis is not only an empirical hypothesis: it is also a hypothesis about the child's empirical hypotheses about the world and others.

It may be objected that the empirical phenomena $(a)-(c)$ could equally be explained by the hypothesis that the child uses the Core Rule in self-ascribing experiences, and then infers to the occurrence of experiences in others by using the principle that others see something to be the case if and only if he himself does. I suggest, however, that at these early stages the child has no conception of what it is for another person to see something to be the case other than that such other-ascriptions can be reached by applying the Core Rule to others. If that is the child's conception of other-ascriptions and their correctness-conditions, it will indeed be a consequence of the procedures for self- and other-ascription of experiences that he sees something to be the case if and only if another person does. But the child does not have an independent conception of perception for which this coincidence is believed to hold.

The empirical phenomenon of Ignorance of Sources would not be possible if to have the concept of seeing-that is to think of it as a kind of knowledge that has visual perception as its source. That way of thinking would make Ignorance of Sources for the case of knowing-that into some kind of conceptual impossibility. But it is not impossible under the Core Rule, for two reasons. First, to say that someone is following a rule does not imply that they can conceptualize the rule they are following, let alone that they know that they are following that rule. In fact, if someone could follow a rule only if he could conceptualize what rule it is that he is following, the Core Rule could not possibly be part of an account of what it is to have the concept of seeing, since under that condition the thinker would have to conceptualize the input conditions, which would require him already to have the concept of seeing. But the idea that one can conceptualize a state because one is sensitive to its instances seems entirely coherent and plausible.

The second reason that the Core Rule permits Ignorance of Sources is this. While seeing-that is indeed a kind of knowledge, the Core Rule does not imply that someone who thinks of his own seeings-that has to think of them as a kind of knowledge. The Core Rule requires someone who has the concept of seeing-that and applies it to himself to be sensitive to the boundary between those of his states that are seeings-that and those that are not. It does not require him to think of those states as states of knowledge. Doing that requires him to take a further step, to connect up his concept of seeings-that with his conception of knowledge. These two philosophical points bring the philosophical conception advocated here into very close alignment with the empirical explanation of Ignorance of Sources given in the paper by Wimmer, Hogrefe, and Sodian already cited.[31] The Core Rule is a philosophical, constitutive account that makes intelligible their empirical explanations.

The fact that the Core Rule also provides a means for ascribing perceptions to other people is of more general philosophical significance than making some sense of the empirical data of acquisition. The fact that one can use the Core Rule in other-ascription shows how a possession-condition for a concept, while being essentially first-personal, can nevertheless contain the seeds of a procedure for other-ascription. This is one very clear way in which a concept can be shown to be unambiguous as between first- and third-person applications, while still displaying an explanatory primacy for the first-person case in the account of possession. The possession-condition for the concept of seeing that I have offered entails that one could not be capable of self-ascriptions of seeings without both having the resources to grasp, and having the materials for a procedure for making, other-ascriptions of seeing.

If someone other-ascribes in accordance with the Same Rule Hypothesis, he is taking one step to seeing the other person as 'another I'. Other-ascribing in accordance with the Same Rule Hypothesis does not, however, take a thinker the whole distance to thinking of the other person as 'another I'. Travelling the whole distance also involves thinking of the other as capable of self-ascribing too, that is, capable of moving from the states ascribed in accordance with the Same Rule Hypothesis to self-ascriptions, in accordance with the Core Rule itself. Here the subject has to think of the other person

---

[31] Wimmer et al. (1988).

as employing the first-person way of thinking. That is, in so thinking of the other person, our subject has to refer to, and not merely to employ, the first-person way of thinking.[32]

The ways of coming to make other-ascriptions for which the Core Rule provides the starting point dovetail very smoothly with simulationist approaches to the procedures by which we make psychological attributions to others. In the case in which one attributes a perceptual state to someone standing right next to one, one may not even need to imagine being in some other state before being in a position to make an ascription to him of a seeing. Slight difference of angle, and individual differences aside, what you see to be the case is what he sees to be the case. When one is considering someone situated in space or time differently from you, you imagine what it would be like to be there. In imagining this, you are in fact imagining having certain perceptions, but you do not need to have the concept of perception in order to engage in such imagining. Making a transition from these imaginings—'there's a tree over there, and a gate to the left'—and applying the Core Rule in the imagined situation, you move to a self-ascription in the imagined situation, or even directly to an other-ascription, using the Core Rule as applied to another—'another I' again. As before, we prescind from individual differences in perceptual mechanisms, something whose intelligibility is made possible by the use of the relation of identity of psychological state, as discussed in section 3 above. In such ascriptions of seeings to others, one makes use of the Core Rule. This is to be distinguished from formulating the rule, which is what one would be required to do at some level or other if one were ascribing by means of a theory-theory approach.[33]

The Same Rule Hypothesis was put forward as an account that could explain children's developing understanding of another person's perception. But applying the Same Rule in other-ascription, however tempered with qualifications about same conditions, or perspective, can never capture our full, mature understanding of what it is for another person to be seeing. We understand the hypothesis of the inverted spectrum, that what I see as red, you see as green. We understand this hypothesis even in the case in which your situation and perspective on an object are precisely those in which I see

---

[32] See Peacocke (1981).

[33] This does not conflict with the point that the theory-theory may give the correct account of what it is to be in a given psychological state. Here we are just talking about the procedures we actually employ in other-ascription.

it as red. Applying the Same Rule in other-ascription of experience builds in an implicit presumption of sameness of experience in two people in the same given external conditions and relations. No doubt in pre-philosophical thought we rely on the Same Rule, which is why it is a surprise when the hypothesis of the inverted spectrum occurs to us, or is suggested to us. But we certainly understand it. A formulation of a possession-condition for the concept of seeing that would make it unintelligible would be erroneous.

Actually there would already be an instability in a variant of the concept of seeing that treated first-person ascriptions in accordance with the Core Rule, together with the additional conditions we noted for counterfactuals, and offered only the Core Rule applied in the third person for other-ascription. As I noted, the understanding of counterfactuals about one's own experience involves grasp of a sameness-relation for experiences. If one has some grasp of that sameness-relation, it is, to say the least, not clear why the condition for another to be seeing that *p* should not simply be that the other is in the same state one is in oneself when one sees that *p*, where one's understanding of the latter involves the Core Rule. In fact, if this identity-condition were not met for correct other-ascriptions of seeing, then it would not after all be the same property that is attributed in first-person and third-person ascriptions. And indeed it would not be the same property if the full account of our understanding of the third person were given by the Core Rule applied in the third person, with surrounding qualifications, since the property predicated in other-ascription would be one for which spectrum inversion is a priori impossible.

We should conclude that, contrary to Wittgenstein, grasp of a sameness-relation plays a crucial part at two points in the understanding of predications of seeings. It plays a part both in our understanding of first-person predications when embedded in counterfactuals and other modals, and in our mature understanding of third-person predications. I suggest that grasp of identity, applied to a given category of item, is not to be reduced to grasp of something else. The fact that the Core Rule applied in the third person cannot capture the full extent of our understanding is itself just one plank in support of the case for such irreducibility. Saying there is irreducibility is, however, consistent with one's saying much more about what such grasp involves (as we aimed to in Chapter 1 section 4, in linking abductive reasoning and grasp of identity in the case of observational concepts). Further development of this position for any given domain of conscious states needs to supply this further elucidation. At the very least, the further development has to say how the thinker latches on to the property itself, whose application in the third person is in question. A thinker's grasp of the Core Rule says how his own case provides a means of doing so. It is uniquely the property of seeing that *p*, nothing weaker or stronger, that is the basic one that the thinker must have for use of the Core Rule to result in a true self-predication. The claim that a thinker's understanding involves some grasp of an identity-relation is also one answerable to what it can explain about his judgements and other actions. This explanatory power can be present without any reduction of identity to something else.

5. THE MODEL GENERALIZED

When the Core Rule is embedded in a possession-condition for the concept of perception, the result is an instance of a general form of account. In the general account, the thinker is in some intentional state S with the content *p*. This state is one with representational content: in being in the state, it seems to the thinker that *p* holds of the world. The thinker then makes a transition from his

S-ing that *p*

to the self-ascription

I S that *p*.

We can call this general schema the "Outside-In" model. There are two variants of the general Outside-In model, according as the state S is factive or not. Are there any other instances of the Outside-In model, of either variant?

I suggest that certain concepts of action provide another instance of the Outside-In model, even in its stronger, factive variant. Suppose the thinker makes a self-ascription of the form

I am ϕ-ing.

Instances of this will be *I am walking, I am typing, I am moving from the waiting room to the exit, I am working out the sum of this column of numbers.* These instances are not all ones that in themselves imply that the subject's ϕ-ing is an action. You might be moving from the waiting room to the exit on a moving walkway, onto which you had stepped unintentionally. I do, however, want to suppose, as part of the specification of the range of cases about which I am talking, that the subject has the kind of distinctive awareness of ϕ-ing that is made available by its in fact being an action on this particular occasion (on which more in the following Chapter 7).

This kind of awareness can be present even when one is not perceiving that one is ϕ-ing. One can be aware that one is raising one's arm, even when one's afferent nerves are severed, and there is no proprioceptive feedback, and one is turning one's head away from one's arm so that one cannot see it either. This distinctive phenomenology of action is what makes possible illusions that one has raised one's arm even when, unknown to oneself after some terrible accident, one has no arm. The phenomenology of action involves states with representational content.

A natural first suggestion would then be that another Core Rule that is an instance of the Outside-In model is one in which the thinker moves from a judgement *I am ϕ-ing* based on an action-awareness of ϕ-ing to a judgement

My ϕ-ing is an action.

Here it is important to distinguish between self-ascribing agency and making a self-ascription of an intentional ϕ-ing. As John Campbell remarked to me, something can be an action without the agent doing it intentionally. His example is that of the beginner at golf who has been told many times not to move his head when swinging the club, but who yet does so, and of course does so unintentionally. His moving his head is still an action; and he will have an action-awareness of it in this example. So the above Core Rule is right only for self-ascriptions of actions, and not for the more restricted class—even within bodily movements—that are intentional.[34]

Though this covers correctly a wide range of examples, it is too strong if it is meant to imply that every case of present-tense self-ascription of an action can be made by this route. We need to treat the cases of basic and non-basic actions differently. I may perform an action of transferring one-third of my assets to my son. But there is no distinctive action-awareness of transferring one-third of my assets to my son. The action-awareness in such a case is action-awareness of moving my hand, and (say) of signing my name. I need not have any action-awareness of conditions involving proportions of my assets.

---

[34] If we are strict on this point, such examples should also lead us to distinguish the events that initiate actions from tryings. The beginner at golf was not trying to move his head, but this action had an appropriate kind of initiating event of the sort required for it to be an action.

Where ϕ-ing is an action (-type) that is basic for the subject, we have the preceding Core Rule for the case of basic actions. From the subject's judgement based on action-awareness

I am ϕ-ing

for a basic action-type, the subject can rationally move to the judgement

My ϕ-ing is an action.

There is a Core Rule for ascriptions of action in the case of non-basic actions too. Suppose that ψ-ing is a non-basic action-type for the agent. Suppose too that there is some basic action-type ϕ such that

(1) the subject has an action-awareness of his ϕ-ing, and

(2) in ϕ-ing, the subject is ψ-ing, and

(3) the subject means to be ψ-ing as part of his plan in ϕ-ing.

From the action-awareness in (1), and the conditions (2) and (3), the subject may make a rational transition to the self-ascription

My ψ-ing is an action.

(Here known but unintended consequences must, for the purposes of (3), not be understood as part of the agent's plan.)

The ability to follow the Core Rule in the case of non-basic action involves a sensitivity, on the part of the thinker, to the nature of his own plans. In this it takes a significant step beyond what is involved in following the Core Rule for the case of basic actions. The capacity to follow the Core Rule for non-basic actions thereby represents an intermediate state, located between that of having no sensitivity in one's judgements to one's own plans and decisions, at one extreme, and having full conceptualization of one's own plans, decisions, and intentions, on the other extreme.

The Core Rule for the action case involves transitions a thinker is entitled to make. When these transitions are made from action-based awareness that he is ϕ-ing, these transitions will be truth-preserving. They will also be capable of yielding knowledge that his ϕ-ing is an action when the further conditions (2) and (3), for the non-basic case, are also known.

The explanatory attractions of the Outside-In model applied in the action case parallel some of those that are present for the Core Rule in the case of the concept of seeing. You do not have perceptions of your apparent action-awarenesses—they do not become an object for you, any more than your seeings do. Apparent action-awareness also has the phenomenology of success. Perceptual experience can make rational judgement overrule this impression of success; but it is overruling that is required. Even in the case of actions that one can perceive that one is performing, there is a way of thinking of them made available by action-awareness that does not require one to perceive them. One can see oneself clenching one's own fist. But one can still think *this clenching* (a way of thinking of the event made available by action-awareness of it), and refer thereby to one's action, provided that one tries and succeeds, even in a case in which one's arm, wrist, and hand are fully anaesthetized. Action-awareness makes possible such demonstrative ways of thinking of particular events.

To all of this it may be objected that there is a fundamental asymmetry between the perception and action cases. There cannot be a case of seeing that *p* without the subject being in a subjective, conscious state that can give him reason to self-ascribe a seeing-that *p*. The phenomenology is intrinsic to the very nature of the state in question, and this makes possible the Core Rule. But, the objection runs, no such point holds for apparent action-awareness. We can conceive of possible worlds in which there are events that are mental initiations of actions, caused appropriately by the subject's mental states, but which do not generate the distinctive phenomenology of ordinary actions. Awareness, so the objection runs, is in the action case an add-on, in the way it is not a mere add-on for the state of seeing something to be the case.

I reply that we must remember the informational states operative for blindsight subjects, the states which make them "guess" correctly when asked what shape is in front of them, even though they have no visual experience as of anything in front of them. A sensitivity to *such* states should not be included in the possession-condition for the concept of seeing! Though this stage of the chapter is not the place for a development of the case, this point does not seem to me to be a merely stipulative one, of no fundamental philosophical significance. Seeings, as conscious states, can have a rational bearing on the thought and action of a subject. They could not function as reasons without this conscious character. Similarly, the occurrence of action-awareness, as crucial in the phenomenology of action, is essential to the subject's non-inferential conception of some events in the world as those that he is controlling. Our conception of ourselves as agents would be very different, and would have a theoretical rather than an immediate character, if action lacked this conscious dimension. The phenomenology of action that conscious states sustain gives us reasons for making judgements about which actions we are performing in the normal, non-pathological cases. I therefore contend that the objector is mistaken in thinking that seeing and acting differ in respect of the importance of phenomenology to our concepts of them.

What is true is that we have no single word in English to pick out the conscious actions that stand to action in general, whether conscious or not, as seeings stand to perceptual informational states, whether conscious or not (as in the blindsight cases). It is also true that the general concept of action, applying as it does also in the non-conscious case, has a somewhat different architecture than that of seeing. A full statement of the possession-condition for the general concept of action should respect that point. But all this is entirely consistent with the fact that our concept of action does involve an element of action-awareness in some subcases: much as the fact that observational concepts like *square* apply to objects too small to see (even in principle) is consistent with their involving a perceptual element in some subcases, as they do.

In the case of the concept of seeing, we identified a practice of using the same rule in other-ascriptions of seeings as is used in self-ascriptions. There is something analogous in the case of basic actions. You can perceive the movement of someone else as being of a kind that you yourself can perform. This is not a matter of personal-level inference, but is rather part of the content of your experience of the other person's movement. When you see someone waving in a certain way to hail a cab, you see his action as of a kind that you could perform. If asked to wave in the way he waves, you could do the same, without any inference or calculation. The famous "mirror" neurons identified by Gallese, Rizzolati, and their colleagues are likely to be involved in the possession of such capacities to act and to perceive.[35] Such underlying representations are also the sort of resource required for the explanation of the ability, even of newborns, to imitate such gestures as sticking out one's tongue.[36]

Suppose a subject sees someone else as performing an action of kind φ that is basic for the subject himself, and suppose too that this perception is of a sort that involves the subject experiencing the other's action as of a basic kind

---

[35] Rizzolati et al. (1996); Gallese et al. (2004); Freedberg and Gallese (2007).
[36] Meltzoff and Moore (1977); Meltzoff (2002).

that he could perform himself. In such a case, our subject can move from the third-person content

That person is φ-ing

to the conclusion

That person's φ-ing is an action.

In making this transition, our subject would be applying the same rule in the third-person case as he applies in self-ascription, that is, the same rule as he applies in the first-person case. The only differences between the first-person and the third-person cases are that the awareness is perception as of another's action, and that "that person" is substituted for "I". Again, our subject thinks of the other person as another I. The ability to see another's actions as ones of a sort one can perform oneself supplies the cantilevering from the case described in the Core Rules to the case of other-ascription.

The scope for errors in ascriptions of actions in the basic case is in certain respects narrower than the scope for errors in ascriptions of seeings. What a third person sees to be so depends on several of his relations to the state of affairs in question, particularly his spatial relations. But in the case of action, nothing plays quite the role of these spatial relations. There are no spatially wholly separate objects and events distinct from a subject, his body, and his own states and events in which the subject must stand in certain spatial relations for an event to be one of the subject's actions. Correspondingly, there is no scope for analogues of mistakes about such relations.

Again, as in the case of perception, our full understanding of agency in other-ascription is not exhausted by the use of the same rule. We know that an expert in yoga, in moving into exotic bodily configurations, is performing an action. We even see him as performing actions, even though we neither see nor think that he is doing something we could do ourselves. We do, however, think of those exotic movements and positions of his as being similar in certain respects to things we can do ourselves. We think of them as produced in the same sort of way as things we can do ourselves. Once again, it is grasp of a sameness-relation that extends understanding beyond what can be reached by use of the same rule in self- and other-ascription. With grasp of this sameness relation, we can also make sense of the idea that organisms that are totally unlike humans are also agents. But we build out to our understanding of that case from the case in which we ourselves are agents.

Under this approach, the concepts of an action and of action-awareness are first-personal in the deeper sense I tried to articulate in the case of seeing. A philosophical account of one's general understanding of what it is for an arbitrary person to be acting makes reference to what is involved in making first-person ascriptions of these properties, so thought of.

6. WIDER ISSUES

I conclude by remarking on two features present in this treatment of self- and other-ascription of certain psychological properties that are of wider application and interest.

The Core Rule in both the perception and the action cases is truth-preserving; it is so a priori; it is so as a result of the nature of the states and concepts involved in the respective Rules. Other things equal, it is adaptive to follow truth-preserving rules. It also, if the present approach is correct, comes with the very possession of the concept of perception that one follows a truth-preserving rule. So in acquiring the concept of perception, one has not only the ability to discriminate in thought between those situations in which someone is perceiving something to be the case and those in which he is not; one also has an ability to apply this distinction correctly. These points suggest a general account of the relations between grasp of transitions that are a priori, and adaptive advantage. Some special form of truth-preservation comes with possession of the concept, and brings adaptiveness in its train.

The other feature of this treatment involves a connection between the external individuation of mental states and epistemological relations on the other. Both perceptual experiences and action-awarenesses are plausibly externally individuated. What gives them the content they have is constitutively dependent upon certain of their causes, in certain circumstances, in the case of perceptual experiences, and upon certain of their effects, in certain circumstances, in the case of action-awarenesses. There is, unsurprisingly, a connection between external individuation of a mental state and what enjoyment of that state entitles one to judge. At the first order, perceptual experience and action-awareness entitle one to make judgements about the external world and about what one is doing, respectively. But if the present approach is correct, external individuation also bears upon the entitlement to make second-order judgements, about one's own mental states—about whether one is perceiving, and whether one is acting. This follows immediately if the externally individuated mental states mentioned in the input to the Core Rules provide an entitlement to judge the contents that are the output of the Core Rules. The Core Rules show how the occurrence of mental states that are externally individuated can lead to knowledge of those very mental states that are externally individuated, and can do so in rational ways.

7

Mental Action

This chapter is built around a single, simple idea. It is widely agreed that there is a distinctive kind of awareness each of us has of his own bodily actions. This action-awareness is different from any perceptual awareness a subject may have of his own actions; it can exist in the absence of such perceptual awareness. The single, simple idea around which this chapter is built is that the distinctive awareness that subjects have of their own mental actions is a form of action-awareness. Subjects' awareness of their own mental actions is a species of the same genus that also includes the distinctive awareness of bodily actions. More specifically, I claim:

(1) Much conscious thought consists of mental actions.

(2) A thinker's awareness of those of his mental events that are mental actions is a species of action-awareness. This I call the "Principal Hypothesis".

(3) The Principal Hypothesis can provide a clarification and explanation of a range of features and phenomena present in conscious thought.

(4) The Principal Hypothesis is a resource that can be used in addressing various classical philosophical issues about the mental, self-knowledge, and the first person. In particular, the Principal Hypothesis allows a treatment of concepts of mental actions along the lines of the Target Account of Chapter 5.

Gilbert Ryle once asked: 'What is Rodin's *Le Penseur* doing?'[1] My answer in this chapter is that he is literally doing something, is engaged in mental action; and our task is to say more about what this involves.

My strategy will be first to articulate some distinctive features of bodily action-awareness; then to characterize the range of mental actions; and to argue that all of these distinctive features of action-awareness in the bodily

---

[1] Ryle (1971*b*).

case are present also for mental actions. I will go on to consider some of the attractions and consequences of the Principal Hypothesis; to draw upon it in an account of our understanding of our own and others' mental actions, in a way that accords with the role of reference and identity in understanding discussed in earlier chapters of this book; to apply it in the characterization of some pathological states; and finally to consider some aspects of its significance for the nature of first-person thought and rationality. Much of this chapter is a contribution to philosophy of mind and the metaphysics and epistemology of one part of mental life, and could be accepted independently of the account of understanding I have been offering. So if you have read this far, but have doubts about the presented theory of understanding, there may still be something for you in what follows.

1. THE DISTINCTIVE FEATURES OF ACTION-AWARENESS

(*a*) You can be aware that you are doing something without perceiving that you are doing it. If you have had a strong injection in preparation for a root canal operation at the dentist, you may have no sensation in and around your mouth and your jaw. If you are asked to open your mouth, you can do so, and you will be aware that you are opening your mouth. This awareness exists even though you do not perceive your mouth or your lower face at all. You can be aware that you are opening your mouth without seeing or feeling your mouth, and without any of the sensations or perceptions of your own body from the inside (that is, without any proprioception). A person whose afferent nerves have been severed or have suffered decay may still be aware that he is extending his arm and pointing to the right, even though he is looking the other way, and does not perceive his own arm at all.

The same kind of action-awareness that is present in these exceptional circumstances is also something we enjoy in normal bodily action in more ordinary circumstances. Your everyday awareness that you are moving your hands, turning your head, or opening your mouth is not purely perceptual.[2] Even if it is true that action-awareness requires some general capacity to perceive, action-awareness on a particular occasion that you are doing

---

[2] This kind of awareness is the subject of Marcel (2003) and Peacocke (2003*c*).

something does not require you to perceive, on that occasion, that you are doing it.

(*b*) The content of your action-awareness is that you are doing something. It is not merely a consciousness that something is happening (though of course that is implied by the content).

This fact arguably parallels a corresponding truth about the content of perceptual states. Perception is as of states of affairs in the objective world, states of affairs of a sort that cause perceptions. If action-awareness is caused by tryings, this awareness is as of what's the case when those tryings successfully cause events in the objective world. What is then the case is that one is doing something.

(*c*) The content of the action-awareness is representational in the sense that in enjoying action-awareness, it seems to the subject that the world is a certain way. This seeming is belief-independent. It may seem to the unfortunate person whose arm is, unbeknownst to him, severed in a car accident that he is moving his arm, even though he has no sensation in it. This seeming has a false content. The seeming, just like a visual illusion, can persist after the subject knows his unhappy situation. In my view, action-awareness should not be identified with any kind of belief, whether first- or second-order.

Bodily action-awareness is to be distinguished from mere awareness of trying to do something. Suppose you are trying, but failing, to unscrew a tight lid on a jar. You are aware that you are trying to unscrew it. You have no awareness, either real or apparent, of the bodily action of unscrewing it. It may be that in certain circumstances, when there is no information to the contrary, tryings cause apparent action-awareness. That does not make apparent action-awareness identical with awareness of trying. It means only that what the latter kind of awareness is awareness of can itself cause apparent awareness of bodily action. Apparent awareness of successfully doing something is distinct from apparent awareness of trying to do it.

Those who hold that there is non-conceptual content at the personal, conscious level will be attracted to the idea that some awareness of bodily action may have an at least partially non-conceptual content. I myself see nothing intrinsically problematic in the idea that an animal without concepts, but with non-conceptual mental representations of the world, may have a form of non-conceptual awareness of its bodily actions. The content of the awareness should be captured in a form that specifies the change in location or properties of the bodily parts that are involved in the apparent action. Such contents could be integrated into the scenario content possessed by perceptual states that I used in earlier work.[3] Such a conception is not essential to the main theses of the present chapter, however. Thinkers like John McDowell, who hold that all personal-level conscious content is conceptual, could also recognize the existence of belief-independent action-awareness.[4] They would simply insist that its content is conceptual too.

(*d*) The content of the action-awareness is both first-personal and present-tensed. The content is of the form *I am doing such and such now*. When you take such an awareness at face value, and judge *I am doing such-and-such now*, your judgement is identification-free in a familiar sense. It is not the case that you are making this judgement only because, for some mode of presentation *m* other than the first person, you judge that *m* is doing such-and-such now, and you also accept that you are *m*. There are further distinctions to be drawn here, and I will return to them.

(*e*) (*i*) Action-awareness makes available demonstrative ways of thinking of particular actions. You can think of a movement demonstratively, as *this movement*, a way of thinking of a movement made available by your action-awareness of the movement.

(*ii*) The reference of such demonstratives is determined by which movement is caused by one's trying. It is not determined by its relations to one's perception of the movement, if indeed any such perception exists. Nor is the reference determined by which movement one believes it to be. There may be no such movement, even though one believes there is; or one may be wrong about which movement it is one has made. You can think to yourself, while making a certain gesture with your hand, *This is the victory gesture Churchill made*, where the demonstrative is made available by apparent action-awareness on this particular occasion. The demonstrative refers to the movement (-type) you actually make. If your efferent nerves have been rerouted, your thought that this is the victory gesture Churchill made may be false, even though you know perfectly well which type of movement it was that Churchill used as a victory gesture. You are just wrong in thinking that *this* movement (action demonstrative) is an instance of that movement-type you know so well.

(*iii*) There is a distinction in the case of action-based modes of presentation which parallels that between the demonstrative and recognitional

---

[3] Peacocke (1992, ch. 3).   [4] McDowell (1994, Lectures I–III and Postscripts).

in the case of perceptual modes of presentation. The action-awareness based demonstrative *this movement* requires that one enjoy at least an apparent action-awareness at the time of thinking. Otherwise it is not even available for use, just as a perceptual demonstrative is not available for use in the absence of perceptual experience. But there is also a way of thinking of a certain type of movement, made available by the fact that one can reliably make the movement. One can use this type of way of thinking even when one is not trying to make the movement so thought of. *I could make such-and-such gesture*, one may think, in the process of deciding how to act.

2. THE NATURE AND RANGE OF MENTAL ACTIONS

Events that are mental actions include instances of the following kinds:

decidings

judgings

acceptings

attendings to something or other

calculatings

reasonings

tryings.

Some types of mental event are such that instances of the type may or may not be mental actions. Such is the case with imagining. Imagining in your mind's ear Beethoven's Hammerklavier Sonata may on a particular occasion be a mental action. On another occasion, that sonata may equally come to your auditory imagination unbidden—your imagining may be a hindrance to what you are trying to do. In this respect, imagining as a type is like the bodily type of making marks on the carpet. When someone is making marks on the carpet, that may or may not be something she is trying to do.

Within the class of mental events, what makes an event a mental action? For a mental event to be a mental action, it must consist of an event which either is, or constitutively involves, a trying. If 'constitutively involves' is allowed to count as a reflexive relation, this criterion can be simplified. To be a mental action, a mental event must constitutively involve a trying.

Every mental action involves success in something at which one may in principle fail. You may find that you cannot bring yourself to believe that *p* (for instance, that your friend is lying to you); you may find that you cannot bring yourself to try to do something; you may find that you cannot bring yourself even to decide to do something. Sometimes lack of success is obvious to the would-be agent himself. In other cases, an agent may have an illusion of success. A subject may think he has formed the belief that *p* when in fact he has not. No amount of affirming to himself that *p* will guarantee that he has succeeded in storing the content that *p* amongst his beliefs. This fact is the ground of possibility of one sort of self-deception.

The success or failure of our attempts at mental action depends upon all sorts of subpersonal conditions to which we do not have independent access, in the way in which perception gives us independent information on whether our attempts at bodily action have been successful. The real possibilities of continuing, ordinary error about some of our mental states are in this respect far more extensive than the real possibilities of such error about our bodily actions. By contrast, a situation in which someone is self-deceived on the issue of whether he has really unscrewed the lid off the jar would provide material for a Monty Python-like script.

The condition I have offered for a mental event to be a mental action is the same condition as I would offer for a bodily event to be a bodily action: it must constitutively involve a trying. Mental actions and bodily actions are actions in exactly the same sense. The differences between them are the differences between the bodily and the mental.

I have unified mental and bodily actions by their common relation to tryings, but someone sceptical that this is the right account of action could still accept the other main claims of this chapter. That sceptic could still agree that mental action-awareness is a species of the same genus of action-awareness that includes bodily awareness of bodily actions. The sceptic would just be offering a different account of what makes something an action, whether bodily or mental.

Tryings themselves featured on the above list of mental actions. This does not involve a vicious regress (nor a non-vicious one either). An unacceptable regress would be generated by the conjunction of the following propositions: tryings are actions; and for an event to be an action, it must be caused by a prior trying. That last proposition is false, however, which is why there is no regress of that sort. Tryings themselves are one of the best counter-examples to the thesis that for an event to be an action, it must be caused by a prior trying.

Though the main concern of this chapter is action-awareness, the recognition that there is a range of mental action-types that includes both judgement and decision already has consequences for a range of philosophical and psychological issues, independently of theses about action-awareness. I give four examples, which should help to locate this position about mental actions in a wider philosophical and psychological landscape.

Outright judgement, something that seems not to be a matter of degree, has often seemed to play a special role in the formation of propositional attitudes.[5] This appearance is both understandable and correct if judgements are mental actions. A mental action involves a trying, and whether you are trying to do something is not itself a matter of degree. You are either trying or you are not. What it is you are trying to do may vary in degree: you may be trying to write a long letter or a short letter, to make a lot of money or a modest sum. But whether you are trying or not is not a matter of degree. Since trying involves the occurrence of an event, an initiating event which produces an effect, it is not surprising that it should not be a matter of degree. It is not a matter of degree whether such an initiating event occurs.

There is such a thing as trying harder or less hard to do something, and this distinction does get a grip in the mental realm as well as in the bodily. But no one who advocates the importance of degrees of belief would be tempted to identify greater degree of belief with (say) lower degree of effort in trying to make an outright judgement. Such theorists would want to contrast degrees of belief with outright judgements, however the members of each of these categories may be reached.

These points about judgement apply also to decision and to the other mental-action-types. Deciding to do something cannot be a matter of degree. Again, there can be variation in degree in respect of what it is that one is deciding to do; but that is a different matter.

Not every case in which you come to believe something involves mental action. By default, we take many experiences, memories, and utterances of other people at face value. What they represent as correct goes straight into our store of beliefs without any mental action. So I am not saying that every time we form a belief, even a conscious belief, there is mental action. It is, however, characteristic of beliefs, as opposed to more primitive representational states, that they can be assessed and reviewed. Such assessment and review does involve mental action.

---

[5] For one good statement of this position, see Harman (1986, ch. 3, sect. 'All-or-Nothing Belief', pp. 22–4).

A second consequence of acknowledging the existence of mental actions that include judgements concerns the idea of concepts as distinguished by norms for making judgements in which those concepts are applied. These concept-distinguishing norms can then be seen as norms of rational action. They are norms of action applying in the special case in which the action is a mental action, that of judgement.

A third consequence concerns the philosophy of mind and action more generally, and it bears upon the existence of the phenomenon of akratic judgement. Knowing or having evidence about what it is rational to think, all things considered, or having information about what is most likely to be the case, never entails that the thinker will perform a certain *action*.

We know this very well from the case of bodily action. If judgements and decisions are mental actions, exactly the same point applies to them too. Akratic belief, and other akratic mental actions, are just as possible as akratic bodily actions. They are possible for the same reasons as in the bodily case. Mental action has all the frailties of subjection to desire, self-deception, and wishful thinking that bodily action also suffers. Mental agency is not in a privileged position vis-à-vis bodily agency. This may be humbling, but it also puts us in a much better position to explain the range of phenomena that actually occur.

A fourth consequence concerns the unified theoretical treatment of areas that have not always been considered instances of a single kind. Daniel Kahneman writes of his own and Amos Tversky's work on the two topics of intuitive thinking and of choice that it 'highlights commonalities between lines of research that are usually studied separately'.[6] If both judgements and choices are mental actions, we should be ready for the possibility that, as mental actions, some of the characteristics of the mechanisms producing them are the same. In deliberating what to think, our deliberation is about a mental action, what to judge; in deliberating between options, we are deliberating about what to choose, equally a mental action.

Kahneman summarizes his views by saying that 'In particular, the psychology of judgement and the psychology of choice share their basic principles and differ mainly in content.' Kahneman draws a distinction between what he calls 'System 1' and 'System 2'. This distinction maps on to, and can help explain empirically, some of the distinctions I have drawn. His System 1 is 'fast, parallel, automatic, effortless' and it delivers what Kahneman calls

---

[6] Kahneman (2003: 717).

'impressions'. These 'impressions' are not mental actions. In this respect his comparison of them with perceptions is wholly apt. Like perceptions, they just occur to the thinker. Judgements are the output of Kahneman's System 2 and of them he writes: 'In contrast, judgements are always intentional and explicit even when they are not overtly expressed.'[7] This is a clear classification of judgements as actions. We will later make use of Kahneman's distinction between Systems 1 and 2.

3. THE PRINCIPAL HYPOTHESIS AND ITS GROUNDS

The Principal Hypothesis, as I formulated it, states that a thinker's awareness of those of his mental events that are mental actions is a species of action-awareness. If mental actions are literally actions, it should not be surprising that a subject's awareness of them is of the same kind as other examples of action-awareness.

All the distinctive features of action-awareness we noted for bodily actions are also present for mental actions. We can run briefly through them, with the same lettering as above.

(*a*) Since you do not have perceptual experiences of your mental actions at all, and you have a distinctive awareness of them, you can certainly have this awareness without perception of them.

(*b*) Your awareness of your mental actions, such as your awareness that you are deciding, that you are calculating, and the like, is not merely an awareness that something is happening. It is an awareness that you are doing something, an awareness of agency from the inside.

(*c*) The awareness is representational: it seems to you that you are deciding, calculating, and so forth. Correspondingly there is such a thing as taking the world to be as this awareness represents it as being.

(*d*) The content of your awareness of your mental actions is first-personal and present-tensed: you are aware for instance that you are calculating now. An expression of this awareness with the first-person pronoun would be counted by Wittgenstein as a use of "I" as subject. Your belief that you are calculating now does not rest on two beliefs, for some mode of presentation

---

[7] Kahneman (2003: 689 ff.).

m other than the first person, that *m* is calculating now and that you are identical with *m*.

(*e*) (i) Mental action-awareness makes available to the thinker particular demonstrative ways of thinking of those mental actions. One can think '*this judgement*', '*this calculation*', and these demonstratives in thought refer to the particular mental actions awareness of which makes the demonstratives available in thought. This action-awareness makes available to a thinker ways of thinking of her own mental actions. These ways of thinking are essential to self-scrutiny and critical reflection on her own mental actions.

(ii) One may have an apparent awareness of a mental action which misrepresents the mental action. When, for instance, there is a sufficiently complex structure of desires and/or emotions leading to self-deception, one may think one is judging something when one is not, and may be judging something entirely different, or nothing at all.

(iii) We noted an analogue, in the case of bodily action, of the distinction between demonstrative and recognitional modes of presentation in the perceptual case. There is a corresponding distinction between two ways of thinking of mental actions. *This deciding, this calculation, this judgement* are all demonstratives in thought that refer to particular mental actions. But there is also a way of thinking of a type of mental action, for example the action-type of judging that London is burning, that is individuated by its connections with one's ability to engage in mental actions of that type. It is that way of thinking of a type that one employs when one thinks "If it is reported on the news that London is burning, of course I will judge that London is burning; but not otherwise". In normal cases, when one tries to perform a mental action of this type, one succeeds. One does not normally perform mental actions of these types by doing something else. These are the analogues in the mental case of a species of basic action.[8]

4. THE PRINCIPAL HYPOTHESIS: DISTINCTIONS AND CONSEQUENCES

I now turn to some attractions of the Principal Hypothesis, and some theoretical possibilities and reflections that it suggests.

---

[8] On basic actions, see originally Danto (1963), and, for refinements, Goldman (1970, chs 1 and 2).

One of the attractions of the Principal Hypothesis is that it assimilates those conscious events that are mental actions to a wider class whose members equally share some of the distinctive features of conscious mental actions. One of the most distinctive features is that such mental actions as judging, deciding, and the rest have the phenomenology of doing something, rather than involving the phenomenology of something being presented as being the case, as in perception, or as of something occurring to one, as in unintended imagination, in which cases the subject is passive. This active phenomenology is present for bodily action too. The action-awareness of raising one's arm is equally not that of being presented with some fact, but is rather a phenomenology of one's doing something. The position I am developing is, then, in head-on disagreement with the view that the character of conscious thought involves only states that are sensory or, like imagination, individuated by their relations to sensory states. That opposing view is well formulated (though not fully endorsed) by Jesse Prinz, who writes, 'When we introspect during thought, all we find are mental images, including auditory images of natural-language sentences (subvocal speech). With no phenomenal traces of nonsensory representations, it is tempting to conclude that all thought is couched in perceptual imagery.'[9]

Here are three cases, subjectively different from one another, in which exactly the same words—for instance, "Meeting tomorrow!"—may occur in your mind's ear:

(*a*) The words may just passively occur to you; this could be memory or unbidden imagination.

(*b*) You may be judging that the meeting is tomorrow, on the basis of remembered evidence.

(*c*) You may be making a decision to convene the meeting tomorrow.

The difference between these three—imagining or remembering, judging, and deciding—is certainly not something within the phenomenology of passive imagination or presentation. Nonetheless, it is a feature of your consciousness that you are, for instance, judging something rather than forming an intention. It is equally a feature of your consciousness if you are merely passive in this respect. Action-awareness is given as action-awareness, and is subjectively different from merely passive states. Any description of your conscious state is incomplete if it omits the characteristics of action-awareness.

---

[9] Prinz (2002: 103).

'No difference in imagistic or presentational phenomenology' does not imply 'No difference in phenomenology at all'.

The point applies even when there are no mental images or perceptions involved at all. Someone, Rodin's *Penseur* with his eyes closed, may be passively drifting in thought, and nothing may come to his mind; or he may be thinking hard about how to solve some theoretical or practical problem—and equally nothing may come to mind. These are very different total subjective states. The person who is concentrating on finding a solution to a problem is actively trying to do something in thought; and this contributes to the phenomenology of his state.

Correspondingly there is a difference in imagining being in these two states. This is what one would expect if imagining, from the inside, being in a certain state is subjectively imagining what it is like to be in that state. Imagining drifting aimlessly in thought is different from imagining concentrating on solving a problem.

Recognition that there is a distinctive category of mental action-awareness can account for many of the features of conscious thought that so engaged Gilbert Ryle in his late writings on the topic.[10] Someone so inclined could devote a whole paper (or more) to this topic. Here I just give two examples.

Ryle repeatedly emphasized that neither the occurrence of any one particular event involving the imagined uttering of words, or visualizing of scenes, or anything else of the sort, or any disjunction thereof, is what constitutes judging, when out on a drive, that the petrol (gas) station at the next village may be closed for Sunday.[11] In my view, Ryle is right about this. Under the Principal Hypothesis, his point is just what one would expect. None of the things Ryle rightly cites as insufficient for judgement involves action-awareness of judging, which is something additional to, and not ensured by, any amount of word-imagining, picturing in one's mind's eye, and the like.

The other example involves Ryle's long-standing (perhaps even fatal) attraction to 'adverbial' theories of mental phenomena. He notes that in the case of bodily events, some of them have 'thick' as well as thin descriptions. His example is that a hitting of a ball with a golf club may also be a 'practice approach shot', and 'a piece of self-training' (p. 474). He says these thick descriptions involve 'intention-parasitism', and that the same phenomenon is found amongst mental events, which may, in the case of

---

[10] See esp. Ryle (1971*b,c,d*).
[11] See Ryle (1971*c*: 393 ff.). Page references in the text are to Ryle (1971*a*).

a composer, be tryings-out, modifications, assemblies, and in the case of other projects in thought, may be serving many other purposes. He rightly concludes that descriptions of mental events involving intentionality on the part of the thinker will not be determined by neutral characterizations of the subjective contents of imaginings and visualizings; and that the intentional characterizations may be correct for many different kinds of imaginings and visualizings (pp. 476–9). What Ryle calls intention-parasitism is possible only where there is mental action. From the standpoint of the present chapter, there is nothing either adverbial (or higher-order, for that matter) in a mental event's being a mental action. To be a mental action, the event must have the additional property of having been produced in the right way by the subject of the event. When it is so, it is then possible for the 'thick' descriptions that Ryle mentions to get a grip. (The 'intention-parasitism', in so far as I understand it, is also not necessary for an event to be a mental action: I may actively imagine the Hammerklavier Sonata on a whim, and not in pursuit of some further purpose.)

In current philosophy of mind, there is a range of kind of states each of which is recognized as having representational content, in the sense that in being in one of these states, it thereby seems to the subject as if that content is correct. This seeming may be overruled by judgement, or it may be taken at face value. In either case, the state's possession of a representational content should not be identified with the subject's judging that content (or a corresponding content) to be correct. States currently recognized to possess such representational content include at least the following three kinds. There are perceptual states, in which, in having an experience in a particular sense modality, it seems to the subject that the world is a certain way. There are states of pure thought, in which it strikes one as the case that (say) the American Declaration of Independence was signed in 1776, where this purely propositional impression does not need to correspond to any personal memory. There are representational states of personal memory, in which one has a memory of, say, walking on the beach at Big Sur, and it thereby seems to one that one was there. To this list of kinds I suggest that we should add action-awareness. Your apparent action-awarenesses of raising your arm, of judging that it is time to leave, of calculating the sum of two numbers, each represent you as doing these very things. And just as a memory-impression may be a memory of your perceiving something in the past, and that represents you as so perceiving, a memory may also be of your doing something, and represent you as having done that thing. A memory of walking along a beach will commonly do both. To give a correct account of the relation between these states and the kinds of content they can contain, and to do so in a way that provides a philosophical resource, is a general challenge. I will return to it in the particular case of action-awareness and its contents.

When a subject has an action-awareness that he is φ-ing, for example, that he is turning the left-hand knob, all the contents of the that-clause contribute to the character of his awareness. There is the action-type of turning, different from that of pushing or pulling, and which he is aware of performing. Similarly, action-awareness of judging is different from action-awareness of coming to a decision. But the intentional objects of the action also contribute to the awareness too. One is aware that one is turning this knob rather than that one (both demonstratively given in thought). Similarly, one is aware that one is judging one complete propositional intentional content rather than another; and that one is coming to one decision rather than another.

In earlier writing I drew a distinction between being the object of attention, and occupying attention.[12] In conscious thought, your attention is occupied, but there need not be anything which is the object or event to which you are attending (not even an apparent object). The Principal Hypothesis contributes to an explanation of this difference. In ordinary action-awareness of bodily action, such as your awareness of raising your arm, your action-awareness need not involve your attending to your arm, or to its rising, even though your conscious action can certainly occupy your attention. If conscious thought is action-awareness, we would expect the same. The action of which you are aware in a distinctive way—making a judgement, forming an intention—does not involve the making of the judgement, or the formation of the intention, being the object of your attention. Rather, as in the case of bodily action, making the judgement, or forming the intention, occupies your attention.

5. HOW DO WE KNOW ABOUT OUR OWN MENTAL ACTIONS?

The distinctive way in which a subject comes to know of his own mental actions is by taking an apparent action-awareness at face value. You judge that it will rain. When so judging, you have an apparent action-awareness

---

[12] See Peacocke (1998c).

of your judging that it will rain. By taking this awareness at face value, you come to know that you judge that it will rain. In another case, you may have an apparent action-awareness of your calculating the sum of two numbers; by taking this awareness at face value, you come to know that you are engaged in calculating the sum of two numbers; and so forth.

Apparent action-awareness is, I emphasized earlier, a belief-independent event. A thinker may or may not endorse in judgement the content of an apparent action-awareness. Since action-awareness is not the same as judgement or belief, a self-ascription of an action made by taking an apparent action-awareness at face value is not reached by inference. It is no more an inferential than a perceptual judgement made by taking a perceptual experience at face value is inferential.

Because action-awareness is not judgement or belief, a self-ascription of a mental action made by taking an action-awareness at face value is a counter-example to the principle that knowledgeable mental self-ascriptions must be made by observation, by inference, or by nothing.[13] On the present view, that is a spurious trilemma. Action-awareness is not perception, and can exist in the absence of perception of the action of which it is awareness. Judgements based on action-awareness are not reached by inference, since action-awareness is not judgement or belief. And judgements based on action-awareness are not based on nothing, since action-awareness is a real state of consciousness, available for rationalizing certain judgements. We should draw the conclusion that the model of observation is not the only model available for a substantive, non-inferential epistemology of first-person mental ascriptions.

These points apply equally to self-ascriptions of bodily actions too. The trilemma "by observation, by inference, or by nothing" is similarly inapplicable to knowledge of one's bodily actions, when based on action-awareness. This fact should increase the credibility of the view that taking apparent action-awareness at face value is a means of rational judgement that we need to recognize in cases beyond those of mental action.

The mental events of which we have an action-awareness, according to this account, are events with an externally individuated content. The conceptual contents of these mental events, such as judgements or decisions, will in general be externally individuated. It may still be felt that there is a problem in the idea that we can be aware, in any way, of such contents of our mental

---

[13] The first sharp formulation of this view known to me is in Boghossian (1989: 5).

events. This feeling ought at least to have been put in question by the arguments of the preceding chapter. For perceptions have contents that are externally individuated; we do know without having to investigate our environmental relations what the contents of our perceptions are; and the Core Rule of the preceding chapter gives the beginnings of an explanation of how this can be so. Nonetheless, it may still be felt that we can be immediately aware only of the 'intrinsic' properties of our mental events.[14] If this were so, it would be an obstacle to the present account of the self-ascription of mental actions. I think that this objection can be satisfactorily addressed only in the presence of a theory of the nature of the ways in which we think of the intentional contents of our own attitudes. I return to precisely this issue in section 5 of the next chapter, after we have in front of us a treatment of the way in which we think of the contents of our intentional states.

As far as I can see, the thesis that we come to know of our mental actions by our action-awareness of them is neutral between conceptions of the type of action-awareness as conceptual or as non-conceptual. The thesis can consistently be accepted by the believer in non-conceptual content, and can consistently be accepted by his conceptualist opponent. In this area, there may seem to be a special problem for the friend of non-conceptual content. If the content of a judgement or decision, say, is conceptual, as it is, how can the action-awareness of making the judgement or decision be non-conceptual? Here we must distinguish what the awareness is of at the level of reference, and how events, things, and properties at the level of reference are given in consciousness. A characterization of a state's content as non-conceptual has to do with how things are given, not which things are given. A state of consciousness can have a non-conceptual content concerning things that include concepts. This is something we should already recognize independently to be possible if we grant that there can be conscious thinking by children who do not have concepts of concepts and do not have concepts of intentional contents built up from concepts. It is one thing to be employing concepts, and have conscious states whose content involves those concepts. It is a further thing to conceptualize those intentional contents themselves.

Is action-awareness philosophically explicable in terms that do not involve reference to subjective, conscious states and events? I call the claim that it is so explicable the "Reducibility Thesis". Under the Reducibility Thesis, however it is developed, action-awareness is not something fundamental,

---

[14] Such a view is expressed by Crispin Wright (2001: 342).

and to understand the role of action-awareness in our thought we must look to more fundamental conditions that do not involve consciousness. Any epistemological role played by action-awareness would then be played by these more fundamental conditions not involving consciousness. But I dispute the Reducibility Thesis.

How might the Reducibility Thesis be developed? Can we say that action-awareness consists in no more than an action's being a result of the operation of rational agency? That would need qualification on several fronts.

(*a*) Making photocopies is an action of mine, but I need not have an action-awareness that I am making copies. My action-awareness is of pressing certain buttons on the machine. To accommodate this, the Reducibility Thesis could be confined to types of action that are basic for the agent, actions the agent does not, in the content of his intentions, do by doing something else. The defender of the Reducibility Thesis would need to make this restriction to basic action-types both for bodily actions and for mental actions.

(*b*) The Reducibility Thesis would also have to make some accommodation of what Brian O'Shaughnessy calls sub-intentional acts.[15] Tapping your toes, moving your tongue are actions. You can become aware of them, and indeed come to have a distinctive action-awareness of them, but it is not clear that that action-awareness was already there when the actions were first performed. The defender of the Reducibility Thesis may make various moves at this point. One would be to insist that there is action-awareness even in these cases, but its content does not go even into short-term memory. Another would be to hold that the Reducibility Thesis holds only for the fully intentional acts of a rational agent. Both of these responses would need some work to become convincing; but let us leave speculation on how that might be done, because there is a deeper, and quite general, problem for the Reducibility Thesis.

It seems there could exist a being whose movements and whose changes in mental state are sensitive to the content of its beliefs and values, but whose tryings and actions, both bodily and mental (if actions they be), do not involve any action-awareness, either real or apparent. These beings would have to perceive their bodily actions, through vision, touch, or proprioception, to know that they are occurring. Would such subjects be exercising rational

---

[15] O'Shaughnessy (1980, vol. ii, ch. 10: 'The Sub-Intentional Act').

agency as that notion is understood within the terms of the Reducibility Thesis? If these subjects are counted as exercising rational agency, then the notion of rational agency employed in the Reducibility Thesis is so thin that it seems incapable of capturing action-awareness at all. But if such subjects are not so conceived of possessing rational agency, it seems that action-awareness, of both bodily and mental actions, has to be conceived as a coordinate element in rational agency in its own right.

I conclude that an explanation of the epistemology of action, both bodily and mental, has to go beyond materials that could equally be present in cases that involve no awareness on the action side. We need to recognize a coordinate, and irreducible, element of consciousness in rational agency and action-awareness as we actually have it. While it is right for an account of self-knowledge to emphasize the role of agency in certain kinds of self-knowledge, in my judgement such an account will work only in the presence of a background presumption that we have an action-awareness of our bodily and mental actions. We return to some of these issues in section 10 of this chapter.

6. CONCEPTS OF MENTAL ACTIONS AND THEIR EPISTEMOLOGICAL SIGNIFICANCE

It is widely accepted that there is a range of observational concepts—concepts of shape, size, orientation, colour, texture, amongst others—that are individuated in part by the fact that certain perceptual experiences give reasons to apply these concepts to objects or events presented in those perceptual experiences.[16] Theorists differ on how this individuation works, but there is less disagreement that there is some such individuative link between these concepts and perceptual states. What makes such an individuative link possible is in part the existence of perceptual states with representational content. I suggest that the representational content of action-awareness provides a similar resource for the individuation of certain concepts of mental action. Some concepts are individuated in part by the fact that action-awareness gives reason to apply these concepts.

One clause in a formulation of the possession-condition for the concept *judging that p* should treat the case of first-person application in the present

---

[16] My own way of developing such views is given in Peacocke (1992, ch. 3; 2001*a*), but many others hold a view of the type given in the text.

tense. It should state that, in the absence of good reasons for doubt, an apparent action-awareness of his judging a given content gives reason for a thinker to accept *I judge that p*. Here, the action-awareness in question has a content to the effect that the thinker is himself judging that *p*. When the action-awareness is awareness of a judgement, and a thinker self-ascribes in accordance with this possession-condition for first-person ascriptions of judgements, his self-ascriptions are sensitive to the event's being a judgement. Quite generally, making a judgement in accordance with one of the clauses of a possession-condition for a concept in the content of the judgement is a way of coming to know the content of the judgement in question.[17] The action-blind subjects considered towards the end of the preceding section could not, incidentally, exercise this concept of judgement in making ascriptions to themselves (if indeed they could possess concepts at all) since they lack action-awareness of their judgements.

An account of possession of these mental-action concepts must also have a clause dealing with third-person ascriptions. To understand third-person ascriptions of these concepts is to have tacit knowledge that their correctness requires the subject of the attribution to be in the same state the thinker is in himself, when a first-person attribution is correct. Under this approach, the bridge from first-person ascriptions to third-person ascriptions is once again built using tacit knowledge involving grasp of an identity-relation, along the lines discussed in Chapters 1 and 5. As with other accounts built according to this model, it follows that understanding the third-person ascriptions does not immediately, and without further empirical information, put a thinker in a position to know what would be evidence that someone else is performing a particular kind of mental action. It also follows that the thinker does not conceive of mental actions in general as events of a type that enjoy a certain role in a thinker's psychological economy. Once again, and for reasons parallel to the other cases we discussed, a thinker has to work out what distinctive role events of a particular mental-action-type play (if indeed there is such a general role). Theorists may, however, present other, competing accounts of the bridge to the third-person case, consistently with accepting the first-person clause I have been offering.

Does the first-person clause I have advocated embody a perceptual model of the self-ascription of certain attitudes? It does not. Action-awareness is not perceptual awareness; a subject can have action-awareness of something

---

[17] A principle I proposed and argued for in Peacocke (1992: 157 ff.; 1999).

without having any perceptual awareness of it. It is no consequence of the present view that when judging in accordance with the relevant possession-conditions, one perceives or observes one's judgements or decisions. Nor does the present view postulate intermediaries that would somehow be an obstacle to knowledge of one's own judgements, decisions, and other mental actions.

In the case of genuine perception of material objects and events, one would insist that a subject perceives an object or an event itself in a certain way. Far from perception inserting an intermediary that prevents access to the material objects and events themselves, it is perception that makes possible such access to the events and objects themselves. The same is true of action-awareness. We should take the grammar at face value. In the bodily case, the subject is aware of his action itself, his clenching his fist, say, and he is aware of it as his clenching his fist. It is as wrong to think of action-awareness as some epistemically problematic intermediary preventing access to the events and objects themselves as it is wrong to think of perceptual experience as an epistemically problematic intermediary between subjects and the world.

Action-awareness that one is φ-ing is a factive notion. It implies that one is φ-ing (arguably it also implies that one knows one is φ-ing). As some of the earlier examples show, there is such a state as mere apparent awareness that one is φ-ing, a state whose content can be false. Someone might argue that all we, as agents, ever have is mere apparent awareness that we are φ-ing. This is a form of the argument from illusion in perception, applied here on the side of action.

The argument in the action case is no more sound than its perceptual cousin. When an apparent action-awareness that you are φ-ing stands in the right complex of relations to your φ-ing, the apparent action-awareness *is* genuine awareness that you are φ-ing. The complex of relations in question is different from those involved in the perceptual case. The relations in question run predominantly from the mind to the world in the action case, rather than the opposite direction of the perceptual case. But the fallacy involved in the argument from illusion is the same in both the perception and the action cases.

Even if the treatment I am offering is not vulnerable to the argument from illusion, it may be thought that it is still open to the objections McDowell has raised against what he calls 'hybrid' accounts of knowledge.[18] As applied

---

[18] McDowell (1998).

to the present subject matter, the complaint would be that on the offered account, there could be a pair of cases in both of which the subject has the apparent action-awareness that entitles him to self-ascribe a mental action, yet in one of these cases the self-ascription is true, and in the other the self-ascription is false. The objection, to summarize it, is that if this is possible, the self-ascription cannot amount to knowledge in the first case. This is not a chapter about general epistemology, so I will not divert the discussion into what would need to be an extended consideration of the status of hybrid theories. The main message of this chapter is the role of action-awareness in the knowledgeable self-ascription of mental actions. That message can certainly be incorporated into a McDowellian epistemology if one so wishes. That incorporation would proceed by first insisting that in genuine action-awareness that one is φ-ing, the subject's mind is embracing the fact that he is φ-ing. The position would then go on to say that the subject, in judging that he is φ-ing, is simply taking this factive state at face value, is endorsing its representational content. Action-awareness that one is φ-ing would, on this McDowellian incorporation of the point of this chapter, play the same epistemic role in relation to certain self-ascriptions of actions as perceptual awareness that p plays, on his account, in attaining perceptual knowledge that p. On the McDowellian approach, in the case in which the subject has a mere apparent action-awareness, the kind of state which gives his reason for making his self-ascription of φ-ing is not the same as the kind in which it is genuine awareness of his φ-ing. So the alleged objections to hybrid theories would not get a grip. I am not endorsing this McDowellian approach. The issues involved in assessing it are orthogonal to the main theses of this chapter. My point is just that the idea that action-awareness of our mental events is important for the epistemology of some mental self-ascriptions can be acknowledged on both McDowellian and non-McDowellian positions in general epistemology.

Though action-awareness is distinct from perceptual awareness, there is a parallelism of abstract structure in the perception and action cases on the view I am advocating. There is a structure of rational entitlement in which the entitling state has representational content; and one can be mistaken about whether the content of the entitling state is correct (or whether it is really a factive state that one is in). If the preceding chapter is correct, there is also a systematic parallelism between the self-ascription of perception and the self-ascription of action (Chapter 6 sections 1 and 5). There is a danger here that we may endorse the following fallacious argument:

Mental actions are not given to their subject under a perceptual mode of presentation.

Hence,

One possible source of error is absent for mental actions that is present for perceptual beliefs about the external world; that is, self-ascriptions of mental actions have a certain domain of infallibility that perceptual beliefs do not.

The premiss of the argument just displayed is true. What follows the 'that is,' in the conclusion is false. An apparent action-awareness can have a false content, just as an apparently perceptual experience can have a false content. (In the case of mental action, this is the ground of the possibility of one form of self-deception: it may seem to one that one is forming a belief when in fact one is not.) The fact that action-awareness is not perceptual awareness does not give it any kind of infallibility, however limited, that perceptual awareness lacks. The premiss of the fallacious argument rightly alludes to the distinction between action-awareness and perceptual awareness. This difference in kind does not by itself produce any kind of philosophically significant restriction on fallibility. If there are restrictions, their sources lie elsewhere.[19]

The modest amount I have said so far about mental actions and concepts of them fits a broadly rationalist model of entitlement. The possession-condition for concepts of mental actions contains a clause about first-person present-tense ascription that says that the thinker has reason for making such ascriptions in the presence of suitable apparent action-awareness. This accords with a general model under which an entitlement to make a transition to a given judgement always has some a priori component that is founded in the nature of the contents involved in the judgement and the reasons for it, and in the nature of the mental states involved in the transition. Here the relevant a priori component is found in a transition (strictly, in the terminology of *The Realm of Reason*, it is an instance of the relatively a priori). A thinker is entitled to take the content of an event of apparent action-awareness at face

---

[19] I may have been guilty of the fallacy identified in this paragraph. There is a whiff of it in my contribution to a symposium with Tyler Burge on self-knowledge (Peacocke 1996, esp. p. 126): 'brute error is impossible. It is impossible precisely because, in these psychological self-ascriptions, there is nothing that plays the role that experience plays in genuine observational knowledge of physical objects.'

value, in the absence of reasons for doubt. The claim of the existence of some a priori component in every entitlement was the general position I defended in the early chapters of *The Realm of Reason*.

We do need, however, to have a much better understanding of how exactly apparent action-awareness provides a thinker with entitlement to make judgements about his own actions. The understanding we seek should explain how relying on apparent action-awareness furthers the goal of making judgements that are true.

In the second chapter of *The Realm of Reason*, I distinguished three levels at which one can characterize the entitlement-relation. There is, first, the level of instances of the relation. There is, next, a second level of true generalizations about the relation, generalizations that have as instances truths at the first level of characterization. At a third level are the principles which explain why those generalizations at the second level are true (and thereby also explain the instances). The third level, as the explanatory level, is the one we should seek to elaborate further in the case of action-awareness and the self-ascription of mental actions.

What makes an apparent action-awareness one of clenching one's fist, or raising one's arm, or judging or deciding some particular thing, is that, when these and the subject's other mental states are properly connected to the world, they are caused by events (tryings) that cause a clenching of the fist, a raising of one's arm, or a judging or deciding of some particular content. That is, the mental states of apparent action-awareness are relationally, and in a certain sense externally, individuated. What makes them the states they are is the fact that when all is functioning properly, and the states are properly embedded in relation to the subject's other mental states, his body and the external world, they have a cause which also causes what they are as of—what they represent as being correct. My own view is that the easiest way for such complex, relationally individuated states to occur is for states of their kind to have evolved by a selection process, one which favours the occurrence of those states whose representational content is correct. In taking apparent action-awareness at face value, one is judging that things have come about in what is in fact the easiest way for them to come about.

Under this approach, once again it appears that although action-awareness is distinct from perceptual awareness, the structure and underlying expla-nation of entitlement-relations involved in relying on action-awareness is arguably the same as that underlying perceptual entitlement. The outline just given of why there is an entitlement to take certain action-awarenesses at face value is entirely parallel to an argument that there is an entitlement to take certain observational contents of apparent perceptual experience at face value.

This outline of how action-awareness entitles a thinker to make self-ascriptions of bodily and mental actions is given for the neo-rationalist approach to entitlement that I myself favour. That approach is opposed to purely reliabilist accounts of entitlement that do not include rationality requirements that are distinct from considerations of reliability. But it is only fair to note that pure reliabilists, and no doubt reliabilists of other stripes, could equally accept the importance of taking apparent action-awareness at face value in the account of how we come to know our own mental actions. Taking apparent action-awareness at face value is not at all something proprietary to neo-rationalists; it can serve many other comers too.

7. IS THIS ACCOUNT OPEN TO THE SAME OBJECTIONS AS PERCEPTUAL MODELS OF INTROSPECTION?

Current philosophers of mind often agree that models of introspection that treat it as a form of perception are untenable. I too have repeatedly emphasized that action-awareness is not perceptual awareness. But action-awareness, as a source of self-knowledge, does involve a conscious state that stands in complex causal relations to what it is an awareness of. Action-awareness is also, as I have equally emphasized, to be sharply distinguished from judgement that one is performing a certain action. It is also to be distinguished from awareness merely of trying to perform the action. So there is a pressing question: do the objections to perceptual models of introspection, suitably adapted, apply equally to action-awareness models of first-person knowledge of mental action?

One of the most interesting and general arguments against perceptual models of introspective knowledge has been developed by Sydney Shoemaker in the second of his Royce Lectures, 'Self-Knowledge and "Inner Sense" ', in the lecture entitled 'The Broad Perceptual Model'.[20] Because of its significance and generality, and the depth at which it addresses these issues, I

---

[20] Shoemaker (1996*b*). Page references in the text are to this work.

will examine Shoemaker's arguments in some detail. Shoemaker's discussion of the perceptual model of introspection includes the following theses:

> Shoemaker's Thesis (1): Under the perceptual model, 'the existence of these [perceptually known] states and events is independent of their being known in this way, and even of there existing the mechanisms that make such knowledge possible' (pp. 224–5).

Shoemaker calls his Thesis (1) the 'Independence Condition' (my capitals). I agree that the Independence Condition must be a commitment of any conception worthy of being called perceptual.

> Shoemaker's Thesis (2): The Independence Condition implies the possibility of what Shoemaker calls 'self-blindness'.

To be self-blind with respect to certain mental facts or phenomena is to be able to conceive of them—'just as the person who is literally blind will be able to conceive of those states of affairs she is unable to learn about visually' (p. 226)—but not to have introspective access to them. The possibility of such self-blindness, Shoemaker writes, 'I take to be a consequence of the independence condition that is built into the broad perceptual model of self-knowledge' (p. 226). I call his Thesis (2) the "Thesis of the Independence/Self-Blindness Link", or the "Link Thesis" for short.

> Shoemaker's Thesis (3): Self-blindness is not a genuine possibility in respect of pains; nor in respect of perceptual experience; nor in respect of the will and intentional action; nor in respect of beliefs (sections II, III, IV, and V of the Second Lecture respectively).

Shoemaker elaborates: 'it is of the essence of many kinds of mental states and phenomena to reveal themselves to introspection' (p. 242). It follows from his Thesis (3), together with his Thesis (2), that the Independence Condition is false for pains, perceptual experience, the will, intentional action, and beliefs. It also follows in turn by modus tollens from Thesis (1) that the perceptual model of introspection is false.

> Shoemaker's Thesis (4): The correct account of the relation of these mental events and states (pain, experiences, intentions, actions, beliefs) to awareness of them needs to draw on the distinction between the core realization of a state and its total realization (pp. 242–3).

The core realization comes and goes as the mental state comes and goes. 'The total realization will be the core realization plus those relatively permanent features of the organism, features of the way its brain is "wired", which enable the core realization to play [the causal role associated with that state]' (pp. 242–3). Adding rationality, intelligence, and possession of the concept of belief to a first-order belief enables the core realization of the first-order belief to play a more encompassing role. When this surrounding material is present, a first-order belief and the second-order belief that one has that belief have the same core realization. The total realization of the first-order belief is a proper part of the total realization of the self-ascriptive belief that one has the first-order belief (p. 243).

If Shoemaker's arguments in his Theses (1) through (4) are sound, their applicability is not restricted to the perceptual model of introspection. They apply to any subject matter for which the Independence Condition is fulfilled, and for which self-blindness is not a possibility. This generalizable character of Shoemaker's argument is part of its interest.

It certainly appears that, if Shoemaker's argument is sound, it must generalize to apply against the action-awareness account of our knowledge of our own actions (bodily or mental). Action-awareness of a particular action is certainly distinct from the action itself. The real or apparent action-awareness lies on a different causal pathway from the action itself. The awareness is caused by an initial trying, or some initiating event, which trying or event also causes the effects (the arm's rising) that are required for there to be an action of the kind in question. Even if there is an argument that tryings must, at least in central cases, involve awareness of those tryings, the trying and the awareness of trying is distinct from action-awareness. The relation between some constitutive components of the action and the action-awareness of the action is causal. It is not a real option to say that there are no causal-explanatory elements at all in the action-awareness account.

But this then seems to leave it at least metaphysically possible that there be actions without the distinctive kind of action-awareness that we enjoy. This is precisely the case of action-blindness we considered two sections back. What makes an event in that envisaged world an action is the fulfilment of the same condition as makes something an action in the actual world: it is caused in the right kind of way by a trying. The actions in this non-actual world would be explained by their agents' contentful intentional states (conceptual or non-conceptual). To fail to acknowledge a category of actions in this possible world would be to miss an explanatorily significant category of events. Thus there is indeed a plausible case to be made that there can be actions without action-awareness; and if that case is good, then Shoemaker's Independence Condition is met for actions.

So if Shoemaker's general argument is sound, it would follow that the action-awareness account is committed to the possibility of self-blindness in respect of such mental actions as judgements, decisions, and the rest. That is what his Thesis (2), the Thesis of the Independence/Self-Blindness Link, implies. It is this Link Thesis on which we need to focus in assessing the bearing of Shoemaker's argument on the action-awareness account of knowledge of our mental actions.

Whenever something is impossible, one should ask: what is the explanation of the impossibility? If self-blindness is not possible in respect of certain states and events, it may be that the explanation of the impossibility traces to the conditions required for possessing concepts of those states and events, rather than being explained by the failure of the Independence Condition. Actually it seems to me that further reflection on Shoemaker's own initial illustration of a genuine case of self-blindness, of the genuinely blind person who is able to conceive of the states of affairs that she cannot see to obtain, supports this alternative explanation. The blind person can conceive of objective states of affairs involving objects, events, their properties, and spatial relations only because she is capable of perceiving these things and properties in at least some other sense modality—by touch and hearing, for instance (or else because she was once able to see, and knows what it would be to have visual experience of objective states of affairs). If we are asked to entertain the possibility of someone who is supposed to have the conception of spatial, material objects and events while also lacking all such perceptual faculties, and lacking all knowledge of what it would be like to have them, it seems reasonable to question whether that is a genuine possibility at all. It is such faculties that make possible the thinker's possession of concepts of objects and events that may be perceived in one or more sense modalities. If this is so, then there could not be someone who is capable of no perceptual states at all, yet has the concept of objects and events he cannot perceive. The explanation of this impossibility has, however, nothing to do with failure of the Independence Condition. The Independence Condition holds as strongly as ever for conditions concerning external objects, events, and many of their properties and relations. It would be quite wrong to move from the impossibility of someone who both lacks all perceptual faculties and conceives of objects and events he cannot perceive to the conclusion that the existence of material objects and events is not independent of our ability to conceive of them, to perceive them, or to know of them. Their existence is so independent, in all these respects.

Structurally, the position here is as follows. The claim of the possibility of self-blindness with respect to some states of affairs is a claim of the form $\lozenge$ (p & ~q), a claim that it's possible that the subject has the concept of those states of affairs and yet does not have a certain kind of access to them. When self-blindness is not possible, we have something of the form ~$\lozenge$ (p & ~q) holding. A proposition of that last form is equivalent to the corresponding proposition of the form $\square$ (p → q). The explanation of this necessity's holding may simply be that, necessarily, whenever the conditions for the subject's possessing concepts of those states of affairs hold, the subject also has a certain kind of access to them. Such access may be involved in the possession-conditions for the concepts in question. This can all be true consistently with the Independence Condition's still holding for the states of affairs in question.

A case which seems to me clearly to exemplify this possibility is that of pains and beliefs about pains. An animal can have real pains (not just some surrogate or proto-pains), without having the concept of pain, and hence without having any ability to think about its pains as pains. The existence of pains is independent of their being known about, as the Independence Condition requires. Self-blindness is nevertheless arguably impossible for the state of being in pain. The explanation for this is the point that part of what is involved in having the concept of pain is a willingness to judge, and judge knowledgeably, that one is in pain when one is in pain, where the pain itself makes rational the thinker's judgement. This explanation does indeed not have anything to do with a failure of the Independence Condition.

These points also highlight the fact that the sense in which pain is something essentially open to introspection—a consideration Shoemaker uses in the intuitive defence of his Thesis (3)—is to be distinguished from the claim that its nature is constitutively dependent on what its possessor would judge about it in specified circumstances. Introspection is a matter of the occupation and direction of attention, rather than something to be characterized at the level of judgement.

This consideration of the case of pain shows two things:

(*a*) There are relatively uncontroversial instances in which we have the Independence Condition holding, consistently with the impossibility of self-blindness. It follows that we cannot take the failure of the Independence

Condition as the explanation of an impossibility of self-blindness. Shoemaker writes of introspection, contrasting it with perception, that 'the reality known and the faculty for knowing it are, as it were, made for each other—neither could be what it is without the other' (p. 245). We are committed to disagreeing with this in one direction: pain could be what it is independently of the presence of the capacity for, and the nature of, thought about pain. The concept of pain is, however, certainly made for knowing about pains. The explanation of the impossibility of self-blindness in the case of pain has more to do with the nature of the concept of pain than with the nature of pain.

It would be wrong, however, to say that the explanation has nothing at all to do with the nature of pain itself. It is because pains are conscious, subjective events that pain itself is capable of featuring in the possession-condition for the concept *pain*.

(*b*) The second lesson is that if, as is also widely accepted, we do not perceive our pains but simply experience them, the Independence Condition can hold even in a case in which the perceptual model itself fails.

An explanation of the impossibility of self-blindness in the case of one's own mental actions is analogous in some respects to that just given for the case of pain, and is disanalogous in other respects. The explanation is partially analogous in respect of the role played by the possession-conditions for such concepts as those of judgement and decision. To possess the concept of judgement involves applying it to oneself in response to one's action-awareness of one's own judgements. If a thinker is capable of doing this, he will not be self-blind in respect of his mental actions. His ability to conceive of judgements, decisions, and other mental actions as such is constitutively dependent upon the kind of awareness that underlies his ability to come to know of them in a certain way (or at least to know what it is like to have such awareness).

It would be an objection to this account of the nature and limits of the impossibility of self-blindness in the case of mental actions if there were a different account of possession of the concepts of judgement, decision, and other mental action-types, an account that does not give an essential, constitutive role to action-awareness. I do not know how such an account might run. Could an alternative account talk of the thinker's tacit knowledge of an individuating role for judgement, or decision, or some other action-type, in a psychological economy? Such tacit knowledge seems unnecessary in simply making a knowledgeable present-tense self-ascription of an action in rational response to an action-awareness of one's performing such an action.

For third-person (or other-tense) ascriptions, once one has the role of action-awareness in the first-person, present-tense case, a thinker's understanding of the other cases can consist simply in his tacit knowledge that they are correct if their subject is in the same state as someone who is genuinely action-aware of his performance of the action-type in question. In my judgement, this description of the tacit knowledge is more faithful to what has to be explained than attribution of tacit knowledge of a quite specific psychological role for the action-type in question. In so far as ordinary thinkers are able to reach conclusions about the role of a mental action-type in a thinker's psychology, it is by way of application of this identity-condition.

A major respect in which the cases of pain and action-awareness are disanalogous is that in making a self-ascription on the basis of action-awareness, a subject is endorsing the content of representational state. Pain is not, in my view, a wholly representational state (or at least, it is not necessary for the purposes of this account that it be so, unlike the case of action-awareness). This difference means that we need an account that addresses the question of why we are entitled to take the representational content in question at face value, as touched upon in the preceding section. Once again, although action-awareness is not perceptual awareness, the need for such an account is something shared with the case in which a perceptual experience is legitimately taken at face value.

To summarize this critique to this point: (*a*) There are counter-examples to Shoemaker's thesis that the Independence Condition implies the possibility of self-blindness; (*b*) there are alternative explanations of the impossibility of self-blindness, to the extent that it is impossible, consistently with rejection of the perceptual model of introspection; and (*c*) the explanation of the impossibility of self-blindness has more to do with the nature of the concepts involved in thought about these mental states and events, than in the nature of the events themselves.

What, however, of Shoemaker's own positive explanation of the impossibility of self-blindness in the cases he discusses? There is some reason to doubt that the distinction between the core and the total realization of a state, and Shoemaker's proposal about its extension in cases of introspective knowledge, can do quite the work he requires of it. Shoemaker's view is that the core realization—the realizing state that comes and goes as what it realizes comes and goes—is the same for the mental state thought about and the self-ascription of the state. But since a judgement that one is in a certain kind of mental state requires employment of one's concept of that state (and of oneself, and of the present), the structured state that realizes this judgement is much more plausibly identified as something causally downstream from the mental state that verifies the content of the judgement about oneself as correct. The realizing state must have sufficient structure for it to realize judgements of a structured intentional content, involving concepts combined in a quite specific way. I will not pursue this further here, mainly because the issues are not specific to awareness and self-knowledge. I just note that this second objection will be compelling to those who see something in the arguments, marshalled some years ago in debates about the language of thought by Jerry Fodor and Martin Davies, to the effect that the causal-explanatory powers of states with intentional content require corresponding structure in their realizing states.[21] While it is true that Shoemaker includes in his total realization whatever it is that realizes possession of particular concepts, that point would not be enough to meet the concerns of these critics. When someone makes the judgement that he is in pain, it is not merely that he possesses the concept of pain. The state that realizes his judgement must also realize the activation or use of his concept of pain, and thus be ready for inferential interactions involving the concept in other premisses. Simply being in pain falls short of that. The distinction becomes vivid when for, instance, one thinks one is in pain when the dentist approaches with some terrifying instrument. The dentist then says, 'I haven't even touched you yet!' In the patient's rush to judgement, he judges that he's in pain, and the realization of this will involve the activation of concepts, and the placing of symbols for the concepts, suitably combined, into the 'belief-box' on theories endorsing the existence of a language of thought. But the subject is not really in pain (nor is a possession-condition relating possession of the concept of pain to the occurrence of pain undermined by such impulsive cases). The most natural treatment of such examples is to say that, even for core realizations, the core realization of pain is distinct from the core realization of the judgement that one is in pain.

8. CHARACTERIZING AND UNIFYING SCHIZOPHRENIC EXPERIENCE

Our Principal Hypothesis states that a thinker's awareness of those of his mental events that are mental actions is a species of action-awareness,

---

[21] Fodor (1975; 1987*b*); Davies (1991).

with all the distinctive characteristics of action-awareness. The Principal Hypothesis has some significance for our understanding of the phenomenon of schizophrenia. The Hypothesis contributes to a correct characterization of what it is that the schizophrenic subject lacks. It is equally essential to providing a deeper unification of some of the symptoms of schizophrenia. The distinctions drawn upon in elaborating the Hypothesis are also relevant to current psychological theories in their explanation of the occurrence of schizophrenia.

I divide the significance of the Principal Hypothesis for schizophrenia into five different headings.

(*a*) What the schizophrenic subject lacks in the area of conscious thought is action-awareness of the thoughts that occur to him. To enjoy action-awareness of a particular event of thinking is to be aware, non-perceptually, of that thinking as something one is doing oneself. The awareness of one's own agency that exists in normal subjects is missing in, for example, the schizophrenic experience of 'thought-insertion'. One schizophrenic subject famously reported: 'The thoughts of Eamonn Andrews [a UK television presenter in the 1960s] come into my mind. He treats my mind like a screen and flashes his thoughts on to it like you flash a picture.'[22]

It is important to characterize the schizophrenic's consciousness as lacking action-awareness. It is not merely that these subjects report that their conscious mental events are caused by external, intervening agents. Even when they no longer report that they are so caused, because they are persuaded of the non-veridicality of these conscious events, these subjects' experience of passivity persists. Action-awareness is still absent, whatever the schizophrenic subject's own beliefs, if any, about why he is having mental events from which the action-awareness is absent. Precisely because action-awareness is, like perception, belief-independent, it cannot be restored simply by altering someone's beliefs.

The schizophrenic condition is also sometimes characterized as a 'failure to distinguish between ideas and impulses arising from within the subject's own mind and perceptions arising from stimuli in the external world'.[23] But subjects do draw the distinction. The ability to draw the distinction is implied by the subject's own description of thought-insertion just quoted. It is in part because the distinction is drawn that the conscious states of

---

[22] Frith and Johnstone (2003: 36).   [23] Frith and Johnstone (2003: 37).

schizophrenia are so alarming to their unfortunate subjects. The right way to formulate the point about the distinction rather involves action-awareness. The schizophrenic subjects lack the action-awareness in thought present in normal subjects, an awareness that, in its representational content, draws the distinction between events produced by oneself and events produced by others in the right place.

(*b*) The Principal Hypothesis provides a straightforward unification of some of the symptoms of schizophrenia in thought and some of its symptoms in bodily action. Some schizophrenic subjects experience delusions of control of their body by an external agency. 'It is my hand and arm that move, and my fingers pick up the pen, but I don't control them. What they do is nothing to do with me.'[24] Sean Spence asked subjects with delusions of control to perform a simple bodily task of holding a lever and producing a random sequence of movements. They performed this task normally, but still reported that their movements were controlled by alien forces.[25]

The Principal Hypothesis states that awareness of mental actions is action-awareness of the same sort as occurs in bodily action-awareness. Subjects who lack action-awareness of the thoughts they are in fact producing must have some kind of impairment of the mechanism that, in healthy subjects, produces action-awareness. But if action-awareness in the bodily case is awareness of exactly the same kind as in the case of conscious mental actions, it is to be expected that some cases of impairment of the mechanism producing action-awareness would affect awareness of bodily actions too. This is just what one finds. Symptoms that might otherwise seem somewhat diverse, and might even raise doubts about whether there is a single underlying condition of which they are both manifestations, are in fact unified by the Principal Hypothesis.

(*c*) Some of the phenomena of schizophrenia highlight, and cannot be properly characterized without, the distinction between action-awareness and awareness of goals and intentions. The idea of a defect in awareness of goals and intentions has sometimes played a large role in some earlier theorists' explanation of schizophrenia. It played such a role in Christopher Frith's 1992 account in *The Cognitive Neuropsychology of Schizophrenia*.[26] But we should remember the subjects in the Spence study just mentioned, in which subjects succeeded at simply bodily tasks they were instructed to carry out, but still

---

[24] Frith and Johnstone (2003: 37).   [25] Frith and Johnstone (2003: 37); Spence et al. (1997).
[26] Frith (1992; see the summary pp. 133–4, and earlier in the same chapter).

experienced delusions of control. These subjects knew their goal and their intention—it was to perform the task the experimenter had requested. Their abnormality is not in failing to represent their goal or intention correctly, but in their lack of action-awareness of their bodily actions as their own.

(*d*) There is a theory proposed by Irwin Feinberg, and developed further by Frith and Johnstone, which proposes for schizophrenia an analogue of Helmholtz's famous 'corollary discharge' in visual perception.[27] Helmholtz offered an explanation of why the world does not seem to move when you move your eyes, even though the image of objects moves on the retina as your eye moves. According to Helmholtz, just prior to a movement of your eyes there is a corollary discharge caused by the attempt to move the eyes, and this discharge permits a computation of the location of objects in the environment that takes into account the movement of the eyes. Frith and Johnstone write that 'Patients with delusions of control and related symptoms have problems that suggest that they cannot monitor their own movements in the normal way.'[28] When we regard consciousness of mental actions as a species of action-awareness, such awareness can be accounted for in this explanatory structure. The natural conjecture, given all the evidence to date, is that:

(*i*) When there is no corollary discharge, there is no action-awareness of the movement in question as one of your own actions, and this applies quite generally, both in bodily and in mental cases. If the corollary discharge theory is correct, this hypothesis would explain the absence of action-awareness in schizophrenic subjects, again both in bodily and in mental cases.

(*ii*) If the corollary discharge is caused by trying to perform the action in question, in normal subjects, that explains why, when there is no evidence to the contrary, trying itself causes an (apparent) action-awareness. Computationally, it is for the agent exactly as one would expect it to be when there is action. This would also explain the apparent action-awareness in trying to move a severed limb. It may also explain some illusions of having formed a belief.

(*e*) There is a syndrome of symptoms in schizophrenia having to do with a loss of will, an absence of spontaneous action and thought, and blunted emotional responses. Action-awareness is the most obvious and fundamental

---

[27] See Frith and Johnstone (2003); Feinberg (1978); Helmholtz (1962).
[28] Frith and Johnstone (2003: 133).

manifestation in conscious life of oneself as a successful agent. When this awareness is lacking, it is not surprising that a subject's sense of himself as an agent should suffer, and that he should be less motivated to action and spontaneity. When your actions, however extensive, are experienced only passively, it is hard to conceive of yourself as a successful agent. Absence of action-awareness is not an isolated phenomenon of consciousness, but has ramifying effects, both for the emotions of the schizophrenic subject and for his self-conception.

Obviously there is much about schizophrenia that the Principal Hypothesis does not explain. A full understanding has to explain the prevalence of the impression of control by alien agencies and forces. Why an absence of action-awareness should lead to this specific kind of illusion needs an empirical explanation by resources going far beyond those of the Principal Hypothesis. My position is only that we need the distinctions I have been drawing to characterize and unify the schizophrenic phenomena. We will not have a proper empirical explanation of the phenomena without an accurate characterization of what it is that has to be explained.

9. THE FIRST PERSON IN THE SELF-ASCRIPTION OF ACTION

I now turn to the role of the first person in action-awareness. I define a use, on a particular occasion, of the first person in thought as a "use of "I" as agent" as one in which that use occurs in a first-person judgement made simply by taking the representational content of an apparent action-awareness at face value. The uses of the first person in the judgements *I am pressing the button* and *I judge that Bush will be re-elected* will be uses of "I" as agent when made by taking the corresponding action-awarenesses at face value.

Uses of "I" as agent are uses of "I" as subject, in the sense employed by Wittgenstein in *The Blue and Brown Books*, and later so well elucidated in Sydney Shoemaker's important papers.[29] As we noted, in ordinary circumstances, when a thinker uses "I" as agent in a judgement *I am φ-ing*, his judgement does not rest on a pair of beliefs that m is φ-ing, for some m distinct from the first person, together with an identity belief *I am m*. I do not

---

[29] Shoemaker (1984*b*,*c*).

have first to judge *that person is pressing the button*, or *CP is pressing the button*, before I am in a position to judge *I am pressing the button*. Action-awareness already has a first-person component in its intentional content. If the thinker is taking that awareness at face value, no such identity belief is needed for the thinker to be in a position to make a self-ascription of the action in question. The case quite unlike that in which my belief *My car alarm is sounding* is based on the two beliefs *That car's alarm is sounding* and *I am the owner of that car*. In Shoemaker's terminology, judgements *I am φ-ing* involving the use of "I" as agent are immune to error through misidentification relative to (the first occurrence of) the first person.

For enthusiasts about these distinctions, this is arguably a case of what Shoemaker calls de facto immunity.[30] In a world in which devices or Wilder Penfield-like persons intervene after one's tryings, and, by means of some randomizing mechanism, may or may not make their intended bodily and mental effects come about, there could regularly be incorrect apparent action-awarenesses. In such a world a thinker could introduce a demonstrative "That A agent", that refers to whoever is the agent of the event of which the subject has a token action-awareness A. This is the action-analogue of the demonstratives for times and places I imagined in *Sense and Content* for cases in which there are massive time-lags in perception, or perceptions as from places other than one's current location.[31] In those circumstances, one could reasonably wonder "Am I identical with that A agent?" But this is no more our actual situation with respect to agency than is the corresponding situation for the invented temporal and spatial demonstratives. Whatever the correct explanation of the phenomenon, contingent features of our actual circumstances can have a bearing on what is required for coming to make a judgement reasonably.

The existence of a use of "I" as agent and the nature of the conscious states on which these uses are based can help explain some of the illusions, in the history of philosophy, to the effect that there exists a transcendent subject whose transcendent operations affect the spatial world, and the mental world. In the apparent action-awareness *I am φ-ing* itself, the subject is not given as having a location in the spatial world, nor as having spatial or material properties. This applies to predications of bodily actions of φ-ing, as well as to mental actions. The apparent action is bodily, but the subject who is represented as doing it is not represented in the awareness as a spatial object, or as having spatial properties, itself.

---

[30] Shoemaker (1984c)   [31] Peacocke (1983: 125 ff.).

It would be a terrible fallacy—one of those non sequiturs of 'numbing grossness'—to conclude from this fact that the subject referred to in such thoughts and awarenesses does not have a spatio-temporal location and does not have spatio-temporal and material properties. It would be a fallacy even to conclude that the subject referred to does not need to have such properties. But it would be a brave person who, on reading the works of those who have postulated a transcendental subject, concludes that no such fallacious transition is hovering over their writings. This is particularly so in the case of those writers who have placed some species of agency in a noumenal realm.

As is often the case with the postulation of transcendental subject matters, the motivation for the postulation involves a genuine insight, misapplied. It is right to hold that much thought is mental action, and so must be explained in the same general way that other action is. It is wrong to think that a transcendent subject is either necessary or possible in explaining these distinctive phenomena.

The case of action-awareness is a distinctive one amongst the range of phenomena that can generate illusions of transcendence, in that the intentional content of the awareness itself contains the first person. A wide range of other cases that generate the illusion have the property that in *Being Known* I called 'representational independence'.[32] When self-ascribing a perception, or an occurrence of a passive thinking to oneself, one does not normally rely on a conscious state which represents oneself as enjoying that mental state. Rather, one moves rationally from that mental state itself to a self-ascription. There are thus two rather different ways in which it may come to seem that "I" refers to something without spatial or material properties. One way is for the transition to a judgement to move from a state which does not contain the first person in its intentional content (or not as standing in the relation self-ascribed). The other is for the rationalizing state to contain the first person in its intentional content, but for that content not to represent the subject as having spatial and material properties. Described in the abstract, this case might seem to be of questionable possibility; but it is this possibility that action-awareness realizes.[33]

---

[32] Peacocke (1999, sect. 6.1).

[33] It also follows that a different explanation of the entitlement to the transition must be given in the case of action awareness than in the representationally independent cases. In Peacocke (1999) I offered what I called the 'delta account' (sects 6.2, 6.3). The account above of entitlement for

While all uses of "I" as agent are uses of "I" as subject in our ordinary circumstances, the converse is not true. There are uses of "I" as subject, even uses in the self-ascription of attitudes, that are not uses of "I" as agent. An example of Richard Moran's illustrates the possibility.[34] You may come to the conclusion that you believe that someone has betrayed you on the basis of information about your feelings, emotions, and other judgements. As Moran writes, 'insofar as it is possible for one to adopt an empirical or explanatory stance on one's own beliefs, and thus to bracket the issue of what their possession commits one to, it will be possible for one to adopt this stance to anything theoretically knowable, including private events or attitudes that one may be somehow aware of immediately, without inference'.[35] Suppose then you come to the conclusion that you believe that a certain person has betrayed you, and your evidence for this self-ascription consists of your other mental states that, in self-ascribing, you use "I" as subject. The evidence might, for instance, include your emotions of anger or irritation at the person, and your self-ascriptions of the mental states that form the evidential basis for your belief about your beliefs will then involve uses of "I" as subject. Your inferential judgement "I believe that person has betrayed me" would, in these circumstances, not be reached by some identity inference from two premises of the form "*m* believes that that person has betrayed him" and "I am *m*". The self-ascription does, in ordinary circumstances, involve a use of "I" as subject. But it is not a use of "I" as agent based on an action-awareness of judging that that person has betrayed you. There is, in the example, no such action-awareness, and no such judgement for there to be an action-awareness of.

In this example, the self-ascription in "I believe that that person has betrayed me" uses "I" as subject because the premises from which it is reached also use "I" as subject. But the same propositional evidence about some person given in a third-person way *m* could equally, and in normal circumstances, support the conclusion "*m* believes that that person has betrayed him". By contrast, when one self-ascribes a belief on the basis of action-awareness, such awareness involves the first-person essentially. Reliance on action-awareness is a way of coming to ascribe an attitude that one can, in ordinary circumstances, use only in ascribing attitudes to oneself. In this respect, it is unique to the first person.

---

the case of action awareness, which in abstract structure more closely parallels that for perceptual judgements, is quite different from the delta account.

[34] See Moran (2001, ch. 3 sect. 3: 'Avowal and Attribution').   [35] Moran (2001: 92).

10. RATIONAL AGENCY AND ACTION-AWARENESS

Rational agency and action-awareness are coordinate elements in being a rational subject. Neither element seems to be definable in terms of features of the other.

The idea that the nature of action-awareness could be explicable without reference to rational agency is immediately puzzling. As we emphasized, an apparent action-awareness has a representational content whose correctness requires that the subject of the awareness be the agent of the event which the awareness represents the subject as producing. The correctness of the apparent awareness requires rational agency. If the apparent action-awareness is correct, there will be rational agency. Further, if the apparent awareness is apparent awareness of some state of affairs whose existence is independent of the apparent awareness, as it seems to be, the prospects for reducing rational agency to features of action-awareness are poor.

What of the converse direction? Can action-awareness be reduced to other features of rational agency? In section 5 of this chapter, I argued against the idea that action-awareness can be reduced simply to rational agency itself. Can it instead be reduced to a thinker's knowledge of his intentions? Is a thinker's knowledge of what he is doing really explained by his knowledge of his intentions in acting?

There are at least two problems with this idea. The first is that a thinker can intend to act at a given time; may know that that time is now; but may yet fail even to try to act. When the thinker does try to act, how does he know that he is trying? It is no defence of this position to say that he is aware that he is trying. Trying itself is a mental action, and awareness of it is a case of action-awareness, the phenomenon that this account was trying to explain in terms of knowledge of intentions.

Some of the examples given earlier show that even if we grant that the subject knows that he is acting, his knowing that he is intending to φ does not imply that he has an action-awareness of φ-ing. In operating the photocopying machine, I know that I am intending to make a good copy of a document. I do not have an action-awareness of making a good copy of the document. Only by opening the lid of the machine and perceiving the result do I become aware that I have made a good copy, if I have. The same applies even when it is not a question of operating machines whose results are not immediately open to view. If I am novice at Greek, then whether I have successfully written a Greek letter zeta, or traced its shape correctly in the air, may not be something I know or am aware of simply by having an operative intention to do so. You do not know what you are really doing simply by knowing your intentions in acting.[36] Action-awareness continues to be an essential and irreducible element in our knowledge of what we are doing.

As we stand back from the details of these issues, the deep question that emerges is why there is a connection between rational agency and awareness. It is an instance of a more general connection of which we need a better understanding. In the case of the non-mental world, we know that a rational subject can judge and act only on what he is aware of. We do not expect the informational states of the blindsight subject, however reliable, to explain his rational decisions and actions. If they do explain his decisions and actions, it is not by rational transitions of thought. What applies to the non-mental world holds here equally for the mental world. A rational subject can make decisions and mental self-ascriptions, and keep track of his own mental events and states, only if he is aware of them. The awareness may be of a distinctive kind, as I have been arguing that it is, but the general principle still holds. Further investigation of this territory should include exploration and explanation of these internal connections between awareness and the rationality of thinkers.

---

[36] This case appears to be a counter-example to what Richard Moran calls 'Anscombe's Condition': 'If he can only know what he is doing by observing himself, that would be because, described in *these* terms (e.g. clicking out the rhythm [while pumping water]) his action is *not* determined by his primary reason, is not undertaken by him as the pursuit of some aim. Otherwise, he would know what he is doing in knowing his practical reasons for adopting this aim.' See Moran (2001: 126–7). My own view is that Moran's fundamental insights on the role of agency in a range of cases of self-knowledge can be integrated with an account of the essential role of action awareness in such self-knowledge.

8

Representing Thoughts

The recent chapters of this book have taken for granted the ability to think about Thoughts and their constituent concepts without hitherto elucidating that ability. The capitalization of 'Thoughts' I continue to use to indicate propositional conceptual intentional contents, Fregean *Gedanken*, to distinguish them from mental events, including thinkings, that have these Thoughts as their contents. This ability to think about Thoughts was presupposed in the discussions of self-ascription and in the discussion of other-ascriptions of actions, judgements, and other events and states with conceptual intentional content. In making such self- and other-ascriptions, a thinker is engaged in thinking about Thoughts. It is time to offer some elucidation of this capacity. I will also be arguing that a good elucidation of this capacity puts us in a position to answer the doubts, still present in some distinguished contemporary writers, about the reconcilability of privileged self-knowledge with externalism about intentional content.

A philosophically satisfying account of thought about Thoughts must include, but must also go beyond, the philosophical logic and formal semantics of a language ascribing thoughts about Thoughts. A satisfying account must say something substantive about what it is to possess concepts of Thoughts and their constituent concepts. What it says must of course dovetail with the philosophical logic and formal semantics. In fact it may aim to ground some features of the more formal account.

In discussing thought about Thoughts, we are entering issues surrounding the Fregean hierarchy of concepts. This is a topic on which many of the leading writers on meaning of the past sixty years have published views, including, in order of publication, Church, Kaplan, Davidson, Dummett, Burge, and Terence Parsons.[1] A resolution of issues about the hierarchy of concepts turns on the resolution of a series of issues that are of much

---

[1] Church (1951); Kaplan (1964); references for the other authors are given as they are mentioned later in this chapter.

wider significance in the theory of thought, in epistemology, in metaphysics, and in the philosophy of mind. The acceptability and nature of a Fregean hierarchy of concepts involves the correct way of conceiving of the relation between concept and reference. It involves some conception of how thinkers are capable of thinking of abstract objects like concepts and Thoughts. Correspondingly, evidence drawn from substantive theories of understanding is pertinent to the assessment of treatments of the Fregean hierarchy. I will try to draw out some of these connections in what follows.

I begin with a puzzle.

1. THE PUZZLE

When Karl believes

(1) Bush is powerful

he believes something about the world: about a man and his power. In so believing, Karl thinks about Bush in a particular way, a way that we can write <Bush>. Equally we can write <is powerful> for Karl's way of thinking of the property of being powerful; and in general, we can write <A> for the concept that is the sense of the expression A (if it has a sense). Under the classical Fregean treatment, the sentence

(2) Karl believes that Bush is powerful

states that Karl stands in a certain relation to a Thought built up from concepts. If we use '^' as a symbol for predicational combination of concepts, then according to the classical Fregean account, (2) states that

(3) Bel (Karl, <Bush> ^ <is powerful>).

If John believes what (2) states, that is, if John believes that Karl believes that Bush is powerful, then according to the classical, hierarchical Fregean account, the following is true:

(4) Bel (John, < Bel> ^ <Karl> ^ <<Bush>> ^ <<is powerful>>).

(I simplify the symbolic formulation for legibility.)

I start with a tiny question: what is the relation between Karl's way of thinking about Bush and John's way of thinking about Karl's way of thinking about Bush? Are they identical? More generally, is <A> identical with <<A>>? If they are not identical, what is the relation between them?

Despite its brevity, the question of whether <A> = <<A>> has extensive ramifications and theoretical significance. Some have held that Fregean
theories are unable to give any satisfactory answer to this question, and have
drawn the conclusion that the notion of sense is not suitable for giving
an account of the content of propositional attitudes.[2] But addressing the
question goes beyond the issue of the theoretical utility of the notion of
sense. Any answer to the question must draw on a conception of the relations
between two intertwined abilities we possess: the ability to think about the
world in certain ways, and the ability to think about how we and others are
thinking about the world.

It is intuitively plausible that the ability to think about any Thought as
the Thought that p requires the ability to employ that same Thought p in
first-order thinking about the world. If this is so, why is it so? We need a
general theoretical explanation of this intuitive truth. How, in the enterprise
of philosophical explanation, are we to conceive of the connection between
the complex of relations required to think about something in the world in
a given way, on the one hand, and the ability to think about that very way
itself on the other?

The question of whether <A> = <<A>> has, more specifically, been
a puzzle because there seem to be compelling reasons for a negative answer,
and there seem to be compelling reasons for a positive answer. I group the
considerations in support of the distinctness of <A> and <<A>> under
the heading "Thesis". I group the considerations in support of the identity
of <A> and <<A>> under the heading "Antithesis".

Thesis

<A> cannot be <<A>> because:

(*a*) Each concept is individuated by the fundamental condition for something to be its reference. This Fregean conception, emphasized by Dummett,
is one that I have been endorsing and whose consequences I have been
exploring from Chapter 2 onwards in this book.[3] The conception applies just
as much to concepts of concepts as it does to concepts of ordinary objects.

---

[2] Davidson (2001*b*,*c*).
[3] See Dummett (1973: 93 ff.; 1981, esp. 42–5). This Dummettian point about sense–reference
relations is being used in this first consideration for the Thesis in support of a conclusion about the
hierarchy of senses that Dummett elsewhere rejects.

The condition for being the reference of a first-level concept <A> must, together with the world, determine something at the level of reference (an object, in the case of singular concepts). By contrast, the condition for being the reference of a concept <<A>> must, together with the world, determine a concept, rather than something at the level of first-level references. Since these conditions determine different references, given the way the world is, they must be distinct. Hence, given the individuation of a concept by the fundamental condition for being its reference, these conditions correspond to distinct concepts. So <<A>> is not <A>. We can call this "the condition-for-reference argument".

(*b*) A concept is, as Evans said, a way of thinking of something.[4] A way of thinking cannot be both a way of thinking of a thing, and also a way of thinking of a concept of that thing. Hence <<A>> is not <A>. This is "the way-of-thinking argument". This intuitive argument was presented to me in correspondence by Tyler Burge, and features in his Postscript to 'Frege and the Hierarchy'.[5]

(*c*) Concepts, according to some (but by no means all) theorists of concepts, are individuated by their possession-conditions.[6] Whatever the condition a thinker must meet to possess the concept <A>, it involves only his ability to think about the world. But to possess <<A>> the thinker must have the ability to think about concepts. So <A> and <<A>> have distinct possession-conditions; and hence are distinct concepts. This is "the possession-condition argument".

Under some approaches to concepts, namely those that accept all the characterizations of concepts given in these three arguments, these three arguments are different perspectives on a single underlying idea. The idea underlying these arguments for the Thesis is that the very essence of concepts, whose three characterizations in terms of reference-conditions, ways of thinking, or possession-conditions can be shown to be equivalent, is incompatible with a given concept having such different things as an object and a distinct concept as its reference.[7]

This concludes the arguments for the Thesis.

---

[4] Evans (1982, ch. 1).   [5] Burge (2005*c*).

[6] Peacocke (1992, chs 1 and 2), and the less stringent treatment, that still respects the idea that concepts are individuated by their possession-conditions, in Ch. 4 above.

[7] For a defence of the equivalence of these three conceptions of sense, see Peacocke (1997).

Antithesis

<A> must be <<A>> because:

(*a*) When you understand "believes" (for instance) and any arbitrary term *a* and sentence *s*, you are thereby in a position to understand the sentence "*a* believes that *s*". The simplest explanation for this, the argument runs, is that <<A>> is the very same concept as <A>. This is the argument from understanding propositional-attitude contexts.[8]

(*b*) If <A> were distinct from <<A>>, there would be an infinite hierarchy of concepts. Concepts and concepts of concepts are in a one–many relation: for anything at all, including concepts, there are many concepts of it. There would then be no explanation of how we can grasp this hierarchy, for, it is said, we have been given no principle that generates it. Thus Davidson, 'Theories of Meaning and Learnable Languages', and 'On Saying That'.[9] Yet if the Fregean hierarchy exists, there would have to be some principle generating the members of a higher level from the members of the next level down, since we can understand arbitrary long embeddings of propositional attitudes. Since there is, seemingly, no such generating principle, if we are going to use the notion of a concept at all, we had better hold that <A> = <<A>>. This is the argument against a hierarchy from the absence of a generating principle.

(*c*) There are many inferences whose validity is, apparently, most easily explained by the hypothesis that <A> = <<A>>. From

(5) John believes that Karl believes that Bush is powerful

it seems to follow that

(6) There is some proposition <*p*> such that John believes that Karl believes that <*p*>, and <*p*> is the proposition that Bush is powerful.

Similarly, from (5) and (7)

(7) It is true that Bush is powerful

it certainly seems to follow that

---

[8] See Peacocke (1996).   [9] Davidson (2001*b*,*c*).

(8) Something John believes Karl believes is true.

If, quite generally, <A> is <<A>>, and in particular <Bush is powerful> = <<Bush is powerful>>, both these arguments are validated, without any supplementary premises or principles.[10] The clause "that Bush is powerful" always refers to the same thing, however deeply it is embedded. But if the Thought <Bush is powerful> were distinct from the Thought <<Bush is powerful>>, then the arguments would need additional premises for validity, which apparently they do not. In natural language, we apparently treat a given clause of the form "that *p*" as having the same reference whether it is embedded in one or arbitrarily many operators, be they operators of propositional attitudes or such operators as "It is true that", "It is probable that", and the like. The phenomenon is not peculiar to English. It occurs in other natural languages, including French and German. The challenge is rather to find a natural language that does behave in accordance with the Fregean hierarchy of concepts. I label this the "argument from inferences".

That concludes the arguments for the Antithesis.

2. A PROPOSAL

If we could show how the canonical concept of a concept *s* is uniquely determined by *s* itself, and could explain the principle by which it is determined, we would meet the need for a generating principle. Now there are special cases in which a concept of something is determined by the thing itself. One such class of special cases is that of certain concepts of certain abstract objects. In these cases, a person thinks of an object under the very condition that individuates that object. The number 0 itself is individuated by its being the unique number *n* of which it holds that necessarily there are *n* things that are F iff $\sim\exists x(Fx)$. That fact about the number 0 is a truth of metaphysics, about the nature of numbers. But there is a corresponding truth at the level of thought. To think of a number as 0 is to have tacit knowledge that it is the unique number *n* such that necessarily there are *n* things that are F iff $\sim\exists x(Fx)$. An analogous point can be made about thinking of a number as 1. The number 1 is individuated by the fact that it is the unique number *n* such that necessarily there are *n* things that are F iff

---

[10] This was an argument I developed in Peacocke (1996).

$\exists x \forall y (Fx \leftrightarrow y = x)$. Thinking of a number as 1 involves tacit knowledge of that same individuating condition. Here we have some examples at the level of individuals of a phenomenon that also occurs for properties and relations: that of thinking of property or relation in a way fixed by what makes the property or relation the property or relation it is.[11]

So, there are some cases in which a canonical concept of an object is determined by the object itself. Does anything analogous hold for canonical concepts of concepts, for concepts of concepts and Thoughts?

I argue that it does. I use the notation "can(F)" for the canonical concept of the concept F. At the level of metaphysics, can(F), like any other concept, is individuated by its fundamental reference rule. This is in accordance with the earlier claims of this book, particularly Chapter 2. In the case in which F is a first-level concept, the fundamental reference rule for can(F) will state a condition for an arbitrary concept to fall under can(F). A plausible first attempt to state that condition is this:

(*) For an arbitrary concept C to fall under can(F) is for the fundamental condition for something to fall under C to be the same as the fundamental condition for something to fall under the concept F.

(*) makes clear that the canonical concept of F, can(F), unlike other ways of thinking of a concept, is determined by the concept itself. This is so because the fundamental condition for something to fall under the concept F is determined by the concept itself, rather than some mode of presentation of the concept F.

Can we then say at the level of thought, in parallel with the numerical example, that to think of a concept under the canonical concept of F, under can(F), is to have tacit knowledge of what (*) states? I call this claim the Leverage Account of what it is to be employing can(F) in thought. It leverages the materials of a condition for something to be a concept F of one level into the materials of an account of what it is to be a particular concept, the canonical concept of F, at a higher level in the Fregean hierarchy of concepts.

There is a wrinkle we have to consider in assessing what the Leverage Account involves. Quite generally, knowing that something is the same as the

[11] For more discussion of some other examples, see Peacocke (2000). Issues concerning thought about numbers are very delicate, and there are close limits to the extent to which the points in the text can be generalized to other, even canonical, ways of thinking of natural numbers. To think of something as 5, for instance, does not necessarily involve thinking of it as the successor of 4. When you see, without counting, that there are five mugs on the table, it is a further step, and a further thought, that the number of mugs there is the successor of 4.

thing that is G is not yet knowing which thing it is. If I know that your car is the same colour as John's, that does not put me in a position to know the colour of your car if I don't know the colour of John's car. If we say that having the canonical concept of F is having tacit knowledge of what (*) states, then the same issue arises, since that content involves tacit knowledge that something is the same as the fundamental condition for a thing to fall under the concept F.

One way to address this issue is simply to delete the descriptive reference in (*) to the fundamental condition for an object to fall under F, and replace it with the specific condition that is the fundamental condition for an object to fall under F. Suppose we also say that the resulting condition, after this replacement, for something to fall under can(F) is tacitly known. That has the consequence that a thinker cannot possess the canonical concept of F if he has only an incomplete grasp of F, since this proposal writes the full, correct condition for an object to fall under F into the reference-condition for can(F). This does not accord with our actual practices of concept-ascription. Someone may well use can(F) in wondering about the correct extension of the concept F: "I wonder whether the concept *number* applies only to what is finite?" I think there is a respectable function to be served by a theory that says what full understanding would consist in. Maybe there is also a way of thinking of a concept F available only to those who have full understanding of that concept. But that way of thinking of the concept cannot be the one we actually employ in thinking about the concept when our understanding is only partial.

The response to the issue I favour is to hold that a thinker could not have the concept F itself (as opposed to some mode of presentation of F) in the content tacitly known in knowing what (*) states unless he has enough of a grasp of the reference-condition for F to be attributed with attitudes containing F in their content. Such a thinker knows some, but maybe not all, of what is involved in the fundamental reference-condition for F. If we understand the Leverage Account in combination with this thesis, then there is no obstacle to possessing can(F) while also having only a partial understanding of F. Such a thinker can combine tacit knowledge of (*) with those parts of the fundamental reference rule for F that he does know, together with other information, to reach judgements whose contents contain the concept can(F).

Under the Leverage Account so conceived, it is a distinctive feature of the canonical concept of F that a thinker cannot possess that canonical concept unless he has at least a partial grasp of the concept F itself. This is part of the answer to the question of how the ability to think of the world is intertwined with the ability to think about one's own and others' Thought about the world. In this distinctive feature, the canonical concept differs from indefinitely many other concepts of the concept F. Such concepts of concepts as *Einstein's favourite concept*, or *the legal concept specified on the title page of such-and-such book*, are concepts that a thinker can possess without possessing the concepts to which they refer, and without knowing which concepts they are. By contrast, someone who possesses the concept *the concept number* must have at least a partial grasp of the concept *number*, and knows which concept *the concept number* refers to. In certain respects, then, as Jerry Fodor once remarked to me, applying the functional concept *the canonical concept of…* to a concept is analogous to applying quotation marks to an expression. If you understand quotation marks, and perceive an expression of the form "___", you know what that whole expression refers to.

Another consequence of this conception is that whatever contributes to the individuation of the concept F thereby also contributes to the individuation of the concept can(F). In particular, if F is externally individuated, can(F) will also be externally individuated. This fact has an epistemological significance in the philosophy of mind I will take up in section 5 below.

Attribution of tacit knowledge of some content is justified by what attribution of that tacit knowledge explains. What does tacit knowledge of the fundamental reference rule (*) explain?

One very straightforward class of transitions in thought explained by tacit knowledge of (*) is the thinker's willingness to move from

   a is F

to

   a falls under the canonical concept of F;

and conversely. Tacit knowledge of (*) explains the willingness to make this transition, since if something is F, it evidently falls under a concept the fundamental condition to fall under which is the same as the fundamental condition for an object to fall under F (and conversely). The fundamental reference rule (*) in effect correspondingly lifts reasons for judging that something is F up one level of the Fregean hierarchy to reasons for judging that something falls under can(F).

A philosophically more interesting engagement of tacit knowledge of (*) arises in its interaction with mental states in whose content the concept F itself features (rather than any mode of presentation of the concept F). Consider a thinker who makes a transition from his action-awareness of

> judging F*a*

to the self-ascription

> I judge that F*a*.

In attributing this content to his judgement, he is thinking of the concepts *a* and F under their respective canonical modes of presentation. If the thinker has a sensitivity to which of his mental states contain the concept F rather than some other concept, this sensitivity can be combined with tacit knowledge of (*) to explain the thinker's ability to make such self-ascriptions—and, in the right circumstances, thereby to gain knowledge of the content of his mental states. The characterization of the states to which the thinker has to be sensitive does not require him already to think of the concepts *a* and F under their canonical concepts. The sensitivity is just to the presence of *a* and F themselves in the content of the mental state. Actually, the same applies to the concept of judging too. Grasp of this concept involves an ability to be sensitive to the distinction between those events that are judgings and those that are not. The capacity of a thinker to be sensitive to the presence or absence of some feature itself, and the presence of this capacity in the account of mastery of some concept of that feature itself, seems to me to be a widespread phenomenon in the theory of concepts. It was present for the feature of a mental state of being a seeing in the account of grasp of the concept of seeing in Chapter 6. It will be present for any account of a particular mental concept conforming to the model of that chapter. For anyone who believes in the existence of a level of non-conceptual representational content in perception, and holds that observational concepts are individuated by their relations to such contents, this phenomenon of sensitivity to a feature without prior conceptualization thereof is present even in that basic case.

It is very plausible that part of the subpersonal explanation of how it is that a thinker is able to enjoy such content-sensitivity in his grasp of the canonical concept of a concept is that the subpersonal realizations of the relevant mental states to which he is sensitive contain some representations in a subpersonal, Fodorian language of thought, structured representations that have the Thought in question as its assigned concept. I agree with those who say that it is hard to see how there can be any other explanation of all the phenomena in which mental states with content are implicated.[12] It matters, however, that the sensitivity mentioned in the account of the ability to employ a canonical concept of a Thought does not merely involve subpersonal sensitivity to the occurrence of a particular formula in the subpersonal language of thought. By itself, such a subpersonal sensitivity is neither necessary nor sufficient for the capacity with which we are concerned. It is not sufficient, because that sensitivity in a subject whose subpersonal symbols meant something different would not be the sensitivity we require, which is a sensitivity to a concept itself in the content of a mental state. It is not necessary, because any other symbol for the same Thought would equally serve. The particular subpersonal structured symbol whose sense is a given Thought is implicated in the realization of our subject's capacities; but it does not exhaust them. The capacities are characterized in content-involving terms. The sensitivity to the occurrence of mental states containing a given content will be a sensitivity to a state whose content is individuated in part by its relations to other states, and, very often, in part by its relations to the subject's environment. The occurrence of particular expressions in the language of thought cannot by itself ensure the obtaining of these relations. The states of affairs and events in whose empirical explanation canonical concepts of concepts are involved will also be individuated by their relations to other states, and (often) to the environment. Symbolic forms are by themselves inadequate to explain these effects too. These should be seen as familiar points about explanation by content-involving states, personal or subpersonal.[13] They are simply applied here in the context of thought about concepts and Thoughts.

It might be asked: why do we need the Leverage Account and its tacit knowledge of (*) at all? Do we not already have an account of thought about concepts in a good theory of the possession-conditions of those concepts, along the lines of either *A Study of Concepts*, or some of its variants, rivals, or successors? But those accounts do not by themselves meet the need that we have been discussing, the need for an account of ordinary thought about Thought. Ordinary, non-philosophical thought about concepts does not involve any explicit knowledge or belief about what the possession-conditions of those concepts may be. It does not involve any explicit conception of possession-conditions at all. A theory of possession-conditions is a (modest)

---

[12] Fodor (1975); Davies (1991).   [13] Hornsby (1986); Peacocke (1993*c*).

kind of theoretical construct. When we reflect upon what the specific possession-condition for a given target concept may be, we have to have a way of thinking about that target concept, as the concept it is, in advance of knowing or even conjecturing what that possession-condition may be. I suggest that our understanding, when engaged in such reflection, as in other thought about the concept, is simply given by our tacit knowledge of the reference rule (*).

Perhaps someone will insist that ordinary thinkers, in thinking about a concept as the concept it is, draw upon tacit knowledge of the possession-condition that individuates it. I think such tacit knowledge is in principle possible, but hold that it is not the basis of the ability to think about concepts in the canonical ways in question here. Tacit knowledge is properly invoked to explain correct performances, in the presence of the right background conditions. But people can make all sorts of mistakes about the features of concepts, and what is involved in having attitudes involving them, that they would not make if they had such tacit knowledge. Such mistakes are entirely consistent with their still thinking about the concept *man*, as the concept *man*, or about whatever other concept is in question. To have tacit knowledge of the fundamental reference rule (*) is not to have tacit knowledge about the conditions for possession of a concept. Possession-conditions and reference rules are of course connected, but the connection is substantive, and having knowledge of the fundamental reference rule (*) for can(F) is not the same as knowing, even tacitly, the possession-conditions for the concept F.

We have here a state of affairs structurally similar to those we discussed when considering the canonical concept of pain (Chapter 5 section 9) and the canonical concept of seeing (Chapter 6, end of section 2). Since we have a recognitional capacity for events that are our own pains and our own seeings, we have a way of thinking of them for which it is an open question what their role is in a thinker's psychological economy. I argued that to think of an event as a pain, or as a seeing, is not thereby to think of it, even tacitly, as whatever plays such-and-such role in a thinker's psychological economy. In effect, I have just been arguing a similar case for the rather different category of canonical thought about a given concept F, canonical thought made available by the thinker's own grasp of the concept F itself. Though concepts are quite different sorts of things from mental events and conscious states, it is true both of concepts and of conscious states and events that we stand in a special relation to them that makes available canonical ways of thinking of them that cannot be identified with an instance of the form "whatever has such-and-such role". The same point applies *pari passu* for canonical ways of thinking of meanings, in the cases in which meaning can be identified with concepts as understood here.

To summarize: on the Leverage Account, for each concept F, there is a canonical way of thinking can(F) of the concept F. This canonical way is uniquely fixed, under that account, by what individuates the concept F itself.

Under the Leverage Account, the subject's ability to think about concepts and Thoughts at all is explanatorily posterior, as a constitutive matter, to his ability to employ first- (or lower-) level concepts and Thoughts.

The Leverage Account can be iterated up the hierarchy of concepts. We can say that

> (**) For an arbitrary concept C to fall under the concept can(can(F)) is for C to be such that: the fundamental condition for something to fall under C is the same as the fundamental condition for an object (entity) to fall under can(F).

Just as is the case one level down, the canonical concept can(can(F)) is individuated by the concept can(F) itself on this account, and not by some mode of presentation of can(F). It is clear that this approach can be iterated up the hierarchy to any finite level. It gives a generating principle for fixing the canonical concept of a concept from the latter concept itself. Tacit grasp of this generating principle will allow thinkers to understand arbitrary embeddings of propositional-attitude verbs.

3. HOW THE SOLUTION TREATS THE CONSTRAINTS THAT GENERATE THE PUZZLE

The Leverage Account accepts all of the arguments for the Thesis that <<A>> must be distinct from <A>.

The condition-for-reference argument could be expanded, in the presence of the Leverage Account. Consider the case in which F is a first-level concept, true or false of objects. Suppose, following Frege, that we take the reference of a concept to be a function whose range consists of truth-value. Then under the Leverage Account, the condition for something to be mapped by the reference of can(F) to the True certainly requires it to be a concept. This is certainly distinct from the condition required for something to be mapped to the True by the reference of F, which will (on the Fregean view) require it to be an object, meeting whatever condition is determined by the first-level concept F. The conditions required for something to be the reference of can(F) are distinct from the conditions for something to be the reference of the first-level concept F, just as the condition-for-reference argument maintained. The same argument could be reproduced further up the hierarchy.

The Leverage Account can also endorse the second, intuitive, argument for the Thesis in terms of ways of thinking. If a way of thinking is individuated by the fundamental condition for something to be its reference, a way of thinking of a concept cannot be the same as a way of thinking of something that is not a concept.

The third argument, from the distinctness of the possession-conditions for $<<A>>$ and $<A>$, is also underwritten and validated on the Leverage Account. The possession-condition for the canonical concept of a concept involves tacit knowledge of (*), that involves the ability to think about concepts. The possession-condition for the concept so thought about does not involve relations to contents, but only relations to the world itself (or possibly to lower-level attitudes and Thoughts). So the possession-conditions for $<<A>>$ and $<A>$ are distinct, as the third argument for the Thesis maintained.

The Leverage Account as formulated already has the resources for responding head-on to the first of the two arguments for the Antithesis. The first of those arguments, the appeal to understanding propositional-attitude contexts, cited the fact that when you understand "believes" (for instance) and any arbitrary term *a* and sentence *s*, you are thereby in a position to understand the sentence "*a* believes that *s*". Contrary to the argument in the Antithesis, however, the explanation of this fact is not that $<<A>> = <A>$. It is simply that any concept uniquely determines the canonical concept of that concept, in the way described in the Leverage Account. Because thinkers are able to employ a canonical concept of a concept that is uniquely determined by that concept, as long as they have the general ability to move from a concept to its canonical concept, they will be able to understand any sentence of the form "*a* believes that *s*" as soon as they can understand its constituents. Understanding the propositional-attitude form just involves appreciation that if *s* expresses the Thought $<p>$, then "*a* believes that *s*" expresses the Thought $<\text{Bel}>\ ^\wedge\ <a>\ ^\wedge\ <<p>>$.

The Leverage Account supplies the generating principle for the hierarchy demanded in the second argument for the Antithesis. So for the first two arguments marshalled in the case for the Antithesis, the Leverage Account can explain why the considerations they adduce, though correct in themselves, do not support the thesis that $<<A>>$ is identical with $<A>$.

The status of the third argument for the Antithesis, from the validity of inferences, is more complex. The two transitions from (5) to (6), and from (5) and (7) to (8), are validated under the Leverage Account if we add the premiss, uncontroversial on the account, that

$<<p>>$ refers to the Thought $<p>$.

So, when we say (6) above follows from (5), (6) is understood as meaning that

(9) There is some Thought $<p>$ such that there is a concept $<<p>>$ that refers to $<p>$, and such that John believes that Karl believes $<<p>>$, and $<p>$ is the Thought that Bush is powerful.

I have abbreviated some formalities for simplicity.

This, however, is far from an adequate answer to the third argument for the Antithesis. The point of that argument was that *no* additional premiss, however obvious, should be needed—the language behaves as if "that *p*" refers to the same thing, however embedded, functioning as a complex term for the same Thought wherever it occurs. This was precisely the consideration that was influencing some of my earlier writings on this topic.[14] So this challenge has not yet been fully addressed.

A first step towards addressing the challenge involves a consideration about canonical concepts of concepts more generally. It is very plausible that if *s* is a concept of an abstract object *x* that is determined by what individuates *x*, as in the example of the numbers 0 and 1 we considered above, then what Quine in 'Quantifiers and Propositional Attitudes' called 'exportation' is valid for it.[15] That is, if someone believes F(*s*), then she believes of the object *x* that it is F. This is also in the spirit of what Kaplan argued in 'Quantifying In'.[16] If this is correct, then it applies also to canonical concepts of Thoughts. From

(10) *a* believes $<John>$ ^ $<believes>$ ^ $<<p>>$

it would then follow that

(11) Concerning the Thought $<p>$: *a* believes John believes it.

[14] Peacocke (1996).   [15] Quine (1976*a*: 190).
[16] See Kaplan (1969, sect. VIII) on 'standard names'.

The form of transition saliently instantiated by the step from (10) to (11) is one that will concern us further. I label it "exportation of concept"—since that is what it is. Exportation of concept involves the same relation between concepts of concepts and concepts one level below them that Quine labelled 'exportation' in the case of concepts of objects vis-à-vis the objects themselves.

We can put the validity of exportation for canonical concepts of concepts to work. It contributes to a partial explanation of the validity of the inferential pattern from (5) to (6) above in the argument for the Antithesis; and it does so in a way consistent with the soundness of the arguments for the Thesis. It contributes to an explanation of validity, because we can export on the canonical <<Bush>> ^ <<is powerful>> in the premiss

Bel (John, <Bel> ^ <Karl> ^ <<Bush>> ^ <<is powerful>>)).

Nonetheless, the defender of the Antithesis may reasonably insist that this is still not a full explanation of the datum he cited. For, to say it one last time, this point does not address the intuition that *no* additional premiss is needed in English to explain why the transition from (5) to (6) is valid. I offer a second step and a fuller explanation, drawing on additional resources, in the next section.

Issues about partial understanding also produce interesting wrinkles here too. It is a question whether exportation is valid, even for standard names, when understanding is merely partial. Consider someone who only partially understands "aleph-two". He may know that it is a name (strictly, a description) of an infinite number, but may know no more than that. It may be true to say of him in English "He believes that aleph-two is larger than the number of natural numbers". But does he have relational beliefs, of aleph-two, that it has such-and-such properties? There is certainly some resistance to saying so. This resistance is increased when we reflect that what motivates relational ascriptions in some other cases of standard names of abstract objects is grasp of the notation of such a kind that the thinker knows where some number comes in an ordinal or cardinal system. Precisely that is lacking in the case of our thinker who only partially understands "aleph-two". There is an intuition in favour of saying that he has beliefs to the effect that aleph-two is thus-and-so; but does not know of any particular infinite number that it is thus-and-so (and in particular does not know that it is aleph-two). The Quine-like treatment of exportation is correct only if we tacitly assume a background of sufficient understanding, an assumption that goes beyond what is required for correct *de dicto* attributions. In this particular corner of the territory, however, canonical concepts of concepts and Thoughts are better-off than concepts like *aleph-two*. If grasp of the canonical concept of the concept F involves tacit knowledge of the reference rule (*), which in turn requires possession of the concept F, one cannot employ can(F) in thought without possessing the concept one is thinking about, and knowing which concept it is. By contrast, knowing that an infinite number is two up in the aleph-ordering falls short of knowing which infinite number it is, if your grasp of the nature of the aleph-ordering is weak.

4. RELATION TO SINGLE-LEVEL TREATMENTS

In his book *Frege: Philosophy of Language*, Michael Dummett proposes a well-known alternative to the Fregean infinite hierarchy of concepts. This alternative is also considered, amongst other alternatives, in Terence Parsons's discussion of these issues.[17] On this alternative, the notion of a concept is not abandoned, but it exists at only one level. According to this treatment, in sentences such as our (2) above

(2) Karl believes that Bush is powerful

the words "Bush" and "is powerful", at those occurrences, not only denote their usual senses (as Frege said), but they also express their normal senses (as the Fregean hierarchy denies). Under this Dummettian treatment, in

(12) John believes that Karl believes that Bush is powerful

"Bush" at its occurrence there, doubly embedded, denotes its normal sense, rather than a canonical concept of a sense. As Dummett writes about his emendation of Frege's theory,

With this emendation, there is no such thing as the indirect sense of a word: there is just its sense, which determines it to have in transparent contexts a reference distinct from its sense, and in opaque contexts a referent which coincides with its sense. There is therefore no reason to think that an expression occurring in double *oratio obliqua* has a sense or a reference different from that which it has in single *oratio obliqua*.[18]

---

[17] Parsons (1981). Parsons's most extended exposition there is of a two-level theory of sense that distinguishes ordinary sense from indirect sense.
[18] Dummett (1973: 268).

There are at least two different approaches to giving a formal object-language suitable for a conception on which there is only one level of sense.

One approach employs a notion of denotation that is relativized to linguistic context. Here the object-language itself is non-hierarchical. Whether an expression has its normal reference, or refers instead to its normal sense, depends upon the sentential context in which it occurs. This style of approach is what Tyler Burge calls 'Method I' in his 1979 paper 'Frege and the Hierarchy'.[19] The type of object-language it employs is one for which I argued one can give an adequate truth-theory language in 'Entitlement, Self-Knowledge and Conceptual Redeployment'.[20]

The other style of approach to giving a formal object-language suitable for a conception on which there is only one level of sense is to introduce terms—simple or complex, variables or constants—that correspond in the formal language to expressions of English consisting of that-clauses. This is Burge's 'Method II' in 'Frege and the Hierarchy'. Under this treatment, denotation does not for these purposes need to be treated as relative to linguistic context. In a formal language that makes explicit to which concepts and Thoughts a subject stands in various relations, under this second form of single-level treatment, (12) could be regimented thus:

> (12S) Believes (John, <Karl> $^\wedge$ <Believes> $^\wedge$ <Bush> $^\wedge$ <is powerful>).

We can call the single-level language in which (12S) is cast "SL".

By contrast with both of these styles of approach, under the treatment with the Fregean hierarchy explicitly articulated in the object-language, as we said, (10) would be regimented

> (12H) Bel (John, < Bel> $^\wedge$ <Karl> $^\wedge$ <<Bush>> $^\wedge$ <<is powerful>>).

Henceforth I distinguish "Bel" and "Believes" in order not to prejudge any issue of the identity of the respective belief-relations used by the different kinds of treatment. I reserve "Bel" for the explicitly hierarchical language.

Is there a translation scheme between formulae of the single-level language SL of (12S) and the hierarchical language of (12H)? There is; in fact there

---

[19] Burge (2005c).　　　[20] Peacocke (1996).

is more than one. I distinguish a superficial translation scheme and a deeper translation scheme.

The superficial translation scheme is the one that is simply obvious from the notation itself, independently of any substantive theses about concepts. In any sentence like (12S), we can add to expressions like "<is powerful>" additional pairs of pointed brackets, according to this rule: we add one additional pair for each embedding of the occurrence of the expression within the versions of expressions that are traditionally regarded as creating oblique contexts. Unembedded occurrences are left unchanged. If we then also change "Believes" to "Bel", the result is a translation from a sentence of the single-level language to a sentence of the hierarchical language. Applying these rules to (12S) yields (12H) as its translation.

The significance of this translation lies in the fact that the defender of the hierarchy could, if he so wished, use the same sentences as this form of single-level theorist, but regard these sentences as legitimate only in so far as they have a translation into his hierarchical language. The friend of the hierarchy could insist that the translation into the hierarchical language makes perspicuous and explicit the structure that exists in the realm of concepts and Thoughts.

This is, however, a superficial translation scheme from the point of view of answering the argument from inferences, because the scheme does not in itself, independently of any further theses, involve any commitment to the idea that when (12S) is true, John is really related by a belief-relation only to the Thought <Bush> $^\wedge$ <is powerful> itself, as opposed to a concept of that Thought.

If the principle of exportation of concept of the preceding section is correct, however, there is also a deeper translation scheme available for the single-level language SL. This deeper scheme does imply that in the translation of (12S), a belief-relation is represented as holding between the subject and the Thought

<Bush> $^\wedge$ <is powerful>

itself. Exportation of concept implies that when someone has an attitude to a content containing a canonical concept of a Thought, he has the corresponding *de re*, relational attitude to that Thought itself. This applies to the concept

<<Bush>> $^\wedge$ <<is powerful>>

as it is mentioned in (12H). In the presence of these claims, (12H) implies (12HR):

> (12HR) Concerning the Thought $<p>$, namely $<$Bush$>$ $^\wedge$ $<$is powerful$>$, Bel (John, $<$Bel$>$ $^\wedge$ $<$Karl$>$ $^\wedge$ $<p>$).

Under the deeper translation scheme, (12S) is translated as (12HR). (12HR) manifestly involves a relation to the Thought $<p>$ itself. The general rule for the deeper translation scheme can be given in two steps. First, we take a sentence of SL and translate it into a sentence of the explicitly hierarchical language in accordance with the previously mentioned, more superficial, translation scheme. We then export on the canonical concepts corresponding the most deeply embedded that-clauses. (We could of course also validly export on intermediate that-clauses, and for some inferences, it will be important to do that.)

If we use the deeper translation scheme, we can speak with the user of the single-level language SL. The Dummettian language is undeniably more concise, less cumbersome, than the explicitly hierarchical language. Under the deeper translation scheme, the language is not even misleading in representing the truth of (12S) as involving a relation to the embedded Thought $<p>$. We can speak this way without denying the fundamental arguments for the hierarchy, the arguments for the Thesis.

The deeper translation scheme finally puts us in a position to take a second step in answering the argument from inferences that featured in the case for the Antithesis. That argument appealed to the validity of the transition from

> (5) John believes that Karl believes that Bush is powerful

to

> (6) There is some proposition $<p>$ such that John believes that Karl believes $<p>$, and $<p>$ is the proposition that Bush is powerful.

(5) is regimented in SL as (12S), and (12S) in turn is, under the deeper scheme, translated as (12HR). But (12HR) immediately logically implies (6), as required. It does so, crucially, without relying on any additional premises special to the subject matter. The transition from (12HR) to (6) relies only on first-order logic with identity.

Similar considerations apply to the other illustration mentioned in the argument from inferences, that from (5) together with

> (7) It is true that Bush is powerful

it follows that

(8) Something John believes Karl believes is true.

Under the deeper translation scheme, (5), (7), and (8) are translated respectively as (12HR), (13HR), and (14HR):

(12HR) Concerning the Thought $<p>$, namely $<$Bush$>$ $^\wedge$ $<$is powerful$>$, Bel (John, $<$Bel$>$ $^\wedge$ $<$Karl$>$ $^\wedge$ $<p>$)

(13HR) Concerning the Thought $<p>$, namely $<$Bush$>$ $^\wedge$ $<$is powerful$>$, True ($<p>$)

(14HR) There is some Thought $<q>$ such that Bel (John, $<$Bel$>$ $^\wedge$ $<$Karl$>$ $^\wedge$ $<q>$) and True ($<q>$).

(14HR) follows from (12HR) and (13HR), again without any additional premisses special to the theory of concepts, just as the argument from inferences demanded. This explains away the last consideration offered in support of the Antithesis, consistently with acceptance of the philosophical case for the hierarchy.

Experts on the regimentation of propositional attitudes will have realized for some pages that I have been suppressing a complication. When Karl has the belief that Bush is powerful, Karl stands in a propositional-attitude relation to the Thought $<$Bush$>$ $^\wedge$ $<$is powerful$>$ itself, and not to a Thought given under a mode of presentation. When John has a belief about Karl's belief, matters stand differently. When John believes that Karl believes that Bush is powerful, John is thinking in a quite particular way of the Thought to which Karl stands in the belief-relation—he is thinking of it under its canonical concept. The English sentence "John believes that Karl believes that Bush is powerful"—our (5)—is most naturally read as attributing to John use of this way of thinking of the Thought to which Karl stands in the belief-relation. But our regimentation (12HR) does not in itself imply that John is thinking of the relevant Thought in this way.

(12HR) and a certain background assumption do jointly imply that John is thinking of the Thought that way. The Background Assumption is that a thinker can have a *de re* attitude about a Thought only by thinking about it under its canonical concept. Under the theses of this chapter, this in turn implies that a thinker can have of *de re* attitudes about a Thought only if he is capable of judging and having other attitudes to that Thought. The Background Assumption seems to me to be true. It is hard to conceive of what it would be to have a *de re* attitude to a Thought without having the ability to think that Thought. Intuitively, it seems that if someone were not able to think the Thought in question, he would be able to have only *de dicto* attitudes concerning the Thought. If the Background Assumption is true, there is no gap between the truth of (12HR) and the truth of (5). If the Background Assumption is correct, it too iterates up the hierarchy of concepts. To have a *de re* attitude about the canonical concept of a Thought is to think of that canonical concept under its canonical concept; and so forth. For those who like symmetry in their theories, we can note that if the Background Assumption is true, we have for canonical concepts not only the exportation transitions we discussed earlier, which export a term outside a propositional-attitude verb, but also a kind of importation inference. When a thinker has a relational, *de re* attitude to a Thought, we can pull to the inside of the scope of the relevant propositional-attitude verb the term canonically specifying that Thought.

But suppose we wanted to give an account of the English sentences that does not presuppose the truth of the Background Assumption—how should we then proceed? I will not go into great formal detail at this stage of the chapter, but I mention one line of development to illustrate further possibilities. In his paper 'Reference and Propositional Attitudes', Brian Loar argued some years ago now that some terms within the scope of propositional-attitude verbs make what he calls 'a dual contribution' to the truth-conditions of the whole in which they occur.[21] In some cases, it is important to recognize that a term both contributes a concept or mode of presentation to the intentional content of the attitude, and also indicates that the subject of the attitudes stands in some relational attitude to the reference of the same term. Loar's point could be applied to canonical concepts of Thoughts and concepts. In the translations like (12HR) through (14HR) from the single-level language SL, we have taken only the reference of the canonical concepts of Thoughts as relevant to the truth-conditions. But in considering the issue of translations back to sentences of SL, there are advantages in regarding the canonical concepts as making exactly the kind of dual contribution that Loar describes. They both specify how a thinker is thinking of a Thought—precisely what we were discussing in the previous two paragraphs—and, by their reference, which Thought it is he is ascribing to the subject whose attitudes he is thinking about. So on a more complex implementation of the deeper scheme,

---

[21] Loar (1972).

our translations would not merely be sentences like (12HR) through (14HR). In the more complex scheme, they would include those conditions, but also add explicitly how, for instance, John is thinking of the Thoughts he is attributing. Instead of (12HR), we would have something which says:

> Concerning the Thought $<p>$, namely $<$Bush$> \wedge <$is powerful$>$, John believes of it, under the concept can($<p>$), that it has the property that Karl stands in the belief-relation to it.

This can be formalized straightforwardly. Corresponding formalizations will still validate the transition from (5) and (7) to (8).

However we implement the deeper translation scheme, either in a simple or in this more complex fashion, the single-level language SL used in formulae like (12S) raises semantical and formal issues that need to be addressed. I make a start on these in the Appendix to this chapter. SL is closer in some respects to natural language, and this makes it attractive as a means of describing embedded attitudes. But this closeness and attractiveness should not be taken as evidence in support of a single level of concepts. The very existence of the deeper translation scheme that legitimizes use of SL undermines any idea that the single-level language is intelligible only if there is a single level of concepts. Hierarchies of sense and understanding need not be reflected in hierarchies of expressions in our natural language. The theory of actual linguistic structures is one thing. The philosophical theory of concepts and understanding is another.

5. AN APPLICATION: RECONCILING EXTERNALISM WITH DISTINCTIVE SELF-KNOWLEDGE

One application of the Leverage Account is in answering arguments that externalist treatments of intentional content cannot be reconciled with a subject's having a distinctive kind of knowledge of his own mental states. Twenty years have now passed since intensive discussion began about the reconcilability of distinctive self-knowledge with the external character of intentional content. The first decade of such discussions has by no means quieted the objections of those who say that some theories of self-knowledge make such reconciliation impossible, so that we must either abandon those theories, or reject externalism about content. The questions arise sharply for the action-awareness account of our knowledge of our own mental actions offered in Chapter 7. Is that an account that makes such reconciliation impossible? And if it does not, what is its positive account of the nature of the reconciliation?

Specific doubts about the possibility of reconciliation on certain models of self-knowledge have been concisely articulated, and endorsed, by Crispin Wright, writing about halfway (1996) through this twenty-year period. Wright considered the model of self-knowledge as inner observation, and wrote:

> I want to say that ... in the sense in which an image or mental picture can come before the mind, its intentionality cannot.[22]

> Both a sunburned arm and a triangle can be presented as ordinary objects of observation, and each sustains, *qua* presented under those particular respective concepts, certain internal relations: the sunburned arm to the causes of its being in that condition, and the triangle to, for instance, other particular triangles. And the point is simply that while the identification of the triangle as such can proceed in innocence of its internal relations of the latter kind ... recognition of the sunburned arm as just that cannot proceed in like innocence but demands knowledge that its actual causation is as is appropriate to that mode of presentation of it.[23]

Wright attributes to Wittgenstein, and finds convincing, the point that

> the internal relations to the outer, of whatever sort, are all of the latter—sunburn-style—kind; and hence there is indeed a standing puzzle in the idea that an appropriate characterization of them, incorporating such intentionality, is somehow vouchsafed to their subject by something akin to pure observation.[24]

Does Wright's objection apply equally to the action-awareness account? In the perceptual case, as Wright implied, there is a partition between properties such as that of being sunburned that cannot be known to be instantiated simply by taking perception at face value, and those such as shape, colour, orientation, surface texture, and so forth, which can be known to be instantiated simply by taking perceptual experience at face value. (A state's representing these latter properties is also a matter of its external relations—a fact, incidentally, that should give us pause about the direction in which the argument is going.) An analogous partition of properties, as thought about in given ways, can be made for action-awareness. I cannot, from action-awareness alone, come to know that the copying machine whose lid I am closing was manufactured in Taiwan. Knowing that requires knowledge

---

[22] Wright (2001: 342).   [23] Wright (2001: 343).   [24] Wright (2001: 343).

of its history that is not given in action-awareness. But action-awareness can make available knowledge that I am closing the machine's lid, at a certain speed, with a certain force, and that I am doing it now. So, in the case of mental actions, the crucial question to address is this: is the intentional content of a mental event or state to be grouped with the property of being made in Taiwan, or is it to be grouped with the properties which you can know about simply from your action-awareness?

The intuitive, pre-theoretical answer to this question is that we have an action-awareness of the full intentional content of our judgements, decisions, and other mental actions. We are aware that we are judging that New York is hot in the summer; we are aware that we are deciding to spend the summer in a cooler place. A judgement with that intentional content may also be a manifestation of a neurosis, may be an unconscious excuse for not staying in New York, or many other things that are to be grouped with the machine's being made in Taiwan. But in ordinary cases, the intentional content of the judgement, decision, or whatever mental action-type is in question does seem to be so available. What is the explanation of this fact?

Whatever the explanation, it will have to have a certain generality. When we know what we are judging or deciding, on the basis of action-awareness, we know the content of our judgement or decision, whatever its conceptual constituents. You can have an action-awareness of your judging that p, whatever the content p may be, whether the conceptual content p is observational, theoretical, moral, or anything else. As we noted earlier, in such judgements about the content of mental states, you think of the conceptual constituents of the content judged under their canonical concepts. You think of the concept *hot* under its canonical concept; and so forth.

We can now focus on the transition a thinker makes in passing from

an action-awareness of his judging that New York is hot in the summer

to his judgement of the following intentional content, where the concepts referred to are thought about under their canonical concepts:

<Judge> ^ <I> ^ (can(<hot>) ^ can(<New York>) ^ can(<in the summer>)).

(Purists can add notation for the canonical concept of ^, predicational combination in Thoughts, but I will abstain in the interests of legibility. On the concept expressed by "I" as used in thought, see Chapter 3.) This transition from the action-awareness to the judgement is a priori valid. In any context in which the thinker has a genuine, and not merely apparent, action-awareness of judging that New York is hot in the summer, it will also be true that he judges that it's the concept *hot* that he judges New York to fall under in the summer. The same applies to the canonical concept of any other concept F in place of the concept *hot*, however externally or historically individuated the concept F may be. This explanation has the required generality.

This transition in thought from action-awareness to judgement is totally different in character from the transition, unwarranted without further information, from

a perception of a reddish arm

to a judgement

this arm is sunburned.

This latter transition does, just as Wright said, need further information about the causes of the redness on the arm if it is to be valid. By contrast, the preceding transition involving action-awareness does not need any further information for its legitimacy. No further information is needed, under the Leverage Account, because if the conceptual constituents of the content of the judgement of which there is action-awareness are externally individuated, so are the canonical concepts of those constituents. For the transition involving action-awareness, the reason-giving state and the judgement for which it gives reason are equally externally individuated. There is not even an apparent leap from what is internally individuated to what is externally individuated.

There may be a sense of unease about this reconciliation of externalism and the distinctive knowledge of mental actions, a sense that there is some kind of cheating going on. This unease may stem from the thought that the treatment given here is like that of someone who insists, correctly, that the recognitional concept of water is externally individuated, and that we know our thoughts are water-thoughts. There is a clear sense in which one can possess a recognitional concept of water without knowing which liquid it is, in the sense of not knowing its chemical composition. Does a similar objection apply against the account I have offered of action-awareness of the conceptual contents one is judging? Is the account consistent with the thinker's not knowing which concepts are in question?

I reply that because one is employing the canonical concept of a concept in making judgements about the contents of one's thoughts, one does, by contrast with the chemical characterization of water, know which concept is in question. It is precisely the force of the Leverage Account to make it clear that any such seeming gap is really closed. Under the Leverage Account, you know as much about which concept is in question when you think of it as *the concept F* as there is to know. (You may learn more by philosophical investigation about the nature of the concept, but that is not a matter of further determination of which concept is in question. You already knew that in fixing on just one concept to investigate.) All the conditions that contribute to the individuation of the concept F itself contribute to the individuation of the canonical concept of F. From the Leverage Account, as noted, reasons for making first-order judgements containing the concept F are transmitted to reasons for making suitably corresponding judgements containing the higher-order concept *the concept F*. Any requirements on knowing which concept that are met when one is simply using the concept F will equally be met when one uses the canonical concept of the concept F. It is always an answer to the query "Which concept is in question?" to say "It's the concept F", where this answer employs the canonical concept of F, rather than some descriptive mode such as "the concept discussed in Chapter 5 of such-and-such book".

There will, for any given concept, be empirical conditions met by a given thinker who employs that concept, conditions not extractable simply from the nature of the concept itself. They will include such matters as the nature of that particular thinker's mental representations underlying his possession of the concept, and the particular computational procedures involving it that he employs. There is manifestly an important area of study that consists in the empirical investigation of these empirical matters involving concepts as possessed by particular thinkers. But precisely because these empirical conditions can vary across thinkers that share the same concept, these empirical conditions are not what constitute the nature of the concept itself. A thinker's ignorance of these empirical matters of mental representation does not impugn her knowledge of which concepts are in question when she thinks *I judge that New York is hot in the summer*.

It is a striking feature of the canonical concept of a concept that it has two characteristics whose coinstantiation rests on a merely empirical truth. The canonical concept has the individuating properties specified in the Leverage Account. Our minds and conscious states are also such that we can rationally apply the canonical concept of a concept in response to conscious states, such as action-awareness and passive thinking, whose content involves the very concept of which it is a canonical concept. It seems to be a precondition of rational, critical thought that these two characteristics go together. Rationality requires us, on occasion, to consider for instance whether our conscious judgement that Fa was made in an epistemically responsible fashion. Investigation of this issue involves drawing on our tacit knowledge (or tacit partial knowledge) of the condition for something to be F. Such a rational exercise of thought is possible only because the canonical concept of F is one we can apply in rational response to conscious mental states whose intentional content contains the concept F.

Canonical concepts of concepts are far from the only concepts some of whose distinctive applications rest on empirical facts. The way we think of a type of bodily movement, when we perceive it made by someone else, yet also perceive it as an action of a type that we ourselves could make, provides another type of example. No doubt the underlying ground of the possibility of such concepts involves the now-famous mirror neurons identified by Rizzolati and his colleagues mentioned earlier. It is an empirical matter that there are such representations in our psychology. They make possible much that would not otherwise be possible. To deny the existence of ways of coming to apply concepts that rely on empirical facts would rule out large tracts of human thought and experience. This applies equally to our ability to know about the intentional content of our own mental actions and our other conscious states.

Appendix: Semantical and Formal Issues

The main text of this chapter has concentrated on core philosophical issues about concepts of concepts, and their relation to understanding. So as not to interrupt the flow of that discussion, I have collected some more technical issues in this Appendix. The technical issues are nonetheless important, and sometimes pivotal. Some of the stances taken in the recent literature would, if correct, undermine various features of the position for which I have been arguing. Other stances on formal or semantical issues would rule out the single-level language to which I have said that a defender of the Thesis (in section 1 above) can have access. These formal and semantical issues may be technical, but they are not technicalities.

I start with the most pressing questions for the position I have developed here, and then open the discussion into a consideration of the relation of this position to some others in the literature.

> *Question 1.* Does a hierarchy of canonical concepts collapse into, or at least make available, a single-level account of sense and concepts?

In his early paper 'Frege's Hierarchies of Indirect Sense and the Paradox of Analysis', Terence Parsons argues that the hierarchy does so collapse.[25] He classifies as 'rigid' any theory that holds that 'the customary sense of an expression uniquely determines its indirect sense' (p. 44). The theory I have offered is certainly rigid in this sense. In Parsons's notation, $s_1[A]$ is the customary sense of A; $s_2[A]$ is the unique indirect sense of A, what I have called the canonical sense of $s_1[A]$; and, where a and b are senses, $a(b)$ is the result of 'applying' the sense a to the sense b. (This last embodies a controversial conception of sense and/or controversial interpretation of Frege; but we can equally construe $a(b)$ as the predicational combination of sense a with sense b for purposes of the present discussion.) Parsons goes on to argue that

A rigid theory can be converted into a theory that associates with each expression only one sense, as follows. We define '*the* sense of A', i.e., '$s[A]$', as follows:

---

[25] Parsons (1981). Page references in the text are to this work.

(i) If A is a name or a sentence or a predicate or an extensional sentence operator, then $s[A] = s_1[A]$.

(ii) If A is an indirect sentence operator, then $s[A] =$ that function which maps an arbitrary sense x to $s_1[A](s_2[B])$, where B is an expression such that $s_1[B] = x$. (p. 45)

I do not dispute that we can define the operation Parsons specifies; but I do not think that that shows the hierarchy is eliminable or redundant. The complex sense $s_1[A](s_2[B])$, in terms of which '*the* sense of A' is individuated, involves a second-level sense, and could not be grasped by a thinker unless he grasps the canonical sense of a first-level sense. It seems to me that we do not have a reduction of senses to a single level if an account of what it is to grasp senses in that single level involves grasp of senses at other levels. To insist that that is irrelevant to reduction is to set sense loose from its essential connections with grasp of sense or understanding, by intentional agents and thinkers. This is of course not a criticism of Parsons if his intentions were either purely definitional, or were concerned with a kind of ontological reduction that is not constrained by considerations of understanding. Parsons does, however, (in passing) write that a variant of this approach just described turns out to be the theory 'that Dummett says Frege should have given' (p. 45). Dummett certainly was intending to offer an alternative to the hierarchy.

Question 2. Do representations in the single-level language SD together with obvious truths imply falsehoods?

As we noted in the main text, under the treatment Tyler Burge called 'Method II', a language designed originally for only a single level of sense formally uses terms in the position corresponding to the complete sentences of English that are embedded in propositional-attitude operators. In his 1979 paper 'Frege and the Hierarchy' Burge argued that, in the presence of other Fregean principles, this treatment implies that if someone believes one truth, he believes every truth.[26] If sound, this is effectively a *reductio* of Method II when developed without a hierarchical language, in the presence of the other Fregean principles.

I accept that Burge's argument is valid given his premises and his interpretation of the language. I also accept, though for other reasons, the conclusion that Burge draws from this argument (and others), that there is good reason to introduce a hierarchy of concepts. The pressing question that

[26] Burge (2005c: 271–2). Page references in the text are to this work.

arises for my position is this: why do not representations in the language SL, such as my (12S)

(12S) Believes (John, <Karl> ^ <Believes> ^ <Bush> ^ <is powerful>)

not equally fall victim to Burge's *reductio*? For in the formulae of SL, the English sentences embedded in propositional-attitude contexts are certainly represented by terms. The term "<Bush> ^ <is powerful>" is one such; the term "<Karl> ^ <Believes> ^ <Bush> ^ <is powerful>" is another.

I am going to quote the initial statement of Burge's argument in full. (I change the numbering of examples to avoid confusion with numbered examples already used; the altered numbering is indicated by square brackets.) Burge started by considering an example of double embedding of the sort we have been considering:

(15) Igor believes Bela believes Opus 132 is a masterpiece.

He continued (pp. 271–2):

Let us assume then that 'α' (which denotes the proposition that Opus 132 is a masterpiece) represents 'Opus 132 is a masterpiece' as it occurs in [15]. [15], we shall assume, asserts a relation of belief between Igor and the proposition that Bela believes that Opus 132 is a masterpiece. I shall denote this proposition by the expression '$\Gamma_1(\beta_1, \alpha)$'. Thus on our assumptions, [15] is formalized as

[16] Believes (Igor, $\Gamma_1(\beta_1, \alpha)$)

By the principle of extensionality, the denotation of '$\Gamma_1(\beta_1, \alpha)$' is a function of the denotations or extension of its parts. I shall assume that 'β_1' denotes the sense of 'Bela' and that 'Γ_1' denotes the sense of 'believes'—a function from β_1 and α to the relevant proposition.

We assume the principle that a given sense is associated with a unique denotation or extension. Thus the proposition $\Gamma_1(\beta_1, \alpha)$ is associated with (or, in Church's terminology, is a concept of) a unique denotation or extension, its truth value.

We assume that this truth value is a function of the unique denotations or extensions associated respectively with the senses that determine the proposition. ... Let 'β' express β_1 and denote Bela; let 'Γ' express Γ_1 and denote what 'believes' denotes (or have its extension). Let α_0 express α and denote its truth value. (We suppose that truth value to be truth.) Then '$\Gamma(\beta, \alpha_0)$' expresses $\Gamma_1(\beta_1, \alpha)$ and denotes its truth value. 'Believes' originally applied to persons and propositions. But on our assumptions it has come also to apply to persons and truth values. This leads to absurdity in short order.

For given the classical substitution laws of Method II, we may substitute any expression that denotes truth for 'α_0' in '$\Gamma(\beta, \alpha_0)$' and preserve the truth value of

'$\Gamma(\beta, \alpha_0)$'. (We speak of both sentences and propositions as having truth value.) But '$\Gamma(\beta, \alpha_0)$' supposedly expresses the proposition that Bela believes Opus 132 is a masterpiece. So it seems to follow that if Bela believes Opus 132 is a masterpiece, he believes every truth.

The argument shows that on these assumptions 'Opus 132 is a masterpiece' in [15] cannot be represented by a term 'α' denoting the proposition that Opus 132 is a masterpiece.

Representations such as (12S) in the single-level language SL are not vulnerable to this argument because one of the assumptions of the argument fails for SL. Terms of SL such as "<Bush> $^\wedge$ <is powerful>", "<Opus 132> $^\wedge$ <is a masterpiece>" denote Thoughts, or complex concepts. Those Thoughts or complex concepts do also have truth-values; but those truth-values *are not the denotations or semantic values of these terms in the language SD*. SL is nevertheless still an extensional language. The denotation of the complex term "<Opus 132> $^\wedge$ <is a masterpiece>", a complex Thought, is a function of the denotation of its constituent terms "<Opus 132>" and "<is a masterpiece>" (and of the denotation of the functor '$^\wedge$'). There is no difficulty on this view in the formula

(17) Believes (Bela, <Opus 132> $^\wedge$ < is a masterpiece>)

being true, while the formula

(18) Believes (Bela, <The Continuum Hypothesis> $^\wedge$ <is independent of> $^\wedge$ <the axioms of ZF>)

is false. The Thought denoted by the term "<Opus 132> $^\wedge$ <is a masterpiece>" is distinct from the Thought denoted by the term "<The Continuum Hypothesis> $^\wedge$ <is independent of> $^\wedge$ <the axioms of ZF>".

Can it be objected to this argument that we can still make the substitution of any true sentence for 'Opus 132 is a masterpiece' in the English sentence 'Bela believes Opus 132 is a masterpiece'? That would be begging the question against SL in the absence of the assumption that the terms that correspond to complete sentences denote truth-values. The hypothesis is that formulae of SL, like (17) and (18), translate the corresponding English sentences; and under that hypothesis, substitution of sentences with the same truth-value within "believes that" contexts is clearly not always going to preserve truth-value. The translations of (17) and (18) into the explicitly hierarchical language, under the deeper scheme, simply underwrite this point.

Does the rejection of the assumption on which the *reductio* rests make the solution offered by SL un-Fregean? The complete sentences of SL, as opposed to terms for Thoughts, can and should be regarded as denoting truth-values, in classical Fregean fashion. And the fully hierarchical language into which I have suggested some deeper translation schemes for sentences of SL seems to me wholly Fregean. What I have resisted is the substitution of a complete sentence such as "Opus 132 is a masterpiece" (as opposed to a term) in the position of "<Opus 132> ^ <is a masterpiece>" in such SL-formulae as (17). In the formulae subject to Burge's *reductio*, unlike SL, complete sentences can occupy the same positions as terms for Thoughts. (This is legitimate under his assumptions about denotation and semantic value.) We could if we so wished design an extension of the language SL, a language SL+, one that does allow such substitutions of a sentence in certain term-positions of formulae of the unextended language SL as well-formed. But the reference (semantic value) of the sentence thus allowed in term-position would have to be its normal sense. This reference-shift too would also seem to be entirely Fregean in spirit.

Conclusion

I have argued that fundamental reference rules for concepts can provide a substantive account of understanding. They can support a realistic treatment of truth and reference, and can do so in a way that is superior to justificationist, pragmatist, and pure conceptual-role theories of content. In so far as the account I have offered is along the right lines at all, it fits squarely into the tradition that attempts to elucidate and apply the classical Fregean conception of sense as given by truth-conditions.

Sense and Thoughts are of interest in themselves; but they are also an indispensable starting point for other programmes of inquiry. Even in Frege's own case, his interest in an account of sense was generated by the need for an account of the sense of sentences that could be integrated with, and support, a theory of the deductive relations of those sentences. Our need today for a substantive account of particular senses reaches much wider. Each of the following current issues in philosophy and its adjacent cognitive sciences requires a substantive theory of sense for its resolution:

> the correct general form to be taken by a non-circular, explanatory account of the acquisition of a concept;

> the correct account of rule-following in applying a particular concept;

> the conditions under which acceptance of a complete conceptual content is, in the presence of additional information, justified, and what is involved in knowing it;

> the nature of the explanatory powers of the truth of a complete conceptual content, and its consequent role in sound abductive inference;

> the constraints on the mental representations involved in grasp of a given conceptual content following from the nature of grasp of that content;

the possibility, if such exists, of sound transcendental reasoning in the philosophical theory of conceptual content based on the nature of grasp of those conceptual contents.

Whether or not the particular treatments of this book are correct, I hope that some variant of the approach in terms of fundamental reference rules will be a resource for further investigation of all of these issues.

References

ALBRITTON, R. (1968), 'On Wittgenstein's Use of the Term "Criterion": Postscript (1966)', in G. Pitcher (ed.), *Wittgenstein: The Philosophical Investigations* (London: Macmillan).

ANSCOMBE, G. E. M. (1975), 'The First Person', in S. Guttenplan (ed.), *Mind and Language* (Oxford: Oxford University Press).

ARISTOTLE (1995), *Selections*, trans. T. Irwin and G. Fine (Indianapolis: Hackett).

ASTINGTON, J., HARRIS, P., and OLSON, D. (eds), (1988) *Developing Theories of Mind* (Cambridge: Cambridge University Press).

BAILLARGEON, R. (1987), 'Object Permanence in 3.5 and 4.5 Month Old Infants', *Developmental Psychology*, 23: 655–64.

——— (1993), 'The Object Concept Revisited: New Directions in the Investigation of Infants' Physical Knowledge', in C. Granrud (ed.), *Visual Perception and Cognition in Infancy* (Hillsdale, NJ: Erlbaum).

BLOCK, N. (1978), 'Troubles with Functionalism', in *Minnesota Studies in the Philosophy of Science*, ix, ed. C. W. Savage (Minneapolis: Minnesota University Press):

——— (1986), 'Advertisement for a Semantics for Psychology', *Midwest Studies in Philosophy*, 10: 615–78.

BOGHOSSIAN, P., (1989) 'Content and Self-Knowledge', *Philosophical Topics*, 17: 5–26.

BRANDOM, R. (1994), *Making It Explicit: Reasoning, Representing, and Discursive Commitment* (Cambridge, Mass.: Harvard University Press).

——— (1997), 'Study Guide', in Sellars (1997).

——— (2000), *Articulating Reasons: An Introduction to Inferentialism* (Cambridge, Mass.: Harvard University Press).

BREWER, B. (1995), 'Compulsion by Reason', *Proceedings of the Aristotelian Society Supplementary Volume*, 69: 237–53.

BROAD, C. D. (1975), *Leibniz: An Introduction* (Cambridge: Cambridge University Press).

BURGE, T. (2003), 'Perceptual Entitlement', *Philosophy and Phenomenological Research*, 67: 503–48.

——— (2005a), 'Frege on Sense and Linguistic Meaning', in Burge (2005b).

——— (2005b), *Truth, Thought, Reason: Essays on Frege* (Oxford: Oxford University Press).

——— (2005c), 'Frege and the Hierarchy', in Burge (2005b).

BURGE, T. (2007*a*), 'Individualism and the Mental', in Burge, *Foundations of Mind, Philosophical Papers*, ii (Oxford: Oxford University Press).

——— (2007*b*), 'Intellectual Norms and Foundations of Mind', in Burge, *Foundations of Mind, Philosophical Papers*, ii (Oxford: Oxford University Press).

CAREY, S. (1982), 'Semantic Development: State of the Art', in E. Wanner and L. Gleitman (eds), *Language Acquisition: The State of the Art* (Cambridge: Cambridge University Press).

CASTON, V. (2002), 'Aristotle on Consciousness', *Mind*, 111: 751–815.

CHOMSKY, N. (1966), *Cartesian Linguistics: A Chapter in the History of Rationalist Thought* (New York: Harper and Row).

——— (1980), *Rules and Representations* (New York: Columbia University Press).

——— (1986), *Knowledge of Language: Its Nature, Origin and Use* (New York: Praeger).

CHURCH, A. (1951), 'A Formulation of the Logic of Sense and Denotation', in P. Henle, H. Kallen, and S. Langer (eds), *Structure, Method and Meaning: Essays in Honor of H. M. Sheffer* (New York: Liberal Free Press).

CRAIG, E. (1976), 'Sensory Experience and the Foundations of Knowledge', *Synthese*, 33: 1–24.

CRIMMINS, M. (1992), 'Tacitness and Virtual Beliefs', *Mind and Language*, 7: 240–63.

DANTO, A. (1963), 'What We Can Do', *Journal of Philosophy*, 60: 435–45.

DAVIDSON, D. (2001*a*), *Inquiries into Truth and Interpretation*, 2nd edn (Oxford: Oxford University Press).

——— (2001*b*), 'Theories of Meaning and Learnable Languages', in Davidson (2001*a*).

——— (2001*c*), 'On Saying That', in Davidson (2001*a*).

DAVIES, M. (1981), *Meaning, Quantification, Necessity: Themes in Philosophical Logic* (London: Routledge and Kegan Paul).

——— (1987), 'Tacit Knowledge and Semantic Theory: Can a Five Per Cent Difference Matter?', *Mind*, 96: 441–62.

——— (1989), 'Connectionism, Modularity and Tacit Knowledge', *British Journal for the Philosophy of Science*, 40: 541–55.

——— (1991), 'Concepts, Connectionism and the Language of Thought', in D. Rumelhart, W. Ramsey, and S. Stich (eds), *Philosophy and Connectionist Theory* (Hillsdale, NJ: Erlbaum).

DENNETT, D. (1978*a*), *Brainstorms* (Montgomery, Vt.: Bradford Books).

——— (1978*b*), 'Where Am I?', in Dennett (1978*a*).

DUMMETT, M. (1973), *Frege: Philosophy of Language* (London: Duckworth).

——— (1976), 'What Is a Theory of Meaning? (II)', in G. Evans and J. McDowell (eds), *Truth and Meaning: Essays in Semantics* (Oxford: Oxford University Press).

——— (1978*a*), *Truth and Other Enigmas* (London: Duckworth).

——— (1978*b*), 'The Realist of the Past', in Dummett (1978*a*).

——— (1981), *The Interpretation of Frege's Philosophy* (London: Duckworth).

—— (1991), *The Logical Basis of Metaphysics* (Cambridge, Mass.: Harvard University Press).

—— (2004), *Truth and the Past* (New York: Columbia University Press).

—— (2005), 'The Justificationist's Response to a Realist', *Mind*, 114: 671–88.

—— (2006), *Thought and Reality* (Oxford: Oxford University Press).

EDGLEY, R. (1969), *Reason in Theory and Practice* (London: Hutchinson).

EVANS, G. (1982), *The Varieties of Reference* (Oxford: Oxford University Press).

—— (1985*a*), *Collected Papers* (Oxford: Oxford University Press).

—— (1985*b*), 'Understanding Demonstratives', in Evans (1985*a*).

FEINBERG, I. (1978), 'Efference Copy and Corollary Discharge: Implication for Thinking and its Disorders', *Schizophrenia Bulletin*, 4: 636–40.

FIELD, H. (1977), 'Logic, Meaning and Conceptual Role', *Journal of Philosophy*, 74: 379–409.

—— (1996), 'The Aprioricity of Logic', *Proceedings of the Aristotelian Society*, 96: 359–79.

—— (2001*a*), *Truth and the Absence of Fact* (Oxford: Oxford University Press).

—— (2001*b*), 'Which Undecidable Mathematical Sentences Have Determinate Truth Values?', in Field, *Truth and the Absence of Fact* (Oxford: Oxford University Press).

—— (2001*c*), 'Apriority as an Evaluative Notion', in Field (2001*a*).

FINE, K. (2003), *Reference, Relation and Meaning*, John Locke Lectures, Oxford University, 2003 <http://www.philosophy.ox.ac.uk/misc/johnlocke/index.shtml>, accessed 11 June 2007.

FODOR, J. (1975), *The Language of Thought* (New York: Thomas Crowell).

—— (1987*a*), *Psychosemantics: The Problem of Meaning in the Philosophy of Mind* (Cambridge, Mass.: MIT Press).

—— 'Appendix: Why There Still Has to Be a Language of Thought', in Fodor (1987*a*).

FREEDBERG, D., and GALLESE, V. (2007), 'Motion, Emotion and Empathy in Esthetic Experience', *Trends in Cognitive Sciences*, 11: 197–203.

FREGE, G. (1953), *The Foundations of Arithmetic*, trans. J. L. Austin (Oxford: Blackwell).

—— (1964), *The Basic Laws of Arithmetic* (Berkeley: University of California Press).

—— (1977), 'Thoughts', in Frege, *Logical Investigations* (Oxford: Blackwell).

—— (1979), *Posthumous Writings* (Oxford: Blackwell).

—— (1984*a*), 'Logical Investigations Part I: Thoughts', trans. P. Geach and R. Stoothof, in *Gottlob Frege: Collected Papers on Mathematics, Logic and Philosophy*, ed. B. McGuinness (Oxford: Blackwell).

—— (1984*b*), 'Compound Thoughts', in *Gottlob Frege: Collected Papers on Mathematics, Logic and Philosophy*, ed. B. McGuiness (Oxford: Blackwell).

FRITH, C., (1992), *The Cognitive Neuropsychology of Schizophrenia* (Hove: Erlbaum).

FRITH, C., and JOHNSTONE, F. (2003), *Schizophrenia: A Very Short Introduction* (Oxford: Oxford University Press).

GALLESE, V., KEYSERS, C., and RIZZOLATI, G. (2004), 'A Unifying View of the Basis of Social Cognition', *Trends in Cognitive Sciences*, 8: 396–403.

GEACH, P. (1972), *Logic Matters* (Oxford: Blackwell).

GOLDMAN, A. (1970), *A Theory of Human Action* (Princeton: Princeton University Press).

GOODALE, M. A., and Milner, A. D. (2004), *Sight Unseen* (Oxford: Oxford University Press).

GOPNIK, A., MELTZOFF, A., and KUHL, P. (1999), *How Babies Think: The Science of Childhood* (London: Weidenfeld and Nicolson); pub. in North America as *The Scientist in the Crib* (New York: Perennial, 2001).

_____ _____ _____ (2001), *The Scientist in the Crib* (New York: Perennial).

GREEN, B. (2004), *The Fabric of the Cosmos: Space, Time and the Texture of Reality* (New York: Knopf).

GREGORY, R. (1970), *The Intelligent Eye* (London: Weidenfeld and Nicolson).

_____ (1974), *Concepts and Mechanisms of Perception* (London: Duckworth).

HARMAN, G. (1965), 'The Inference to the Best Explanation', *Philosophical Review*, 74: 88–95.

_____ (1986), *Change in View: Principles of Reasoning* (Cambridge, Mass.: MIT Press).

_____ (1999*a*), 'Meaning and Semantics', *Reasoning, Meaning and Mind* (Oxford: Oxford University Press).

_____ (1999*b*), *Reasoning, Meaning, and Mind* (Oxford: Oxford University Press).

HELMHOLTZ, H. VON (1962), *Treatise on Physiological Optics* (New York: Dover).

HIERONYMI, P. (2005), 'The Wrong Kind of Reason', *Journal of Philosophy*, 102: 437–57.

HILL, C. (1998), 'Peacocke on Semantic Values', *Australasian Journal of Philosophy*, 76: 97–104.

HORNSBY, J. (1986), 'Physicalist Thinking and Conceptions of Behaviour', in P. Pettit and J. McDowell (eds), *Subject, Thought and Context* (Oxford: Oxford University Press).

HORWICH, P. (1998), *Truth*, 2nd edn (Oxford: Oxford University Press).

ISHIGURO, H. (1990), *Leibniz's Philosophy of Logic and Language*, 2nd edn (Cambridge: Cambridge University Press).

JACKSON, F. (1986), 'What Mary Didn't Know', *Journal of Philosophy*, 83: 291–5.

JAMES, W. (2002), *The Meaning of Truth* (first pub. 1909; Mineola, NY: Dover Publications).

_____ (2003), *Pragmatism: A New Name for Some Old Ways of Thinking* (first pub. 1907; New York: Barnes and Noble).

JOHNSON-LAIRD, P. (1983), *Mental Models* (Cambridge, Mass.: Harvard University Press).

KAHNEMAN, D. (2003), 'A Perspective on Judgement and Choice: Mapping Bounded Rationality', *American Psychologist*, 58: 697–720.

KAPLAN, D. (1964), *Foundations of Intensional Logic*, UCLA Dissertation (Ann Arbor: University Microfilms).

——(1969), 'Quantifying In', in D. Davidson and J. Hintikka (eds), *Words and Objections: Essays on the Work of W. V. Quine* (Dordrecht: Reidel).

——(1989), 'Demonstratives', in J. Almog, J. Perry, and H. Wettstein (eds), *Themes from Kaplan* (New York: Oxford University Press).

KELLMAN, P., and SPELKE, E. (1983), 'Perception of Partly Occluded Objects in Infancy', *Cognitive Psychology*, 15: 483–524.

LEIBNIZ, G. (1951), 'Reflections on Knowledge, Truth and Ideas', in *Leibniz: Selections*, ed. and trans. P. Wiener (New York: Charles Scribner's Sons).

——(1969), *Leibniz: Philosophical Papers and Letters*, ed. L. Loemker (Dordrecht: Reidel).

——(1981), *New Essays on Human Understanding*, trans. P. Remnant and J. Bennett (Cambridge: Cambridge University Press).

LEWIS, D. (1973), *Counterfactuals* (Oxford: Blackwell).

LOAR, B. (1972), 'Reference and Propositional Attitudes', *Philosophical Review*, 81: 43–62.

MCDOWELL, J. (1994), *Mind and World* (Cambridge, Mass.: Harvard University Press).

——(1998), 'Knowledge and the Internal', in McDowell, *Meaning, Knowledge and Reality* (Cambridge, Mass.: Harvard University Press).

MARCEL, A. (2003), 'The Sense of Agency: Awareness and Ownership of Action', in J. Roessler and N. Eilan (eds), *Agency and Self-Awareness: Issues in Philosophy and Psychology* (Oxford: Oxford University Press).

MASANGKAY, Z., McCLUSKEY, K., et al. (1974), 'The Early Development of Inferences about the Visual Percepts of Others', *Child Development*, 45: 357–66.

MELI, D. (1993), *Equivalence and Priority: Newton versus Leibniz* (Oxford: Oxford University Press).

MELTZOFF, A. (2002), 'Elements of a Developmental Theory of Imitation', in A. Meltzoff and W. Prinz (eds), *The Imitative Mind: Development, Evolution and Brain Bases* (Cambridge: Cambridge University Press).

——and MOORE, M. K. (1977), 'Imitation of Facial and Manual Gestures by Human Neonates', *Science*, 198: 179–92.

MILNER, A. D., and GOODALE, M. A. (1995), *The Visual Brain in Action* (Oxford: Oxford University Press).

MISAK, C. (2004), *Truth and the End of Inquiry: A Peircean Account of Truth*, 2nd edn (Oxford: Oxford University Press).

MOORE, G. E. (1962), ' "This" and Partial Tautology', in *The Commonplace Book of G. E. Moore 1919–1953*, ed. C. Lewy (London: George Allen and Unwin).

Moore, G. E. (1993), 'Proof of an External World', in *G. E. Moore: Selected Writings*, ed. T. Baldwin (London: Routledge).

Moran, R. (2001), *Authority and Estrangement: An Essay on Self-Knowledge* (Princeton: Princeton University Press).

Nagel, T. (1986), *The View from Nowhere* (Oxford: Oxford University Press).

Nozick, R. (1981), *Philosophical Explanations* (Cambridge, Mass.: Harvard University Press).

O'Shaughnessy, B. (1980), *The Will*, i and ii (Cambridge: Cambridge University Press).

Parsons, T. (1981), 'Frege's Hierarchies of Indirect Sense and the Paradox of Analysis', *Midwest Studies in Philosophy*, 6: 37–57.

Peacocke, C. (1981), 'Demonstrative Thought and Psychological Explanation', *Synthese*, 49: 187–217.

_____ (1983), *Sense and Content: Experience, Thought and their Relations* (Oxford: Oxford University Press).

_____ (1985), 'Imagination, Possibility and Experience', in J. Foster and H. Robinson (eds), *Essays on Berkeley* (Oxford: Oxford University Press).

_____ (1987), 'Understanding Logical Constants: A Realist's Account', *Proceedings of the British Academy*, 73: 153–200.

_____ (1988), 'The Limits of Intelligibility: A Post-Verificationist Proposal', *Philosophical Review*, 97: 463–96.

_____ (1992), *A Study of Concepts* (Cambridge, Mass.: MIT Press).

_____ (1993*a*), 'Proof and Truth', in J. Haldane and C. Wright (eds), *Reality, Representation and Projection* (New York: Oxford University Press).

_____ (1993*b*), 'How Are A Priori Truths Possible?', *European Journal of Philosophy*, 1: 175–99.

_____ (1993*c*), 'Externalist Explanation', *Proceedings of the Aristotelian Society*, 93: 203–30.

_____ (1994), 'Content, Computation and Externalism', *Mind and Language*, 9: 303–35.

_____ (1996), 'Entitlement, Self-Knowledge and Conceptual Redeployment', *Proceedings of the Aristotelian Society*, 96: 117–58.

_____ (1997), 'Concepts without Words', in R. Heck (ed.), *Language, Thought and Logic: Essays in Honour of Michael Dummett* (Oxford: Oxford University Press).

_____ (1998*a*), 'Implicit Conceptions, the A Priori, and the Identity of Concepts', in Villanueva (1998).

_____ (1998*b*), 'The Concept of a Natural Number', *Australasian Journal of Philosophy*, 76: 105–9.

_____ (1998*c*), 'Conscious Attitudes, Attention and Self-Knowledge', in C. Wright, B. Smith, and C. MacDonald (eds), *Knowing Our Own Minds* (Oxford: Oxford University Press).

—— (1999), *Being Known* (Oxford: Oxford University Press).

—— (2000), 'Explaining the A Priori', in P. Boghossian and C. Peacocke (eds), *New Essays on the A Priori* (Oxford: Oxford University Press).

—— (2001*a*), 'Does Perception Have a Nonconceptual Content?', *Journal of Philosophy*, 98: 239–64.

—— (2001*b*), 'Theories of Concepts: A Wider Task', in J. Branquinho, J. Saagua, and A. Marques (eds), *Foundations of Cognitive Science* (Oxford: Oxford University Press).

—— (2003*a*), 'Postscript', in Y. Gunther (ed.), *Essays on Non-Conceptual Content* (Cambridge, Mass.: MIT Press).

—— (2003*b*), 'Implicit Conceptions, Understanding and Rationality', in M. Hahn and B. Ramberg (eds), *Reflections and Replies: Essays on the Philosophy of Tyler Burge* (Cambridge, Mass.: MIT Press).

—— (2003*c*), 'Action: Awareness, Ownership, and Knowledge', in Roessler and Eilan (2003).

—— (2004), *The Realm of Reason* (Oxford: Oxford University Press).

—— (2005*a*), 'Justification, Realism and the Past', *Mind*, 114: 639–70.

—— (2005*b*), ' "Another I": Representing Conscious States, Perception and Others', in J. Bermúdez (ed.), *Thought, Reference and Experience: Themes from the Philosophy of Gareth Evans* (Oxford: Oxford University Press).

—— (2007), 'Mental Action and Self-Awareness (I)', in J. Cohen and B. McLaughlin (eds), *Contemporary Debates in the Philosophy of Mind* (Oxford: Blackwell).

—— (2008), 'Mental Action and Self-Awareness (II): Epistemology', in L. O'Brien and M. Soteriou (eds), *Mental Action* (Oxford: Oxford University Press).

PEIRCE, C. (1940), 'How to Make Our Ideas Clear', in *The Philosophy of Charles Pierce*, ed. J. Buchler (London: Routledge and Kegan Paul).

PERRY, J. (1993), 'Frege on Demonstratives', repr. with Postscript in Perry, *The Problem of the Essential Indexical and Other Essays* (Oxford: Oxford University Press).

—— (2004), 'Selves and Self-Concepts', paper prepared for a conference at New York University, Dec.

PRICE, H. (1988), *Facts and the Function of Truth* (Oxford: Blackwell).

—— (forthcoming), *Naturalism without Mirrors* (New York: Oxford University Press).

PRINZ, J. (2002), *Furnishing the Mind: Concepts and their Perceptual Basis* (Cambridge, Mass.: MIT Press).

PRIOR, A. (1960), 'The Runabout Inference-Ticket', *Analysis*, 21: 38–9.

PRYOR, J. (2000), 'The Skeptic and the Dogmatist', *Noûs*, 34: 517–49.

PUTNAM, H. (1975*a*), 'Explanation and Reference', in Putnam, *Mind, Language and Reality, Philosophical Papers*, ii (Cambridge: Cambridge University Press).

PUTNAM, H. (1975*b*), 'On Properties', in Putnam, *Mathematics, Matter and Method, Philosophical Papers*, i (Cambridge: Cambridge University Press).

——— (1975*c*), 'The Meaning of "Meaning" ', in Putnam, *Mind, Language and Reality, Philosophical Papers*, ii (Cambridge: Cambridge University Press).

——— (1975*d*), 'It Ain't Necessarily So', in Putnam, *Mathematics, Matter and Method, Philosophical Papers*, i (Cambridge: Cambridge University Press).

——— (1978), 'Reference and Understanding', in Putnam, *Meaning and the Moral Sciences* (London: Routledge and Kegan Paul).

QUINE, W. (1976*a*), *The Ways of Paradox and Other Essays*, rev. enlarged (Cambridge, Mass.: Harvard University Press).

——— (1976*b*), 'Carnap and Logical Truth', in Quine (1976*a*).

——— (1976*c*), 'Quantifiers and Propositional Attitudes', in Quine (1976*a*).

REY, G. (1998), 'What Implicit Conceptions Are Unlikely to Do', in Villanueva (1998).

RICKETTS, T. (1996), 'Logic and Truth in Frege', *Proceedings of the Aristotelian Society Supplementary Volume*, 70: 121–40.

RIZZOLATI, G., FADIGA, L., GALLESE, V., and FOGASSI, L. (1996), 'Premotor Cortex and the Recognition of Motor Actions', *Cognitive Brain Research*, 3: 131–41.

ROESSLER, J., and EILAN, N. (eds) (2003), *Agency and Self-Awareness* (Oxford: Oxford University Press).

RORTY, R. (1998), 'Is Truth a Goal of Inquiry? Donald Davidson versus Crispin Wright', in Rorty, *Truth and Progress, Philosophical Papers*, iii (Cambridge: Cambridge University Press).

RUMFITT, I. (2000), ' "Yes" and "No" ', *Mind*, 109: 781–823.

RUSSELL, B. (1919), *Introduction to Mathematical Philosophy* (London: George Allen and Unwin).

RYLE, G. (1971*a*), *Collected Papers*, ii: *Collected Essays 1929–1968* (London: Hutchinson).

——— (1971*b*), 'The Thinking of Thoughts: What Is *Le Penseur* Doing?', in Ryle (1971*a*).

——— (1971*c*), 'A Puzzling Element in the Notion of Thinking', in Ryle (1971*a*).

——— (1971*d*), 'Thinking and Reflecting', in Ryle (1971*a*).

SCHIFFER, S. (1987), *Remnants of Meaning* (Cambridge, Mass.: MIT Press).

——— (2003), *The Things We Mean* (Oxford: Oxford University Press).

SELLARS, W. (1963*a*), *Science, Perception and Reality* (London: Routledge and Kegan Paul).

——— (1963*b*), 'Truth and "Correspondence" ', in Sellars (1963*a*).

——— (1963*c*), 'Some Reflections on Language Games', in Sellars (1963*a*).

——— (1974), 'Meaning as Functional Classification', *Synthese*, 27: 417–37.

——— (1997), *Empiricism and the Philosophy of Mind*, introd. R. Rorty, with Study Guide by R. Brandom (Cambridge, Mass.: Harvard University Press).

SHOEMAKER, S. (1984*a*), *Identity, Cause and Mind: Philosophical Essays* (Cambridge: Cambridge University Press).

—— (1984*b*), 'Self-Reference and Self-Awareness', in Shoemaker (1984*a*).

—— (1984*c*), 'Persons and their Pasts', in Shoemaker (1984*a*).

—— (1996*a*), *The First-Person Perspective and Other Essays* (Cambridge: Cambridge University Press).

—— (1996*b*), 'The Broad Perceptual Model', in Shoemaker (1996*a*).

—— (1998), 'Causal and Metaphysical Necessity', *Pacific Philosophical Quarterly*, 79: 59–77.

SMILEY, T. (1996), 'Rejection', *Analysis*, 56: 1–9.

SPELKE, E. (1998), 'Nativism, Empiricism and the Origins of Knowledge', *Infant Behavior and Development*, 21: 181–200.

SPENCE, S., Brooks, D., et al. (1997), 'A PET Study of Voluntary Movement in Schizophrenic Patients Experiencing Passivity Phenomena (Delusions of Alien Control)', *Brain*, 120: 1997–2011.

STALNAKER, R. (1968), 'A Theory of Conditionals', in N. Rescher (ed.), *Studies in Logical Theory* (Oxford: Blackwell).

STEWART, I. (1996), *From Here to Infinity* (Oxford: Oxford University Press).

STRAWSON, G. (1994), *Mental Reality* (Cambridge, Mass.: MIT Press).

STRAWSON, P. (1954), 'Review of Wittgenstein's *Philosophical Investigations*', *Mind*, 63: 70–99.

—— (1959), *Individuals: An Essay in Descriptive Metaphysics* (London: Methuen).

TYE, M. (1997), 'A Representational Theory of Pains and their Phenomenal Character', in N. Block, O. Flanagan, and G. Güzeldere (eds), *The Nature of Consciousness: Philosophical Debates* (Cambridge, Mass.: MIT Press).

VILLANUEVA, E. (ed.) (1998), *Concepts, Philosophical Issues 9* (Atascadero, Calif.: Ridgeview).

WIGGINS, D. (2001), *Sameness and Substance Renewed* (Cambridge: Cambridge University Press).

WILLIAMS, B. (2002), *Truth and Truthfulness: An Essay in Genealogy* (Princeton: Princeton University Press).

WILLIAMSON, T. (2002), *Knowledge and its Limits* (Oxford: Oxford University Press).

—— (2006), "Conceptual Truth", *Proceedings of the Aristotelian Society Supplementary Volume*, 80: 1–41.

WIMMER, H., HOGREFE, J., and SODIAN, B. (1988), 'A Second Stage in Children's Conception of Mental Life: Understanding Informational Accesses as Origins of Knowledge and Belief', in Astington et al. (1988).

WITTGENSTEIN, L. (1958), *Philosophical Investigations* (Oxford: Blackwell).

—— (1978), *Remarks on the Foundations of Mathematics*, trans. G. E. M. Anscombe, 3rd edn (Oxford: Blackwell).

330   *References*

Wright, C. (1989), 'Wittgenstein's Rule-Following Considerations and the Central Project of Theoretical Linguistics', in A. George (ed.), *Reflections on Chomsky* (Oxford: Blackwell).

—— (1992), *Truth and Objectivity* (Cambridge, Mass.: Harvard University Press).

—— (2001), *Rails to Infinity: Essays on Themes from Wittgenstein's Philosophical Investigations* (Cambridge, Mass.: Harvard University Press).

Yaniv, I., and Shatz, M. (1988), 'Children's Understanding of Perceptibility', in Astington et al. (1988).

Index